PROJECT PLOWSHARE

PROJECT PLOWSHARE

The Peaceful Use of Nuclear Explosives
in Cold War America

Scott Kaufman

WITHDRAWN

CORNELL UNIVERSITY PRESS   ITHACA AND LONDON

First published 2013 by Cornell University Press
Printed in the United States of America

Library of Congress Cataloging-in-Publication Data

Kaufman, Scott, 1969–
   Project Plowshare : the peaceful use of nuclear explosives in Cold War America / Scott Kaufman.
       p. cm.
   Includes bibliographical references and index.
   ISBN 978-0-8014-5125-6 (cloth : alk. paper)
   1. Project Plowshare (U.S.)—History.   2. Nuclear energy—Industrial applications—United States—History.   3. Nuclear explosions—United States—History.   I. Title.

   TK9153.K38 2013
   621.48—dc23   2012009128

Cornell University Press strives to use environmentally responsible suppliers and materials to the fullest extent possible in the publishing of its books. Such materials include vegetable-based, low-VOC inks and acid-free papers that are recycled, totally chlorine-free, or partly composed of nonwood fibers. For further information, visit our website at www.cornellpress.cornell.edu.

Cloth printing   10 9 8 7 6 5 4 3 2 1

To Julie and Lexi

And he shall judge among the nations, and shall rebuke many peoples; and they shall beat their swords into plowshares, and their spears into pruning hooks; nation shall not lift up sword against nation, neither shall they learn war any more.

—Isaiah 2:4

Contents

Preface

While conducting research for a book on President Jimmy Carter's foreign policy, I happened to read about a proposal to use nuclear explosives to construct a sea-level canal in Panama. The topic grabbed my attention. Once I completed my work on Carter, I began to read about what was called Project Plowshare. I discovered not only that few books had been written on this program but that none had fully considered the program's domestic and foreign policy implications. This monograph is the result.

In researching *Plowshare*, I traveled to over a dozen archives throughout the United States. With the exception of papers at the University of Alaska at Fairbanks, the Dwight D. Eisenhower Library, Lawrence Livermore National Laboratory, and the National Archives at College Park, Maryland, these archival collections largely have been ignored. Because, outside of U.S. soil, it was in Panama and Australia where peaceful nuclear explosions came closest to use, this monograph includes manuscripts from both countries, none of which scholars had previously consulted. Additionally, through mandatory review requests, I have been able to get declassified hundreds of pages of documents. Consequently, many of the details about the peaceful-use program were unknown prior to *Plowshare*'s publication.

There are numerous institutions and people I want to thank for their assistance in researching this monograph. In the United States, my appreciation goes to the staffs of the Herbert Hoover, Dwight D. Eisenhower, John F. Kennedy, and Lyndon B. Johnson Libraries; the National Archives and Record Service, including the main branches in Washington, D.C., and College Park, Maryland, and the regional branches in Anchorage, Alaska, and San Bruno, California; the Library of Congress; the Malcolm A. Love Library at San Diego State University Library; and the American Heritage Center at the University of Wyoming. Rachel Seale at the University of Alaska's Rasmuson Library assisted me as I conducted research there. Through her, I was able to meet Dan O'Neill, the author of an excellent book on Project Chariot, who spent time with me discussing my manuscript. Brad Arnold, an archivist at the University of Colorado's Norlin Library, directed me to some very useful collections. Carol Leadenham and Ron Bulatoff helped me with my work at the Hoover Institution, as did Maxine Trost at Lawrence Livermore National Laboratory and Terry Fehner at the Department of Energy Archive. John Krygier, who wrote an article on Project Ketch, gave me access to his research. Harold Brown, one of Plowshare's founders, took time to correspond with me about his role in the peaceful-use program. I needed additional information on people mentioned in documents; here, Charlotte Pendleton at Rasmuson Library and Maureen Booth at the Department of Interior Library were of immense help. In Australia, I want to thank the staffs at the National Archives of Australia, including the main branch in Canberra and regional branches in Sydney and Melbourne, as well as the archivists at the State Record Office of Western Australia in Perth. Xiomara Sarmiento de Robletto at the Foreign Ministry Archive in Panama City provided me enormous help as I conducted research there.

Jaclyn Stanke at Campbell University and Michael McGandy, acquisitions editor at Cornell University Press, read the entire manuscript and offered suggestions for revisions. My appreciation goes out as well to the two anonymous readers and the Cornell University Press Faculty Review Board for their proposed changes.

Throughout, I have received support from current and retired colleagues in the Francis Marion University (FMU) History Department, who have listened to me drone on about the peaceful use of nuclear explosives. Special appreciation goes to Elena Eskridge-Kosmach and Larry Nelson, experts in Soviet and Western U.S. history, respectively, who answered questions during the writing process. I also want to thank Derek Jokisch, professor of health physics at FMU, who spent time discussing with me the civilian use of radioisotopes and how radioactive elements travel through soil and rock.

Completion of this work would not have been possible without financial assistance from a number of sources. The administration at Francis Marion University is strongly supportive of research, and both the FMU History Department and the Francis Marion University Foundation appropriated me with travel funds. I am grateful as well to the Herbert Hoover Library Association, which awarded me the William R. Castle, Jr., Memorial Fellowship; the Lyndon B. Johnson Library, which awarded me a Moody Grant; and the John F. Kennedy Library, which provided me with a travel grant.

Finally, I cannot thank enough my friends and family for their love and support. Numerous friends of mine—Tony Schountz and Rebecca Staudenmaier, Dan and Becky Ashton, Don and Kerri Burchett, Al and Mickie Keithley (my "second parents"), John Hamilton and Stacey Paige-Hamilton, and Eric and Julia Nickell—all opened their doors to me as I traveled from archive to archive, as did my aunt and uncle, Shirley and Barry Michaelson, and my sister and brother-in-law, Heather and Steve Moore. As a member of the Army Corps of Engineers who specializes in environmental matters, Steve was also someone who gave me useful insights into hydraulic fracturing of natural gas. My father, Burton Kaufman, himself a retired history professor, has been a constant source of inspiration and also helped me fine-tune the manuscript. My mother, Diane, did not hang up the phone on me as I called (repeatedly) to tell her and my father about my latest archival discoveries. Finally, my love goes to my wife, Julie; our four-legged "daughter," Lexi; and my in-laws, for putting up with me as I spent hours researching, reading, writing, and revising.

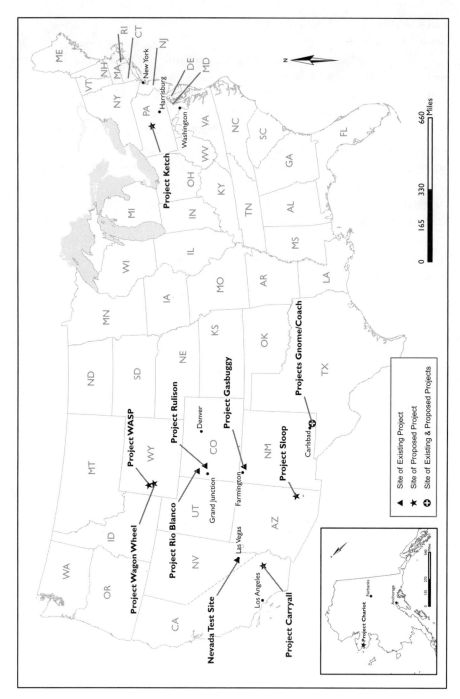

Map 1. Locations of proposed or executed Plowshare tests on U.S. soil.

Abbreviations

AAEC	Australian Atomic Energy Commission
AAIA	Association of American Indian Affairs
ACDA	Arms Control and Disarmament Agency
ACS	Alaska Conservation Society
AEC	Atomic Energy Commission
ANF	Atlantic Nuclear Force
BHP	Broken Hill Proprietary
CBTB	comprehensive test ban treaty
CNI	Citizens' Committee for Nuclear Information
CONOCO	Continental Oil Company
ENDC	Eighteen-Nation Disarmament Committee
EPA	Environmental Protection Agency
EPNG	El Paso Natural Gas Company
Euratom	European Atomic Energy Community
IAEA	International Atomic Energy Agency
ICBM	intercontinental ballistic missile
JCAE	Joint Committee on Atomic Energy
LLNL	Lawrence Livermore National Laboratory
LRL	Lawrence Radiation Laboratory
LTBT	Limited Test Ban Treaty
MLF	multilateral force
NAS	National Academy of Sciences
NATO	North Atlantic Treaty Organization
NEPA	National Environmental Policy Act
NPT	nonproliferation treaty
NSC	National Security Council
NTS	Nevada Test Site
PNEs	peaceful nuclear explosions
R&D	research and development
RPI	Rensselaer Polytechnic Institute
SWRHL	Southwest Radiological Health Laboratory
UAF	University of Alaska at Fairbanks
UAR	United Arab Republic
UCRL	University of California's Radiation Laboratory

UCRL-L   UCRL at Livermore
UNR   University of Nevada at Reno
USGS   U.S. Geological Survey
WASP   Wyoming Area Stimulation Project
WWIC   Wagon Wheel Information Committee

PROJECT PLOWSHARE

Promoting the Peaceful Atom

In April 2010 an explosion took place on British Petroleum's Deepwater Horizon oil rig, killing eleven people and causing millions of gallons of petroleum to contaminate the Gulf of Mexico. As BP attempted to find some means to stop the spill, CNN reporter John Roberts suggested in an off-the-cuff remark, "Drill a hole, drop a nuke in and seal up the well." Roberts drew criticism from the Barack Obama administration and atomic experts, who said such an act "would be not only risky technically, with unknown and possibly disastrous consequences from radiation, but also unwise geopolitically," for it risked a violation of past treaties "at a time when President Obama is pushing for global nuclear disarmament."[1]

The criticism directed toward Roberts reflected a long-held view that nuclear weapons were (and are) the purveyors of death and destruction. When he witnessed the successful testing of the atomic bomb in the New Mexico desert in July 1945, J. Robert Oppenheimer claimed that he recalled the words of the *Bhagavad Gita*: "Now, I am become Death, the destroyer of worlds." The United States then used two atomic bombs against Japan in August 1945, killing hundreds of thousands of people. With the Soviet development of its own nuclear explosives in 1949, the United States expanded its atomic arsenal, and American officials made the threat of nuclear annihilation part of their strategy aimed at containing communist aggression. Indeed, during a crisis with communist China in 1955, President Dwight D. Eisenhower told reporters that atomic weapons should be employed "just exactly as you would use a bullet or anything else." The comment upset America's European allies, who believed the president too willing to risk starting World War III.[2]

It was that same president, however, who two years earlier had advanced a different, more benign use for nuclear explosives. Calling his proposal Atoms for Peace, he suggested one might put the atom toward civilian use, such as power production. His proposal grabbed the attention of scientists at the Atomic Energy Commission (AEC) and the University of California's Radiation Laboratory—later renamed Lawrence Radiation Laboratory and then Lawrence Livermore National Laboratory. Together, they developed a program run out of Livermore but administered and funded by the AEC called Project Plowshare. The scientists took the name from the Bible's book of Isaiah 2:4: "They shall beat their swords into plowshares, and their spears into pruning hooks; nation shall not lift up their sword against nation, neither shall they learn war anymore."

Plowshare was more than just a name, though. It was an article of faith. It was not that Plowshare's champions wanted the United States to eliminate its nuclear stockpile, although many of those involved in the program encouraged efforts to check the atomic arms race with the Soviet Union. Rather Plowshare's defenders truly believed that they could control the atom and use it to benefit rather than destroy humankind. Those who were part of or supportive of the program contended that "peaceful nuclear explosions," or PNEs, could excavate harbors and canals, stimulate the production of gas and oil, provide storage facilities for water or fuel, help gain access to deeply buried ores, create heat that could be captured for power production, and generate new atomic elements and isotopes for general use. As an example, after listing the numerous potential uses for PNEs, AEC Commissioner Willard Libby told an audience at the California Institute of Technology in 1958 that nuclear explosives produced more energy at a lower cost than conventional devices. "In addition, of course," he said, "they are easier and safer to place and handle."[3]

One could accuse Libby of hubris, and certainly self-confidence drove Plowshare's defenders. But hubris fails to fully account for the commitment individuals such as Libby made to the peaceful-use program. Plowshare's proponents also saw in themselves the personification of progress and modernity. Thanks to science, people living in the mid-twentieth century had electricity for their homes, ever faster and more efficient modes of transportation, mass-produced goods, treatments for once incurable diseases, and radio and television. The atom could play its part in moving the United States, and indeed the world, down the road of progress and modernization by helping industry, building an advanced transportation infrastructure for any country desirous of one, and developing new isotopes for medical purposes.

Offering Plowshare services to interested parties, however, required money. Nuclear devices released potentially dangerous radioactive fallout, and so it was necessary to create "cleaner" technology. Furthermore some projects might require dozens of atomic explosives. Plowshare's champions thus sought to embrace what Eisenhower called the "military-industrial complex" by seeking corporate and congressional support. To get the private sector and Capitol Hill to open up their pocketbooks, proponents of the peaceful atom asserted that their technology could do a better job than conventional explosives, more quickly, and with fewer dollars. Realizing the economic argument might not be enough to get lawmakers' ears, Plowshare scientists and their allies added that the program was imperative to national security.

Importantly, Plowshare's advocates did not see national security as solely an excuse to get money from Congress. Just as they believed the peaceful atom would promote progress and modernity, so they were certain it could help protect the United States. As those involved in Plowshare saw it, national security had geopolitical, military, and economic connotations. In a world where Soviet-inspired communism appeared to pose a direct threat to U.S. prestige and credibility, Plowshare seemed to offer a response. By proving the utility of the peaceful atom, the United States could demonstrate to the world that its technological know-how remained far ahead of that of the Soviet Union. Consequently foreign nations would want to remain on Washington's side so they could share in what the United States had to offer them. "The Communists might develop Plowshare before we do" and offer to use PNEs "to help their friends with gigantic nuclear projects," wrote the physicist Edward Teller in 1962. "The consequences of such aid would be an economic penetration a hundred times more extensive than those following the Soviet offer to help Egypt construct the Aswan Dam."[4] To Teller and his ilk, this fear became real in 1965, when the Soviets began their own version of Plowshare.

Militarily, the peaceful-use program offered a way to halt the proliferation of atomic weapons. By the mid-1960s the United States, the Soviet Union, the United Kingdom, France, and communist China all had acquired atomic bombs, and there was the possibility of other nations following suit. "Our deepest obligation to ourselves and to our children is to bring nuclear weapons under control," President Lyndon B. Johnson stated in February 1967. "If we fail to act now, nation after nation will be driven to use valuable resources to acquire them. Even local conflicts will involve the danger of nuclear war."[5] The problem was that some countries wanted the right to acquire atomic explosives for what they asserted were civilian projects. If the United States could furnish Plowshare technology to those states—with the caveat that the explosives themselves remain under U.S. control—then nonnuclear countries would have less reason to develop atomic devices. In turn the possibility of nuclear war, even at a local level, would be significantly curtailed.

In the event armed conflict did break out, Plowshare again offered advantages. One of the reasons for the passage of the National Interstate and Defense Highways Act in 1956 was to allow for the transport of troops and matériel from one part of the nation to another in time of war. It might be possible to use the atom to construct similar projects more quickly and for less money than conventional explosives. Furthermore, should the superpowers engage in open warfare, the Kremlin certainly would want to knock out the Panama Canal, which, because of its lock-based system, would be hard to repair; in turn, moving maritime resources between the Atlantic and Pacific would become much more difficult. Another possibility was that Panamanians themselves, upset with U.S. control of the Canal Zone, might attempt to sabotage the waterway. Plowshare's advocates, therefore, suggested employing the atom to construct a sea-level canal, one more impervious to attack than that in the Canal Zone.

Economically Plowshare offered to do more than simply combat the Soviets' efforts to spread their influence worldwide. It could serve Americans by binding together their nation and giving U.S. manufacturers access to markets that previously had been largely inaccessible. From the birth of the republic, Americans had argued that national unity and economic well-being were best served by an extensive transportation system made up of roads, railroads, canals, and ports. Agriculturalists, commented Secretary of the Treasury Robert J. Walker in 1845, "must have the foreign market, or a large surplus, accompanied by a great depression in price, must be the result." Seventy years later President Woodrow Wilson observed that an advanced system of roads "afford[ed] the farmers . . . and the residents in villages the means of ready access to such neighboring markets as they need[ed] for the economic benefit."[6] By constructing harbors and canals and clearing the way for new roads and railroads, the peaceful atom could further secure America's economic future.

That bright economic outlook, however, was threatened by the inaccessibility of important metals and the overreliance on foreign sources of fuel. If Americans did not get access to ores, gas, and oil buried deeply under U.S. soil, they could find themselves at the mercy of foreign suppliers of those same goods. President Eisenhower suggested as much when he told reporters in 1957, "The whole present approach to this business of regulating oil imports, arises out of one thing—consideration of the national security." The president added, "[Although] in [an] emergency the Western Hemisphere can supply the petroleum requirements of the Western World for a limited time . . . we can do that only if there is continued exploration and maintenance of reserves in this country."[7] By employing the atom, Americans could get at otherwise unreachable metals, oil, and natural gas and protect the nation's economic independence.

Driven by their hubris, dedication to their vision of modernity, and determination to defend the nation's security, the AEC conducted twenty-seven Plowshare explosions between 1957 and 1973, spending an enormous sum of money in the process. By 1963 the Commission was devoting $1 million a month to prove Plowshare's utility, or just over 30 percent of all the money it assigned to its peaceful and weapons programs. Four years later that rate had risen to 53 percent.[8]

To their dismay, however, Plowshare's champions never saw their program achieve the promise they believed it held for the United States or the peoples of the planet. Part of the problem was forces beyond the control of those who wanted to prove the potential of PNEs. White House officials had what they regarded as priorities more important than the peaceful use of the atom. Domestic and international pressure to stop both testing and the proliferation of nuclear technology made Washington pause when deciding whether to hold a Plowshare test or offer peaceful-use services to other parties. When the international community during the 1960s codified restrictions to testing and the spread of atomic technology, many in the U.S. capitol became even more wary of supporting peaceful-use experiments that might foment a domestic or international backlash.

Yet even on those occasions when the political or international support for Plowshare appeared greatest, the program faced the challenge of acquiring the necessary funding. Desirous to avoid large deficits, both the executive and the legislative branches refused to budget all the money the AEC and its friends wanted for Plowshare, favoring instead other initiatives. Confronted with a financial shortfall, the scientists and politicians who promoted the peaceful use of atomic explosives had no choice but to turn to projects in which they could expect the greatest help from industrial sponsors. But here too peaceful-use proponents did not get the monetary backing they sought.

Plowshare's champions, however, were not solely the victims of forces beyond their control. Indeed, they sowed the seeds of their beloved program's destruction. In a relationship also analogous to that of the military-industrial complex, the AEC contracted out work to attendant laboratories and private industry, where, the Commission believed, it could conduct its work in an environment largely free from accountability. When the AEC and its allied labs and corporate entities unexpectedly found themselves the target of public scrutiny and criticism, they fought back by trying to ignore detractors or, when that failed, lying or charging opponents with being uninformed, antiprogress, anti-American, or somehow communist. Rather than quiet their adversaries, such tactics created a coalition of scientists, politicians, laypersons, and even industrialists who, from the grassroots on up, challenged PNEs. In fact the modern environmental movement was built on a reaction to the activities of the AEC and its allies. Unable to gather the necessary economic and political support, the Commission staged its last Plowshare test in 1973, and by the end of the decade the U.S. government had defunded the program.

Project Plowshare covers the life of the peaceful-use program from Eisenhower's suggestion to apply the atom to civilian projects to the program's eventual demise. For much of its two-decade life span, Plowshare's advocates called for a balanced program, one designed to prove the numerous nonmilitary applications for nuclear explosives. However, the overwhelming majority of energy and money went toward excavation projects. This was no accident. It was the construction of a sea-level isthmian canal that became Plowshare's centerpiece, and every blast designed to clear earth or create "cleaner" devices had some relation to the waterway. When an atomic-built canal proved impossible, the scientists, industrialists, and civilian officials involved with Plowshare made a last-ditch and ultimately futile effort to save their program by turning to stimulation of energy resources.

What is most amazing is that Plowshare survived as long as it did and received the funding it did despite intense, widespread opposition. In that respect, *Project Plowshare* is more than just the story of budgetary appropriations, the science of the atom, or the intense debates over whether to conduct individual tests. It is also the story of the power of an idea, one determinedly advertised by its advocates as new, innovative, and beneficial to the United States, if not the world.

A Plan of Biblical Proportions

At 10 a.m. on September 19, 1957, a nuclear blast shook a mesa at the Nevada Test Site (NTS), located about sixty-five miles northwest of Las Vegas. Willard Libby, a member of the AEC, recalled that he and other observers who had positioned themselves about two and a half miles away heard "a muffled explosion" and felt "a weak ground wave." The entire "mountain jumped about six inches," a "ripple . . . spread over [its] face," and some rocks rolled down the formation's slopes. The explosion generated shock waves equivalent to those of an earthquake of approximately 4.6 on the Richter scale, and seismographs as distant as Alaska registered vibrations.[1]

What Libby witnessed and the seismographs recorded was Project Rainier, the first underground nuclear explosion conducted on U.S. soil. Rainier's significance, however, went beyond where it took place. Since the late 1940s American scientists had given thought to using atomic explosives for peaceful purposes, and a few months before Rainier they had assigned the idea the name "Plowshare." Yet throughout, proponents of using the atom in civilian projects faced an increasingly vocal and influential movement to ban nuclear testing because of the dangerous radioactive fallout such explosions generated. For those who believed in Plowshare's potential, Rainier provided clear evidence that atomic blasts could take place while offering little, if not no, danger to humans.

Genesis

The idea for putting nuclear explosives to nonmilitary use developed from a number of sources. One was the creation of the U.S. Atomic Energy Commission in 1946. Prior to the establishment of the AEC, control over America's nuclear technology was in the hands of the U.S. Army's Manhattan Engineering District, better known as the Manhattan Project. An example of the "military-industrial complex" about which President Eisenhower famously warned in his farewell address, the Manhattan Project brought together government officials, scientists, the armed forces, and industry in an effort to develop the atomic bomb. Within a day of the dropping of the first A-bomb on Japan in August 1945, President Harry Truman called on Congress to create a "commission to control the production of the use of atomic power." Although at first lawmakers considered giving the military much of the control over the new body and to have the commission focus primarily on weapons development, the outcry from both the public and the scientific community prompted Senator Brien McMahon (D-Connecticut) in 1946 to sponsor legislation that would shift responsibility for overseeing America's military and civilian atomic energy programs from the armed forces to civilian officials. Passed by Congress and signed into law later that year, the McMahon Act, also known as the Atomic Energy Act, established the AEC. The Commission consisted of five civilians, all of whom required Senate confirmation to take their posts. Its job was to give priority to the development of nuclear weapons, but it also had the task of encouraging peaceful uses of the atom. To afford the armed forces, scientists, and lawmakers all a say in the new agency's decision making, the McMahon Act divided the AEC into various divisions, among them the Division of Military Applications, headed by an officer in the armed forces,[2] and established two committees. The first was a General Advisory Committee, made up of engineers and scientists, which met at least four times a year and advised the AEC "on scientific and technical matters relating to materials, production, and research and development." Unlike the members of the AEC, those individuals who sat on this committee did not require Senate confirmation. The second was Congress's Joint Committee on Atomic Energy (JCAE). Its job was to oversee the civilian and military nuclear programs. Unlike other agencies of government that sent budget requests directly to the House or Senate appropriations committees, the AEC first had to receive authorization from the JCAE for any budget request; only then would that request move on to the appropriate appropriations committee.[3]

The superpower arms race also had an impact. With the advent of the cold war, the United States took steps to contain the spread of Soviet-inspired communism. Maintaining a monopoly on atomic weaponry was to U.S. officials an

Figure 1.   Ivy Mike, the first test of a thermonuclear explosive, 1952. Photo courtesy of National Nuclear Security Administration, Nevada Site Office.

integral component of containment. But the Soviet test of an atomic bomb in August 1949 threatened containment doctrine. It now became vital for the United States to stay ahead of its superpower rival militarily. As part of that effort, President Truman in January 1950 authorized construction of the "super," or hydrogen bomb. At the end of the year he established the Nevada Proving Grounds as a location for secret tests of new weaponry. Renamed in 1951 the NTS, it was located inside the Tonopah Bombing and Gunnery Range, which encompassed more than five thousand square miles of land in southeastern Nevada.[4]

In 1952 the "super" went from theory to reality when the "Ivy Mike" test occurred at Eniwetok Atoll, located in the Pacific Ocean. Weighing sixty-five tons, Ivy Mike generated a blast equivalent to ten megatons (or 10 million tons of TNT) and left behind a crater over a mile wide and 160 feet deep. What made Ivy Mike unique was that unlike the fission-based atomic bombs dropped on Japan, it employed fusion. In fission an atomic nucleus is split apart, thereby releasing energy. Fusion takes place by combining atomic nuclei; again, the blast releases energy, but in this case, the amount is much greater. Ivy Mike was evidence of fusion's potency, having unleashed an explosion equivalent to some 650 Hiroshima-style bombs.

In the superpower arms race, fusion offered advantages over fission. First, there were the matters of production and cost. To build a fission explosive requires the use of uranium-238. A naturally occurring radioactive isotope, uranium-238 itself cannot be employed in a nuclear device. It must be enriched to create uranium-235 or bombarded with neutrons to generate plutonium-239. Uranium-238, however, is not a common element, and therefore is expensive.

A fusion device is different, relying primarily on deuterium and tritium. Deuterium, which is found in nature, is a form of hydrogen, the most common element on the planet and hence much cheaper to obtain than uranium-235. Tritium is more problematic. It too is a form of hydrogen but is not naturally occurring; this makes it costly to produce. However, by using lithium, a more readily available and less expensive element, and bombarding it with neutrons, one can create the necessary tritium.

There was still a problem. Tritium requires a temperature of 80 million degrees to fuse. This was lower than the temperature required to fuse deuterium but still a challenge in itself. Here fission came into play. In a process still used in today's thermonuclear weapons, a small amount of enriched uranium provides the fission process that, within milliseconds, generates the heat necessary to create and fuse the tritium; that in turn almost instantaneously raises the temperature high enough to fuse the deuterium, and it is the fusion of tritium and deuterium that releases the force of a hydrogen blast. Hence a fusion device requires some uranium. However, since it needs less uranium than one relying solely on fission, a fusion weapon, despite the cost of the tritium, delivers far more bang for the buck than one that employs solely fission. According to U.S. scientists in 1955, a single pound of hydrogen for use in fusion cost only $140, as compared to $11,000 for an analogous amount of uranium-235.[5]

President Eisenhower and his secretary of state, John Foster Dulles, found fusion highly attractive. It was now possible to build nuclear weapons in larger quantity and at less cost than it took to maintain sizable conventional forces in the field, thereby allowing for cuts in defense spending. Fusion also offered greater deterrence value. With ever more nuclear weapons at its disposal, the Eisenhower administration could use the threat of a nuclear Armageddon to convince the Soviets not to try to spread their influence beyond where it already existed. As Dulles put it in January 1954, "Local defenses must be reinforced by the further deterrent of massive retaliatory power."[6] Adding to that deterrent effect was the fact that the United States (as was the Soviet Union) was within a few years of developing intercontinental ballistic missiles (ICBMs). The ability to place very powerful yet small hydrogen warheads on those missiles would permit the U.S.

military to destroy numerous Soviet targets without having to fly aircraft over or physically place launchers near those sites.[7] Ivy Mike, in short, proffered numerous military benefits to the United States.

Yet Ivy Mike also held promise for nonmilitary projects. The atom need not lead the world toward obliteration. Rather, if properly harnessed, it could direct humankind toward a better, brighter future. Scientists had known since the early 1900s that radiation could kill bacteria in food and treat human cancers. In February 1946 Edward Teller, a world-renowned physicist who worked on the Manhattan Project and later became known as the "father of the hydrogen bomb," contended that it was possible to find other civilian uses for the atom, such as producing power. He declared, "Use of radio-elements which are by-products of atomic power plants will have an extremely great influence in science, particularly in medical science."[8] Indeed from Ivy Mike, scientists had discovered two new elements, fermium and einsteinium. Maybe it was possible to generate still others that could be put toward human benefit.

Construction was another possible application. A fission device is very "dirty," meaning it releases a large amount of radioactivity, a considerable portion of which gets into the atmosphere and returns to Earth in the form of fallout. Fusion generates very little radiation, and what radioactivity is released comes from the fission process used to fuse the deuterium and tritium. Thus in addition to its explosiveness, the smaller amount of uranium employed in a fusion device as opposed to one of fission meant fusion produced a "cleaner" blast.[9] If they could further reduce the radioactivity generated in a fusion reaction—in essence, create a totally clean explosive—wondered some scientists, might it not be possible to use the atom to, say, create a hole similar to that at Eniwetok and use it for a harbor? Could they, in short, find creative rather than destructive uses for fusion?

One of the first American scientists to ask such questions was Fred Reines, a physicist at Los Alamos National Laboratory. Shortly after President Truman announced confirmation of the Soviet atomic test, Moscow's foreign minister, Andrei Vishinsky, told the United Nations in November 1949 that his country did indeed possess the power of the atom, but he insisted that the Kremlin had no intention of adopting it for military applications. Rather, he claimed, his nation had used, and would continue to use, nuclear explosives solely for nonmilitary projects, including mining, hydroelectric power, and the construction of canals.[10] While many Americans doubted the Kremlin's professions of benevolence, Reines found the possibility of putting nuclear devices to use in civilian projects intriguing. Writing in 1950 in the *Bulletin of the Atomic Scientists*, Reines admitted that nuclear blasts released dangerous radiation, yet he asked whether it might be possible to use "the bomb in such activities as mining, where the fission products would be confined to relatively small regions into which men would be required to go," or to "divert a river by blasting a large volume of solid rock." Reines was not alone. One of his colleagues, the mathematician John von Neumann, and scientists at the University of California's Radiation Laboratory (UCRL), shared Reines's concept of applying nuclear explosives to civilian undertakings.[11]

So did President Eisenhower. During World War II he had served as commander of Allied forces in Europe. Afterward he led the U.S. military troops occupying Germany, became president of Columbia University, and then commanded the military forces of the North Atlantic Treaty Organization (NATO) in Europe before running for the presidency in 1952. His time at Columbia had given him an opportunity to meet with atomic scientists, from whom he had learned the possibilities of using the atom for the benefit of humankind. At the same time, he had come to understand, especially with the advent of the fusion weapon, that as long as the arms race continued, the planet faced the risk of a war far more catastrophic than anything it had yet seen. "The world," he told his recently appointed head of the AEC, Lewis Strauss, "simply must not go on living in the fear of the terrible consequence of nuclear war." Reinforcing that realization was news in August 1953 that the Soviets had detonated their own hydrogen bomb.[12]

For Eisenhower, the question was how to curtail the arms race while permitting the United States to maintain its nuclear supremacy. An earlier attempt, called the Baruch Plan, had failed. A half-hearted proposal presented by the United States in 1946, the Baruch Plan called for an international organization to control "all atomic energy activities potentially dangerous to world security" through on-site inspections and other measures. The U.S. government insisted, however, that it would not relinquish its nuclear stockpile until after the Soviets halted their atomic research and permitted inspections. Correctly viewing Washington's proposal as an effort to maintain America's nuclear monopoly, and charging it as an infringement of their sovereignty, the Soviets rejected the Baruch Plan.[13]

Looking at that history, Eisenhower and his aides came up with an ingenious idea: promote the peaceful use of the atom. They saw several advantages to such a strategy. It might curb the arms race by having the superpowers assign a portion of their nuclear stockpile to civilian rather than military use. It would shift the emphasis from the danger offered by the atom to the possible benefits that might accrue. More ominously—and left unsaid—an emphasis on the atom's potential for good would make Americans more receptive to an increase in the overall size of their nation's nuclear arsenal, which, in the event of war, could be unleashed against an enemy.[14]

It was with these considerations in mind that in December 1953 Eisenhower proposed in a speech before the United Nations General Assembly what became known as "Atoms for Peace." "Atomic bombs today are more than 25 times as powerful as the weapons with which the atomic age dawned," he explained, "while hydrogen weapons are in the ranges of millions of tons of TNT equivalent." Even so, history had demonstrated "mankind's never-ending quest for peace, and mankind's God-given capacity to build." The United States sought to join that effort for peace. It wanted, the president insisted, "to be constructive, not destructive. It wants agreement, not wars, among nations." Hence he proposed that those countries with fissionable material contribute some of it to an international atomic energy agency, overseen by the United Nations, which would use that technology for "the peaceful pursuits of mankind." The Soviets questioned the speech, pointing out that Atoms for Peace threatened to proliferate atomic technology to nations that did not have it.[15] The U.S. Congress, however, saw merit in Eisenhower's proposal and in 1954 amended the 1946 Atomic Energy Act. The altered law afforded the military full control over the nation's arms policy, while the AEC dedicated more attention than before to the job of promoting peaceful use of the atom.[16]

During the next two years the AEC concentrated primarily on building nuclear power plants. The 1956 Suez Crisis, however, gave those at the Commission reason to take a closer look at employing the atom in construction projects. In July of that year President Gamal Abdel Nasser of Egypt, angered by the Eisenhower administration's decision not to offer money to finance an expansion of the Aswan Dam, nationalized the Anglo-French company that oversaw the Suez Canal, closed the waterway to Israeli shipping, and stated that tolls paid by other nations using the canal would cover the cost of the Aswan project. In October Israel, the United Kingdom, and France launched an attack on Egypt in an attempt to oust Nasser. The Soviets threatened to intervene on the side of their Egyptian ally. Eisenhower believed Moscow was bluffing, but he could not be certain of that; furthermore he was in the midst of a reelection campaign and was trying to generate international condemnation of a recent Soviet intervention in Hungary. The president thus brought pressure to bear on London, Paris, and Jerusalem by cutting oil shipments and financial aid, as well as through a U.S.-supported UN resolution calling for the attackers to stand down. The Israelis, British, and French gave in and withdrew their troops. Afterward a United Nations peacekeeping force moved in.

Though the Suez Crisis lasted only a matter of weeks, it made Harold Brown wonder about additional peaceful uses for the atom. Born in 1927 in New York City, Brown was a brilliant student, receiving his doctorate in physics from Columbia University at age twenty-one. Brown was impatient, serious, and something of a loner; he "spoke and wrote clearly, succinctly, and colorlessly." One Israeli official who years later knew Brown as President Jimmy Carter's secretary of defense commented that he was "almost incapable of small talk."[17]

When he first considered applying the atom to civilian projects, Brown was on the UCRL staff. Originally founded in 1931 by the scientist Ernest O. Lawrence at the University of California as a site for research in physics, the Radiation Laboratory—renamed Lawrence Radiation Laboratory following Lawrence's death in 1958—was one of several places that contributed to the Manhattan Project. In 1952 UCRL established a branch at Livermore (UCRL-L) to compete against the national laboratory at Los Alamos, New Mexico; Brown joined the Livermore staff that same year. Having just witnessed the Suez Crisis, he wondered if it might be possible to construct a sea-level canal across Israel using atomic explosives.[18] In so doing Israel would not have to worry about closure of the Suez waterway, and it would give international shippers an alternative to traveling through Egypt.

In light of the availability of fusion devices, President Eisenhower's call for using the atom for peaceful purposes, and the international ramifications of the Suez Crisis, Brown, with the support of UCRL-L's director Herbert York, proposed in October 1956 a national conference to discuss the peaceful use of atomic explosives.[19] They wanted to bring together scientists not just from the AEC and UCRL, but from other centers involved in nuclear research, including Los Alamos and Sandia Laboratories, the Research and Development (RAND) Corporation, and General Atomics.[20] The proposed conference would assemble scientists working for the U.S. government, nongovernmental organizations, academia, and private industry.

It was at this point that the proposal for using nuclear explosives for peaceful purposes received its name. There are three different, though not necessarily incompatible, versions of how the name was chosen. According to York, Brown came up with it, and Brown himself states that is indeed the case. Teller credited a fellow physicist, Isidor I. Rabi. Rabi, who believed thermonuclear weapons represented "an evil under any light," skeptically commented after hearing of Brown's proposal for a conference on the peaceful atom, "So you want to beat your old atomic bombs into plowshares." In a later account, however, Teller attributed the name to an unnamed scientist from the Los Alamos lab who wanted to know if the purpose of the upcoming meeting was "to 'beat our swords into plowshares.'" Shortly thereafter, Teller said, Rabi made the similar statement, and the name stuck.[21]

The First Plowshare Symposium took place in February 1957. With Teller acting as keynote speaker, the attendees heard about and discussed three broad areas of application for what became known as peaceful nuclear explosions:

power production, the creation of new atomic elements, and earthmoving (also referred to as "nuclear excavation"). Those at the symposium emphasized the need to develop nuclear explosives that would release little or no radioactivity. They believed they could do this by adjusting the amount of fission or fusion used in a blast. Consequently if, for instance, the AEC turned to atomic devices to build a canal, any persons evacuated from the area where the explosions—or, as Plowshare scientists came to call them, "shots"—took place could return to their homes after a brief period of time.[22] The scientists left excited about the possibilities. John Philip, who worked for the AEC's San Francisco office, remarked, "Plowshare instantly appealed to everyone because of its obvious promise of practicality."[23]

The Fallout Debate

Moving Plowshare from conception to inception required traversing several hurdles. One was to determine which agency or agencies should have responsibility for overseeing it. In June 1957 the AEC decided to place the program under the auspices of the Division of Military Applications. The head of the division, General Alfred D. Starbird, was not certain that the Atomic Energy Act permitted the federal government to offer atomic technology to industry. He was certain, however, that he wanted to prevent the "wider dissemination" of what was potentially top-secret information. Hence he forbade giving details on atomic devices to private corporations that might want to use that technology for mining or other civilian-related purposes.[24]

A second obstacle was funding. "The close relationship between the nonmilitary uses program and the weapons program in many areas requiring investigation should frequently permit an integration of task objectives," wrote Starbird. Accordingly he saw no reason to increase funding for the AEC's weapons program. However, he did foresee UCRL-L working closely with the AEC on Plowshare, and so for "work unique to this program to be undertaken by Livermore," he suggested an initial appropriation of $100,000. Within a month UCRL-L "had formally established the Plowshare Project."[25]

The decision to place Plowshare, a program with *civilian* applications, in the hands of the AEC's *military* applications division may have made sense from a security standpoint, but it stood to pose a public relations nightmare. Here Plowshare faced its biggest hurdle: how to avoid a conflict between the desire to use the atom in the name of peace and a growing international movement to ban nuclear weapons tests.

Just as it had been known prior to World War II that radiation could benefit humans, so it was known that the atom could harm humans as well. The geneticist

Herman Muller, for instance, had shown in 1927 that x-rays used to treat cancer also caused mutations.[26] If x-rays could injure, what about fallout? Within a year of the establishment of the NTS, some Americans began to ask this very question. In 1952 the AEC attempted to calm public anxiety, declaring, "These explosives created no immediate or long-range hazard to human health outside the proving ground." But in 1953 physicists at Rensselaer Polytechnic Institute (RPI) discovered an increase in strontium-90 near the campus in Troy, New York, following a major rainstorm. Produced by fission, strontium-90 is a radioactive isotope with a twenty-eight-year half-life. Having a chemical composition similar to calcium, strontium-90 accompanies calcium into the human body, allowing it to get into bone marrow and teeth and cause cancer. After further analysis the scientists at RPI publicly announced in 1954 that the fallout came from explosions at the NTS; the rain had brought the radioactivity from the atmosphere to the soil. The problem was that while there was general agreement that strontium-90 was harmful, no one had conducted a full investigation because of an assumption that it would remain high above the Earth's surface. Therefore other specialists took issue with RPI's findings, leaving the scientific community and the public uncertain about just how serious that hazard was.[27]

It took an accident to convert uncertainty into fact for many observers. In March 1954 the United States tested a hydrogen device, code-named Bravo, at the Pacific island of Bikini. As proof of the advances made in explosive technology, Bravo, though weighing only 10.7 tons—or less than one-sixth the weight of Mike—detonated with a force of fifteen megatons. People witnessed the blast from a hundred miles away, and buildings shook twice as far as that.[28] In at least two respects the test did not go as planned: the force of the explosion was more than twice what scientists had projected, and an unanticipated shift in the wind blew radioactive debris eastward, where it fell on islands as distant as Kwajalein, one of the Marshall Islands and some 175 miles from the blast site. There over two hundred natives suffered radiation sickness, including burns and loss of hair, though none died.[29] More alarming was the fate of the twenty-three men aboard the Japanese fishing boat *Fukuryu Maru*—ironically, *Lucky Dragon*—about eighty-five miles from the Bravo test. Not only did they too suffer radiation poisoning, but one of them passed away a few months later.

This was not the first time humans had suffered radiation sickness. Thousands of Japanese had become ill or died from the aftereffects of the atomic bombs dropped on their country in 1945. Yet outside of Japan many had considered the atomic bombs' use justifiable. Bravo was different. Not only was it far more powerful than the weapons used against Japan, but it had injured and killed individuals in peacetime. Anti-American protests erupted in numerous countries. In the United States newspapers and magazines drew attention to

Bravo's impact on those aboard the *Lucky Dragon*. Strauss, assigned the duty of calming the public uproar over the radioactive fallout, told reporters that despite the unexpected wind shift, the Marshallese were doing fine, the fishermen (all of whom were still alive at this point) would recover as well, and the United States had gained vital military information from the blast.[30]

Strauss then made a mistake. When asked about the destructive power of an atomic bomb, the AEC chair commented in an excited tone about how one fusion weapon could destroy a whole city. "I wouldn't have answered that one that way, Lewis," Eisenhower remarked afterward. Indeed reporters latched onto Strauss's comment, feeding public fear. The magazine *U.S. News and World Report* published a map showing that a single hydrogen weapon dropped on Philadelphia would destroy buildings in Trenton, New Jersey, and Wilmington, Delaware, and cause fallout from New Hampshire to Virginia.[31]

Many in the scientific community joined the uproar. In March 1955 two scientists at the University of Colorado Medical Center, Ray R. Lanier and Theodore Puck, cited a rise in radioactivity in their state resulting from tests at the NTS. A few months later the *Washington Post* reported that Strauss himself had refused to permit Muller to present a paper on the impact of fallout on the human reproductive system at the first International Conference on the Peaceful Uses of Atomic Energy. Held a year earlier in Geneva, Switzerland, the gathering brought together 1,200 nuclear scientists from seventy-two nations who discussed using the atom for power and breeding hardier crops, as well as the possible hazards such use might pose to plants, animals, and humans. Though Strauss apologized, the Lanier-Puck report, followed by assertions that the AEC had purposely tried to conceal from the public information on the danger posed by radioactivity, served to make many wonder if the U.S. government had something to hide. In a scathing editorial in *Science* magazine, George Beadle, president of the American Association for the Advancement of Science, accused Strauss of prohibiting the Muller paper simply because Muller did not agree with him.[32]

One focus of the debate became strontium-90. Understanding the significance of this dispute requires a brief examination of the three measurements of radiation: roentgens, rads, and rems. Exposure to radiation is measured in roentgens, which is the amount of molecular ionization in a centimeter of dry air at the point at which water freezes (32° Fahrenheit). A rad, or "radiation absorbed dose," is the amount of radiation a mass of matter, such as a human body, absorbs. A rem, or "roentgen equivalent in man," refers to the relationship between the dose of radiation absorbed and its biological effect. For perspective, consider that background radiation exposes an average American to about 100 millirem (mrem) per year. However, for people living at higher altitudes, such as Denver, that amount can climb to 170 mrem.[33] These numbers do not include other activities that might expose a person to additional doses, such as tanning, x-rays, or working in or near facilities where radioactive elements are present.

In 1955 the International Commission on Radiological Protection recommended exposing the general public to no more than 1.5 rem annually. (It was reduced in 1960 to an "average" annual dose of 170 mrem beyond normal background radiation, and then to 100 mrem in 1994.)[34] Using those guidelines the National Academy of Sciences (NAS) issued a report in June 1955 denying the findings of the physicists at RPI. According to the NAS, nuclear testing had not appreciably boosted atmospheric radiation. Furthermore at current levels, during his or her lifetime a person would absorb only 0.2 roentgen of strontium-90, or 0.001 below the level considered dangerous. Strauss argued that the report demonstrated nuclear testing did not pose a danger to humans. Libby agreed, contending that it took about ten years for strontium-90 in the atmosphere to fall to Earth; filtering took place as it traveled through the food chain from plants to animals to humans, to the point that when it entered the human body, it caused no harm. But Ralph Lapp, an American physicist who also had served on the Manhattan Project, rejected Libby's conclusions. The amount of atmospheric strontium-90, he asserted, increased with each nuclear test, and it did not dissipate as it went through the food chain. Instead its long half-life led to a buildup of radioactivity in the human body, potentially causing cancer. Furthermore he dismissed the NAS claim that the present level of strontium-90 was well below the danger line. By his estimate "the atmosphere already contained 15 per cent of the total that the world could safely absorb."[35]

No scientist was more outspoken against testing, though, than Linus Pauling. Born in 1901 in Oregon, Pauling received his Ph.D. in physical chemistry in 1925 from the California Institute of Technology and in 1954 was awarded the Nobel Prize in Chemistry for his book *The Nature of the Chemical Bond*. Thin, with an oval face topped by a receding hairline of wavy white hair, a sharp nose, "an animated face and a persuasive smile," the brilliant chemist and biologist was soft-spoken in private but outspoken in public and repeatedly at the center of controversy. While working in California during World War II for the U.S. National Defense Research Commission, he was accused of being pro-Japanese because he and his wife had hired a gardener of Japanese descent. After the war he became a leading opponent of nuclear testing, which generated accusations that he was a communist sympathizer. Mistrust of Pauling's loyalty prompted the State Department repeatedly to reject his application for a passport.[36]

In early 1955 Pauling shocked a television audience when he stated during an interview that fallout caused cancer. He continued to make this charge, proclaiming in April 1957, a month before the United Kingdom tested its first hydrogen device, that ten thousand people would die from leukemia because of radioactivity released in previous atomic blasts; the British shot would doom a thousand more "for every megaton of explosive power released." In May, with the assistance of the biologist Barry Commoner and the physicist Edward Condon, he put together a petition signed by more than nine thousand scientists calling for a cessation of testing.[37]

Such sentiment soon entered the center of American politics. In April 1956, while running as the Democratic nominee in that year's presidential election, Adlai Stevenson called on the United States to suspend atomic tests unilaterally. To do so "would reflect our determination never to plunge the world into nuclear holocaust, a step which would affirm our purpose to act with humility and a decent concern for world opinion." If the Soviets joined a U.S.-led moratorium on testing only to violate it, scientific apparatuses would detect Moscow's deception. Senator Clinton Anderson of New Mexico, who had assumed the chairmanship of the JCAE after the Democrats gained control of both houses of Congress in the 1954 congressional election, seconded Stevenson, at least insofar as testing bombs greater than one megaton.[38]

Eisenhower knew he faced a conundrum. Nuclear weapons offered the cheapest and most effective deterrent to the Soviet threat, but they also risked the greatest harm to the human race if used. Testing of those weapons had aroused a movement that he could not ignore. For Eisenhower, however, a ban on testing was not enough. It had to be part of a broader agreement designed to reduce, if not eliminate, the world's nuclear stockpiles. Yet achieving that goal required international, and particularly Soviet, cooperation, which he did not see forthcoming any time soon. Moscow had rejected his Atoms for Peace proposal, believing that it failed to address the threat posed to the world by atomic weapons. Disarmament talks that began in London in 1954 between American, Soviet, British, Canadian, and French representatives also saw little progress.[39] The president thus concluded that he had no choice but to continue testing to maintain America's atomic superiority over its superpower rival.

Others joined Eisenhower. Vice President Richard Nixon called Stevenson's bid "not only naive but dangerous to our national security." Truman asserted that without continued testing, the United States would find it harder to "guard the peace."[40] While numerous scientists had signed the Pauling petition, many leading names in their fields had refused. Joel Hildebrand, a chemist at the University of California, for example, stated that national security was more important than the risks posed by testing, and Eugene Rabinowitch, the editor of the *Bulletin of the Atomic Scientists*, considered Libby's conclusions "approximately correct."[41]

Some people tried to bring this message to a wider audience. In 1952 General Electric sponsored a short animated film produced by John Sutherland entitled *A Is for Atom*, which pointed to the numerous peaceful uses of the atom, including for medicine, power, and agriculture. Even the cartoonist Walt Disney, with the financial support of the U.S. government, in 1956 produced an hour-long television program called *Our Friend the Atom*. Included was a cartoon in which a fisherman opens a bottle; a genie appears to him in a "mushroom-shaped cloud" and threatens to destroy the world. But the fisherman successfully tricks the genie to return to the bottle. The message was clear: humans could make the atom do their bidding.[42]

It was Edward Teller, however, who led the test ban's doubters within the scientific community. Standing nearly six feet tall, with dark hair, thick eyebrows, and penetrating eyes, Teller had been born in 1908 in Austria-Hungary. At age eighteen he left his homeland for Germany, where he received his Ph.D. in physics from the University of Leipzig. He moved to the United States in the mid-1930s and later worked on the Manhattan Project. From 1956 to 1958 he served on the AEC's General Advisory Committee. Following Lawrence's death in 1958, he resigned his position on the Committee to become director of UCRL-L, serving in that post for two years. Brilliant but vain and impersonal, Teller detested both fascist Germany and the Soviet Union.[43] Determined to maintain America's nuclear supremacy over the Kremlin, he had joined with Lawrence in lobbying for development of the "super," which later became the hydrogen bomb.

Teller's determination to continue testing derived in part from his fervent anticommunism. He and Lawrence not only downplayed the danger posed by fallout but argued that a ban on weapons tests would prevent the United States from knowing if the explosives in question worked. Additionally there was no way to guarantee that the technology of the day could detect Soviet violations of a test ban, if implemented. As far as Teller was concerned, the Kremlin would "find methods to cheat." But he also maintained that any cessation of testing jeopardized the science needed to create a better, more modern world. "Testing," he wrote in his memoir, "has the obvious potential of increasing knowledge. . . . Suppressing knowledge seems to me . . . wrong and impractical. . . . Those who believe that we are not yet ready for some knowledge consider themselves members of a world aristocracy that is ahead of everyone else in its value judgments."[44]

This debate over testing was important in three respects. First, it represented an attempt by advocates of testing to make out opponents as self-centered elitists who stood in the way of discoveries that might help all people. Second, by presenting the debate as a choice between a cessation of testing and defending the security of the United States, Teller and his allies sought, with some success, to give the impression that individuals such as Pauling and Stevenson were anti-American or even pro-communist.[45] Third, the difference of opinion over testing had ramifications for Plowshare. Any test, whether conducted in the atmosphere or on the surface, caused fallout. Even a blast that took place underground might not be fully contained. How, then, could scientists justify blasts for peaceful purposes if they harmed humans? Complicating matters was that Plowshare was under the authority of the AEC's Division of *Military* Applications. How could Plowshare's defenders assure a domestic and international audience that peaceful-use tests were in fact not a cover for developing weapons that could obliterate humankind? If no such guarantee were possible, it was highly unlikely the United States could convince the Soviet Union or any other nation to accept an international moratorium. Both Libby and Senator Anderson realized the problem. Libby "questioned the advisability of including a program for peaceful uses of explosions under military administration." The AEC's general manager, A. R. Luedecke, replied that Plowshare was not large enough to warrant disconnecting it from the Division of Military Applications. Anderson considered such a rationale "unfortunate," for it permitted the Soviets to charge the United States with using peaceful nuclear tests to hide what was really a weapons program. "When General Starbird, as director of Military Applications, signs letters dealing with Project Plowshare . . . it does not tend to refute the Russian claim."[46]

For Plowshare's defenders, Anderson's discomfort was immaterial. What mattered was continued testing that would allow the United States to supplement its technological and numerical atomic superiority over the Soviets. By 1957, though, Teller and other testing advocates had to wonder how much longer they might get their way, for American opinion began to echo the anxieties felt among scientists and politicians. In 1954 and 1956 Gallup polls had found that most Americans wanted to continue hydrogen bomb tests. But when asked in 1957 if the United States should stop such tests if the Soviets agreed to do so, nearly two-thirds of respondents said yes. In that same 1957 poll a majority of Americans said that fallout posed a "real danger" to humans.[47]

Some Americans did more than simply respond to poll questions. There were already some pacifist organizations in the United States protesting nuclear testing, among them the Women's International League for Peace and Freedom and the Religious Society of Friends, but they garnered little notice. That changed as new groups appeared that emphasized the danger posed by atomic weapons. The most famous was the Committee for a SANE Nuclear Policy, founded in November 1957 by Coretta Scott King, the wife of Martin Luther King Jr.; Nobel Prize–winning philosopher and physician Albert Schweitzer; and pediatrician Benjamin Spock. By the end of 1958 it had 25,000 members in 130 chapters throughout the country.[48] These organizations became part of a larger international movement to ban nuclear testing, which included such groups as the Campaign for Nuclear Disarmament, founded in 1957 in the United Kingdom.

Many Hollywood productions reflected the growing international trepidation about testing. American children watched Bert the Turtle, who encouraged them to practice "duck and cover" drills to protect themselves against nuclear attack, and their parents saw movies depicting monsters or giant humans created by nuclear tests. The first such movie, *The Beast from 20,000 Fathoms* (1953), featured a giant dinosaur, unfrozen by nuclear testing in the arctic, unleash havoc on New York City. Similar films followed, including *Them!* (1954), *Godzilla* (1955),[49] *The Amazing Colossal Man* (1957), and *Attack of the Crab Monsters* (1957). Others warned that the peaceful atom was not so peaceful. In the movie *Tarantula* (1955), a scientist who hoped to use the atom to feed animals inadvertently created huge mutations, among them a large spider that attacked humans. Food also played a role in *The Beginning of the End* (1957). This time it was crops grown with the help of the atom that caused grasshoppers to reach enormous size; the insects then rampaged through the city of Chicago.

Eisenhower, who a year earlier had rejected a moratorium on testing, realized he could no longer ignore the weight of domestic and international opinion. Teller, joined by Lawrence and UCRL-L physicist Mark Mills, attempted to convince the president not to buckle. Otherwise it would be impossible to make advancements in nuclear technology, such as the creation of a clean bomb. Though Eisenhower found clean technology intriguing, he told his visitors that he would not allow the United States to be "crucified on a cross of atoms." As a further inducement for the president to engage in serious bargaining, the Soviets offered to discuss a moratorium on testing for two to three years and to accept the American demand for on-site inspections. Eisenhower, however, insisted on tying any moratorium to a cessation of nuclear weapons production. To Moscow that quid pro quo was an attempt to maintain America's nuclear dominance, and the Soviets rejected it. With that the London talks in August broke down.[50]

Project Rainier

Teller and his allies certainly were pleased with the collapse of the London talks. Yet they were cognizant that if they did not meet the ever louder demand to curb fallout, the White House might decide it had no choice but to stop testing unilaterally. The Plumbbob test series, set off between May and October 1957, seemed to offer a way to confront those pressures. All but one of the series took place on or above the ground. The exception was Project Rainier. In early 1956 Teller and Dave Griggs, a geophysicist at the California Institute of Technology, suggested testing nuclear explosives underground. There were several advantages to this, they contended. It would reduce, if not eliminate, radioactive fallout while allowing for advancements in atomic technology. Aerial and ground-level blasts required mobilizing numerous people, such as meteorologists or pilots to conduct sampling of the air, which was both time-consuming and expensive. And weather conditions such as wind speed and direction might determine whether an atmospheric or surface-level blast could take place. For example, a shot might have to be postponed because the wind happened to be blowing toward a populated area. Meteorological conditions, however, would not affect the timing or location of underground explosions. In turn the AEC could set off underground blasts with fewer restrictions as to time and place than those occurring on the surface or in the atmosphere.[51]

Rainier, named after Washington State's famous mountain, received the most attention of the twenty-nine Plumbbob tests, including from Plowshare proponents. Teller had warned that if the superpowers reached a test ban agreement, the Soviets would cheat. One method of cheating was to conduct an underground test in a medium that would absorb as much of the shock waves as possible. Rainier's purpose was to see how easy it was to detect such blasts. Therefore the AEC selected a mesa at the NTS made of limestone, a spongy rock that would retard the explosion's transmission. Scientists then placed the 1.7-kiloton explosive in a room six foot square and seven feet high at the end of a tunnel shaped like the number nine 900 feet underground and 790 feet from the mesa's edge. Afterward workers sealed the tunnel with sandbags. When set off, Libby recounted, the device crushed some 400,000 tons of rock, leaving behind a "spherical cavity" (or "chimney") about 110 feet across and 25 feet high. Though the AEC at first determined no seismographs had detected Rainier beyond two hundred miles from the blast site, within months it turned out that seismologists had recorded it in Fairbanks, Alaska, some 2,300 miles away.[52]

Several things about the Rainier shot intrigued scientists interested in Plowshare. While initially there were fears that the explosion had caused cracks in the mesa through which radioactivity might enter the air, none appeared, and the radiation remained contained within the hill. Moreover when scientists in November 1957 drilled into the cavity from what remained of the tunnel, they found little radioactivity. AEC and UCRL-L scientists surmised that the heat from the blast had melted the rock, and when the rock cooled and rehardened, it trapped the majority of the radiation. Last, even three months after the explosion some holes drilled into the mesa found temperatures as high as 194°F.[53] Capturing that heat and mixing it with water would generate steam, which could then be used to produce electricity.

It now appeared that those who wanted to see Plowshare move beyond conjecture had found the way to make it happen. Rainier had shown, Libby told members of Congress, that PNEs could move earth, dig harbors, stimulate production of stagnant oil fields, provide heat that might be tapped for power, and produce isotopes for numerous human uses without posing the danger of fall-out. Of course, there was the matter of conducting blasts on or near the surface, where they might release radioactivity into the atmosphere. But if, as Teller surmised, scientists could develop a clean explosive, then that concern would become moot.[54] Even without such clean technology available, Rainier had piqued the interest of gas, oil, and mining companies, which wondered if they might apply the atom to their work. Consequently, a 1970s report noted, scientists had good reason "to press for expansion for the Plowshare Project for 1958 and beyond."[55]

Making Plowshare a Reality

About three weeks before Rainier the Soviet Union shocked the world when it announced that it had successfully tested the planet's first ICBM. Then, on October 4, Moscow achieved another milestone with the launch of *Sputnik*, the world's first unmanned space satellite. The impact of these two events on the American psyche was enormous. It seemed the Soviet Union was winning not just the arms race but the space race, giving the Kremlin and communism a boost both in terms of prestige and military might. "It appears likely that the effect [of *Sputnik*] in unsophisticated countries will be to create the impression of Soviet technological and military superiority over the United States," Arthur Larson, the director of the U.S. Information Agency, wrote Strauss later that month. As for "more sophisticated areas such as Europe, the impression may be that the USSR is at least equal." Libby immediately called for boosting the $100,000 appropriation given to UCRL-L for Plowshare research. In December Starbird offered up to an additional $350,000 for Livermore in fiscal year 1958, and the AEC expressed its hope to expand funding for the entire program to $1.6 million the next fiscal year.[56]

Larson meanwhile came up with an idea. "Why not," he asked Strauss, "find a reasonably remote place (such as Alaska, perhaps) which needs a harbor, and do the job with one blast?" Furthermore it made sense to have both the media and the public witness it as proof of American technological skill. Larson acknowledged the possibility of fallout, but the development of a clean bomb would alleviate concerns over radioactivity. "The relatively small amount of fallout from a 90% 'clean bomb' could be handled with little trouble."[57]

Strauss found the proposal intriguing. Born in 1896, the balding, bespectacled AEC chair had worked as a partner in an investment banking company between the wars, joined the naval reserve in 1925, entered the regular service when World War II began, and served as special assistant to Secretary of the

Navy James Forrestal during that conflict. In 1946 he joined the AEC, becoming its chair in 1953. He shared Teller's steadfast anticommunism and endorsed the decision of the Eisenhower administration to strip the security clearance of the physicist J. Robert Oppenheimer, the former head of the Manhattan Project and the "father of the atomic bomb," on the grounds that Oppenheimer had Marxist leanings. He also knew a lot about the atom, having done work on uranium fission before America's entrance into World War II and, after the war, moved the AEC to begin a program of detection that discovered the Soviets' 1949 atomic bomb blast. Amicable in social situations, he was certain of his judgments, rarely willing to question his decisions, and "unduly sensitive to criticism." His combination of warm- and coldheartedness prompted one associate to comment, "He has more elbows than an octopus."[58]

It was Strauss's self-conviction and anticommunism that made him determined to continue nuclear testing, despite the clamor it generated. It was those same traits that made him a devotee of finding peaceful uses for the atom. Strauss had shown from an early age a love for science, particularly physics, and the loss of both of his parents to cancer in the 1930s had made him even more interested in that field because of its relationship to the radiation therapy used to treat cancer patients. Following the Soviet hydrogen bomb test of 1953, Strauss called for developing nuclear power plants in the United States and offering that technology to other nations. In so doing Washington would demonstrate its intellectual prowess, repair the damage done to its prestige because of the Soviets' technological advancements, gain allies abroad, and, in the process, create a better world. As part of this effort Strauss had proposed holding a conference in Geneva in 1954 on peaceful uses of the atom. "A Higher Intelligence decided that man was ready to receive it," he wrote a year after he suggested the Geneva meeting. "My faith tells me that the Creator did not intend man to evolve through the ages to this stage of civilization only now to devise something that would destroy life on earth."[59]

Similar considerations made Larson's suggestion appealing to Strauss as well as other Plowshare proponents. Building a harbor in a remote location such as Alaska could meet the need to prove America's technological know-how in the face of the Soviet ICBM test and *Sputnik* while avoiding the danger of domestic or international reaction from fallout. It would also demonstrate that the United States had the ability to effectively put the peaceful atom to use in civilian construction projects. The country was already well on its way to creating a clean explosive, Strauss wrote in December 1957, for it had atomic devices "with more than 95 percent of their power free from the production of radioactive fallout."[60] If the United States could create an even cleaner explosive before blasting the harbor, radioactivity would be of even less concern. If not, Alaska's distance from the other forty-eight states and its sparse population meant few if any people would be affected. And the successful construction of a harbor might prove to Americans and others the economic benefits offered by Plowshare. In turn there would be far less pressure to ban testing.

Strauss therefore personified the beliefs of those who defended Plowshare. They were overwhelmingly confident that they could control the atom and use it to lead humankind down a path of progress. They regarded those who opposed nuclear tests as insensitive, anti-American, and even pro-communist, individuals who overestimated the danger posed by radioactivity, underestimated the good the atom could bring to humankind, and misjudged the threat posed by international communism. For Strauss and those who thought like him, a harbor project represented the first step in simultaneously creating a better world for all and protecting the nation's security. Moving the harbor project from drawing board to reality, though, proved far more difficult than Plowshare's supporters had anticipated.

Just Drop Us a Card

In mid-August 1958 several Eskimos from the village of Point Hope, Alaska—Daniel Lisbourne, Peniluke Omnik, and Lisbourne's nephew—took Lisbourne's small boat to nearby Ogotoruk Creek to hunt caribou. Located in northwestern Alaska, the eleven-mile stream empties into the Chukchi Sea. It was, and remains to this day, an area rich in plant life and a feeding ground for caribou, which make up a sizable portion of the Eskimos' diet. Unfortunately for Lisbourne, he and his party returned to the village empty-handed. But they did bring back some odd news: there were surveyors camped at the creek. What they were doing at Ogotoruk, of all places, Lisbourne did not know.[1]

The surveyors Lisbourne witnessed were working with the AEC. Motivated by U.S. Information Agency Director Arthur Larson's suggestion to conduct a nuclear excavation blast in Alaska, the AEC had selected for ground zero Cape Thompson, located on the Chukchi Sea about thirty miles southeast of Point Hope. Called Project Chariot, this Plowshare experiment was one of four proposed by the AEC, two of the others having the names Oilsands and Gnome. The AEC and its supporters believed that together these four tests would prove to the world the multitude of uses for the peaceful atom while simultaneously protecting America's military and economic security. The focus for Gnome was heat and isotope generation; for Oilsands and an unnamed experiment, it was the stimulation of petroleum production. Chariot would create a harbor beneficial to the people and corporate interests of Alaska. More important, if successful, it would provide information vital to what would become for much of its history the keystone of the Plowshare program: the construction of a sea-level isthmian canal.

All four tests ran into obstacles. Each of them faced varying levels of resistance from citizens, scientists, politicians, and industrialists. Possibly even more important, these proposed projects ran headlong into a U.S.-Soviet moratorium on nuclear testing. The Eisenhower administration was reluctant to permit any blasts that could allow the Kremlin to claim bad faith on its part. By the middle of 1959 the entire Plowshare program appeared to be in limbo.

Target: Alaska

With AEC Chairman Lewis Strauss's decision to build a harbor using the atom, the UCRL-L started looking for a suitable location in November 1957. There were four criteria the site had to meet. First, it had to be located within the United States. To try to conduct the blast in a foreign country would involve potentially long and complex negotiations that might ultimately fail. Second, the site had to guarantee the "protection of people and wildlife." Third, it had to provide "geologic and engineering requirements for essential experimental data." Such data were necessary for other excavation projects, most notably that of a sea-level isthmian canal. Fourth, it had to offer the potential for "long-term utilitarian value."[2] Hence the blast had to be more than simply an experiment.

Though they considered California and Texas, the AEC and UCRL-L quickly settled on Alaska because of its remoteness and dispersed population. In early February the Radiation Laboratory contacted both the U.S. Geological Survey (USGS) and the Minneapolis-based engineering firm E. J. Longyear Company. From USGS, UCRL-L requested information on the soil and permafrost along Alaska's coastline from Point Barrow to the Arctic Circle in anticipation of a large-scale engineering project. From Longyear, it wanted to know about the possible mineral deposits of the region, suggestions for a site for a deep-water harbor, and an estimate of the traffic using such a harbor a quarter of a century into the future. Wanting to move quickly, Livermore asked to receive both reports by mid-April. This meant that USGS and Longyear had to limit themselves to what they could find in the literature rather than on-site inspection; indeed Plowshare officials denied Longyear authorization to travel to Alaska to survey the coast.[3]

Longyear apparently had little comment about the time constraints it faced. Not so with USGS. George Gates, the head of the Survey's Alaskan Geology Branch, complained at the end of February to a colleague that there was little information on the northwest coast of Alaska, and it made no sense to write "a series of 'quickie' reports based solely upon photo-interpretation and literature search."[4]

David Hopkins, an expert on the Bering Strait who worked at USGS's Western Region headquarters in Menlo Park, California, was even more outspoken when a group from Livermore came to speak with him about Alaska. He could not believe that fellow scientists had in mind such a project knowing that only fifty-five miles separated Alaska and the Soviet Union. If the harbor explosion generated radioactive fallout on Soviet soil, an international incident could result. UCRL-L Associate Director for Testing Gerald Johnson himself admitted years later that such a consideration never entered the minds of those supporting the harbor project,[5] but it also did not deter Livermore and the AEC from proceeding.

The same day Gates lodged his first complaint about the harbor, Strauss began an effort to sell it. Ironically, while Chariot's purpose was supposedly a demonstration of the potential of the atom for *civilian* projects, Strauss first approached the military, namely Navy Secretary Thomas Gates. The AEC head explained that his agency had begun looking at using nuclear explosives to build a harbor somewhere along the 1,600-mile stretch of land between Nome and Point Barrow. He asked whether the navy might find an anchorage in that part of Alaska useful. Unfortunately for Strauss, Gates replied that while the navy had an interest in the Plowshare program, it saw no need for a harbor in that region.[6]

Strauss much have realized that detonating nuclear explosives for a project designed to benefit the U.S. armed forces would have belied claims that Plowshare was peaceful in nature and given the Soviets reason to charge the United States with duplicity. Why he decided to approach the navy rather than the Alaska state government or a private company must remain speculative. There is good reason to believe, however, that his motivation derived from the AEC's relationship with both the White House and the Commission's attendant laboratories. Until 1957 the only one of President Eisenhower's top aides who endorsed arms control was Harold Stassen, whom Eisenhower had appointed in 1955 as special assistant on disarmament. Therefore Strauss had little reason to worry that any Soviet charge of deceit would carry much weight in the Oval Office. Furthermore the cold war necessitated a continuation of the military-industrial complex that had developed during World War II. To provide the armed forces the weapons they needed to defend the United States and its allies, the AEC contracted much of its work to its attendant laboratories, such as Livermore and Sandia. As government contractors, the scientists in these labs could conduct their work without fear of accountability. Even better, if they could sell whatever atomic projects they developed as militarily necessary, they could guarantee themselves a further infusion of cash. It was unlikely that lawmakers or the interested public would fully understand the science behind the endeavor in question, thus giving the AEC and the labs further freedom to maneuver.[7] Nor were Americans likely to question a project marketed as crucial to national security.

Despite Gates's disinterest, planning for the harbor continued. By mid-April UCRL-L and the AEC had the USGS and Longyear reports in hand. The USGS had identified three possible sites between Cape Seppings and Cape Thompson, a strip of territory about twenty miles long.[8] Longyear settled on Cape Thompson, concluding that coal and petroleum existed in large quantities nearby. Although ice would limit use of the harbor to ninety to a hundred days a year, within twenty-five years of its completion it would generate $176 million of exports annually.[9]

Having restricted the location of the harbor to a small area of coastline, representatives from the AEC, UCRL-L, and Holmes and Narver, an engineering and construction firm that had contracted with Livermore, met in mid-May at the firm's headquarters in Los Angeles to begin mapping out what had become known as Project Chariot. They decided to use 2.4 megatons of explosives, with four 100-kiloton devices blasting a channel measuring about 6,000 feet long and 1,200 feet wide, and two one-megaton bombs producing a turning basin of the same length and 3,000 feet in width. The AEC estimated that burying each explosive three hundred to four hundred feet underground would trap about 95 percent of the radioactivity within the site.[10] The truth, though, was that the AEC and UCRL-L were not so sure of their conclusions. Gary Higgins, who succeeded Johnson in 1960, admitted that no one involved in Chariot had given "serious thought of air blast." When asked what the air blast effect of a near-surface one-megaton explosion would have been on Point Hope, Higgins replied, "Well, it would have wiped out everything." Considering that Chariot envisioned using *two* such devices, the impact would have been far greater.[11]

Selling the Shot

With the plan in hand, and with the navy's lack of interest in Chariot, the AEC and its allies turned to selling the explosion to the people of Alaska and determining the exact location for ground zero. In June the Commission publicly announced it had begun to look at the nuclear excavation of a harbor along the Alaskan coastline to take place in 1960.[12] In the middle of the following month a team including representatives from Sandia Corporation, UCRL-L, and the AEC, and led by Edward Teller, headed to Juneau. Arriving unannounced, they learned that the governor, Mike Stepovich, and much of the state legislature were out of town. Therefore the Livermore group split up, with half, including Teller, remaining in Juneau to give a news conference and meet with the local branch of the Rotary Club, while the remainder traveled to Anchorage to hold talks with that city's chamber of commerce. Before giving his first presentation, Teller tried to convince an economist from Alaska, George Rogers, of the viability of the blast. Rogers was not impressed. He explained that any coal in northwestern Alaska that might exist lay far north of the blast site, hauling the coal to Cape Thompson required an expensive transportation system, and the port itself could function only three months out of each year. When Rogers then raised the matter of the Eskimos who lived in the Cape Thompson region and who relied heavily on "hunting and fishing for their living," Teller made clear he had no intention of permitting the indigenous people to stand in the way of progress. "We are not interested in preserving the Eskimo as a hunter," he retorted. "We are interested in giving him the opportunity of becoming a coal miner." Rogers ascertained that he was not the person Teller had hoped for when the latter changed the subject and asked about the best place to buy souvenirs.[13]

Teller's reaction to Rogers's comments was indicative of his vanity, his determination to prove Plowshare's utility, and his unwillingness to allow anything to get in the way of nuclear testing. It was also evidence of his failure to understand the complexities involved in PNEs. Teller, Johnson stated years after Plowshare's demise, was "very smart, very good. He just has no idea what it takes to get something done." Instead he would come up with a design for whatever it was he wanted, assume it worked, and expect others to move to the next step of proving it.[14]

For Teller, Chariot would work. Playing on Japan's interest in importing coal from Alaska, he told his audiences in Juneau that the AEC intended to spend $5 million constructing an anchorage advantageous to businesses by providing a place from which to ship coal. Once again he encountered a less than enthusiastic reception. As with Rogers, the business and governmental officials at the news conference pointed out that a harbor at Cape Thompson would be ice-bound three-fourths of the year; they suggested other in-state locations for a harbor or even a canal. The Anchorage team did not fare much better. The attendees did not take well to a comment by the visiting delegation that the corporate sector would have to foot most of the bill for the project, which could run as high as $100 million. One local businessman quipped, "Economic feasibility and scientific feasibility don't go hand in hand."[15]

Resolute in their determination, Teller and the UCRL-L legation reunited and headed to Fairbanks, where they had arranged a meeting with area business leaders as well as scientists from the University of Alaska at Fairbanks (UAF). In light of the perfunctory reception they had received earlier, the Livermore group, at least publicly, now took the position that it would implement any project—it no longer had to be a harbor—that Alaskans wanted. What they heard startled the university scientists. Though Teller, who led most of the presentation, argued that Chariot "would add even less radiation than the background amount to which all persons are constantly exposed due to cosmic rays," the UAF professors realized that this could still mean a doubling of that exposure. Even a small increase in radiation might harm the human body. The scientists also rejected an assertion Teller made that the shot would not hurt animal life because there would be no animals feeding in the area in the winter. "There are herds of caribou out there," explained Albert Johnson, an associate professor of botany. Teller did not appreciate the challenge. "There can't be," he responded. "What would they eat?" He clearly did not know that caribou during the winter foraged through the snow to get at lichen, grass, and twigs. The UAF scientists suggested conducting environmental surveys to make sure that the blast posed no danger to the regional ecology.[16]

The only group in Alaska that evinced any excitement about Chariot was the Fairbanks media. C. W. Snedden of the city's *Daily News Miner* portrayed Chariot as beneficial to the territory's economy, and a week later the paper's editors championed the shot. "We say to Dr. Teller and his associates: Come ahead, Alaska will be proud to be the scene. . . . Alaska welcomes you, tell us how we can help." Nowhere did the *Miner* ask Alaskans if they wanted Chariot to take place on their soil.[17]

Despite the chilly response they encountered, and notwithstanding their expressed willingness to consider any number of nuclear excavation projects, the AEC and UCRL-L were set on constructing a harbor. While in Anchorage and Fairbanks, neither Teller nor anyone else in his entourage mentioned that in June the AEC had asked the Department of Interior's Bureau of Land Management to remove from the public domain 1,600 square miles of land in the Ogotoruk Creek region, an area significantly larger than Rhode Island; that a USGS team had been on the Arctic Coast taking a closer look at the three sites the Survey had earlier identified; or that Gerald Johnson had led a group of AEC, UCRL-L, and Holmes and Narver officials to select ground zero. Whichever site Johnson chose would be based on a lack of information. Not only had USGS received what it considered insufficient funding for a complete survey, but it had to finish its inspection by July 17, when Johnson was to arrive. "This will give our boys some, but altogether not enough, time to size up the three possible sites," wrote Gates's colleague, G. Donald Eberlein.[18]

Gerald Johnson brought with him six other men to the Cape Thompson site, joining the USGS team of about nine. Impressed by the location, he gave the green light to proceed with preparations for the blast. Holmes and Narver and USGS began setting up a camp, which, along with an airstrip, they completed by mid-August. (It was these people whom Lisbourne and his party had witnessed.) Fourteen men from the Fairbanks-based Philleo Engineering Company, with which the AEC had also contracted, joined USGS in an intensified survey of the area. An enthusiastic Teller wrote Alfred D. Starbird, the head of the AEC's Division of Military Applications, "The preliminary site inspection of the Cape Thompson area revealed that it would be an ideal site for an experiment."[19]

Beyond a conviction to use nuclear excavation at Cape Thompson, Teller's letter was significant in that he said nothing about a project beneficial to the people of Alaska. Quite the opposite: "In discussing the usefulness of such a harbor with groups in Alaska we found no one who could justify at this time the harbor on an economic or military basis." Rather than a project designed to provide "long-term utilitarian value" to the people of Alaska, Chariot had become "a demonstration or an experiment." The message to Starbird, however, was confidential, meaning that few people outside of those involved in Chariot knew that its purpose had changed. For instance, in a letter to Senator Henry Jackson (D-Washington) dated a month later, Teller provided a summation of the Plowshare program, including Chariot, which specifically referred to the intention to construct a harbor in Alaska that would cater to coal and oil interests.[20]

Chariot and a Sea-Level Canal

Even if Chariot had now become an experiment, that was good enough for the AEC and its allies, for the blast could provide information crucial to what became the centerpiece of the Plowshare program, the construction of a sea-level canal somewhere in or near Central America. As Johnson put it years later, Chariot "was tied to the Panama Canal studies, which was driving all of our activity."[21] The idea of building such a waterway dated at least as far back as Vasco Núñez de Balboa, a Spanish explorer who crossed modern-day Panama in 1513.[22] In the late 1800s Ferdinand Marie de Lesseps, the builder of the sea-level Suez Canal, believed he could achieve the same feat in Panama. Landslides caused by the damp dirt, disease spread by mosquitoes, and cost overruns forced him to abandon the project in 1893. In 1903 the United States and Panama signed the Hay-Bunau-Varilla Treaty, which gave Washington the right to construct a canal and to retain a strip of Panamanian land—the Canal Zone—"in perpetuity." Additionally Washington received the right, whether or not Panama consented, to use its armed forces to defend the canal. In return the U.S. government paid Panama $10 million and agreed to an annuity of $250,000 for control of the Zone. Construction of the canal began shortly thereafter, and in 1914 it opened to traffic.

The Panama Canal is not a sea-level waterway. Because of a difference of about eight inches in height between the Atlantic and Pacific Oceans, as well as a need to get through Gatun Lake and the hills that cut through central Panama, the canal uses a series of six locks to raise and lower vessels. Each lock is 1,000 feet long and 110 feet wide and set in pairs, allowing a ship heading in one direction to pass a vessel traveling the opposite way. The entire fifty-mile trip takes a contemporary ship eight to twelve hours, depending on traffic; the busier the canal, the longer vessels may have to wait to pass through a lock. In the event one of a pair of locks requires repair, the travel time would be even longer.

Such considerations prompted some U.S. officials, among them President William H. Taft, to suggest even before the canal's completion the construction of a sea-level waterway. That idea, though, received little attention until World War II, when it became clear that if any of America's enemies succeeded in sabotaging or destroying one or more of the locks, the canal would become effectively useless. Ships cruising between the Atlantic and Pacific Oceans would have no choice but to travel around South America, a longer, more dangerous, and more time-consuming voyage. Before America's entrance into World War II, Congress, realizing the waterway's vulnerability, authorized a study to look into adding a third lock to each pair, and during the war the United States intensified its efforts to defend the waterway.[23]

Although nothing happened to the canal during the war, lawmakers continued to point to its defenselessness. Consequently in 1945 Capitol Hill authorized another study, this one to examine increasing the waterway's security and, in light of the growing number of ships using the canal, its capacity. The study took on added importance following a nuclear test at Bikini Atoll in 1946; the explosion sank ten of a fleet of fifty captured German and Japanese warships as well as obsolete U.S. vessels placed nearby. It became clear that protecting the canal, which was so vital to the United States commercially and militarily, required taking into account not just sabotage and conventional attack but, possibly at some point in the future, a nuclear assault. Hence when the study was issued in 1947, it offered five solutions. Four involved locks, including the third lock proposal, or a modification of the existing lock system. The last, however, suggested turning the existing canal into one that was at sea level. Of the options, the study recommended the sea-level waterway, contending that it was the most impervious to sabotage or attack, as there was no need to worry about rebuilding any damaged or destroyed locks. The problem with converting the lock canal to one that was at sea level was the estimated $2.3 billion cost. Moreover that sum did not include the dollars needed to build "tidal regulating structures," a necessity because of the height difference between the two oceans. Not prepared to spend that kind of money, for the next decade the U.S. government shelved any proposals to upgrade the waterway.[24]

The canal's security, though, never strayed far from the minds of U.S. officials. Panamanians grew increasingly frustrated with the 1903 treaty, viewing the perpetuity clause as an infringement on their country's sovereignty and the $250,000 annuity as too little. In an attempt to assuage Panama, Washington in the 1930s and again in 1955 raised the annuity and gave other concessions. The 1956 Suez crisis made some U.S. officials wonder if the Panamanians might make new demands on Washington that could precipitate a similar predicament in the Canal Zone. As President Eisenhower warned his defense secretary, Charles Wilson, the U.S. government "must be exceedingly careful that the future years do not bring about for us, in Panama, the situation that Britain has to face in the Suez."[25]

Once again attention turned to a sea-level waterway. Such a canal would prove easier to repair should Panama or another power attempt to damage or destroy it. Moreover there were concerns about the existing canal's utility. During World War II U.S. battleships had a difficult time using the canal's locks, and by the mid-1950s some ships, both military and civilian, had become so large that about three hundred of them could not use the waterway. All the while traffic on the canal had increased, with some reports concluding that the waterway would exceed its capacity by the mid-1970s. For these reasons, in 1957 the board of directors of the Panama Canal Company ordered a study to improve it.[26]

That same year Sandia Corporation's Luke J. Vortman proposed at the First Plowshare Symposium the atomic construction of a new isthmian canal. But it was not until 1958 that the suggestion received serious consideration. "I recently made a liaison visit to the University of California Radiation Laboratory," U.S. Army Major General Louis Heath wrote William E. Potter, the governor of the Canal Zone, in March. There Heath learned about Plowshare, which "convinced [him] that there is an expanding possibility of successful use of atomic explosives in this sort of work." He encouraged Potter to learn more about "this project." Whether Heath's letter had an impact is not clear, but by September of that year the Canal Company indicated its interest in using the atom to build "a second canal."[27]

The Panama Canal Company report came out in September 1958. Evaluating some thirty possible routes and both conventional and nuclear methods of constructing a new waterway, the study recommended use of the atom. Most of the routes examined had too many people living nearby to make them candidates for a PNE. But there were five where the United States might safely apply the atom: route 1, through the Isthmus of Tehuantepec in Mexico; route 8, located in Costa Rica close to the Nicaraguan border; route 16, the San Blas, located in Panama "at the narrowest part of the Isthmus"; route 17, called the Sasardi-Morti, in the Darien region of southern Panama; and route 25, the Atrato-Truando in northern Colombia. Of the options, the two that drew the most attention were routes 17 and 25. They were short, thus saving time and money for shippers. Unlike route 16, they did not have a terminus close to a major city. They were also cheaper. Compared to the estimated $2.5 billion to build a new waterway using conventional means or the $4 billion cost to use nuclear excavation along routes 1 or 8, a nuclear-excavated canal along the Atrato-Truando would run about $1.25 billion; the Sasardi-Morti was cheaper still, at about $750 million. Yet the survey did not discount the other options. For instance, the Tehuantepec route, though pricey, had the advantage of proximity to the United States and U.S.-based shippers.[28]

Of course, constructing a canal with the atom required time. Surveys of the land and biological studies had to take place, the explosives had to be constructed and emplaced, and following detonation conventional equipment had to connect the craters and provide the finishing touches. The entire process alone could take up to ten years. Moreover whether built in Panama or elsewhere, the United States could anticipate potentially difficult negotiations over such matters as sovereignty, annuities, defense of the waterway, and whether to abandon the original canal. Even if Panama decided to continue managing the lock canal on its own, the competition it faced from a U.S.-operated sea-level waterway—one that offered safer, faster travel—certainly would cut into the $60 million Panama made each year in tolls and annuities, with potentially disastrous effects on that nation's economy. Furthermore by the fall of 1959 the United Sates faced one other consideration. "Planning for the nuclear excavation of a canal across the Isthmus," noted the State Department, "must take into account the current negotiations in Geneva for a treaty for the discontinuance of nuclear weapons testing."[29]

A Test Ban and Changes at the Top

The negotiations in Geneva had seemed dead in the water just a couple of years earlier. But in March 1958 the Soviet Union announced a unilateral suspension of nuclear testing. This was no spontaneous declaration. Nikita Khrushchev, who had served as first secretary of the Soviet Communist Party, had become premier following a struggle for power. Meanwhile the United States was on the verge of starting a new series of weapons tests, called Hardtack II. Khrushchev's intention was to use the moratorium as a way to build international pressure on Washington to follow suit, thereby forcing cancellation of Hardtack. If the White House refused, then the Kremlin could justify a resumption of testing.[30]

A month later Linus Pauling again entered the picture. Pauling, who for some time had warned of the threat posed by strontium-90, had turned his attention to carbon-14, concluding that carbon-14, a radioactive isotope generated by atomic blasts, was as much as two hundred times more dangerous to humans than strontium-90. He announced his findings in early April at an international scientific convention, and later that month the *New York Times* publicized his conclusions. The AEC immediately rejected Pauling's assertions, yet it could not discover any proof they were incorrect. Willard Libby, a chemist and member of the AEC, could only argue, "There must be something wrong someplace."[31]

The Soviet announcement and the unceasing debate over the perils of fallout stepped up worldwide calls for the United States to stop its own testing and raised two serious questions for Washington. One was how to proceed with Chariot. To authorize the blast without at least some advance warning would generate international condemnation of the White House and give the Kremlin a propaganda victory. Therefore in June Foy Kohler, the deputy assistant secretary for European Affairs, let the counselor of the Soviet embassy in the United States, Sergei Striganov, know about Chariot, and shortly thereafter the AEC issued a press release. Not surprisingly the Soviets issued a strong rebuke, accusing the United States of trying "to evade permanently the cessation of such experiments" as well as "to set up a legal camouflage for the continuation of nuclear tests." Moreover the Kremlin warned that radioactivity from the blast might be deposited on Soviet soil.[32]

The second question facing the White House was whether to join the Soviets in a test suspension. Teller and others had warned that the Kremlin would cheat if the superpowers stopped testing, and Eisenhower had commented that a poorly supervised testing agreement would endanger U.S. security. By April 1958, however, the president had begun to reconsider. Getting wind of Moscow's plans to announce a moratorium, Secretary of State John Foster Dulles, who up to this point had opposed a cessation of testing, now suggested the United States declare a suspension before the Soviet Union did. Doing so, Dulles stated, "would make a great diplomatic and propaganda sensation to the advantage of the United States." Then, in April, the atomic physicist Hans Bethe declared it possible to detect tests smaller than two kilotons, thereby accounting for some 90 percent of all nuclear blasts, and the president's science adviser, James Killian, called an adequate inspection system "feasible."[33]

None of this was good news for Strauss. At one time President Eisenhower had relied on his AEC chief when it came to nuclear matters, thereby giving Strauss enormous influence over White House decision making regarding a test ban. But following the uproar within the United States caused by the Soviet launching of *Sputnik*, Eisenhower had established the Presidential Science Advisory Committee, many of whose members, among them Killian, desired a test ban. Dulles now appeared to favor a ban too. Consequently Strauss found himself with far less influence than he once had in the Oval Office.[34] Despite the AEC head's objections, and assured that he now had the ability to detect almost any effort by the Soviets to cheat on a test ban, in April Eisenhower told the American public and Khrushchev of his preparedness to halt further tests. Shortly thereafter representatives from the three nations with nuclear bombs—the United States, the United Kingdom, and the Soviet Union—began preliminary talks in Geneva to determine the feasibility of ending testing.[35]

Strauss's resistance to a cessation of testing played a part in costing him his job. The *New York Times* commented in May 1958, "Mr. Strauss seems to be at odds these days with just about everyone who counts in official Washington."[36] This was true. His arrogant and uncompromising personality had indeed turned powerful figures against him, among them Clinton Anderson (D-New Mexico), who served in the U.S. Senate from 1948 to 1973. For just over twenty years of that period Anderson was on the JCAE, including two stints as its chairman (1955–56 and 1959–60).

Anderson and Strauss had first clashed over the idea of developing a clean bomb. It was impossible to devise a perfectly clean explosive, Anderson charged, and no matter how sanitized it was, a nuclear device would kill thousands of people. Indeed he believed that the military, with the AEC's collaboration, was actually making bombs "dirtier"—developed to generate more fallout—so as to kill even more people if used. To the senator, this was evidence of a larger effort by the AEC to keep the JCAE uninformed of what exactly the Commission was doing. He got confirmation of his suspicions when the Commission initially declared that no seismographs over a few hundred miles from the September 1957 Rainier blast had recorded it, then later admitted that seismologists had detected the shot well over two thousand miles away. Why, Anderson wondered, would the AEC present the lower number unless it wanted to raise doubts about the ability to detect nuclear blasts from long distances and so undermine any hope of enforcing a ban that might include underground explosions? "For me," the senator wrote years later, "the [Rainier] episode was one more piece of evidence for the belief that Lewis Strauss was untrustworthy."[37]

Strauss reciprocated the sentiment. He rejected Anderson's contention that the AEC had not kept the JCAE informed, telling President Eisenhower, "[Anderson] does not always do his homework [and] knows, or remembers, remarkably little of what we do." As for any personal animosity Anderson had toward him, Strauss could not ascertain the cause. "I suspect that only a psychiatrist could explain it," he wrote. "However, I have particular resentment toward him since I believe him to be a sick man."[38]

Having served his five-year term as head of the AEC, Strauss was due for reappointment in June 1958. He asked Eisenhower not to submit his name to Congress. For a variety of reasons, including his part in the effort to strip the security clearance of the physicist J. Robert Oppenheimer, he explained, "I have acquired the hostility of a small but vocal coterie of columnists." But he also pointed to Anderson's "almost psychopathic dislike for [him]." As the deadline for his re-appointment neared, Strauss submitted his resignation, which Eisenhower accepted.[39]

Strauss's successor was John A. McCone. Born in 1902 in San Francisco, McCone had gone on to make a fortune building ships during World War II and had been a friend of Eisenhower's since serving in the late 1940s as deputy to Defense Secretary James Forrestal. He had a fighter's spirit but was also gracious and charming, and observers believed that he would repair the strained relationship that had developed between the AEC and JCAE. The Senate quickly approved his nomination. As it turned out, McCone got along better at a personal level with his contemporaries, but he showed little difference with Strauss on such matters as nuclear testing.[40]

McCone became a member of a newly established body called the Committee of Principals, the purpose of which was to develop U.S. policy on nuclear testing. Its other members included Secretary Dulles, CIA Director (and Dulles's brother) Allen Dulles, Defense Secretary Neil McElroy, and Killian. Given its membership, it is not surprising that the Principals faced a split in their ranks over nuclear testing. This became clear two months after Strauss's resignation, when the delegates at Geneva issued a report stating that it was possible to use a system of 160 to 170 control stations placed around the globe as well as on-site inspections to detect nuclear explosions, including underground tests as small as five kilotons. Though the report was ambiguous on several issues, including the specifics of the on-site visits, Eisenhower now felt confident enough to consider a public statement offering to begin formal test ban talks with the Soviets. If those negotiations went well, the State Department favored a one-year suspension, while the Department of Defense, though not supportive of a ban, expressed a willingness to back one "if the President decided that political considerations" mattered most. Meanwhile the Joint Chiefs of Staff and the AEC wanted to continue testing unabated.[41] Cognizant that he had the cards stacked against him, McCone urged the president to include in any call for a test ban an exception for explosions for peaceful purposes. Secretary Dulles realized such a provision provided a "possible loophole" for the Kremlin to violate a moratorium, but he believed it more important not to "deny to mankind, perhaps forever, the possibility of using this vast new power for human betterment."[42]

On August 22, 1958, the president issued his statement offering a one-year moratorium, with annual extensions if the Soviets showed good faith in stopping their own tests. But taking up the suggestion made by McCone and Dulles, he proposed that any test ban treaty "deal with the problem of detonations for peaceful purposes, as distinct from weapons tests."[43] A week later Khrushchev expressed his willingness to open such discussions in October.[44]

Project Oilsands

The U.S. moratorium and improvement in superpower relations offered to cause difficulties not just for Chariot, but for other Plowshare experiments. Though nuclear excavation of a canal was the keystone of the peaceful-use program, from Plowshare's inception scientists had considered the application of the atom to other areas. One was the stimulation of energy resources. Just as with Chariot, the AEC hoped to elicit corporate interest, allowing it to contract out services and to save money by having the private sector assume some of the cost. The Commission had in mind two experiments. One, not yet named but costing an estimated $2.6 million, aimed to acquire oil from deeply buried shale. Both Humble Oil and Dow Chemical Company expressed interest, but no firm was willing to appropriate funding for such an experiment, either desiring more data or insisting that the AEC pay the full price tag.[45]

Another test, called Oilsands, offered more promise, for in this instance the AEC already had an industrial sponsor in the form of Richfield Oil Company, a subsidiary of U.S.-based Sinclair Oil. In September 1958 Richfield approached both the AEC and the State Department about using the atom to exploit tar and oil sands it controlled in the Athabasca region of Canada's Alberta Province. The area, encompassing some seventeen thousand square miles, "contains," said Richfield's vice president W. J. Travers, "as much as 600 billion barrels of oil," equal to the world's known reserves. But there were two problems: conventional methods of extraction permitted access to no more than 10 percent of the oil in the sands,[46] and the petroleum's thickness made it difficult to retrieve. The company concluded that a 100-kiloton atomic explosive, buried about 1,500 feet underground, would create a chimney similar to that generated in the Rainier shot and melt the oil into a thin liquid, which would then fall into the cavity. Afterward the company could easily pump the petroleum to the surface.[47]

For Plowshare's champions, Oilsands offered a way to meet simultaneously the communist threat and America's energy needs. The specters of Soviet influence in the Middle East and Arab nationalism had drawn the attention of President Eisenhower and his military and diplomatic aides. Since 1951 U.S. imports of Middle Eastern oil had more than doubled, to 12.6 percent, and Washington did not want to lose access to that vital resource. In the meantime the United States had warily watched as, following the Suez Crisis, President Nasser drew ever closer to the Soviet Union. Also worrisome were Nasser's formation in 1957 of the United Arab Republic, a political union of Egypt, Yemen, and Syria, and that same year a coup in Iraq that brought to power a new government that aligned itself with the Kremlin. Richfield estimated that the reserves in the Athabasca were enough to meet the growing U.S. demand for petroleum for some two centuries, thereby providing, as John S. Kelly of the AEC's Division of Military Applications put it, a means to confront "the Middle East situation." It was almost indisputably for these very reasons that Eisenhower in October 1958 "mentioned with enthusiasm" to Canada's ambassador to the United States, Norman Robertson, "Project Plowshare and particularly the tar sands proposal."[48]

Richfield saw dollar signs in the project. The company estimated the cost of the shot at about $1.25 million but that it would receive $2.6 million in profits if successful. There were the matters of seismic shock and radioactivity, but company officials dismissed both. "The nearest installation," commented Travers, was six miles away, too far to fall victim to the shaking of the earth generated by the explosion. Nor was there any danger of fallout because the blast would be fully contained underground. But what about radioactivity contaminating either the oil or aquifers that provided water for humans, animals, and crops? "The tar sands are made up of bitumen and silica," Richfield officials explained. "The fission products from the explosion would fuse with the silica," and any radioactivity left would consist of krypton and xenon—two toxic gases—which "decay rapidly. . . . The net effect of all of these factors is that there would be no contamination of oil or ground water beyond acceptable limits."[49]

Even if the unnamed oil shale experiment had had an industrial sponsor of its own, there was little chance of it or Oilsands taking place in the near term. The moratorium was now in effect, and U.S.-Soviet relations had shown additional evidence of improvement, marked by Khrushchev's acceptance of an invitation to come to the United States for a summit with the president. Despite his own interest in Plowshare, Eisenhower, as well as the Canadian government, had no intention of allowing tests that the Soviets might charge as a cover for weapons development and that might jeopardize the test ban talks in Geneva.[50]

Project Gnome

The tone of U.S.-Soviet relations affected another Plowshare test, called Gnome. Naming a blast after "mythical dwarfs who guard underground treasure" reflected the Plowshare scientists' certainty as to what their program could accomplish. First conceived in 1958, the $3.2 million experiment envisioned use of a ten-kiloton explosive buried 1,200 feet underground in a salt bed near Carlsbad,

New Mexico. Like Oilsands, Gnome represented an attempt to apply PNEs to purposes other than nuclear excavation. Unlike Oilsands, Gnome had several aims: to determine the feasibility of using a nuclear blast to generate heat for power, to create new isotopes for both civilian and military use, and to learn how an atomic explosion reacted in a medium different from the volcanic tuff in which many tests at the NTS had taken place.[51]

These were the advertised motives.[52] What the AEC did not actively publicize were two additional purposes for Gnome. One was to provide data useful for the U.S. military's seismic detection program, called Vela, the purpose of which was to improve methods of verifying Soviet compliance with a test suspension; indeed the armed forces planned to have Vela officials present should Gnome take place. The second was to garner additional funding for the Plowshare program. Because of the moratorium on testing, scientists working on the peaceful atom had devoted their attention to high-explosives tests and feasibility studies, yet appropriations for those efforts had witnessed a decline. Gnome, slated to take place in Senator Anderson's home state, might change the financial fortunes of the AEC and its allied laboratories. While the senator disliked some people at the Commission, namely Strauss, and favored a suspension of nuclear weapons testing, he strongly supported atomic research and Plowshare, crowing at one point that about 40 percent "of all federal spending in [his] state had some form of atomic connection." If Gnome went well, Anderson would have all the more reason to push for greater funding for the peaceful-use program. UCRL-L officials commented, "We are determined to make Gnome as successful an experiment as possible, believing that a single successful Plowshare demonstration may very well affect decisions on the budget and authorization."[53]

Unfortunately for UCRL-L and the AEC, Gnome faced complications from the outset. The AEC, Livermore, and the U.S. Bureau of Mines put out bids to drill "a pilot hole to log the geology" and accepted that offered by Brininstool Drilling Company, which "proposed to use a churn drill rather than rotary drill." Raymond Harbert of Holmes and Narver urged the AEC to reject the bid, contending that the churn drill would not do the job. Only after it became clear that Harbert was correct did UCRL-L pull Brininstool's bond and hire Water's Drilling Company, based in Artesia, New Mexico.[54]

With that hurdle cleared, others appeared. Nearby farmers worried that radioactivity would contaminate their crops. Also in close proximity were potash mines run by several companies, including International Minerals and Chemicals Company, at least one oil well owned by Shell Oil, and the famous Carlsbad Caverns. International Minerals and Shell warned that seismic shock caused by Gnome might harm their investments or, at the very least, force them to shut down operations for a time, while damage to Carlsbad Caverns could hurt state tourism. Desirous to calm such anxieties, the AEC had the National Academy of Sciences recommend a group of experts to look into the matter further. The panel concluded that because it would be contained, Gnome offered no danger to crops, and the shaking it would create would not be of enough magnitude to pose a threat to the mines, the oil well, or the caverns.[55]

Shell Oil had little comment, but International Chemicals was unpersuaded. In 1957 Senator Anderson and his JCAE colleague, Congressmen Charles Melvin Price (D-Illinois), had sponsored passage of the Price-Anderson Nuclear Industries Indemnity Act, which limited the liability of nuclear power companies for damages caused by accidents. Without such protection, the nuclear industry argued, it risked bankruptcy as a result of lawsuits should such accidents occur. International Chemicals requested that Anderson offer "special legislation" that would make the government fully liable for any damage to its mines. Rather than do so, the New Mexico senator asked the AEC for its thoughts about revising the Price-Anderson Act to give International Chemicals the coverage it wanted. Not surprisingly the Commission refused. Commissioner John S. Graham did not want to set a precedent that "would develop into a requirement for Government underwriting of all future nuclear detonations," the potential cost of which might impair, if not destroy, the Plowshare program. The AEC knew it had to assume some responsibility for damages but, stated Graham, "accepting absolute liability in these matters would be a mistake."[56]

In addition to agricultural and corporate opposition to Gnome, there were the test ban talks. Eisenhower wrote Teller that he wanted to see America's weapons labs continue their research and development efforts—which, though the president did not say so, could mean the creation of new, cleaner explosives for possible use in future Plowshare tests. As for actual peaceful-use blasts, though, the president made clear that no detonations were to take place without his explicit approval.[57]

Still Eisenhower had not outright prohibited planning for any Plowshare shots. At the end of February 1959 McCone updated the president on the preparations for Gnome and indicated that he planned to seek White House authorization to proceed with the blast. He added that the shot required a public announcement as a way to attract bids from contractors who would build the machinery necessary to lower the explosive into the drilled hole. Eisenhower was cautious. On the one hand, the statement would inform "the world that we have given up obtaining an overall nuclear test ban agreement within a year." On the other, he saw no reason to halt preparations for Gnome, with the caveat that the United States would welcome observers from the United Nations or any other UN member state, including the Soviet Union. In so doing Washington could both demonstrate that Plowshare was strictly for peaceful purposes and, hopefully, generate international support for the program. To protect the technology involved, though, the AEC determined to use an older device rather than a newer, more sophisticated one.[58] Since the shot would take place deep underground, in all likelihood the radioactivity would remain contained, as had been the case with Rainier.

Neptune's Impact

As planning for Gnome continued, so did preparations for Hardtack II, which got under way in September 1958 and ended the following month with the start of the test ban negotiations in Geneva. One of the Hardtack blasts was Neptune, which took place on October 14. Positioned into a mesa—not unlike the method used in Rainier—the purpose of the approximately one-tenth-kiloton Neptune explosive was to test the safety features of a warhead the United States planned to use on its new submarine-launched Polaris missile. The AEC had intended to fully contain Neptune, as it had Rainier. Instead the device exploded through the mesa, generating a rock slide that destroyed a trailer near the entrance to the tunnel where the warhead had been placed and left behind a crater. Though Neptune had failed, it provided valuable information for the scientists involved in Chariot. They learned that their notions regarding the proper depth of burial if one wanted to create a crater with a nuclear explosive were incorrect. They now realized that the more deeply buried the device, the larger the crater it left behind. Also, Neptune was a dirty fission explosive, leading one to assume that it had released a significant amount of radioactivity into the atmosphere. But only between 1 and 2 percent of the radioactivity generated by Neptune vented. Plowshare scientists could thus assume that a much cleaner fusion device would have meant even less fallout. Finally, there were those aforementioned blast effects. When a nuclear explosive goes off, it generates seismic waves that can have an impact similar to that of an earthquake. It also releases air shock, or air blast, which is sound waves carried through the atmosphere; depending on the size of the blast and the weather conditions, the jet stream or other atmospheric winds can focus the sound waves to the point where they break windows hundreds of miles from ground zero. The blast effects from Neptune, though, were smaller than those generated by shots buried less deeply.[59] Put together, it seemed more than ever that the AEC could conduct Chariot safely.

One would infer that the knowledge of fusion's cleanliness compared to fission would move the AEC and UCRL-L to use thermonuclear explosives in Alaska to further cut down on what radioactivity was released. Adding to that assumption was the price tag, for a fusion explosive produced more power at less

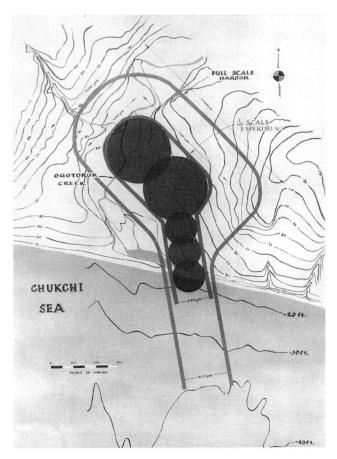

Figure 2. The larger outline depicts Project Chariot in its original 2.4-megaton form. The circles and smaller outline are of the redesigned 460-kiloton version. Diagram courtesy of U.S. Department of Energy.

cost than fission. In fact Livermore had put together a price sheet for its explosives, ranging from about $500,000 for "a few kilotons" to $1 million for "several megatons." A harbor dug with fusion devices certainly would produce a massive blast, one "visible from Siberia," thereby sending a message to the Soviets regarding American technological prowess.[60] Yet Teller proposed to use a fission device instead. The cleanliness of Neptune was one reason. Another, however, was the lack of experience in using fusion for cratering events.[61] True, the AEC had inadvertently created a crater in the Ivy Mike test of 1952, but that was a test with a military purpose, not a civilian one. It is also possible that Bravo was in the back of the minds of AEC and UCRL-L officials. The last thing they needed was to have a repeat of that test, with radioactivity falling over Soviet soil and injuring, if not killing, Soviet nationals. Better to use fission, which, Plowshare scientists believed, they could handle more easily.

Applying the lessons of Neptune, Teller and his colleagues scaled back Chariot. Rather than use 2.4 megatons of explosives, they now needed only 460 kilotons: three smaller explosives of twenty kilotons buried four hundred feet underground to build the channel, and two larger ones of two hundred kilotons each, buried seven hundred feet below the surface, for the turning basin. The blasts would move 4.5 million to 5 million tons of earth and create a harbor 2,700 feet long and 750 feet wide. "From such an experiment," Teller wrote, "we would learn the cratering characteristics of large buried explosions fired simultaneously, the effectiveness of containment or localization of radioactivity, and the suppression of blast effects by burial of the explosive at appropriate depths." As a side benefit the smaller experiment cut down the overall price tag. Private entrepreneurs had shown no preparedness to defray any of the expenses of the blast, and from the start both the AEC and UCRL-L had wanted to avoid pumping a large sum of money into the experiment, as seen in the limited funding they gave to USGS. As revised, Chariot now cost about $4 million, or at least $2 million less than the original design.[62] If the shot went off as the Plowshare scientists hoped, creating a large harbor for less money and with the release of virtually no radioactivity, then they had every reason to expect the successful cultivation of corporate, if not governmental, support for other enterprises, including the sea-level canal.

Yet officials at UCRL-L, now renamed the Lawrence Radiation Laboratory (LRL), and the AEC were troubled, for they had not heard much comment from Alaska about Chariot. They wondered whether the nation's newest state had turned against the blast. In an attempt to discern Alaskans' feelings, as well as to advertise the information they had gained from Neptune and the new rationale for Chariot, two LRL scientists, Harry Keller and Vay Shelton, headed north. Stopping first in Anchorage, they gave "a 'purely informational'" talk to the state's Department of Health. Though Chariot was now an experiment, Keller explained that Cape Thompson lay near "vast, unknown mineral deposits" that might someday "be developed." He played down the danger posed by radioactivity, citing Alaska's "sparse population" and the fact that winds would blow the fallout away from populated areas.[63]

There is no indication the visitors encountered much resistance in Anchorage. Such was not the case when they arrived in Fairbanks for a meeting with the UAF faculty. Florence Robinson, a geologist affiliated with USGS who sat in at the meeting, recalled "a rather hostile atmosphere, particularly from the biologists." UAF's scientists found the new justification for Chariot disconcerting and again raised questions about fallout. Shelton tried to reassure the attendees that no blast would take place until the winds were coming from the east, thereby blowing the radioactivity into the ocean, but to no avail. What right, asked some of the faculty, did a physicist, who had no background in botany, biology, or genetics, and who was in the government's pay, have to tell the scientists knowledgeable in those fields that there was no need to worry? Keller stressed that the AEC and LRL had no intention of approving Chariot if the people of Alaska opposed it. By the next day, biologist Tom English had put together a statement signed by most of his colleagues in the departments of biological sciences and wildlife and supported by the university's president, Ernest Patty, insisting that Chariot not proceed without an environmental survey.[64] Only then would they and the people of Alaska know what effects, if any, a release of radioactivity from Chariot might have on the plants, animals, and humans living in the region.

The antagonism Keller and Shelton found in Fairbanks reverberated through the AEC and the labs involved in Plowshare. In 1958 the Commission's San Francisco office had established a Special Projects Group to oversee the Plowshare program, and it was on that office that Livermore relied for government funding. Facing intense public scrutiny, the AEC encouraged LRL to proceed with Chariot carefully, and Livermore, not wanting to put itself at odds with a key source of appropriations, agreed. Accordingly, Teller and Gerald Johnson proposed to mollify critics by undertaking the types of studies recommended by the UAF scientists. The AEC agreed, and in February it offered to fund a bioenvironmental survey. To oversee it, the Commission established what became known as the Committee on Environmental Studies for Project Chariot. Made up of five (later expanded to eight) people, its head was John N. Wolfe, an ecologist who oversaw the Environmental Sciences Branch of the AEC's Division of Biology and Medicine. Wolfe had visited Alaska previously and understood that the tundra of that territory was not "remote, barren, and climatically rigorous," as long believed, but was an ecological system that consisted of Eskimos and numerous plant and animal species. Pleased with the willingness of the Plowshare scientists to take the welfare of Alaskans into account, the state legislature passed a resolution endorsing the project.[65]

In March Wolfe arrived in Fairbanks with the other members of his committee. The plan was for the bioenvironmental survey to begin in the summer, he stated. He then offered UAF an opportunity to work on some of the studies. At the suggestion of Brina Kessel, a zoologist and acting head of the Department of Biological Sciences, the university hired mammalogist William Pruitt, and Albert Johnson brought ornithologist L. Gerard Swartz on board; Pruitt's and Swartz's jobs were to study the region's mammals and cliff birds, respectively. Johnson himself got the job of overseeing the botanical research. To cover the cost of these surveys, the AEC appropriated $107,000 to UAF.[66]

Thus the university biologists, some of whom had criticized the AEC's Plowshare program, now found themselves under contract with that same government agency. Some, like Pruitt, admitted that the idea of money being available so they could conduct fieldwork was what moved them to accept the contracts. But there was also an understanding that by joining the bioenvironmental studies, the scientists were expected to cooperate. "There was that feeling," Pruitt recollected, "that we were the tame biologists . . . that they had bought."[67]

Atoning for America's Sins

Two months after Wolfe's visit to Fairbanks, LRL and the AEC's San Francisco office sponsored the Second Plowshare Symposium. Marine biologists who attended warned that a sea-level canal would lead to a disastrous intermingling of Atlantic and Pacific life, and other attendees pointed to fallout from excavation projects or contended that it was cheaper to create new isotopes in reactors than in underground blasts. Yet other scientists took issue with such conclusions and were confident that they could prove the numerous benefits offered by peaceful atomic explosions. A future AEC chair, Glenn T. Seaborg, remarked, "Tempers are short and arguments long, and great advantages of a new canal to the human species are often underestimated or forgotten in the heat of conflict."[68]

That same month Teller returned to Fairbanks. Offered an honorary doctorate by UAF's board of trustees, the world-famous physicist also delivered the commencement address. He began by playing down the threat posed by radioactivity. He conceded that fallout was dangerous, but it had been so dispersed in the atmosphere that it "contributes to radiation less than the wristwatch I am wearing on my wrist." In fact, he asserted, radioactivity was safer to humans than drugs bought at a pharmacy, because it was possible to lose or confuse pills. Radioactivity, however, could be controlled and "has the property that it can be readily and easily identified."[69]

Believing he had reassured his audience, Teller turned to the potential benefits of the atom. It could do more than simply provide power to Americans' homes; the atom, when put into a clean nuclear explosive, could also allow humans to reshape the planet as they saw fit. Proclaimed Teller, "If your mountain is not in the right place, just drop us a card. [Thanks to the atom, it was now possible] to blast harbors in otherwise inaccessible coasts, to engage in the great art of what I want to call geographical engineering." And there was one more benefit, which Teller addressed through prayer: "Please God, that by making harbors here in Alaska, perhaps near coal deposits, by exporting this coal cheaper to Japan, the Japanese might become the first beneficiaries of atomic energy, of atomic explosions, as they have been the first victims."[70] Thus in addition to defending American security and creating a better world, Chariot would allow America to atone for its past sins.

Whether atonement was possible remained the question for Plowshare scientists in the middle of 1959. The improvement in U.S.-Soviet relations, marked by their mutual decision to suspend further nuclear testing, had put Plowshare experiments on hold. The Canadian government had yet to approve Oilsands, no one seemed interested in the unnamed oil shale experiment, and outspoken opposition, especially in Alaska, had become a concern to the AEC and its allies. Still, there was reason for optimism. Ottawa had not rejected Oilsands. At some point the Eisenhower administration might give the green light to Plowshare tests. There was every reason to assume Gnome would be fully contained and cause no damage to nearby industrial facilities or Carlsbad Caverns. The biggest question was Chariot, which all sides agreed would cause fallout. Yet Neptune had shown that excavation was possible with minimal release of radioactivity. Further, by funding a large bioenvironmental survey, the AEC could demonstrate it had taken into account criticisms of that blast and, hopefully, prove that it could proceed without endangering humans, flora, or fauna.

A Program on Hold

Les Viereck was a wildlife biologist who had gone into botany and spent a substantial amount of time studying plants throughout much of Alaska. In March 1959 he received a letter from Albert Johnson, a botanist at UAF who had agreed to join the bioenvironmental studies sponsored by the AEC. The purpose of those studies was to determine whether the first Plowshare experiment, Project Chariot, could take place safely. Other commitments prevented Johnson from spending long hours in the field, so he asked Viereck to come on board as his assistant, with Johnson drawing up the investigations and Viereck doing most of the actual fieldwork. Viereck, though not yet finished with his dissertation at the University of Colorado, saw it as an opportunity he could not refuse.[1]

In early June Viereck and a small field party from UAF set up camp at Ogotoruk Creek in northwestern Alaska, the site where the AEC planned to set off Chariot.[2] Others joined them, and by the end of July roughly seventy scientists were living in a camp complete with Jamesway huts, a mess hall, showers, and an automatic laundry. Their numbers included faculty from UAF's Department of Biological Sciences and the University of Washington, as well as officials from Hanford Laboratories, the U.S. Public Health Service, and the U.S. Fish and Wildlife Service. Joining them as an independent contractor was Don Foote, a geographer with extensive experience studying Arctic climates. Two skiffs, two research ships, and nine "weasels"—World War II–era vehicles with tank-like treads designed to travel through snow—took the scientists to their field studies. Two airstrips, the longest of which was 750 feet, were built at the camp. Determining that logistics necessitated larger aircraft, however, workers constructed a 2,200-foot runway about a quarter of a mile away.[3]

The studies assigned to these individuals and entities were extensive, ranging from the ecology of the ocean near the Chariot site to marine mammals and limnology. While not part of the bioenvironmental program, USGS had the job of mapping the geology of the region and assessing sedimentation, water quality, and the possible existence of underground aquifers. In total, the scientists involved conducted forty-two different investigations at a total cost of approximately $1.3 million. Add this number to other expenditures, such as studies to look at the results of the blast—which had not been taken into account in previous cost estimates—and the price tag came to $5.7 million.[4]

Driven by their hubris, their desire to lead the world toward a better future, and their determination to defend U.S. security as they defined it, officials within and outside the AEC made two assumptions: that the investigators could complete these comprehensive studies no later than August 1960 with the appropriations provided and that the studies would alleviate any concerns Chariot's detractors had about the safety of the blast. The shot could then take place later in 1960 or, if necessary, in 1961.[5]

These assumptions proved invalid. Instead by the end of 1960 the AEC found not just Chariot, but the entire Plowshare program, still in a state of uncertainty. Some of the scientists involved in the studies reached the conclusion that Chariot posed a danger to the plants, animals, and people of Cape Thompson, and the handling of their warnings by the AEC's Committee on Environmental Studies as well as the administration of the University of Alaska only served to widen the divide between them and Chariot's defenders. Moreover the ongoing moratorium meant not just Chariot but another Plowshare project, Gnome, remained on hold. The decision of the Canadian government to reject a third Plowshare blast, Project Oilsands, only added to the frustration of those who wanted to prove the possibilities of the peaceful atom.

Trouble with the Natives

As the scientists set up camp, Edward Teller returned to Alaska. The director of the LRL-L branch and one of the staunchest defenders of the Plowshare program, he intended once again to attempt to sell Chariot to the people of the state. Stopping first in Juneau, he tried to call on the governor, William Egan. Egan, though, was ill and could not meet the famous physicist. Instead he sent Jim Brooks of the state's Department of Fish and Game to represent him. Brooks had read about Bravo and other Pacific tests and pressed his guest on the potential threat Chariot posed to the environment. Annoyed by such questions, Teller raised the communist threat. "If Soviet Russia should surpass the United States in the development and use of nuclear energy," Brooks recollected Teller saying, "it would be one of the worst setbacks in his life." Brooks was taken back. "He interpreted my concern and probing questions . . . as being an expression of disapproval at the outset." Brooks assumed that Teller had come to give the Alaskan government a full briefing, and what Brooks sought was "to have all the information [Teller] was willing to give in the area of environmental concern."[6]

Teller found a friendlier reception in his next stops: Elmendorf Air Force Base near Anchorage; Nome, where he met with civic leaders; and Kotzebue High School, where he spoke before a group of students and townspeople. He would have then flown to the Chariot blast site, but the longer runway was not yet complete. Accordingly he flew over it before heading back to California. Throughout he played on two themes: one was an image of Alaskans as having an indomitable spirit that enabled them to conquer and survive the harsh conditions of frontier life; the other, which was more implicit, was that progress originated from the minds of special individuals who were willing to take chances. "Anything new that is big needs big people to get going," he told his audiences, "and big people are found in big states."[7]

In August it was the turn of John N. Wolfe, the chair of Chariot's Committee on Environmental Studies. Joined by other AEC officials at Ogotoruk Creek, he told reporters that the spring, namely March or April, was the best time for Chariot to take place, while his colleagues asserted there was no need to fear any harm to the environment from the blast. These statements could not have pleased Egan. Teller never had answered his questions about the danger posed by fallout, and the AEC had further upset the governor by refusing to pay for a state official to participate in planning for the blast. Now the head of the AEC-sponsored environmental committee had selected a time of year for it to take place. Yet officials from the Commission and LRL had said Chariot would occur only if the people of Alaska favored it. Egan expressed his concerns to Representative Carl Durham (D-North Carolina), the vice chairman of the JCAE, who passed them on to AEC Chairman John A. McCone. "You may be assured," McCone replied, "that the detonation will not be authorized unless there is assurance that it can be conducted without undue hazard to the public health and safety, and the economic well-being of Alaskans."[8]

In one respect McCone's response was a lie, for the AEC had already decided that Chariot was solely an experiment, not a project aimed at providing for Alaskans' "economic well-being." Additionally it was doubtful whether McCone could uphold his promise not to harm "public health and safety." As part of its responsibilities, USGS had to gather core samples, some of which it would study to learn about the mineral composition of the rock, and others that it would send to LRL to get a baseline of the level of radioactivity in the ground. Boyles Brothers Drilling Company, a Salt Lake City outfit, contracted with USGS to dig two samples, one 1,000 feet deep and the other 1,500. Hard rock and cave-ins prevented the company from reaching the requisite depth for either. In August Boyles Brothers decided it would not risk its equipment and gave up. Then, in mid-September, a barge carrying about 1,500 feet of samples, as well as Boyles's equipment, sank, carrying with it nearly all of the equipment and samples.[9]

McCone had no control over the ground conditions or weather in Alaska. Offering the people of the state a comprehensive understanding of Chariot was another matter. Officials from both the AEC and LRL had repeatedly visited Alaska, but none had actually taken the time to brief the Eskimos who resided near the blast site. Point Hope, one of the oldest villages in the Arctic region, had a population of three hundred and lay about thirty miles northwest of ground zero. Kivalina was about the same size and approximately forty miles to the south. Both communities relied heavily on fishing and hunting. The people of Point Hope grasped that Chariot could endanger their livelihood, if not their lives, when Foote explained to them the purpose of his study. Daniel Lisbourne, who had served as the president of the village council, immediately wrote one of Alaska's U.S. senators, Edward Bartlett, expressing his opposition. Bartlett, in turn, had informed the AEC of his constituency's concerns.[10]

The AEC realized it might have trouble on its hands. Teller had charged those opposed to testing with elitism, yet those who championed Plowshare were guilty of the same. Adopting an air of superiority toward anyone who stood in the way of what it regarded as progress, the AEC contacted Foote and asked him to "allay the anxiety of the natives." Replying that he would "be honest with the people within the limits of my own knowledge," Foote met with the Point Hope Village Council in late November. He discussed the plan to build a harbor using nuclear explosives, the potential danger posed by the atom, and the bioenvironmental studies. The village council unanimously declared itself against the experiment and sent a petition to the AEC expressing that sentiment. However, the council offered to reconsider if the Commission could guarantee Chariot's harmlessness; for that reason it asked for the environmental studies to continue.[11]

Ditchdigger and Dissension

The AEC had no intention of seeing Chariot derailed by dissent. Such was evident in the agency's decision to curtail funding for yet another Plowshare proposal, called Ditchdigger. While its specifications remain classified to this day, Ditchdigger referred to both an excavation project and a device, one designed to reduce the amount of radioactivity generated during nuclear excavation. The Plowshare Advisory Committee favored giving Ditchdigger priority over Chariot. Established earlier in the year, the Advisory Committee was made up of engineers and scientists from both industry and the academic community who, as their name suggested, made recommendations relevant to the peaceful-use program. The AEC did not have to heed the Advisory Committee's counsel, and in this case it did not. To the Advisory Committee, Ditchdigger would be important for future Plowshare projects, especially those near populated areas, such as the isthmian canal. To the AEC, delaying Chariot would increase its cost and delay the acquisition of information "essential to the Panama Canal Company and other large-scale excavation studies."[12] In short, what mattered most to the AEC were firing Chariot and getting data from that blast at as low a price tag as possible; developing and testing a cleaner explosive could wait.

The next month Wolfe's committee raised the stakes when it issued a report based on the data so far gathered by the bioenvironmental studies. It again referred to March or April as the best time for the blast. The majority of the plants and small animals at that time lay under snow, most birds had left the region, little hunting took place during those months, and the weather was "generally good." The statement bred condescension among the UAF scientists in the field. In a report he sent to the AEC in November, Foote cited an increase in hunting in the area during March and April to make up for "a decline in marine hunting." Viereck and Johnson, along with two of their colleagues, the mammalogist William Pruitt and the ornithologist L. Gerard Swartz, protested that no environmental studies had taken place during March or April. They pointed out that the region was not "completely snow-covered in the winter" because winds left sizable tracts "bare of snow." "[The Committee's] statement," they declared, "places the *scientific* investigators in an embarrassing position and will cause Alaskan residents who are familiar with the Arctic to mistrust the entire scientific program."[13]

The scientists involved in the bioenvironmental studies were not the only ones questioning the direction Chariot had taken. So were officials from USGS. The Plowshare budget had grown significantly. Appropriations had risen from $100,000 in fiscal year 1957 to $3 million for FY 1959, and then to $6 million for the following year.[14] The latter two figures, however, were less than the AEC had wanted. It had hoped for $4 million for FY 1959 and $11 million for FY 1960, but President Eisenhower, citing a federal deficit that had reached $13.5 billion for FY 1959, insisted on checking government spending. Consequently there was less money available than the AEC had hoped, and some of that was contracted to labs such as LRL and Sandia, both of which were heavily involved in research and development.[15] Every dollar devoted to the bioenvironmental studies cut even further into the laboratories' budgets.

Something had to give. "[The budget] puts us in the position of substantially delaying the development of all of the cheap and clean new explosives that we are working on," complained Gerald Johnson. Also affected was a Sandia proposal to hold at the Chariot site some tests using high explosives to see how the local lithology would affect the cratering process. Deciding that the cost of tests in Alaska was too high, LRL's Cliff Bacigalupi asked the Geological Survey about finding a site in the lower forty-eight states that had similar types of rocks. A USGS geologist, Reuben Kachadoorian, and Ernest Campbell of the AEC's San Francisco office resisted. Permafrost, they wrote, had an effect on rocks, and "there weren't any areas of permafrost in the 'south' states." Bacigalupi replied that his concern was lithological, not whether "the area was underlain by permafrost."[16] The labs apparently got their way, for starting in the spring of 1960 LRL and Sandia conducted several high-explosive tests at the Nevada Test Site, including Toboggan, Buckboard, and Scooter. Only one high-explosive test occurred at the Chariot site, in November 1960, which found that the local geology and lithology had a significant impact on the size of the rocks produced and where they landed.[17] Plowshare scientists certainly would have had a much better picture of what Chariot might do had they held more high-explosive experiments in Alaska rather than the NTS, where permafrost was not a factor. But determined to prove their theories correct, and at as little cost as possible, defenders of the peaceful-use program ignored such considerations.

The AEC Comes to Point Hope

As the AEC, LRL, and Sandia debated where to hold the high-explosive tests, the AEC reached the conclusion that its best hope of allaying any qualms in Alaska was to send several of its own representatives to that state. Therefore in March Russell Ball and Rodney Southwick, both of the Commission's San Francisco branch, and Charles Weaver, from the agency's Albuquerque office, headed north. They had several jobs. One was to visit a number of Alaskan towns and describe and try to generate support for the shot. Another was to explain that the bioenvironmental studies would continue during 1960. Finally, they were to defend a decision to alter the plan for Chariot once again. Now, rather than two

200-kiloton explosives, it would use one, and it would add one twenty-kiloton device. This reduced the total size of the blast to 280 kilotons.[18]

This alteration was significant. Project Toboggan, a series of row-charge experiments, had taken place from November to December 1959 and was to restart in April 1960. Its purpose was to learn if placing charges in a line would create a set of separate craters or a channel. This information was vital to construction of an isthmian canal using nuclear explosives, for connecting a series of craters required more time and money than if the explosions left behind a channel. The AEC and LRL had determined that "reliable information on ditching" necessitated at least four in-line conventional explosives, so LRL decided in December 1959 to change Chariot's blueprint. Adding one to the number of explosives to build the channel and reducing the devices to construct the turning basin by the same number was clear evidence that the AEC and LRL had decided to deemphasize harbor construction in favor of the isthmian canal project. As a February 1960 report on construction of an isthmian canal put it, Chariot would "provide a part of the information required on simultaneous multiple detonations."[19]

Ball, Weaver, and Southwick made their first stop in Anchorage, where they picked up Robert Rausch, an employee with the U.S. Health Service's Alaska office, a member of the Committee on Environmental Studies, and someone who knew the residents at Point Hope. From there they called on a number of Eskimo villages, including Nome, Kotzebue, and Wales. This was the first time anyone from the AEC had met with the indigenous population, and without a doubt the visitors were pleased with their reception. With the exception of Kotzebue, the three men found no hostility to Chariot, and even in Kotzebue the anti-Chariot sentiment was restrained.[20]

Not so in Point Hope. Several of the residents of that village had subscriptions to *Life* magazine, from which they had learned about the effects of the blast at Bikini in 1954 on the residents of the Marshall Islands as well as the fishermen aboard the *Lucky Dragon*. It is almost certain that they were aware of commentary by scientists such as Linus Pauling about the danger posed by fallout. Important as well was that the Eskimos had no written language and Point Hope had no telephones; many of the residents had purchased tape recorders to document their history and send messages. Hence when the three visitors arrived at Point Hope on March 14, they found about a hundred people packed in a local meeting hall, many of them with tape recorders.[21]

Rausch opened the meeting by emphasizing that Chariot would receive approval only if it could take place safely and then proceeded to play down the danger posed by radioactivity. An above-ground atomic test at Bikini Atoll in 1946 had not deleteriously affected the fish, so there was no reason to assume Chariot would. As for the Chariot blast site itself, no one could enter it for a while, but within "several weeks or a few months at most" they could do so "without any harmful effects." Ball seconded his colleague. He assured those in attendance that the AEC had successfully controlled radioactivity to the point that "the numerous small communities surrounding the Nevada test site" had not been "adversely" affected. In fact, added Rausch, a study of cattle that grazed on fields near the NTS had not exhibited any sign of radiation sickness. When someone raised the possibility of a malfunction that could cause a large amount of radioactivity to affect the local population, Ball cited studies showing that many Japanese exposed to fallout from the atomic bomb dropped on Hiroshima suffered no ill effects. He himself had been to Hiroshima and the NTS and experienced no sickness.[22]

Ball was not straightforward with his audience. It had been known for years that radiation at high levels could harm humans. In 1957 Samuel Glasstone had pointed out in *The Effects of Nuclear Weapons*, published by the AEC, "The first definite evidence of an increase of the incidence of leukemia cases among the inhabitants of Hiroshima and Nagasaki was obtained in 1947. . . . The number of new cases reported has increased fairly regularly in succeeding years."[23]

Nor was the Nevada cattle study a good indicator of what a blast might do. This investigation, which had begun near the end of 1957, involved a small herd, numbering no more than fifty. Two years later the AEC concluded that despite numerous tests at the NTS, the cattle were fine. But there were several problems with such a determination. One was the small size of the herd. The second was that some isotopes, especially if carried into the high atmosphere, can take years to reach the surface. Third, scientists had recognized it could take more than two years for cancer caused by radioactivity to appear; the AEC itself should have recognized this from Glasstone's report. Fourth, the cattle in question did not consume contaminated grass or hay; rather they ate food brought to them from off-site. Fifth, the AEC sought to extrapolate the findings of an experiment conducted in a dry, arid environment to one it planned to conduct in the Arctic.[24] That making such a jump was invalid would become apparent within a year.

Furthermore Livermore knew that Chariot would vent an enormous amount of radioactivity. Ten percent sounded like a small number, but the 280-kiloton design would have released into the atmosphere 1.5 billion curies of fission products an hour after detonation. The U.S. Weather Service calculated the percentage was higher, at 30 percent for the 200-kiloton explosive and 40 percent for the smaller twenty-kiloton devices. This would amount to about 27 billion curies. (By comparison, the 1986 Chernobyl disaster in the Ukraine, which may have killed thousands of people, vented 86 billion curies.) While the AEC's scientists hoped they could conduct the blast so that the fallout drifted seaward (and simultaneously away from Soviet territory), there was no way of guaranteeing that.[25]

Maybe Ball assumed that those in attendance had little or no knowledge of the dangers posed by radioactivity. If so, he was wrong. One resident, Alice Weber, pointed out that her husband had fought in World War II, been involved in the "clean-up of Japanese cities," and returned "sick and sterile." In light of what he knew about radioactivity, Keith Lawton, the pastor of the local Episcopal church, asked which of the three scientists had the expertise in radiation biology to back up what Rausch and Ball had said. Ball replied that that person was Allen Seymour, a member of the Environmental Committee who had come with the group to Anchorage. "But," Ball said in a comment suggesting that the AEC had underestimated the erudition of those at Point Hope, "we didn't at that time consider it important enough to bring him up here."[26]

Possibly the biggest concern of the townspeople, though, was the impact of Chariot on their livelihood. Having to stay out of the Ogotoruk valley, even for "two or three weeks," protested Lisbourne, would "cripple the hunting at Point Hope." The area in which Point Hopers could not go would "rapidly shrink in size," replied Ball. "There might be a short period where we would ask you not to come right along the shore line." That happened to be the location of the hunting ground, retorted Lisbourne. "Right close to the shore?" asked Southwick. "Yeah, right there, ya," Lisbourne answered. "There were 19 teams there, right around there, just this week." Ball felt he had a simple answer: to have the environmental studies determine a time to hold the blast when caribou were not present. Lawton now chimed in, explaining that the people of Point Hope hunted daily, and adding that if seal or fish were affected, it would only compound the difficulties faced by the village. Lisbourne pointed out that collecting birds' eggs was important to the Eskimo as well, a practice that generally took place during April, one of the months the Environmental Committee had said was best for the blast. The back-and-forth left the village council convinced the AEC did not have the best interests of Point Hope in mind. After the visitors left, it again voted unanimously against Chariot.[27]

Though the AEC did not want to see Chariot pushed any further off course, it became aware that it might have to delay the shot even further. It was obvious the Commission could expect intense resistance from the local inhabitants, and even members of the bioenvironmental studies had started to register misgivings. Additionally the moratorium remained in place. Teller continued to complain that a test ban only played into Soviet hands, but Eisenhower refused to budge. The president liked Plowshare; a test ban, however, was more important. He permitted "preparatory work" for Chariot to continue but declined to mandate the blast. Such authorization likely would come only if the superpowers could reach an agreement at the Geneva test ban talks to permit peaceful-use explosions. In light of all of those considerations, the AEC decided in early March 1960 to postpone the blast until the spring of 1962.[28]

Implications of a Test Ban Treaty

Whether a test ban agreement was possible remained very much up in the air. The U.S., Soviet, and U.K. delegates were far apart on such matters as the number of control stations placed in each country, who would man them, and the process of deciding which seismic events required on-site inspections. The Hardtack test series compounded matters, for the data produced showed that rather than being able seismically to detect blasts bigger than five kilotons, the threshold was about twenty kilotons. Furthermore Hardtack suggested it was possible to "decouple" explosions, whereby a nation could detonate an explosive in an underground cavity, thereby muffling the blast's seismic signature. Therefore enforcement of a test ban necessitated either more on site inspections or control posts. In April 1959 Secretary Nikita Khrushchev indicated his willingness to discuss a control system and accepted a British suggestion for a quota of on-site inspections. However, fearful that the West would use such inspections as a means of spying on his country, he wanted to keep the number of them low.[29]

Five months later Khrushchev visited the United States. While the Soviet leader and Eisenhower did not discuss a test ban in detail, Khrushchev's junket symbolized the growing rapprochement in U.S.-Soviet relations. In a further step forward, Eisenhower accepted the counsel of his science adviser, James Killian, that since the superpowers did not see eye-to-eye on a ban on all testing, the United States should push for an atmospheric test ban as a first step toward a comprehensive agreement. The British too favored a phased treaty, and in February 1960 they and the Americans at Geneva proposed starting with an atmospheric ban that would include a certain number of annual on-site inspections in the Soviet Union as well as a cessation of all underground explosions above five kilotons. The Soviets indicated their readiness to accept this plan, though they emphasized the need to move toward a comprehensive agreement. Consequently by the spring of 1960 a test ban treaty appeared possible. The only outstanding matters were the length of the ban and the number of inspections.[30]

The test ban had implications for numerous Plowshare projects. By far the most important was the canal. In February 1960 the Panama Canal Company, with the assistance of the AEC, completed another major study of a sea-level waterway. It emphasized, as had earlier studies, the relationship of a sea-level route to commerce and national security and the inability of many ships, both military and civilian, to traverse the existing canal. Quoting construction costs similar to those given in 1958 for each of the five possible routes, it too favored the Atrato-Truando and Sasardi-Morti options, though it did not discard the others.[31]

There was much new in the 1960 study, however. One was the estimated number of nuclear explosions required for each route, which were nothing short of mind-boggling. The San Blas, the shortest of the five options, necessitated 185 devices, totaling 430 megatons. For the Sasardi-Morti, it was 325 explosives and 310 megatons, while the Atrato-Truando called for 610 devices totaling 360 megatons. The most expensive, that along the Nicaragua–Costa Rica border, required 925 explosives equaling 550 megatons. "The total fallout produced," the AEC estimated "will be about 1%," of which half would fall within twenty miles of the blast zone "and essentially all within 75 miles." While this would contribute "only a very small fraction of the worldwide fallout," the Commission admitted that the amount of cesium-137—an isotope produced by fission with a half-life of thirty years and which scientists had known for some time could harm internal organs—and strontium-90 "are among those which will be enriched severalfold in the local fallout." For this reason the AEC foresaw evacuating people from the blast area. While it did not give statistics for every route, it estimated removing five thousand people during the entire nuclear excavation phase along the Sasardi-Morti, with another twenty thousand forced to leave for shorter periods of time.[32]

The AEC played down the environmental and physical threat posed by the excavation process. Contamination of groundwater was not a complicating factor except for that in the craters produced. There "the [strontium-90] may be concentrated by certain living organisms. However, by controlling food production in the canal, on the canal banks, and within a mile or two from the ends of the canal, no damage should result." How the Commission planned on restricting food production, making sure animals did not eat contaminated plants, and preventing humans from consuming those plants or animals it did not say. Rather it called for further study "of the local meteorology, hydrology, and ecological relationships" prior to construction. Nor did it consider air blast or seismic shock as insurmountable problems, although it noted the need for further study of both as well.[33]

The AEC believed it could buttress some of its conclusions with data gathered from high explosives. With regard to fallout, however, the Commission hinted that its job would prove much easier if atomic testing continued. Present technology released only a small part of the radioactivity generated by nuclear blasts, "essentially all of which is deposited within 75–100 miles." That said, "complete elimination of the fissionable material in future explosives would remove even the local contamination problems in the region of the canal." In that case the

Commission would have to evacuate fewer people from the area surrounding ground zero. "Air blast rather than radioactive debris would now dictate the size of the region evacuated. The evacuated area would be controlled for a shorter time."[34]

The test ban negotiations posed trouble for the canal and were largely responsible for killing Oilsands. From the beginning the Canadian government had shown a reluctance to permit a nuclear blast on its soil, partly out of fear that the Soviets would perceive the test as a subterfuge for weapons development. With the endorsement of Canadian public opinion, Prime Minister John Diefenbaker and his new minister for external affairs, Howard Green, intended to do everything possible to move the Geneva talks along. In May 1960 Green announced that Ottawa would not countenance the shot.[35]

Ironically those same negotiations appeared to have put Gnome back on track. While the Kremlin continued to insist on applying the moratorium to all tests, including those held underground, it had shown some softening of its stance. Whereas during a 1958 international atoms-for-peace conference the Soviets had called Plowshare a way to clandestinely test weapons, they said nothing after the Eisenhower administration publicly announced Gnome. Moscow's apparent change of heart may have been related to the general improvement in superpower relations or the opportunity to witness the blast and share in its results. Whatever the thought process taking place in Moscow, it looked like Gnome might indeed get the go-ahead, so preparatory work continued. Holmes and Narver provided technical information, and several New Mexico engineering firms and Reynolds Electrical and Engineering Company oversaw digging the L-shaped shaft that went 1,200 feet beneath the surface and nearly the same distance perpendicularly. Once Gnome received the green light, workers planned to place the explosive at the end of the L.[36]

The AEC's hope for White House authorization of Gnome suffered a serious setback in May, when the Soviet Union shot down an American U-2 spy plane flying over its airspace. At first Eisenhower denied the incident had taken place. Infuriated, the Kremlin disclosed that it not only had found the plane largely intact but had captured the pilot, who had parachuted onto Soviet soil. While the U-2 incident did not cause a breakdown of the Geneva talks, it severely hindered their progress and cast a pall over the earlier improvement in superpower relations.[37] In light of the fact that the Soviets had in the past charged that Plowshare was a cover for weapons development, Eisenhower certainly had no intention of approving any peaceful-use blasts that might serve to further increase U.S.-Soviet tensions. Gnome, as well as Chariot, remained in abeyance.

UAF and the Citizens' Committee for Nuclear Information

All the while, resistance to Chariot mounted. In June 1960 Foote sent Wolfe another report on his findings, now based on a year's worth of data. He confirmed the importance of caribou hunting in the vicinity of Ogotoruk Creek to the Eskimos of Point Hope. Furthermore if Chariot blew radioactivity landward, it would restrict the Eskimos' access to that important hunting ground for an unknown period. He wrote several people, including Wolfe and Pruitt, that he was now convinced its "severe climate," proximity to birds' nesting grounds, and importance to the Eskimos as an area for hunting made Ogotoruk Creek "probably one of the worst locations in the North American arctic for an experiment like Chariot." He added, "I am not in favor of how Project Chariot has been and continues to be presented to the local inhabitants of northwest Alaska, the Alaskan public and the American public." Believing the Environmental Committee was untrustworthy, he questioned whether he should resign from the bioenvironmental studies. Viereck was even more outspoken, explaining to a friend that he would continue with the environmental survey for "one more year in the hopes of being of some use in getting the thing called off completely." Wolfe tried to calm down his scientists, urging Viereck, Swartz, Johnson, and Pruitt to be patient, as much data still required evaluation. Yet he insisted on the safety of the blast, contending that the fallout would not pose a threat to the caribou and asserting that the evidence he had received from them confirmed March and April as the best time for the explosion.[38]

The objections to Chariot among UAF scientists such as Foote and Viereck developed a national voice in the middle of 1960 through the Greater St. Louis Citizens' Committee for Nuclear Information (CNI). Its founder was Barry Commoner. A native of Brooklyn, Commoner had received a Ph.D. from Harvard University in 1941, served in the U.S. Navy during World War II, and then joined the faculty of Washington University in St. Louis, where he taught plant physiology. He had become a critic of nuclear testing because of the danger fallout posed to humans. Yet other scientists, such as Teller, denied such a threat existed, leaving the public uncertain where the truth lay. To Commoner, the way to handle this situation was for scientists to do more than simply gather data. It was also their job to interpret that data and address possible inaccuracies and alternative interpretations. Providing average citizens with a more complete and objective picture would allow them to make an educated decision,[39] if not use that knowledge to influence officials in Washington.

It was for these reasons that Commoner, in conjunction with members of the St. Louis community and fellow scientists, founded CNI in April 1958. Its members included both scientists and laypersons, whose job it was to present information rather than take a position on an issue. According to its mission statement, "CNI does not stand for or against particular policies. It presents the known facts for people to use in deciding where *they* stand on the moral and political questions of the nuclear age." In so doing, Commoner's biographer wrote, CNI "helped to pioneer the science information movement."[40]

CNI could anticipate a sizable audience. The Eisenhower administration, working closely with Congress, had taken steps to meet the challenge posed by the Soviet launch of *Sputnik* in 1957. That same year saw the founding of the National Aeronautics and Space Administration. In 1958 Eisenhower signed into law the National Defense Education Act, which increased federal funding for educational programs at all levels, particularly those in science, math, and foreign languages. But while Americans favored using math and science to stay ahead of the Soviets in the space race, they were much more ambivalent about applying such knowledge to the atom. Americans tended to look favorably on using the atom to generate energy. In 1957 the nation's first nuclear power plant opened in Shippingport, Pennsylvania, to great fanfare. The following year Ford Motor Company unveiled plans for the Nucleon, an atomic-powered car, and General Atomics initiated Project Orion, a program to employ the atom to propel a rocket into space.[41] Although neither the Nucleon nor Orion got beyond the testing stage, 1958 did witness the U.S. Navy's launch of the *Nautilus*, the world's first nuclear-powered submarine. Popular culture reflected this interest in using the atom as a fuel source. Nuclear-powered spacecraft appeared in such movies as *Destination Moon* (1950), *Invaders from Mars* (1953), and *Enemy from Space* (1957). In *Atomic Submarine* (1959) a nuclear-powered sub successfully destroyed an alien flying saucer threatening Earth.

At the same time, Americans had become more critical of nuclear weapons. When the American Institute of Public Opinion asked in 1958 whether the "continued testing of hydrogen bombs will likely result in a threat to the health of future generations," a plurality of Americans (46 percent) said yes. Reinforcing that sentiment was the result of a five-year study conducted by a trio of scientists at Columbia University, which found that the level of strontium-90 in humans had risen by 33 percent. Children were especially vulnerable, the study pointed out, recording ten times as much strontium in their bones as adults.[42]

Moreover Americans had grown increasingly fearful of the possibility of nuclear war. Between 1958 and 1959 the United States matched the Soviets' apparent lead in space and weapons technology by launching its own satellite and ICBM. The superpowers now had the ability to cause enormous destruction to the planet with the simple push of a button. Even if leaders in Moscow and Washington avoided such a conflict, accidents could happen, as a family in Florence,

South Carolina, discovered in March 1958, when a U.S. Air Force jet inadvertently dropped an atomic bomb that fell on their farm just outside of town. The weapon itself was not armed, but the triggering device detonated, destroying the farmhouse and leaving behind a crater thirty-five feet deep and seventy-five feet wide.[43] It was accidents like these that gave organizations like Committee for a SANE Nuclear Policy further proof that nuclear weapons were a danger and testing had to end.

Once again popular culture reflected this anxiety. The genre of nuclear war replaced that of the atom-created monster, as seen in films such as *Red Alert* (1958), *The World, the Flesh and the Devil* (1959), and the powerful *On the Beach* (1959). In *Red Alert* a U.S. Air Force general, determined to destroy communism, ordered his fleet of bombers to attack the Soviet Union; only by sheer luck was a nuclear exchange averted. The latter two films addressed the aftereffects of such a conflict. *The World, the Flesh, and the Devil* depicted a planet almost totally devoid of life because of a nuclear war. *On the Beach,* based on a 1957 novel by Nevil Shute, portrayed the people of Australia, the only survivors of a nuclear holocaust, awaiting the arrival of a deadly cloud of radioactive fallout.

Prevailing anxieties about the danger posed by atomic explosives, combined with CNI's lack of partisanship, brought the new organization widespread notoriety. Within a year it had become highly regarded for its analyses of nuclear technology. Committee members appeared on St. Louis radio and television programs, and national and international news organizations, such as the British Broadcasting Corporation, used CNI's monthly bulletin, *Nuclear Information,* to address issues related to the atom.[44]

CNI's audience was soon to learn about Chariot. Commoner and his CNI colleagues had long been critical of Teller, who, they charged, "failed to conform to the standards of validity which are customary in scientific work." Teller was, as Commoner put it, a "scientific charlatan" who downplayed the danger posed by fallout. "When we learned that Teller had gone up to Alaska," Commoner recalled, "that was a challenge that we couldn't resist." He requested from Wolfe any data gathered from the bioenvironmental studies, but the Environmental Committee head refused to turn them over because they were still incomplete. Instead he suggested that Commoner contact the field scientists, which CNI did.[45]

In June CNI devoted its newsletter to Chariot, summarizing both the experiment's purpose and the Plowshare program. The committee took issue with the claim that nuclear excavation was cheaper than conventional. It determined that up to ten kilotons the price tag was not much different. Beyond that, atomic devices could move more dirt at less cost, but the outlays commonly quoted by the AEC, such as half a million dollars for an explosive of several kilotons, failed to include environmental studies or removal of the broken rock. Additionally, PNEs caused fallout and seismic shock and could contaminate groundwater used for drinking. CNI also pointed out that Chariot could severely harm the hunting grounds of the Eskimo who lived near the blast site. The committee concluded that while Chariot might provide "experimentally interesting" information, nuclear excavation was "risky and probably impossible for a long time to come."[46]

Internecine Warfare

Chariot still had its defenders. While most people in Point Hope opposed the blast, a few, such as Allen Rock, who managed the Point Hope Lodge and Restaurant, had no such objections: "As far as I'm concerned, they can shoot it off tomorrow." The Fairbanks media also continued to speak in favor. In August Albro Gregory, a reporter for Fairbanks's *Jessen's Weekly*, cited "misinformed people" as the cause of criticism against Chariot. Calling Wolfe "an eminent scientist," he wrote that the blast posed little danger to "'this bleak spot on the snow-covered outlands' where 'an occasional Eskimo or caribou walks.'"[47]

Yet for Chariot's champions, the message coming from Rock and Gregory meant little in the face of what had become an organized national grassroots movement against the experiment. The AEC fought back with an intensified propaganda campaign. On August 11 LRL's Gary Higgins arrived in Point Hope hoping he might yet convince the locals to give up their resistance to the blast. After explaining the rationale for reducing the size of the explosion and changing it from one designed to create a usable harbor to an experiment, he attempted to reassure the residents that the amount of radioactivity released posed no threat to human life, that if something did go wrong—which he called "inconceivable"—the government would give the villagers a choice between moving or staying put, and that Chariot would not take place if it posed a "serious hazard to life or property." Yet he admitted that the shock wave would likely break the windows of homes on Cape Thompson and that the people of Point Hope would have to abandon their homes for at least a year until the radioactivity died down to a safe level.[48] The reaction of the residents is not known, but they could not have failed to notice a contradiction in the declaration that the shot posed no threat to human life yet required them to leave their homes for at least a year. Nor could they have been happy to give up their way of life for an experiment they opposed.

Wolfe and two other members of the Environmental Committee followed with a national message a few days later. "I would say," Wolfe told reporters at a news conference held near Cape Thompson, "that there are no biological objections to the shooting on the basis of our investigations." After spending what now amounted to $2 million on the studies, there was "no evidence that the detonation would damage the Eskimos' relationship to their environment or livelihood." Further studies would be nice, he acknowledged, "but there is a point of diminishing return," and so delaying Chariot much longer made little sense.[49]

Wolfe's statement infuriated the field scientists. The Environmental Committee chair, wrote Viereck, "has been rather two-faced," and his statements about Eskimo hunting in the region "is a real slap at Don Foote." Pruitt informed Foote that Wolfe had read his (Foote's) report yet had ignored what Foote had written. Foote decided enough was enough. So far, he wrote Viereck, the field scientists had not done a good job of bringing "our case to the public." It was vital that they learn about radiation biology and "stall for time" so they could gather even more data. They could then go public, pointing out that the Plowshare scientists could not be certain how much radioactivity Chariot would generate or where it might be deposited and noting the harm that would befall the local Eskimo population. Foote raised as well the international repercussions of Chariot. Whereas Teller and others believed blasts like Chariot were designed to keep the United States technologically ahead of its cold war rival, they could in fact endanger rather than enhance U.S. security, if not put the entire planet at risk. The Alaska experiment, Foote wrote, "would provoke the Russians": "If they start testing again so will we and LRL is back in business—and the rest of us, I sincerely fear, are in mortal danger. The more I read the more I am convinced there should be *no more nuclear explosions* for quite some time."[50]

The internecine warfare within the bioenvironmental program placed Brina Kessel, the chair of UAF's Department of Biological Sciences, in a difficult position. She shared the frustrations of her colleagues in the field. The AEC, she complained to Wolfe, wanted to keep costs down, meaning that scientists like Pruitt had received a salary below that given a full-time UAF scientist. The lack of financial support, moreover, limited the university's ability to conduct complete studies. Nevertheless she had to keep in mind the welfare of her department and institution. Hearing that Viereck had become increasingly "rabid" about the environmental studies, she wrote Johnson, "I'm concerned from the departmental and University standpoint, and also for him personally. . . . Basically I don't care what he does providing it doesn't reflect on the Department or the University."[51]

Complicating matters for Kessel was the new university president, William Wood. A former public school teacher and administrator, he had arrived at the University of Nevada at Reno (UNR) in 1954, where he served as academic vice president and later president. Like many Americans, he had seen the Soviet launch of *Sputnik* in 1957 as a danger. Responding to that threat, he declared, necessitated "university leaders, industrialists and heads of government agencies" joining forces "in pursuit of the same objective, establishing and maintaining a top,

Figure 3. Don C. Foote, who became one of the staunchest critics of Project Chariot. Photo courtesy of the Alaska and Polar Regions Department Archives, University of Alaska–Fairbanks.

world-scale leadership position in science and industrial technology for America." As part of that effort, he had helped secure large grants for UNR, including from the AEC. When President Ernest Patty retired from UAF in 1960, Wood applied for the job, touting in his application that he had accomplished "more in the promotion of scientific studies and scientific research than any of our good people in the scientific fields." In Wood UAF saw a person who could draw government funding, fueling the university's growth and stature.[52]

After trying for some time, Kessel finally met with Wood in October and brought the new president up to date on the difficulties she had had with Wolfe and the AEC, the progress of the bioenvironmental studies, and the criticisms aired by some of the field scientists. "[The] talk with Dr. Wood didn't go exactly as I had expected," she wrote Johnson. Wood saw no reason to cut off the relationship with the AEC, as the Commission seemed happy with the progress of the studies, and added, "[Since the university is] looking forward to a big expansion in northern research in the biological sciences in the near future, we should not jeopardize these opportunities." Here Kessel had reason to agree with the new president. But to her surprise, Wood expressed his frustration with "'obstructionist' activities" by some of the scientists, suggesting that UAF not "rehire members of the staff that felt so strongly against the activities of the agency that was providing money for their research (meaning Pruitt and possibly Les [Viereck])." Indeed, Wood continued, it seemed to him that "staff members who spent so much time and emotional energy fighting something like this so intensely were putting that much less effort into their scientific work." While Kessel did not entirely agree with that assessment, she understood that Wood's concern was UAF's long-term well-being.[53]

Kessel's refusal to stand up to Wood sullied her relationship with the university's field scientists. Years later Johnson called Kessel "a very authoritarian type person" who had "lost her faculty sensibilities and instincts to a large extent [and] became a bureaucrat." He was happy that he had received a grant that permitted him to work in Norway from July 1960 to the middle of 1961, for otherwise "there's a very good chance [he] would have been out." Pruitt shared Johnson's sentiment. Kessel, he commented, was most concerned with trying to "protect her own ass" rather than her fellow scientists. From Kessel's point of view, though, it was members of the faculty who were the problem. "Pruitt is getting more and more difficult," she told Johnson. "Every real headache I have can be traced back to him." Pruitt's trouble was his refusal to accept "'authority,' and anyone or anything that represents authority over his activities is something to be fought." Viereck's "basic difficulty" was "overdoses of idealism."[54]

For Viereck, it had become too much. "I feel now," he wrote, "that the whole biological program is merely a means for the AEC to go ahead with the Project over the protests of the public." Furthermore it appeared to him "that much of the results of the biological program were determined before the studies were ever started."[55] He therefore no longer wanted any part of those studies and so wrote Wood in December. He took note of the comment made in 1959 that March or April was the best time for Chariot to take place, the Environmental Committee's January 1960 statement, and Wolfe's declaration in August that the blast posed no threat. There was no doubt, he wrote, that the AEC and LRL had "predetermined" the when and where of the experiment.[56]

The AEC and the Environmental Movement

As 1960 came to an end the *New York Times* noted, "[Chariot] still is in the problematical stage, for two reasons." One was the moratorium on testing between the United States and the Soviet Union. The other was the AEC's need to gather more information, such as from high-explosive tests that would give the agency a better idea how the local geology might affect the outcome of the nuclear blasts when they occurred.[57]

On the latter score the AEC had begun to make some headway with tests such as Toboggan and Buckboard. The moratorium was another matter. The suspension of testing had played its part in Canada's refusal to sanction Oilsands. Hopeful of success at Geneva, President Eisenhower had permitted planning for Chariot and Gnome to continue, but he withheld authorization for either. The U-2 incident made him even more cautious about taking steps that could worsen superpower relations.

Though the AEC could not control decision making in Ottawa or Washington, it had not helped its cause. Determined simultaneously to prove what the peaceful atom could accomplish and protect America's well-being, the Commission and its allies had long ignored critics of nuclear testing or assailed them as uninformed, unenlightened, or communist dupes. The resistance to Chariot put the AEC on notice that it might have to change its tactics, but it was very slow in recognizing that fact.[58] If anything, the old ways persisted. The Commission had funded bioenvironmental studies aimed at quelling fears about the potential danger posed by Chariot, only seemingly to disregard the findings of the scientists involved in those studies when they suggested the blast posed a threat to the people and environment of the region. Consequently those same scientists began to turn against the agency with which they had contracted, aligning themselves with members of the anti–nuclear testing movement. The AEC was also lax in acknowledging the complaints of the local Eskimos, and even then did not give their objections much credence.

The AEC's actions actually served to undermine its efforts in the long run. After World War II Americans gave little attention to environmental protection. They focused more on containing communism and coming to grips with the burgeoning civil rights movement. They also placed great faith in science, which they believed "would fix everything"; for example, the discovery of the pesticide dichlorodiphenyltrichloroethane (better known simply as DDT) offered a means of killing insects that devastated crops. As American industry pumped out pesticides, consumer goods, and military hardware, pollution became a growing problem. But warnings issued by conservationists like William Vogt and Fairfield Osborn received little notice.[59]

Americans' lack of interest in the environment began to change in 1962, when the ecologist Rachel Carson published the book *Silent Spring*. While there is no evidence that Carson was aware of Plowshare, she was cognizant of the danger of nuclear fallout, including strontium-90.[60] The core of her argument, however, was the harm to animals and humans caused by DDT and other insecticides. Though assailed by the pesticide industry, *Silent Spring* became a best-seller. Most scholars agree that her work set the stage for the modern environmental movement. Over the next decade the U.S. government banned DDT, passed laws to protect air and water quality, and established the Environmental Protection Agency (EPA).

There is reason to argue, though, that Carson's impact was so great thanks to Americans' growing sensitivity over radioactive fallout.[61] It was such sensitivity that had generated the grassroots opposition that forced the AEC to start funding the Chariot bioenvironmental studies three years before *Silent Spring* landed on bookshelves. On this score Teller and Commoner found common ground. To Teller, the bioenvironmental survey "laid the foundation for the environmental studies that have become commonplace today." Commoner wrote, "Chariot can be regarded as the ancestral birthplace of or at least a large segment of the environmental movement."[62] What the AEC could not have known was that the movement it helped engender would repeatedly come back to haunt it as it pressed forward with Plowshare.

4

From Moratorium to Test Ban

John F. Kennedy's accession to the presidency made Plowshare's defenders nervous. He had joined Adlai Stevenson's call during the 1956 presidential campaign for a ban on nuclear testing and in 1959 had rejected a proposal by would-be Republican presidential nominee Nelson Rockefeller for a resumption of underground tests. That same year, Kennedy had warned about "fall-in": the threat to humans, he stated, came not just from radioactive fallout but from radioactive waste that ended up in water and food supplies. Such comments prompted Thomas E. Murray, formerly a member of the AEC, to attempt to pin down the Massachusetts senator about a month before Americans went to the polls. In an open letter he asked whether, if elected, Kennedy would permit the recommencement of underground nuclear testing. "I do not agree that underground nuclear weapons tests should be resumed at this time," the Democratic candidate wrote in a published response. Should he become president, he would make every effort "to conclude an effective international agreement banning all tests with effective international inspection and controls—before ordering a resumption of tests."[1]

As it turned out, Kennedy largely continued President Eisenhower's Plowshare policy. Desirous to see the test ban negotiations at Geneva achieve fruition, the new chief executive did not want to permit any nuclear tests that might lead the Soviet Union to charge the White House with bad faith. Hence he withheld authorization of Project Chariot. The breakdown of the test ban negotiations in August 1961, however, did not help Chariot's defenders. Opposition to that blast in Alaska and beyond remained powerful; the two shots for which Kennedy did

71

give the green light, Gnome and Sedan, did not go as well as anticipated, thereby raising additional questions about Chariot, and the AEC obtained from Sedan the data it believed it could have gotten from the Alaska experiment.

The Cuban missile crisis of October 1962, which brought the superpowers to the brink of nuclear war, moved them to resume the test ban talks, and, determined to see those negotiations succeed, Kennedy authorized only two more Plowshare tests, both of them held at the NTS. The ratification in September 1963 of the Limited Test Ban Treaty (LTBT), which placed prohibitions on radioactive fallout, added yet another roadblock to Plowshare tests. By November of that year, when an assassin's bullet took the president's life, the entire peaceful-use program once again appeared stuck.

The Test Ban Talks

Kennedy was the son of a wealthy Massachusetts family with a long-time connection to the Democratic Party. He had graduated from Harvard University a year before America's entrance into World War II and then served with the U.S. Navy during that conflict. He later gained fame for saving fellow sailors when a Japanese destroyer sank his gunboat. In 1946 Kennedy ran for and won one of his state's seats in the U.S. House of Representatives. After serving three terms he was elected to the U.S. Senate. In 1960, in one of the closest presidential elections in the nation's history, Kennedy defeated his Republican rival, Vice President Richard Nixon.

Kennedy wanted to see the test ban talks succeed, but they had become bogged down by the time of the election. Certainly the chill in U.S.-Soviet relations caused by the 1960 U-2 incident had an impact, but one must wonder whether the negotiations might have succeeded without that incident. The superpowers still remained far apart on such matters as the number of on-site inspections, with the Soviets settling upon a number of no more than three on their soil each year. In an attempt to break through the deadlock, a group of countries, with the support of the United Nations, formed the Eighteen-Nation Disarmament Committee (ENDC) in early 1961. But on-site inspections remained a sticking point, with the United States and United Kingdom favoring a minimum of twelve annually.[2]

How to achieve a breakthrough became an issue for the Kennedy administration. During a meeting of the Committee of Principals—an Eisenhower administration institution that Kennedy preserved—in early March 1961 the president's chief arms control negotiator, John J. McCloy, suggested permitting the Soviets the right to examine any explosives the United States might use for Plowshare, though he hedged on actually providing blueprints. He realized that this could mean using "obsolete devices," for which top-secret technology was not a concern, and consequently restricting the peaceful-use program, but it would at least permit Plowshare to proceed. Secretary of Defense Robert McNamara, Central Intelligence Agency Director Allen Dulles, and the new AEC chairman, Glenn T. Seaborg, endorsed the suggestion.[3]

The White House decided to include this motion in a proposal to Moscow later that month. If it appeared the Soviet Union, United States, and the United Kingdom were on the verge of solving other areas of disagreement, the administration offered to ask Congress to revise the Atomic Energy Act and permit internal inspection by Soviet officials of devices used for Plowshare projects. The White House did have two caveats: it would permit both Soviet and British officials to look at blueprints of the devices but not to copy those blueprints, and although those other officials could be present at the blast itself, they could not "install instruments and receive data." On April 4 the Soviets expressed their willingness to accept these demands, and two weeks later the United States and the United Kingdom submitted a draft treaty, Article XIII of which addressed peaceful-use tests.[4] Disagreements, however, persisted on other aspects of the talks.

Throughout, President Kennedy had remained reluctant to give the go-ahead to any Plowshare explosions, believing that otherwise the Soviet Union would charge the United States with chicanery and resume its own tests.[5] This was bad news for Plowshare. The AEC assumed that if it did resume PNEs, the White House would insist it employ only older devices, the technology of which it could disclose to the Soviets. In the meantime the Commission knew it could not ask for sizable appropriations for tests the White House would nix. Therefore it decided to request only $6.5 million for FY 1962 for Plowshare.[6]

Restricting the Plowshare budget and using only "disclosable" devices had widespread ramifications for the peaceful-use program. Lack of funding meant deferral of Limestone, a proposed nuclear explosives experiment aimed at creating a chemical reaction. Ditchdigger also was deferred; aside from the lack of money, it would have involved new and therefore nondisclosable technology. Since new technology seemed unlikely to receive approval for use in Plowshare experiments, the AEC reduced funding for research and development. If there was any good news, it was that there was enough money in the budget to continue the Chariot bioenvironmental studies and preparations for Gnome and to undertake preliminaries for a new excavation experiment called Wagon.[7]

The Alaska Conservation Society and UAF

The purpose of those bioenvironmental studies had been to allay any fears that Chariot would harm the ecology or the people of the Cape Thompson region. But instead the scientists conducting the fieldwork, particularly those from UAF, had found evidence belying repeated AEC statements that Chariot could take place safely. Organizations such as the Greater St. Louis CNI gave such findings a national and even international audience.

More voices chimed in. In 1959 the Alaska state legislature had passed a resolution supporting the blast. But in February 1961 the state's house of representatives endorsed a resolution submitted by Jacob Stalker, whose district included ground zero, calling for a halt to further preparations for the shot until "the safety of the people and wildlife in the area could be guaranteed." Arthur Grahame, a reporter for *Outdoor Life* magazine, a national publication that catered to hunters and fishers, commented, "Alaska is the 'dream' hunting ground of most American sportsmen," yet the spot the AEC had selected was "comparatively close to excellent game and sport and commercial fisheries." In fact, one guide who hunted polar bears threatened a $10,000 lawsuit if Chariot prevented him from continuing his avocation.[8]

Despite growing public notice of their warnings, the scientists from UAF had grown frustrated with the AEC-sponsored Committee on Environmental Studies, as well as with UAF's administration, both of which they believed twisted or ignored the data they submitted. Making their work even more difficult were budget constraints. Facing monetary limitations, John Wolfe, chair of the Chariot Environmental Committee, called for cutting back several of the ongoing studies, including investigations related to caribou, cliff birds, and botany. Brina Kessel, the chair of UAF's Department of Biological Sciences, resisted. She insisted that the Committee had never given her or the UAF scientists "any direction . . . as to the emphasis desired." Wolfe refused to budge. He permitted additional funding only for studies already approved but that either had not yet begun or had "started late in 1960."[9]

Then came what for the UAF field scientists was the last straw when, in March, the Committee on Environmental Studies published a draft titled "First Summary Report." For reasons that remain unclear, the Committee relied only on data from the first year's fieldwork, even though information was available from the second. It also ignored objections from the field scientists, who contended that its methodology was flawed. The report gave the impression that the Cape Thompson region was largely devoid of life and that the people who did live there relied on caribou less than was actually the case. It concluded, "The chance of significant biological costs . . . appears exceedingly remote." Harm from fallout was "negligible, undetectable, or possibly nonexistent in areas distant from the excavation."[10]

Because the Environmental Committee habitually disregarded their conclusions, geographer Don Foote had the previous year suggested he and his fellow investigators make their data public. They now took that step, writing up a history of Chariot and summaries of their studies for the Alaska Conservation Society (ACS). Founded in 1960 in Fairbanks, ACS was the first environmental organization in the state. Its newsletter, the *News Bulletin*, went to its membership list of about 420, just over half of whom lived out of state. The organization devoted the March 1961 issue to Chariot, tracing its change from a harbor project to an experiment; detailing the wildlife, fauna, and inhabitants of the Cape Thompson region; and addressing the possible damage Chariot might bring. It was obvious, the ACS concluded, that the Eskimos' way of life would face disruption, possibly permanently, "in certain undefined areas for unstated periods of time. Until the AEC makes definite statements as to what these restrictions will be no one can begin to approach the problem of what Project Chariot will mean to the future of the native people." The ACS printed a thousand copies of its newsletter, mailing it not just to members but to officials in Washington as well.[11]

The *News Bulletin* fomented a backlash from the University of Alaska's administration. Kessel, herself an ACS member, was shocked to receive the newsletter. "I, of course, don't mind [the field scientists'] opposition to Chariot, but I *do* mind the lack of ethics involved here," she wrote to UAF botanist Albert Johnson. Kessel was angry that her faculty in the field had acted without first letting her know or without receiving authorization to publish their data and had presented their findings "in a biased manner": "They have done exactly what they have objected to the AEC doing." William Wood, UAF's president and someone who wanted to avoid shaking up his institution's relationship with the AEC, had earlier sought to get rid of those scientists causing trouble for his administration. Botanist Les Viereck had resigned, and now Wood, with Kessel's approval, turned his attention to mammalogist William Pruitt. "Brina," Pruitt wrote Foote, "informed me that my contract was not being renewed [for] being biased, untruthful, using data without permission, secretive, etc." Unless he got work elsewhere, Pruitt would find himself unemployed after January 1962.[12]

The *News Bulletin* became part of the increasingly broad effort to stop Chariot. Between May and July the Sierra Club—the nation's oldest environmental organization—the National Parks Association, and the Defenders of Wildlife issued public statements or resolutions opposed to the blast.[13] Here was proof of the environmental movement adopting a national consciousness. It is further evidence that Rachel Carson's *Silent Spring*, generally credited with pioneering the modern environmental movement, built on a foundation that already existed.

CNI versus AEC

There was something in the ACS *News Letter* that had not received attention before: a link between radioactivity, caribou, and the high level of strontium-90 found in the bones of Eskimos. It had been known for some time that strontium-90 could cause cancer, but why Eskimos seemed more likely to have significant quantities of it in their bodies remained a mystery. Biologist Eville Gorham pointed to an answer. Conducting research in northwestern England, he discovered that some plants readily absorbed radioactive fallout. It also happened that sheep in the region had a "high concentration of strontium-90" in their bones. His conclusion, which he published in May 1958, was that the sheep ate the plants, absorbing ever more strontium-90. Research under way in Norway found a similar association, particularly among caribou, which relied heavily on lichen for sustenance. "The chief practical conclusion to be drawn from this work is that animals feeding on mosses and lichens may well exhibit high intakes of radioactive fall-out," Gorham reasoned.[14]

The key word here is *may*. At this point scientists had yet to make a definitive connection between strontium-90 concentrations in lichen and caribou. It did in fact exist. Similar to fungus, lichen are unlike other plants in that they soak up nutrients from the air rather than soil or groundwater. This made them excellent receptacles for radioactivity generated by Soviet tests, which then drifted over Alaskan territory. Caribou rely heavily on lichen for their diet, resulting in a buildup of radioactive elements such as strontium-90 in their bones.[15]

Barry Commoner began to put the data together. The head of CNI, which had long warned of the danger posed by fallout, Commoner also had a Ph.D. in plant physiology. He had read the ACS newsletter, the reports on strontium levels in lichen and caribou, and Foote's research demonstrating that the Eskimos on Cape Thompson depended on caribou for their diet. He was also aware of emerging evidence that people living in Alaska had more strontium in their bones than those residing in the lower forty-eight states. Based on these data, Commoner reached several conclusions. First, the strontium count among the Eskimo resulted from eating caribou that had consumed fallout-laden lichen. Second, Chariot would add to the environment an indeterminate amount of strontium to that which already existed. Third, that increased exposure to strontium among the residents in the Point Hope region would increase the likelihood of their getting cancer.[16]

These judgments became part of the June issue of CNI's monthly bulletin, *Nuclear Information*. Dedicated to Chariot, it included reports from Foote, Pruitt, and Viereck, as well as articles by Commoner and Michael W. Friedlander, a physicist at Washington University. Commoner addressed the lichen-caribou-Eskimo connection; Friedlander cited uncertainties regarding the amount of fallout generated by Chariot, which could range from a release of only 1 percent to as high as 25 percent: "Thus, conservative judgment of the fallout expected from Chariot would require that the AEC estimates be multiplied by 10." Another factor was wind speed and direction, which could "raise the [strontium-90] levels in the fallout zone to anywhere from 3 to 30 times their present levels."[17]

Not everyone accepted CNI's findings. Wolfe said there was no unequivocal link between lichen, caribou, and humans and denied the existence of "lichen patches sufficient to support caribou during the winter." Edward Teller too rejected the CNI report, commenting that the radioactivity found in Eskimos' bones was "about one-fifth of the maximum permitted dose for massive populations and . . . as little as one-fiftieth of the dose which is judged for individuals." *Science* magazine had its own objections. It reproached the AEC for calling its first summary report "preliminary" yet publicizing it anyway. Hence the report had to "be judged to some extent on the impression it leaves with the general public." Still *Science* believed CNI also deserved criticism. Prediction, the magazine noted, fell within a range from 0 to 100 percent right or wrong. Friedlander contended that as much as 25 percent of radioactivity released by Chariot might return to Earth as fallout and that the AEC's figure might be off by a factor of ten. But multiplying 25 by 10 equals 250, and it was impossible for the AEC to be 250 percent incorrect. Rather the AEC's estimate could not be off by more than a factor of four. This was still significant, but not as significant as being ten times off the mark. As for the danger posed by strontium, *Science* took note that CNI could not give any firm estimate as to how much the Eskimos' exposure to that isotope might increase. Even in the worst-case scenario, though, it was likely that the amount of strontium the Eskimos would absorb would be "negligible," comparable to that received by someone who consistently watched television. The *Christian Science Monitor*'s Robert Cowen tried to adopt a middle ground. Looking at what the AEC and CNI had to say, he found it "hard to escape the conclusion that both reports are colored by the prejudices of their authors. They are opening shots in what is likely to be a strong public debate over the merits and dangers of the Chariot program."[18]

Cowen's remark about "a strong public debate" was prophetic. Media coverage of Chariot showed a recognizable shift following the CNI bulletin's publication.

Prior to mid-1961 newspapers within and outside of Alaska, including the *Anchorage Times*, the *Fairbanks Daily Miner*, and the *New York Times*, had focused on the explosion itself and whether it made scientific or economic sense. There was virtually no coverage of the indigenous peoples who lived near ground zero, let alone the possible harm that might befall them or the ecology of the region as a result of Chariot. Following publication of *Nuclear Information*'s June issue, however, the press began to pay far more attention to the Eskimos and the impact of Chariot on them and their way of life. The *New York Times* "for the first time" issued "a damning indictment of the science surrounding the project," with special focus on the possibility of the Eskimos suffering from consumption of radioactive caribou meat.[19]

Joining the debate was the Department of Interior. In June, Sharon Francis contacted Viereck. An assistant to that department's new secretary, Stewart Udall, she was also a member of the Alaska Conservation Society. "Through my associations with [Udall], I have realized that Chariot is a subject which would interest him keenly," she wrote. She had started to gather information on the blast and asked Viereck for any other data he could provide, particularly data related to the possible harm to the environment and people of Cape Thompson.[20]

Udall was indeed someone who would have an interest in Chariot. Born in 1920 to a prominent Arizona family, he had served as a Mormon missionary, fought with the U.S. Army Air Corps during World War II, and afterward got a degree in law from the University of Arizona. In 1954 he had run on the Democratic ticket and won a seat in the U.S. House of Representatives. During the 1960 Democratic National Convention he got his state's delegates to support Kennedy over Lyndon B. Johnson of Texas. For his loyalty, the president-elect offered Udall the secretaryship of the Department of Interior, making the Arizonan the youngest person in U.S. history to hold that post.[21]

Prior to entering the Kennedy administration, Udall had exhibited a strong interest in the environment. He told members of the House in 1960, "The one overriding principle of the conservation movement is that no work of man (save the bare minimum of roads, trails and necessary public facilities in access areas) should intrude into the wonderful places of the National Park System." He was an avid hiker who, as secretary, led treks as long as fifty miles. His interest in conservation tied to his desire to help Native Americans, whom he praised for their reverence for nature. "It is ironical that today the conservation movement finds itself turning back to ancient Indian land sites, to the Indian understanding that we are not outside of nature, but of it," he explained in his 1963 book, *The Quiet Crisis*. "From this wisdom we can learn how to conserve the best parts of our continent."[22]

Knowing he had potentially powerful allies at Interior, Viereck was more than happy to help. He showed Francis's letter to Pruitt, and the two separately wrote her. Viereck suggested that Francis consult published materials on Chariot, and both pointed to the shortcomings of the Environmental Committee's "First Summary Report." Viereck also charged that Udall's predecessor, Fred Seaton, had acted illegally when the Interior Department's Bureau of Land Management accepted the AEC's application in 1959 to withdraw 1,600 square miles of land from the public domain without first holding a public hearing. "The Eskimo must have some legal right to this land," he declared, "so at least [a] public hearing should be held."[23]

The Eskimos had come to realize that the law might be on their side. Viereck's difficulties with the AEC had come to the attention of the Association of American Indian Affairs (AAIA). The first organization in the United States devoted to defending Native American rights, it was formed in 1922 as the Eastern Association on Indian Affairs but had changed its name after World War II. In July an AAIA delegation arrived in Point Hope. One of the visitors, La Verne Madigan, explained that the 1884 Organic Act forbade activities that "disturbed" lands Alaska's indigenous peoples "use or occupy" and left it up to Congress to decide "the terms under which persons may acquire title to such lands." The 1958 Statehood Act reaffirmed the earlier law. While Capitol Hill had not specified what "right" the Eskimos had to the land, lawmakers had not denied that they had a right. Moreover the Eskimos had never signed any treaty ceding the territory in question to the U.S. government. Madigan suggested the Point Hopers write the Interior Department "a letter in protest," and in return the AAIA would provide legal counsel. The village council did just that, threatening to "resort to legal channels" if the U.S. government failed to defend their legitimate claim to the land. Shortly thereafter AAIA hired Harold Green, an attorney and former member of the AEC, to represent the residents of Point Hope.[24] Thus the Eskimos had someone who not only understood the law as it related to their land rights but who was also knowledgeable about how the Commission worked.

The threat of legal recourse had the desired effect. The Point Hope Village Council's letter "touched [Udall] profoundly," Francis wrote Viereck in mid-August. The secretary planned to write back and offer his assistance to help the Eskimos "defend their rights." Francis also put the AEC on notice. During a briefing conducted by John S. Kelly, chief of the AEC's Peaceful Nuclear Explosives Branch, and AEC Commissioner Leland Hayworth, she "succeeded in making the gentlemen from the AEC highly nervous about why Secretary Udall should or would be interested personally in Chariot."[25]

The Impact of Gnome

August 1961 was an important month for Plowshare. Ever since its inception, the program had received criticism because the AEC's Division of Military Applications oversaw it. In an attempt to emphasize Plowshare's peaceful purpose and avoid connections to weapons development, the Commission established a new Division of Peaceful Nuclear Explosives. That same month the Kremlin announced it intended to resume testing. Their rationale remains unclear, but the Soviets justified testing in part on the grounds that the United States intended to hold PNEs as a cover to develop America's weapons technology.[26]

Both the military's Joint Chiefs of Staff and the AEC had long pushed for a resumption of testing on the grounds that the moratorium posed a threat to America's nuclear supremacy and, by extension, its security. Earlier in the year the AEC had determined that if the test ban talks broke down, it would seek authorization for new peaceful-use explosions. As the bioenvironmental studies were not yet complete, and with the resistance to Chariot growing ever more intense, the Commission turned to Project Gnome, an underground test in New Mexico that it expected to be fully contained. With the moratorium on testing apparently dead, the AEC requested and received approval from Kennedy to proceed.[27] Barring any interruptions, Gnome would be the first Plowshare experiment.

New Mexicans met word that the Oval Office had given Gnome the green light with mixed feelings. Citizens in the town of Carlsbad, stated the local newspaper, were "quietly jubilant." Democrat Thomas G. Morris, the state's only representative in the U.S. Congress, commented, "As Alamogordo had become the symbol of the beginning of the A-Bomb, so would Carlsbad symbolize the beginning of peaceful uses of nuclear explosives." International Minerals and Chemicals Company, which owned potash mines nearby, and Carlsbad Caverns were less enthused. International Minerals and several other potash firms ordered their workers to come to the surface during the blast, while the National Park Service decided to keep visitors away from the caverns when the shot took place.[28]

Gnome was the seventh in a series of tests called Nougat. To keep the $5.5 million experiment within budget, the AEC had reduced it to five kilotons, determining the alteration would not affect the results. The White House had invited all UN members to witness the experiment, and some four hundred observers, including representatives from thirteen nations—but not one from the Soviet Union, which refused to send a delegate—along with scientists, lawmakers, and journalists, were present when it took place on December 10. The event did not go as planned. Daniel Lang, a reporter for the *New Yorker*, wrote that almost immediately after the blast, "all of us who were watching . . . could tell that something had gone wrong." It was not the surface dust the explosion had shaken free or the shock wave those present felt. "Rather, it was the sight of thick and steadily thickening white vapor at the scene of the firing that made us think that plans had miscarried." AEC official Richard Elliott immediately ordered everyone back to their automobiles and said they might have to evacuate the area.[29]

What happened? Just before the blast, gophers had disabled two radiation detectors by eating away the plastic covering electric cables. The explosion itself turned out to be stronger than anticipated. Most important, radioactivity vented into the atmosphere. Just as in the case of Rainier, the AEC in Gnome used a buttonhook, linking the surface to the explosive via a tunnel that took at least one sharp turn and that, prior to the blast, was sealed. The shape of the tunnel and the seal were designed to prevent radioactivity from reaching the surface. Whereas in the case of Rainier, in which the buttonhook was shaped like a 9, Gnome's looked like an L, with an elevator shaft linking the surface to a tunnel that ended in an eight-by-ten-foot room housing the explosive. When Rainier took place, rocks collapsed into the tunnel, further sealing it and preventing any radioactivity from venting. But the Gnome blast did not block the tunnel, and radioactivity was able to get around the other seals into the elevator shaft, where it reached 10,000 roentgens an hour, well above the level considered safe for humans. "Chemical samples over ground zero were severely damaged," *Time* magazine reported. Photographs taken by *Life* magazine were ruined; local officials closed down a nearby highway for several hours and washed seven cars to remove radioactive contamination; a helicopter tracking the cloud of radioactive debris as it headed toward the northwest had "to return to base when the craft's instruments showed that it was being contaminated"; the cashier of at least one local restaurant in Carlsbad received instructions "not to touch the money of anyone who had been to the test"; and for several months afterward the AEC bought feed for ranchers whose land was in the fallout's path.[30]

Driven by their hubris and their resolve to create their vision of a more modern world, AEC officials ignored such setbacks. Instead, believing they had taken adequate measures to protect the local population, the Commission focused on the positive, insisting that it achieved about 70 percent of the objectives it had sought in Gnome and assured individuals living in the area that the radioactivity released posed no threat. It appears that the amount of fallout was within safe limits, though there is some debate on this point.[31] Even so the AEC could not ignore that the results were disappointing and disturbing. It found no evidence that the blast had produced a "heat reservoir" that it might tap for power. Prior to the blast it had confidently assumed that Gnome would not vent, only to have it do so. If the AEC could not ensure the safety of Plowshare shots designed to keep all of the radioactivity contained underground, how could it guarantee that a shot like Chariot, which the agency admitted would release some radiation into the atmosphere, would not be equally or even more dangerous?[32]

The Eskimos at Point Hope raised these very questions. Daniel Lisbourne, the president of Point Hope Village, wrote the *Anchorage Daily Times*, "I am deeply more opposed to Project Chariot after the unforeseen incident occurred at Project Gnome blast in New Mexico, which did not go as expected. It is more probable that a lot more things could go wrong with a 280-kiloton job as planned at Ogotoruk Creek."[33]

Enter Interior

The AEC must have been aware that Gnome's outcome would reflect poorly on it and the Chariot experiment. And there was more bad news. A month before Gnome took place *Science* magazine published the initial findings of a three-year study sponsored by CNI to determine the exposure of children to strontium-90. The assumption was that since young children required a greater amount of milk in their diet than adults, their teeth would reflect how much strontium had built up in their bodies. After collecting over 67,000 teeth, some of them from other countries, and using 1,335 for its study, CNI confirmed a significant increase in strontium in children's teeth following the first U.S. hydrogen bomb test. This discovery, which received wide play,[34] was certain to add to the growing national pressure against Chariot.

More bad news followed. The USGS, the duties of which included an assessment of Chariot's impact on local water supplies, learned that under certain conditions, such as wind speed and direction, radioactivity could enter the water supplies and food chain of Cape Thompson. The AEC then separately determined that because of the winds, the fallout cloud would pass over land to the south of the blast area. There was no environmental data from that region, requiring a set of new studies. Consequently the Commission pushed the blast date back to the fall of 1964.[35]

All the while the battle between the UAF field scientists on the one hand and the UAF administration and AEC on the other continued. In December 1961 Pruitt submitted his final report to Kessel. She deleted virtually all his commentary attesting to the reliance of the Eskimos on caribou as well as his citations of literature demonstrating a strontium-lichen-caribou-human link. Kessel then sent Pruitt's report to the Environmental Committee. While she noted on the cover that she had modified his findings, Pruitt was irate over Kessel's "censorship" of his conclusions. Observed L. Gerard Swartz, an ornithologist who had worked with Pruitt on the bioenvironmental studies, "I had never seen a scientist treated that way before."[36]

UAF botanist Albert Johnson had his own take. Kessel had changed the report "so as to avoid antagonizing the AEC." There may be some truth to that assessment. For some time Kessel had found herself caught in the middle of the struggle between the field scientists and the AEC and UAF administration. In the fall of 1961 Pruitt had submitted a progress report delineating the relationship between radioactivity, lichen, and caribou. Wolfe found Pruitt's analysis "disconcerting" and even "misleading." He warned Kessel in November that the university's receipt of the money the AEC still owed it was "contingent upon the receipt of a satisfactory [final] report." He also had made Wood, who wanted to maintain cordial relations with the AEC, aware of his objections.[37] While Kessel herself had complaints against Pruitt, she certainly wanted to avoid putting herself on the wrong side of a quarrel with the AEC and her university's president.

As Pruitt fought with his superiors, matters reached a head at Interior. Francis and an Interior Department colleague, Joseph Carithers, had turned over the materials they had gathered to Roger Revelle, Udall's science adviser. After going through it, Revelle concluded in late January 1962 that it was one thing to affect human lives for national security purposes, such as had occurred in 1954, when the United States moved people from the Marshall Islands to protect them from fallout. "No such justification exists for Project Chariot," he wrote. "One can argue that the Marshall Islanders have actually benefited from being moved to an atoll with more abundant rainfall and possibly a more fertile surrounding ocean. But the Eskimos cannot be moved because there is literally no place for them to go." In light of that fact, as well as the deleterious impact Chariot could have on the livelihood, and even the lives, of the Eskimos, he would support Chariot only if "the Atomic Energy Commission can guarantee that no radioactivity will be released into the atmosphere."[38]

Fully briefed by his aides on the Chariot blast, Udall decided it was time for his department to bring its full weight to bear. "In granting any land withdrawal, this Department, to discharge its responsibilities, must determine that the use is appropriate," he wrote Seaborg, "and that the citizens inhabiting the land receive every consideration." For this reason he asked for the right to have Interior take part in analyzing the findings of the bioenvironmental studies. Seaborg promised to produce the findings.[39]

Udall's interest in Chariot may explain why the Bureau of Indian Affairs, one of the agencies under Interior's purview, decided it was time to take a greater interest in the matter. Francis had observed the Bureau's silence on the Plowshare experiment, even though its main job was to defend the welfare of Native Americans throughout the country. Now, possibly under prodding from a secretary more activist than his predecessors, the Bureau began to move. Indian Affairs, commented program assistant Frances Miller, was "conspicuously absent from the list" of agencies involved in the bioenvironmental studies. With evidence the Eskimos would suffer ill effects from Chariot, either directly or by eating caribou meat tainted with radioactivity, it was time for the Bureau to consider whether Chariot was "in the interests of the natives." Miller emphasized, *The Bureau should be determining its position now.* Francis was pleased. "The Bureau of Indian Affairs, at the Washington level," she wrote Foote, "is beginning to see its responsibilities in Alaska as going far beyond a 'housekeeping' level."[40]

None of this bode well for the AEC. The Bureau of Land Management had yet to approve the AEC's 1,600-square-mile land-withdrawal request. If Udall calculated that Chariot posed a threat to the ecology or inhabitants of Cape Thompson, he could deny the land withdrawal and kill Chariot. At the very least the AEC recognized that a face-off between it and Interior "could lead to lengthy interagency and legal discussions which would be adverse to the Plowshare program."[41]

End Game for Chariot

As Interior flexed its muscles, Foote made Francis aware of an article Paul Brooks and Foote's brother, Joseph, had begun to prepare. Entitled "The Disturbing Story of Project Chariot," it appeared in the April 1962 edition of *Harper's* magazine. The authors remarked that if the AEC had set aside land half the size of Rhode Island in the continental United States—similar to what it was doing in Alaska—"if it had proposed to detonate nuclear explosions which would affect the immediate livelihood and traditional property rights of several hundred American farmers or cattlemen," and "if there were one chance in a thousand that the radioactive fallout would contaminate ranches or commercial fisheries, the story would have made banner headlines." But because Point Hope was "farther from Washington, D.C., than is the coast of Africa" and was inhabited by a quiet group of people, no one seemed to care. In an attempt to make Americans care, the authors traced the story of Chariot, described the reliance of the people of Point Hope on caribou meat, pointed out that Chariot had changed from a proposal to build an economically viable harbor to simply an experiment, and explained that the blast might radically alter, if not destroy, the local residents' way of life. While the AEC rejected the authors' findings,[42] the negative publicity, coming on top of that already in the public arena, did not help.

On May 13 the *New York Time's* Lawrence E. Davies reported that scientists conversant on the subject had determined that "Project Chariot may well be dead, killed by adverse publicity about its effects on Alaskan Eskimos and their

Figure 4. The crater created by Project Sedan. Photo courtesy of National Nuclear Security Administration, Nevada Site Office.

hunting grounds." Davies did not know how correct he was. Focused on creating a better world as they defined it while protecting American security, the AEC and Lawrence Radiation Laboratory had tried to quell the opposition to Chariot by ignoring or rejecting the arguments of the blast's opponents. Instead, their efforts had backfired and generated an organized and vocal nationwide anti-Chariot movement. The AEC and LRL now reached the conclusion that Chariot was a public relations and monetary liability. On April 30, LRL director John Foster asked the AEC to cancel Chariot. The question was how and when to make the announcement without creating political reverberations that might endanger the entire Plowshare program. The AEC provided the answer: "The public announcement of the decision to cancel Project Chariot should be carefully timed to coincide with a convincing event which documents the technical rationale for this decision. Project Sedan will be such an event."[43]

Project Sedan was a cratering blast and the first of a series of tests called Storax, set to begin in July 1962. Sedan called for using a 100-kiloton device, making it the largest underground nuclear explosion on U.S. soil up to that point. It had two purposes: primarily it was to provide information necessary for nuclear excavation of large projects, such as Chariot or a sea-level isthmian canal; secondarily it would produce data for the Vela program. Set off 635 feet underground on July 6 at the NTS, Sedan sent a cloud of debris nearly three miles into the air, displaced about 12 million tons of earth, and left behind a crater 320 feet deep and nearly 1,300 feet wide. Seismographs three hundred miles away recorded the event. According to the AEC, the crater trapped 95 percent of the radioactivity, while the remainder fell "close to the test site."[44] It appeared that the safe construction of a canal or other major excavation projects were possible without posing a significant threat to public safety.

At least, that was what the AEC wanted the public to know. In fact the results were not nearly so encouraging. The radioactive dust cloud created by the explosion was twice as big, rose significantly higher, and "deposited nearly five times as much fallout on and near the test site" than the Commission had anticipated. Fire trucks had to hose down seven miles of a nearby highway to remove fallout. It also happened that that same day Robert Pendleton, a radiologist from the University of Utah, was conducting fieldwork with some graduate students at a canyon approximately twenty miles southeast of campus. "We were measuring levels of radioactivity in different environmental situations," he recalled. "A cloud of radioactive material came over and all the measurements began to go nuts. I recognized that we were getting fallout and took the students off the hill and back down into the valley." The dust itself was so thick that when it passed over Ely, Nevada, about two hundred miles from the NTS, the city had to order street lights turned on, and "intense radiation" fell all the way to the East Coast, including iodine-131. With a half-life of eight days, iodine-131 can cause damage to the thyroid and produce thyroid cancer. Analyzing the blast's effects, Pendleton wrote, "We found radioactive iodine in all of the children, milk and vegetation that we measured in the whole northern section of the state." LRL-L associate director Gerald Johnson himself admitted that iodine-131 "poses a special health problem under conditions of immediate usage" and "will dictate a much greater limitation on permissible release of radioactivity than was anticipated."[45]

There was a debate within the AEC over whether to publicize LRL's findings. John W. Gofman, a professor of medical physics at the University of California at Berkeley who from 1963 to 1969 also served as one of LRL's associate directors, recalled that after Sedan, he received a call to come to Washington, D.C. Meeting with several others at the AEC's main office, he learned that Harold Knapp, who worked for the Commission's Division of Biology and Medicine, planned to publish a report about the exposure of Utahans to iodine-131, which, Knapp calculated, was "like a hundred times what we said anybody would get."

Gofman and others believed there was no reason why Knapp should not publish his findings. "We're going to be a bunch of liars," declared Charles Dunham, who worked on medical research for the Commission. "The AEC will weather this," Gofman and others replied, for "they've weathered all kinds of storms before." Dunham's effort to have him participate in "a cover-up" angered Gofman. As it turned out, Knapp's report received little attention, possibly because the U.S. Public Health Service, though cognizant that the amount of iodine, cesium, and strontium had "increased 'very markedly' after the Sedan blast," said there was no reason for worry.[46]

In August, after having spent $3.9 million on Chariot, the AEC announced it had officially "put off" that blast. It declared that it had successfully obtained information it otherwise would have received from Chariot through other shots—namely, Sedan. It insinuated that the bioenvironmental studies played no part in its decision making, a claim the *Christian Science Monitor* at the time found misleading and that Gerald Johnson in 1969 all but admitted was untrue: "An important and perhaps key difficulty in the path of the Plowshare program was demonstrated by the Chariot experience, namely the relevance of public information." Anxiety about fallout, Johnson continued, proved "difficult to alleviate, particularly in view of lack of support for the harbor." Another factor in the AEC's decision making was the realization that when the permafrost around the crater thawed, the slopes would become unstable and potentially collapse. It is also highly likely that the Commission did not want to risk another embarrassment similar to that which had taken place following Gnome and Sedan. The following year, the AEC withdrew its request to remove public land for the Chariot shot.[47]

The LTBT

By the time of Chariot's permanent deferral, the Geneva talks had shown little progress. On August 27 the United States and the United Kingdom submitted the two draft treaties at the ENDC. The first, a comprehensive test ban, would reduce the number of control posts and on-site inspections by an unspecified number, though the United States indicated it preferred between eight and ten of the latter. The second, a limited test ban, would permit only underground tests, thereby making moot the need for on-site inspections and control posts. The Kremlin rejected both. Anything short of a comprehensive agreement would permit Washington to continue tests designed to improve its nuclear technology. Yet Moscow was also resolute in its unwillingness to accept more than three on-site inspections as part of a comprehensive ban.[48]

It would take events in the Caribbean to break through the impasse. Learning in mid-October 1962 that the Soviet Union had placed nuclear missiles in Cuba, President Kennedy announced a naval blockade of Cuba to prevent the arrival of additional warheads and threatened military action if the missiles already in Cuba were not removed. For nearly a week, the world community watched to see if the crisis might turn into a full-scale nuclear conflict between the superpowers. On October 28, however, the two nations reached an agreement by which the United States would not attack Cuba in return for Moscow's removal of the missiles.

The Cuban missile crisis triggered a thaw in superpower relations. During those tense days, Kennedy and Khrushchev sent each other over a half-dozen messages, which, as the crisis neared its end, included talk of arms control. The ENDC began to show signs of progress, albeit slowly. For the first time the Kremlin tabled unmanned seismic stations, so-called black boxes, to verify compliance with a test ban. On-site verification, however, remained a sticking point. Moscow still insisted on no more than three per year; Washington maintained that was too few, favoring at least twice that many. The Soviets also wanted to restrict the square mileage open to such inspections so as to protect the secrecy of its military installations.[49]

Then there was the question of peaceful-use explosions. The draft treaties submitted in August 1962 by the United States and the United Kingdom stated that such blasts could take place under provisions established by annexes to be submitted later. No such annex was forthcoming until February 1963, when the Arms Control and Disarmament Agency (ACDA) proposed that the AEC give an "International Control Commission" four months' notice of any Plowshare tests, fully weigh any "comments received from members of the commission," allow for observation of the preparations of the test and the test itself, and permit internal and external inspection of the device used.[50]

ACDA's proposal put it at odds with the AEC's chairman. Born in 1912, Glenn Seaborg earned a Ph.D. in chemistry from the University of California at Berkeley and afterward joined his alma mater's faculty. He had won the Nobel Prize in Chemistry in 1951 for his role in discovering several new elements, including plutonium, americium, and berkelium. Afterward he was instrumental in identifying others, among them einsteinium and fermium. He served four years on the AEC's General Advisory Committee and then, from 1958 to 1961, was the University of California's chancellor. With the end of Eisenhower's term in office, John McCone had decided to call it quits as AEC head. Kennedy therefore phoned Seaborg, offering him the post.[51]

Seaborg had mixed feelings about a test ban treaty. "I personally strongly favored arms control in general and a test ban in particular," he wrote. But he could not ignore his colleagues on the Commission, who saw a close connection between nuclear testing and national security, or "the Joint Committee on Atomic Energy, which tended to be more hawkish than many in the administration." Moreover, he was as strong a defender of Plowshare as had been his predecessors. To him, the peaceful-use program, if successful, could offer much to the United States, if not the world.[52]

ACDA had a very different vision. The agency's origin is a matter of debate. Seaborg traced it to the last years of the Eisenhower administration, when Hubert Humphrey (D-Minnesota), chair of the Senate Disarmament Subcommittee, called for stepping up efforts to reduce the number of weapons worldwide. Another account credited Richard Neustadt, formerly a special assistant to President Harry Truman who became one of Kennedy's advisers. It is clear that as a candidate, Kennedy wanted more attention devoted to disarmament, and following the president's inauguration McCloy suggested establishing an independent government body that would focus solely on disarmament and arms control. Both Kennedy and members of Congress concurred, and in September 1961 lawmakers passed and the president signed legislation establishing ACDA.[53]

ACDA considered Plowshare a threat to its arms control mandate, hence its call for revealing the design of nuclear devices. Seaborg rejected the suggestion. He wrote ACDA deputy director Adrian Fisher that the importance of cutting down on fallout had become clearer than ever as a result of Chariot, Gnome, and Sedan. Doing so required the AEC to use America's cleanest and thus most technologically advanced explosives. To permit full inspection of those devices, Seaborg argued, would give away top-secret technology. He therefore suggested deleting the design provision while adding another permitting between five and six PNEs per year. Without those changes, insisted Seaborg, Plowshare would suffer. ACDA director William Foster rejected that reasoning. As worded, the treaty and annex permitted Plowshare tests. Moreover, revealing device design was not a certainty, for the other parties to the treaty might agree that some blasts did not require inspection of the explosive. The quota, for its part, was a bad idea. "To make such a proposal," Foster wrote, "would subject us to a barrage of propaganda that we are not sincere in our desire for a test ban," and the Soviets would reject the quota unless they received the same, thereby permitting Moscow a chance to develop weapons under the guise of peaceful-use experiments.[54]

Undeterred, Seaborg presented his case to the Committee of Principals at a meeting on April 17. He offered to limit Plowshare blasts to fifty kilotons and to accept only "three or four" peaceful nuclear explosions annually instead of five to six.[55] Jerome Weisner, Kennedy's special adviser on science and technology, had problems with Seaborg's presentation. He found "an inconsistency in saying we would not worry about a few 50 kiloton thermonuclear explosions by the

Soviet Union under guise of peaceful uses but that we were concerned about the possibility of undetected small yield underground tests." Both he and Mc-Cone, who had returned to Washington to replace Dulles as director of the Central Intelligence Agency, suggested putting off Plowshare in the name of getting a test ban treaty. Seaborg took issue with the idea that it was either Plowshare or a test ban, believing the AEC's proposal and the safeguards it had in mind permitted both.[56]

Unwilling to adopt the AEC's solution, ACDA offered two possible resolutions of its own designed to permit Plowshare to proceed while meeting the AEC's concerns. The Commission's proposal, stated ACDA, made large projects like an isthmian canal impossible, for they would necessitate far more than five or six blasts annually and of a size much bigger than fifty kilotons. But other possibilities existed. Mining ore, generating heat, and stimulating oil production required deeply buried devices that stood little chance of releasing radioactivity, so it did not matter whether the AEC used fission or fusion. Even building some canals and harbors was possible. At the Nevada Test Site, "deep underground shots . . . have been observed to create crater-like depressions in the surface of the earth" without fallout. Those depressions could provide the foundation for "small harbors and, possibly, canals." And as fission devices were obsolete and their design well known, the United States would not risk divulging important information by making those explosives available for full inspection. If, however, the AEC insisted on utilizing cleaner fusion bombs, then ACDA offered its second option: disclosure of the design's details. Granted, lawmakers might resist. But ACDA did not believe the risks were that great for, given their own knowledge of atomic weaponry, "Soviet scientists surely already understand the design at this time." Simply put, ACDA concluded, the choice was to continue Plowshare under the guidelines established by the peaceful-uses annex or to adopt an AEC alternative that would anger the Soviets and test ban proponents in Congress, risk weapons development, and ultimately cripple Plowshare.[57]

As the principals continued their debate over the peaceful atom, progress toward a test ban continued. In April, Kennedy and U.K. Prime Minister Harold Macmillan offered to send a senior official to Moscow to break through the impasse at Geneva on such matters as on-site inspections. Outwardly Khrushchev took a hard line. His withdrawal of the missiles from Cuba the year before had drawn criticism from within and outside the Soviet Communist Party. Not wanting to be seen as weak, he felt he had no choice but to reject the West's position on inspections and charge Washington and London with not seriously favoring a test ban. However, the Soviet leader realized the importance of working toward a ban and in May expressed his preparedness to begin talks in Moscow.[58]

In a June 10 commencement address at American University, Kennedy announced the resumption of the test ban negotiations and his selection of W. Averell Harriman as the American representative. He also made clear to his aides that he wanted to hold off on any further tests, as they could undermine those talks. However, he allowed preparations for Plowshare experiments, including a 100-kiloton excavation blast planned for southwestern Idaho called Schooner, to continue.[59]

The negotiations resumed on July 15. Khrushchev offered to accept a treaty similar to that proposed by the United States and the United Kingdom the previous August. In so doing, the delegates in Geneva could put aside on-site inspections and control posts, the two issues that had stalled their negotiations. The Western powers responded with a draft for a limited test ban. The Soviet delegation offered objections on provisions permitting the right to pursue Plowshare tests and granting a signatory the right to withdraw from the treaty on national security grounds. Harriman presented a solution. The Senate would never ratify a treaty that had no withdrawal clause, he explained. He thus suggested, with White House approval, that in return for Moscow's acceptance of the withdrawal clause, the United States would remove its peaceful-use provision. The Kremlin agreed.[60] With those matters resolved, and after three weeks of bargaining, the U.S., U.K., and Soviet delegations signed the LTBT.

Interpreting the LTBT

The immediate question was whether the LTBT prohibited Plowshare. Article I banned all testing in the atmosphere, outer space, underwater, and "in any other environment if such explosion causes radioactive debris to be present outside the territorial limits of the State under whose jurisdiction or control such explosion is conducted." John A. McKesson of the Foreign Service believed the LTBT made Plowshare shots illegal, but the AEC's John Kelly was less certain. He queried whether "to be present" referred to even a single atom, to a larger, though undetectable amount, or something more.[61]

In an effort to protect Plowshare, the AEC adopted a liberal interpretation. There were two reasons for this. First, the peaceful-use program had suffered some additional embarrassments. One was Project Coach. Designed to generate new elements and isotopes, Coach would permit the AEC to maintain a "balanced program" that paid attention to "both scientific and engineering applications" of the atom. The shot also had military applications, for the armed forces thought it possible to use some isotopes to create "smaller, lighter" explosives that had "other special features" (though it is not clear what those features were). The AEC chose to hold the blast at the Gnome site on the grounds that the necessary facilities were already there, "the site is available for immediate use," and the Commission had "extensive knowledge of local geology and hydrology." There was the need to figure out what went wrong with Gnome, but the AEC could use the safety studies prepared for that experiment as a basis for Coach. Hence, making use of the Gnome site meant a savings of both "time and money." Furthermore, it is likely the Commission believed use of the Gnome site might permit it to obtain data on some of the experiments that it had failed to get when Gnome went awry. But persistent problems "related to developing a suitable neutron-producing nuclear device" forced the AEC to postpone Coach.[62]

Nor did at least two of the three underground tests at the NTS, Projects Anacostia (5 kilotons), Kaweah (3 kilotons), or Tornillo (.38 kilotons) offer reason for optimism at the AEC. Anacostia and Kaweah had the purpose of creating new elements and providing data for Coach, while the AEC hoped Tornillo would help it develop cleaner explosives. Anacostia took place in November 1962, before Kennedy ordered a suspension of testing, while the others received the president's authorization after the test ban negotiations returned to the ENDC in early 1963. It is unclear if Tornillo accomplished its objective, but it is known that the AEC failed to get from Anacostia and Kaweah the desired results.[63] Add these failures to that of Coach, and the Commission had all the more reason to adopt a more liberal interpretation of the LTBT, one that would permit it to pursue tests a more restrictive reading would prohibit, perform one or more unquestionably successful experiments, and, as a result, rescue a Plowshare program so far marred by a lack of achievement.

Second, the AEC still hoped to accomplish the isthmian canal project. It appeared more and more that the United States and Panama were on a collision course. Riots had broken out in the Canal Zone in late 1959, after Panamanian students attempted to place their flag in the Zone. Furthermore, the two nations remained at odds over other matters, such as what Panama still charged as an unfairly low annuity. Consequently officials in Washington had every reason to wonder if Panama might take action similar to Egypt in 1956. In that case the best solution to defend America's interests was construction of a sea-level waterway.[64]

How much the LTBT affected Plowshare became a bone of contention among scientists who testified before the Senate as it considered ratification. Despite setbacks, the program's defenders remained confident that they could prove the economic, diplomatic, and military benefits the peaceful atom offered to American security. The problem was the limited test ban, which Plowshare's champions attested was too constraining. The counterargument was that by curtailing weapons testing, the LTBT offered diplomatic and military benefits, for it would meet calls for stopping radioactive fallout, slow Soviets' advancements in weapons technology, and improve relations between two nations that a year before had come close to a nuclear exchange. So which was more important for America's well-being: Plowshare or the LTBT?

To Seaborg, it was the LTBT, but he also believed that in its wording, the treaty did not prohibit all underground tests. Instead, he told the Senate Foreign Relations Committee, it disallowed only those tests that permitted "a quantity of radioactive debris" large enough to be detected to fall over another's borders. This meant that completely contained Plowshare experiments could continue. Constructing a sea-level canal in Panama was another matter. Seaborg admitted that building it likely could not take place under the LTBT as written. Panama was so small that even the cleanest of devices would deposit radioactivity beyond its borders in amounts that the AEC itself considered unacceptable. This meant that before sea-level canal construction could take place, the LTBT, if ratified, would require amending, as permitted under Article II. But that could become a long, drawn-out process. According to the LTBT, all parties to the treaty had to see the text of the amendment. Then, if one-third or more of the signatories agreed that the proposed amendment should receive consideration, the three original members (the United States, the Soviet Union, and the United Kingdom) had to "convene a conference," which all the other parties to the treaty could attend. The treaty did not specify when or where that conference would have to meet.[65] Finally, a majority of the LTBT's adherents, including the three original signatories, had to accept the amendment for it to go into effect.

The AEC hoped that by the time the United States successfully altered the treaty, it would be in a position to move quickly on canal construction. In fact it appears that upon his return from Moscow, Harriman told Seaborg that "in due time it would be possible to amend the treaty in order to liberalize the rules for Plowshare projects." The AEC head later surmised Harriman had said that to avoid any difficulties with the Commission or the JCAE as the Kennedy administration sought Senate ratification.[66] Yet Seaborg must have been aware from reading the treaty how difficult amending it would be.

Opposite Seaborg was Teller. Speaking before both the Senate Foreign Relations Committee and the Preparedness Subcommittee of the Committee on Armed Services, Teller insisted that there was no way to effectively enforce a test ban, and the treaty restricted testing necessary for weapons development. He also believed the LTBT would undermine efforts to use peaceful atomic technology outside U.S. borders, thereby giving the Russians a chance "to intervene in our dealings with friendly or neutral nations."[67]

The forces for ratification appeared to have the upper hand. Opponents of testing had found a common voice with the burgeoning environmental movement,

Figure 5. Left to right: AEC Chairman Glenn Seaborg, Edward Teller, President John F. Kennedy, Augusta "Mici" Teller. Teller and Seaborg disagreed over ratification of the Limited Test Ban Treaty. Photo courtesy of Digital Photo Archive, Department of Energy, and AIP Emilio Segre Visual Archives.

for both fallout and pesticides posed a threat to animals and humans. The Cuban missile crisis, moreover, remained a vivid memory. Consequently public opinion polls exhibited a steady increase supporting Senate approval, rising from 52 percent in July 1963 to an overwhelming 81 percent two months later. Similarly, of the nearly two dozen witnesses to appear before the Senate Foreign Relations Committee, only three, among them Teller, opposed ratification. The committee itself voted sixteen to one in favor of approval of the treaty by the full Senate. The Preparedness Subcommittee, whose membership and witness list were more restive about the treaty's ramifications, was a different story. Though its recommendation did not carry the same weight as that of the Foreign Relations Committee, it counseled against ratification.[68]

Kennedy threw in his opinion in the hopes of getting Senate endorsement. "The United States will diligently pursue its program for the further development of nuclear explosives for peaceful purposes by underground tests within the terms of the treaty," he wrote Senate Majority Leader Mike Mansfield

(D-Montana) and Minority Leader Everett Dirksen (R-Illinois). "When such developments make possible constructive uses of atmospheric nuclear explosions for peaceful purposes, the United States will seek international agreement under the treaty to permit such explosions." On September 23 the Senate ratified the treaty by a vote of eighty to nineteen.[69] Kennedy signed the LTBT into law two weeks later.

The treaty had an immediate impact on Plowshare. Not wanting to violate the LTBT, the AEC decided to defer Project Schooner in favor of developing "cleaner nuclear explosives." Furthermore President Kennedy issued National Security Action Memorandum 269, dictating that the AEC and Defense Department avoid any blasts that might constitute an infraction. The Memorandum also established the Review Committee on Underground Nuclear Tests, consisting of the national security adviser, the secretaries of state and defense, the head of the AEC, the director of the CIA, the chairman of the Joint Chiefs of Staff, the ACDA director, and the president's special assistant for science and technology, "or their designated representatives," to determine whether any proposed nuclear blasts might breach the LTBT. If the committee decided the explosion did not risk a treaty violation, it would then submit a recommendation to the president.[70] The AEC therefore faced an additional step to achieve approval of its nuclear experiments, during which it almost certainly would face a strong voice of dissent from ACDA.

A Program Again on Hold

On the morning of November 22, 1963, Gerald Johnson explained to a group of individuals, including Merrill Whitman of the Panama Canal Company, that the AEC still hoped to proceed with Schooner, with plans for it to take place in late 1964. "This is not a crucial shot," Johnson explained, "but would help determine certain yields" for the Panama Canal project. Whether the canal project itself went forward was another matter and depended on the interpretation of the test ban treaty.[71]

A few hours later Lee Harvey Oswald shot and killed Kennedy as the president traveled through Dallas in his motorcade. Seaborg, then hosting a delegation of Soviet atomic scientists, received a phone call notifying him of the chief executive's death. "The news threw us all into a turbulence of emotion and confusion," he later wrote. The visitors offered to cancel the remainder of their tour—an offer Seaborg accepted—while the AEC chair mourned the death of his nation's leader and determined what to do when Vice President Lyndon B. Johnson assumed the presidency.[72]

By the time of Kennedy's death, the Plowshare program was once again in limbo. The efforts to create new elements and generate heat showed no sign of progress. Opposition to Chariot and the data the AEC had obtained from Sedan brought an end to the idea of conducting an excavation experiment in Alaska, and the president refused to authorize any similar tests that risked a violation of the LTBT. Consequently the AEC found itself lacking the data it desired to determine the feasibility of nuclear excavation of a new canal.

In some respects these setbacks were beyond the AEC's control. It could not, for instance, stop gophers from eating underground cables or dictate where fallout from Sedan went. Yet the Commission and its allies had not helped themselves. Myopically focused on Plowshare, they ignored or disregarded findings that deviated from what they wanted to hear with regard to Chariot, which only served to strengthen the opposition and turn that blast into a monetary and public relations liability. They remained wedded to the idea that their experiments not only could work if given the chance but would benefit America's national security and create a better world for humankind. With passage of the LTBT, the AEC, LRL-L, and their friends now found themselves split over whether their plans might ever get off the ground.

The Complexities of
Canal Construction

On January 7, 1964, U.S. students at Balboa High School, located in the Panama Canal Zone, began raising the U.S. flag daily outside their institution. This followed a decision by officials in Washington in 1963 to have the U.S. and Panamanian flags fly together at seventeen different locations in the Zone but to remove the Stars and Stripes from outside various public facilities, among them schools. The students knew they had violated their nation's policy, and U.S. students at other schools followed suit. Angered, several hundred Panamanian students paraded into the Zone, with the intention of hoisting their country's flag in front of Balboa High. When as many as five hundred North Americans attempted to stop the approaching marchers, a scuffle broke out, during which the Panamanian flag was torn. A riot ensued, which rapidly spread throughout the country. Snipers began to fire on U.S. troops in the Canal Zone, who received orders to shoot back. Only after four days of fighting had worn down the rioters was order restored, but not before four U.S. soldiers and twenty-four Panamanians had lost their lives and nearly three hundred North Americans and Panamanians had suffered injuries.[1]

The January riots had implications for both U.S.-Panamanian relations and Plowshare. Roberto Chiari, Panama's president, severed diplomatic ties with the United States, charging Washington with "aggression." Lyndon B. Johnson, who had assumed the presidency less than two months earlier, and his aides blamed communist agents for fomenting the unrest and charged Chiari with adding "fuel to the fire" by not using his National Guard to restore order while simultaneously proclaiming that "the blood of the martyrs who perished today will not have been shed in vain." Yet Washington could not ignore the fact that the turmoil was symptomatic of the long-brewing frustration within Panama over U.S. control of the Canal Zone. The White House also understood that failure to make concessions to Panama regarding the Zone could prompt more if not worse disorder and concomitantly endanger the canal and U.S. security. With these considerations in mind, the Johnson administration adopted a two-part response: first, it sought to negotiate a new treaty with Panama that would replace that of 1903; second, it gave more serious consideration than previously seen from the White House to building a sea-level canal,[2] be it in Panama or elsewhere in the Central American isthmus.

One would assume that the interest in nuclear excavation of a sea-level waterway would constitute a boon for Plowshare, and indeed the first two years of Johnson's tenure in office saw a flurry of PNEs. Yet not all of the news was good for Plowshare scientists and their allies. For one, the peaceful-use program had to compete against what the president regarded as more important priorities. Additionally, the LTBT continued to interfere in the plans of Plowshare's proponents. And two important Plowshare-related tests delivered unexpected and unwanted results. By the end of 1965 the United States was well on the way to signing a new treaty with Panama but had made far less progress when it came to constructing a new canal using the atom, let alone determining the viability of Plowshare itself.

A Nuclear-Excavated Canal?

Born in 1908 into a fairly comfortable Texas family, Lyndon Baines Johnson attended Southwest Texas State Teachers' College, graduating in 1930. The future president then got a job as legislative secretary to Congressman Richard M. Kleberg and developed a reputation as a highly capable aide. He successfully ran during a special election in 1937 as a Democrat for a seat in the U.S. House of Representatives, where he remained for the next twelve years. In 1949 he moved into the Senate. Rapidly climbing up the ranks of the Democratic Party, he achieved the position of majority leader in 1954. Seeing in Johnson someone with extensive political connections in Congress and someone who could attract votes from the South, John F. Kennedy selected the Texas senator as his running mate in the 1960 presidential election.

Johnson was one of the most complex personalities ever to serve in the White House, combining intelligence, ambition, and a lust for power with a high level of insecurity and a desire to be loved by all. He was also a consummate politician who effectively used compromise and coercion to achieve his goals. As president his key goals were domestic in nature; in particular he wanted to see more aid given to the poor and needy. This was not just because of his limited exposure to foreign affairs as vice president. For personal and political reasons, Johnson desired to help the disadvantaged. Yet he could not ignore foreign relations. America's burgeoning involvement in the war in South Vietnam demanded attention, and the riots in Panama made the White House realize it had to take heed of its Central American neighbor.

On January 10, while the rioting in Panama continued, Johnson phoned Chiari. Referring to "elements unfriendly to both of us who will exploit this situation"—an obvious reference to Washington's perception that communists were behind the turmoil—the U.S. president asked his Panamanian counterpart to do everything possible "to restore quiet." Rather than promise to end the riots, Chiari blamed them on U.S. "indifference" to Panama. The only solution, he claimed, was "a complete revision of all treaties which affect Panama-U.S. relations."[3]

Johnson appreciated that the United States had to do something about the canal, but he had no intention of acting under Panamanian pressure. Indeed, the mail coming to the White House and a recent Gallup poll indicated that the overwhelming majority of Americans wanted the Johnson administration to take a hard line with the Panamanians. In the Senate, which would have to approve any new treaty, Republicans pointed to "Castro-Communist agents" fomenting the unrest in Panama and insisted that the waterway belonged to the United States. Democrats, for their part, were split over whether to make concessions to the Panamanians.[4] Johnson could see that any new agreement required some tough bargaining on Capitol Hill.

Here is where Plowshare came into play. During a meeting on January 13 with the president, Secretary of State Dean Rusk, Defense Secretary Robert McNamara, and others, Assistant Secretary for Inter-American Affairs Thomas C. Mann suggested what became a central piece of the White House's negotiating position. "A longer range plan should be developed," he stated, "involving negotiations with Colombia and Nicaragua to build a sea-level canal in their territories." If the United States could get approval from one or both countries for construction, "we could return to the Panamanians and tell them we were going to build a sea-level canal either in Colombia or in Nicaragua which would greatly reduce the importance of the existing Panama Canal." Faced with that possibility, Panama "would then be prepared to make a satisfactory deal with us."[5] Thus the threat of digging a sea-level waterway in another nation could give the United States the leverage it needed to obtain a new treaty with Panama acceptable to the U.S. Senate.

Of course, the atom offered one means of building such a waterway. There is not much evidence that Johnson had given nuclear excavation technology a great deal of thought before entering the Oval Office, but it is clear that as president he found it intriguing. Harold Brown, a scientist who helped develop the Plowshare program in the late 1950s and served in the Pentagon during the Kennedy and Johnson administrations, recalled that Johnson "liked big projects like Plowshare and its possible use in creating a new isthmian canal." Furthermore the president shared Mann's conclusion that the threat of a new waterway could give the United States an upper hand in negotiations with the Panamanians. Accordingly he asked for quick delivery of a paper covering the "feasibility, cost, etc., of constructing a sea-level canal by nuclear methods."[6]

To meet Johnson's charge, officials from the State and Defense Departments and the AEC gathered on January 23 and reviewed the findings from the 1960 study on the canal. Their recommendations, issued in February, largely followed those of Mann's. They called for constructing a sea-level canal, forming "a Nuclear Canal Coordinating Committee . . . to monitor and coordinate the actions necessary to implement the policy decision," having the State Department approach Colombia and Panama, and undertaking "a public information program" to promote the waterway's construction. The attendees took note of the restrictions prescribed by the Limited Test Ban Treaty, but they believed that agreement did not pose an insurmountable problem. For one thing, there was the matter of how to interpret its language. Additionally U.S. policy "should not depend on the assumption that the Treaty will last forever." Finally, there was the possibility of convincing the Soviets to permit Plowshare blasts under the treaty's provisions. In the meantime the interagency group suggested "a small cratering shot this spring which would serve as a precedent in going to larger shots."[7]

The AEC had reason to believe that it could finally prove Plowshare's real potential. During 1963 alone, the Commission had sunk nearly one-third of its budget into the peaceful use of the atom. From the military and civilian tests it had conducted, it had determined it could carry out explosions that were 96 percent clean. While the AEC had ascertained that fallout from Sedan had traveled nearly a hundred miles—though in fact it traveled much farther than that—it believed it had developed the means to cut that distance in half and, with further experimentation, could reduce it by half again. Now it had in the White House a president who seemed firmly behind the Plowshare program. Indeed, during just the first six months of 1964 Johnson approved three Plowshare-related atomic explosions at the NTS: Klickitat in February, followed by Ace and Dub in June. The first two, at seventy and three kilotons, respectively, had the purpose of developing cleaner bombs. From the 11.7-kiloton Dub blast, the AEC sought to improve methods of trapping radioactivity.[8]

There is no indication that the Johnson administration debated these blasts or that the public gave them much notice. All were buried deeply, giving an ex-

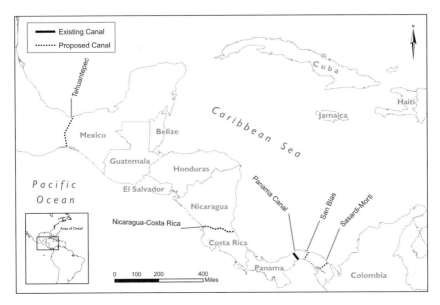

Map 2. The five proposed routes for a sea-level canal.

pectation that they would be fully contained and pose no likelihood of violating the LTBT. Furthermore, at the Nevada Test Site they could take place with little or no publicity. As it turned out, both Ace and Dub vented some radioactivity. Even had they taken place without incident, the fact was that these blasts, and every other underground nuclear explosion, were not truly contained. To gather information about any underground test, be it to determine how clean it was or whether it generated new isotopes, required drilling into the cavity left behind and obtaining samples. During this process some radioactivity entered the atmosphere.[9] What mattered most to U.S. officials, however—and arguably to any signatory to the test ban treaty—was whether the explosion released enough radioactivity at the time of the explosion to pose an LTBT violation, not whether the postshot analysis did so.

Aside from presidential interest and optimism about its ability to curb fallout, the AEC surmised that it could build a canal at lower cost than originally estimated. Having successfully reduced the amount of fission used in its Plowshare explosives and drawing on data from its nuclear tests as well as experiments at the NTS employing high explosives, the Commission now estimated it could set off a ten-kiloton device for $350,000 and one of two megatons for $600,000. This compared with earlier calculations of "$500,000 for a few kilotons" and $1 million "for up to five megatons." Consequently the AEC assumed that it could construct a 60-mile long, 250-foot deep, and 1,000-foot wide waterway across

Panama for about $500 million. This was $250 million less than the 1957 and 1960 canal studies had projected. The appraisal for the 104-mile long channel along the Atrato-Truando route through Colombia had come down to $780 million, or nearly half a billion dollars cheaper than four years earlier. Even the Mexican route, the most expensive of the five candidates for nuclear excavation, had fallen to $1.5 billion from the previous estimate of $2.3 billion.[10]

Not all of the news was positive, though. Appearing before the JCAE in February, AEC chair Glenn T. Seaborg and Gerald Johnson, associate director of LRL, explained that even with full funding for the Plowshare program, the AEC would have to conduct field studies in the nations where nuclear excavation might take place, design and produce special explosives in significant numbers, and, because of the risk of a violation of the LTBT, seek an amendment to that agreement. All told, the Commission and LRL estimated it would be seven to ten years before they would be in a position to start construction.[11]

There was reason to question whether ten or even seven years was overly optimistic. Seaborg himself admitted to the Senate Commerce Committee that it was not clear if the Soviet Union or the United Kingdom—the other two original signatories to the LTBT whose approval were necessary to amend it—would agree to any alterations to that agreement. His only hope was that if those countries realized that the United States had no intention of using cratering technology "to surreptitiously further develop nuclear weapons," then they would accept using the atom to build the waterway.[12]

Furthermore a seven- to ten-year time frame assumed Plowshare got all of the money it needed. In FY 1964 the AEC had budgeted $13.5 million for Plowshare. Of that, $6.725 million was slated for excavation projects, with the remainder designated for Project Coach as well as research and development (R&D). For FY 1965 the Commission had asked for $21 million, only to have the Bureau of the Budget cut that to $11 million. Of that amount, the Commission committed $4.725 million to excavation, $1.1 million to Coach, and the rest to R&D. Seaborg cited difficulties designing the explosive for Coach and the need to work on cleaner explosives to avoid a violation of the LTBT as explanations for the reduced emphasis on excavation projects. Representative Craig Hosmer (R-California), one of Plowshare's staunchest defenders on Capitol Hill, was "shocked and amazed" by the 40 percent cut for excavation. He charged Seaborg with "planting the seeds for losing a lot of" Plowshare scientists, who would become discouraged with the lack of funding; questioned the health of the entire peaceful-use program; and wondered what might happen to Plowshare if excavation suffered another 40 percent decrease. The AEC chair confessed to his journal that the hearing did not go well. "I had some difficulty," he wrote, "defending administration position of delaying cratering shots in view of promises by administration, including myself, before test ban treaty, that we would be able to do crater-ing shots under the treaty."[13]

Defending the White House could prove more difficult if it cut Plowshare's funding further, which was a possibility. President Johnson might have had an interest in Plowshare, but he had what he considered far more important con-cerns. The administration continued to pour resources into South Vietnam to shore up that nation's unstable government. Of even greater priority to the presi-dent than Vietnam was his "war on poverty." Announced in his first State of the Union Address, Johnson planned to fight that war with a plethora of welfare, employment, insurance, and development programs. Indeed according to AEC controller John P. Abbadessa, the Bureau of the Budget reduced the Commis-sion's funding to $11 million for FY 1965 in part because "of a stringent budget." Gerald Johnson told the JCAE that if funding for excavation projects continued at the $4.7 million level it would take just over twenty years for the AEC and LRL to get all of the money necessary to conduct the experiments and develop and stockpile the explosives required for construction of an isthmian waterway.[14]

Then there were the cost estimates, which not everyone accepted. The 1960 canal study had cited a figure of $2.3 billion to conventionally convert the exist-ing canal. However, the governor of the Canal Zone, Robert J. Fleming, believed $1.8 billion was more accurate, and that number "probably could come down even more." As for the quoted $500 million for nuclear excavation across Panama, Fleming cited "uncertainties" such as "potential technical problems" that could "add another several hundred million dollars to the estimate." Furthermore, build-ing a new canal required a treaty. That agreement would include provisions cov-ering "site acquisition, rights of way, indemnification and annuities," and the construction of defense facilities, all of which could take months to work out and would certainly necessitate additional appropriations. Fleming summarized, "We really do not know how much the nuclear solution will cost. But it is obvious that it will be a substantial sum." And none of this addressed the time it might take to amend the LTBT. "When all the factors are considered, then," Fleming wrote, "the nuclear canal is not a short time proposition, but rather a longer one than the conventional canal." Though not willing to give up on the atomic solution, he concluded, "We need much more site information and development work before we can make valid and reliable studies and estimates."[15]

Despite Fleming's doubts and its own unwillingness to fully fund Plowshare, the White House began setting the stage for its two-part approach to Panama, of which the threat of a nuclear-constructed canal in another nation played a part. It made clear it would link economic aid to Panama to the willingness of the Chiari government to cooperate. Then, on March 21, President Johnson pre-sented a fig leaf, offering to "review every issue which now divides" Panama and the United States and strongly hinting to Chiari his willingness to agree to a revision of the 1903 treaty. As a further indication of his seriousness, the president named as special ambassador Robert Anderson, a New York financier who had served as secretary of the navy and of Treasury under President Eisenhower. Chiari, whose National Liberal Party faced an uncertain bid in an upcoming election that May and who wanted to avoid another blow-up in U.S.-Panamanian relations, accepted Johnson's offer. In early April the two nations resumed diplomatic relations, with Anderson staying on at his post while Jack Hood Vaughn, previously the regional director for the Peace Corps in Latin America, assumed the post of regular ambassador.[16]

To make sure Chiari did not suddenly think he held all the cards, President Johnson whipped out the stick again on April 16, announcing an agreement with Colombia to begin surveying land along the Atrato-Truando (route 25). While stating that the United States hoped for similar arrangements with other nations, he made no specific mention of Panama. The announcement and overt omission infuriated the Panamanian government. "It was an ill-timed gesture," complained Octavio Fabrega of that country's Foreign Affairs Advisory Committee, while another member of the same body correctly assessed the statement as "a measure to strengthen the United States bargaining position."[17]

Panama's May election gave the Johnson administration no reason to alter its approach. Under Panama's constitution Chiari could not succeed himself, so he endorsed Marco Aurelio Robles, the National Liberal Party candidate and one of the sitting president's cousins. A wealthy banker who had the nickname "the Rifle" because of his tough nature, Robles had insisted upon changes to the 1903 treaty as early as 1964. Vaughn explained that the new Panamanian president could not dismiss the growing pressure within his country "for changes, here and now, with regard to present canal."[18]

North American use of the carrot and stick thus continued. At the end of June Robert Newbegin, a member of the U.S. delegation negotiating in Panama, told his Panamanian counterparts that although the United States "did not desire to impose some solution upon the Republic of Panama," it was willing to consider "alternatives in another country, possibly Colombia." The way Panama could guarantee that Washington did not turn elsewhere was for Panama to accept an agreement that had a provision for a new canal. Mann repeated that message to Panamanian foreign minister Galileo Solís in July. As a first step toward ensuring that the United States did not go elsewhere to build the waterway, the assistant secretary asked Panama to permit U.S. field studies along the Sasardi-Morti route (route 17) to see if it was a good candidate for nuclear excavation.[19]

Publicly the Panamanians refused to give. Solís told Mann that his nation had yet to fully study the implication of a nuclear-excavated canal, including the possible environmental impact. But in his opinion the United States would want to build a canal where it was easiest and most economical, and here Panama had advantages over Colombia. Privately, though, the Panamanian government had grave concerns about the construction of a sea-level canal, whether built in Panama or elsewhere. The existing lock waterway brought in about $60 million in tolls annually, employed about ten thousand people whose combined payroll was some $35 million, and, in 1963 alone, generated an operating profit of $12.8 million. Should the United States build a new canal and give the old one to Panama, Washington would want to retain control over the new waterway at least until it was paid off. The profit the United States made from the new canal would allow it to increase the annuity paid to Panama. Even so, Panama would experience a loss of income as fewer ships used the old lock waterway. Additionally a sea-level canal required only five hundred to eight hundred people to operate it, meaning thousands of Panamanians would find themselves without work and spending power. It was obvious that the new waterway might wreak havoc on Panama's economy.[20]

Whether a sea-level canal in Panama or anywhere else made sense, let alone how to construct it, could be determined only through thorough surveys of each route. Of the options, the top three were the existing canal, where nuclear excavation was not possible, and the Sasardi-Morti and Atrato-Truando routes. While not out of the running, a canal along the Costa Rica–Nicaragua border was far more expensive than one built in Panama or Colombia. And Mexico was not only costly, but by all appearances that nation wanted nothing short of a canal that it controlled—something the United States would not accept. Although a small group from the Defense Department was in Colombia, a full record of the topography, geography, meteorology, demography, and ecology of each possible location—minus the existing canal, about which much was known already—necessitated far larger teams and, estimated the White House, about three years to complete. Based on information they obtained from the Department of the Army, lawmakers approved $17.5 million for the surveys. On September 22 President Johnson signed Public Law 88-609. It established a five-person body called the Atlantic-Pacific Interoceanic Canal Study Commission, with Special Ambassador Anderson acting as its head. The legislation called for the Commission to issue a report of its findings by June 30, 1968.[21]

As Congress green-lighted the money for the surveys, the AEC and LRL issued a series of studies that gave some indication of what it would take to build an isthmian canal with nuclear devices along the favored routes 17 and 25. Having their new data from previous tests, the number and total power of the explosives were smaller than in 1960. Yet they were still huge. Along the Sasardi-Morti the Plowshare scientists envisioned using 294 atomic devices totaling 160 megatons, fired in fourteen separate detonations. The Atrato-Truando would necessitate 262 explosives, totaling 271 megatons and blown up in twenty-one separate blasts. Each blast would total no more than ten megatons, with the exception of one of thirty-five megatons on the Sasardi-Morti and, on the Atrato-Truando, one of thirty megatons and another of thirty-five megatons. A significant number of the individual devices set off would be in the megaton range. On route 25, for instance, thirteen of the twenty-one blasts required at least a one-megaton explosive. To control fallout and the impact of seismic or air shock, Plowshare scientists proposed having each blast take place about once a month rather than simultaneously.[22]

Assumptions

The AEC and LRL emphasized that they still had much to learn before moving on to the construction phase. Plowshare scientists calculated that the deeper they buried a nuclear explosive, the larger the crater, until they reached what they called "optimum depth," or the point at which the device created the largest possible crater based on its explosive potential. Once buried beyond optimum depth, the explosion became increasingly contained, leaving behind an ever-smaller crater and, eventually, none at all. Yet the AEC and LRL acknowledged that all of these calculations were based on just one test, called Danny Boy. Another example of AEC-military cooperation, the Defense Department had conducted Danny Boy in March 1962 to study the effects of cratering in hard, dry rock. The 0.4-kiloton explosive blasted a crater 214 feet wide and 62 feet deep. According to the AEC, 96 percent of the radioactivity fell within the crater, while most of the remainder was deposited within two miles of ground zero. The data they gathered from Danny Boy convinced Plowshare scientists they no longer needed Project Wagon and so canceled that blast.[23] What the information gathered did not tell them was what might happen if they exploded a bomb in a softer medium, like the clay they would encounter during construction of the canal.

The scientists also wanted to know more about row-charge experiments. As seen in the planning for Chariot, the assumption was that setting off several nuclear devices placed in a line would leave behind a ditch; if that indeed proved the case, it would facilitate canal construction. Starting in late 1959 the AEC had conducted a number of row-charge tests, among them Toboggan, Rowboat, Pre-Buggy I and II, and Dugout. While these experiments proved it was possible to create a ditch with devices placed in a row, all involved the use of high explosives. It was important for the AEC to find out what happened when it placed atomic explosives in a line. Would an atomic row-charge test create a ditch or instead leave behind a series of craters? Would the seismic motion generated by such a test be so great as to cause the lips of the ditch to collapse, thus partially filling it in?[24] Failure to generate a ditch or a collapse of the lips could complicate atomic construction of a waterway.

Seismic shock was also important when considering the impact of PNEs on buildings. The AEC and LRL based most of their seismic findings on "relatively low-yield explosions" in the one- to fifty-kiloton range, and there existed "no experimental data for ground motions from row charges." Nor was much known about the impact of seismic shock on residential buildings: "Tests which involved structural damage are so limited as to be inconclusive." The shaking produced by nuclear explosions at or near the coast might dramatically affect the water, such as spawning large waves, and this too was something on which the scientists had no data. Unmentioned was a March 1964 report by Major William Wray, a member of the Army Corps's recently established Nuclear Cratering Group, who warned LRL that the thirty-five-megaton blast planned for the Darien route would not only cause those parts of the canal already built to collapse, but "would correspond to an earthquake with an intensity of XII (or even worse)."[25]

Plowshare scientists also needed much more information on air blast, particularly that created by row-charge experiments. Winds in the ozonosphere and temperature inversions could increase the intensity of wind blast effects and the distance at which they made themselves felt. Any large-scale construction project had to take into account the monetary and public relations costs of breaking windows or causing other damage to structures away from ground zero. U.S. scientists had learned that "large store windows begin to fail at 2 millibars overpressure," while windows on homes broke "at about 3.5 millibars." Combining a temperature inversion and jet stream winds "can give focusing at ranges of 30–100 miles . . . [and] give overpressures up to 16 times those which would be expected in a homogeneous atmosphere."[26] Hence if the conditions were right, construction of a sea-level canal could cause serious damage to buildings many miles from the explosion.

And what of radiation exposure? The AEC and LRL knew they had to evacuate people living in the area. How many and for how long was a matter of debate. The September studies placed the number at about thirty thousand for either route, though they did not indicate if those removed could at some point return to their homes. In congressional testimony several months earlier Deputy Secretary of Defense Cyrus Vance had cited twenty-five thousand evacuees if the waterway was built in Panama and eighty thousand for the Colombian route. "In each case it would be a temporary removal," he assured lawmakers. Freelance reporter Lawrence Galton placed the number at about twenty-five thousand for the Sasardi-Morti route—he did not give an estimate for the Atrato-Truando—with some evacuated permanently. An internal Johnson administration assessment agreed with twenty-five thousand if built in Panama and sixty thousand in Colombia. This appraisal also made reference to "resettlement and village construction costs,"[27] raising the question whether the number permanently relocated was in fact far larger than assumed by Galton.

The AEC and LRL determined in their September assessments that after evacuation "no persons would be expected to be exposed to radiation in excess of the radiation protection guides of the IAEA [International Atomic Energy Agency]." Yet the scientists based this conclusion on a number of assumptions. One was that improved emplacement and radiation entrapment techniques would reduce the amount of fallout beyond the immediate area around the blast. Weather conditions were also important, and detonating each explosive at the right time "would give a very high probability that the local fallout would fall within the desired sector."[28]

These were dubious assumptions. Neptune and Gnome had both demonstrated that despite precautions aimed at containment, accidents happened. Meteorological conditions could change quickly, meaning there was always the possibility of radioactivity being deposited farther away from the explosion than anticipated. Considering that any nuclear-excavated canal route entailed the use of hundreds of devices set off in numerous blasts, the chance of error increased. Plowshare scientists themselves confessed that "fallout prediction has some limitations."[29]

Even if those scientists made significant headway in answering these questions and fully assessing their assumptions, there remained the matter of a timetable. Starting in March 1964 the Johnson administration had begun the process of increasing economic aid to South Vietnam by $50 million and the number of U.S. military "advisers" from sixteen thousand to over twenty-three thousand.[30] Then, in early August, a few weeks before President Johnson easily won his party's nomination for the November presidential election, the U.S. Navy reported attacks on two of its warships off the North Vietnamese coast. Johnson used the incident to request passage of a resolution granting him power to combat future acts of aggression against the U.S. military. By an overwhelming vote, lawmakers gave the president the authority he sought. Johnson remained wedded to the war on poverty, but the authority afforded to him by Congress opened the door to a costly escalation of the war in Vietnam; that would likely mean further reductions in Plowshare's budget and even more difficulty for those involved in the peaceful-use program to conduct the tests they needed before moving on to building a new canal.

Failure to work out a new treaty acceptable to both Panama and the United States could also complicate plans to build a sea-level waterway. In August,

Mann and Secretary of the Army Stephen Ailes had begun working on a draft treaty to replace that of 1903 and permit the United States to build a new canal outside the existing Canal Zone. This concept, with the approval of the Department of State, soon turned into two separate but interrelated agreements, one on a sea-level waterway and the other on the 1903 pact. By December 1 the two secretaries had prepared a draft sea-level treaty. The State Department meanwhile had made significant progress on the other, which would abrogate the existing canal treaty, recognize Panama's sovereignty over the canal, and terminate shortly after the sea-level waterway opened,[31] thus turning the original canal over to Panama.

Pleased with this progress, on December 18 Johnson announced his intention to "press forward with Panama and other international governments, in plans and preparations for a sea level canal in this area," and authorized the State Department to start discussions on that score. He also proposed that the United States and Panama begin negotiating a new canal treaty. Aware that critics might charge him with succumbing to Panamanian pressure, the president declared, "While the people of the United States have never made concessions to force, they have always supported fair play and respect for the rights of others." Robles praised the speech, proclaiming that it would "create a favorable atmosphere for negotiations." Within a day Washington and Panama had agreed to start the talks the following month.[32]

Project Sulky

The same day President Johnson delivered his speech, the AEC conducted Project Sulky. After Dub the Commission had launched two more Plowshare-related nuclear tests at the NTS. Par, a thirty-eight-kiloton explosive buried 1,325 feet underground and designed to create new elements, took place in October. The following month the twelve-kiloton Handcar experiment, aimed at improving emplacement techniques, went off at a depth of 1,330 feet.[33]

Sulky was different. While the AEC had made calculations regarding optimum depth and full containment, it had not determined what happened if an explosive was buried deep enough not to create a crater but not so deep as to be fully contained. This was an important question, for the data gathered would help Plowshare scientists prepare for future nuclear excavation projects, among them the canal. The 0.1-kiloton test would help provide an answer.[34]

For the first time since the test ban treaty's ratification, the AEC was on the cusp of conducting an experiment it knew would release radioactivity into the atmosphere. But, Seaborg explained to National Security Adviser McGeorge Bundy, the test was "about the smallest scale experiment from which useful cratering information can be obtained." From Sulky the AEC could learn how much radioactivity a blast buried at that depth released as well as where the fallout traveled. He did not believe the LTBT was an issue, for the amount of radioactivity generated would be so small that no nation would detect it unless warned in advance about the blast. Even if discovered, the tiny quantity would not constitute a treaty violation. The AEC chair hoped to conduct the test in February but could defer it "until the fall without impairing the Plowshare program."[35]

Seaborg's request generated a debate within the Johnson administration. The central issue was the interpretation of the test ban treaty, particularly what constituted debris "to be present" outside a nation's borders. The AEC adopted a "de minimis" reading, by which debris existed only if it registered higher than internationally accepted health standards. To the ACDA, though, "present" meant any amount; there was nothing in the LTBT's language "to indicate that the presence of small amounts of debris should be excepted." To risk a violation of the LTBT, continued ACDA, would permit other countries to accuse the United States of bad faith and make it harder to get nuclear nonsignatories, such as France and communist China—the latter appeared on the verge of exploding its own atomic device—to sign on to a test ban. Considering the arguments, Johnson decided in February to postpone Sulky. Doing so would give the AEC more time to find a way to avoid detection of the blast and permit more favorable weather conditions. Most important, the upcoming presidential election was on his mind. To permit the test risked a Soviet charge of an LTBT violation, which could cost Johnson votes among test ban advocates. Furthermore the grazing season was approaching, and radioactivity descending on crops and animals would certainly add to the uproar.[36]

Anticipating eventual presidential approval for Sulky, Seaborg suggested having international observers witness the blast: "We believe that the close-in, first-hand observation of a nuclear cratering experiment by international observers would go far toward allaying the fears of other nations with respect to radioactivity, and would do much to foster an international nuclear excavation." Brown rejected that reasoning. Allowing witnesses meant advertising the experiment's date, thereby increasing the likelihood of the detection of fallout beyond U.S. borders. Washington might also find itself compelled to provide secret information on the device itself. He convinced the White House to hold Sulky and then issue a low-key announcement. In turn the administration could determine if in fact it was detected.[37]

In mid-October Seaborg approached the president about Sulky and, following a determination by the Review Committee on Underground Nuclear Tests that the amount of radiation released would be minimal, received the go-ahead from the White House for execution in December.[38] The day after the December 18 shot, the White House, as planned, issued a simple statement attesting to the size and purpose of the experiment. Unplanned and unmentioned, beyond the acquisition of "data," was the result. The AEC had anticipated the test would "break the surface of the ground in a cratering action." Instead, it left behind "a circular mound of broken rock, roughly 25 feet high and 80 feet in diameter at the top," with a conical depression in the middle. The agency came away with mixed feelings about what had happened. On the one hand, Sulky released so little radioactivity that the AEC concluded there was no way to distinguish it from normal background radiation. Hence it seemed to prove it was possible to conduct nuclear blasts without violating the LTBT. On the other hand, Sulky had not performed as expected, forcing the Commission to go back to the drawing board. "Perhaps this shot was conducted in too conservative a manner in order to be sure of not violating the Test Ban Treaty," Seaborg wrote in his journal.[39]

Project Carryall

Sulky had ramifications not just for the sea-level canal project but for another Plowshare proposal called Carryall. Desirous to save time and money, in the early 1960s the Atchison, Topeka, and Santa Fe Railroad approached the AEC about blasting through the Bristol Mountains in southern California to open a route that would be shorter and quicker than an existing one. It just so happened that the California Division of Highways at this time had its eye on expanding a two-lane road through that same mountain range so it could become part of Interstate 40. The AEC suggested combining the two projects, and both the railroad company and the California state government agreed. Following a feasibility study, the AEC announced the project in December 1963. With a price tag of almost $14 million—Plowshare scientists made sure to point out that this was $8 million less than turning to conventional explosives—Carryall called for using twenty-two nuclear devices ranging in size from twenty to two hundred kilotons and totaling 1.7 megatons. Similar to the planning under way for the Panama Canal, the project envisioned creating a series of interconnected craters by exploding the devices in two stages. The first would take place in the spring of 1967 and the second in the fall of that year, leaving behind a cut two miles long and up to 350 feet deep. Conventional equipment would then complete the undertaking, allowing the railroad and highway to open around 1969.[40]

Carryall was simultaneously a means to an end and an end in itself. If successful, it would represent the nation's first civilian application of nuclear excavation, one that in this case would provide clear benefit to the strategically and economically important U.S. transportation network. It would also assist the isthmian canal project. "All of us involved in the sea-level canal studies have recognized from the outset that a major nuclear excavation project would have to be carried out within the U.S. before we would ask another country to permit one on its territory," Secretary Ailes wrote Seaborg in December 1964. "The Carryall Project appears to be ideal for this purpose." Alone or in combination, Carryall and the sea-level canal would become steps in the broader goal of using the atom to create a better world. Of course, excavation of the canal could not get under way until the LTBT's other signatories supported amending that agreement. Here too Carryall offered promise. As the administration explained, Carryall could "contribute the opportunity, create the interest, and demonstrate the practicality which is necessary to the success of any program of international cooperation in nuclear excavation."[41]

There were several problems with this train of thought. Exploding a hundred tons was one thing; detonating 1.7 megatons—seventeen thousand times that of Sulky—was quite another. The AEC anticipated that 90 percent of the radioactivity would be deposited within five miles of the explosions. Even if that estimate proved accurate, it still meant that up to 10 percent would travel farther, which could affect nearby population centers, among them the cities of Needles, Barstow, and possibly Los Angeles. Even the AEC recognized this and proposed in early 1964 spending another $330,000 to study the issue.[42]

Moreover, the argument that Carryall could lead to a revision of the LTBT was a case of backward logic. It meant risking a violation of the very treaty the AEC wanted to amend to convince other countries to amend it. And because of Carryall's size as compared to Dub, Par, or Sulky, that risk increased exponentially. Because of the proximity of several cities, the AEC would have to announce each series of detonations in advance, giving other countries a chance to prepare detection equipment. Unless the other LTBT signatories agreed not to complain about Carryall, for which there was no guarantee, Washington's only option to avoid a charge of treaty violation was to seek an amendment to it. Even Seaborg had to admit to the JCAE, "I think large projects like [Carryall] would require a modification of the treaty."[43]

Finally, as with the canal project, there was the matter of a timetable. Before proceeding with Carryall, the AEC wanted to conduct several other tests to learn more about the impact of nuclear explosives in different media. Sulky was one, but the agency foresaw others, including one named Schooner and another called Galley. Schooner, a 100-kiloton cratering blast, was to take place in the fall of 1965 in Idaho. Galley, proposed for Idaho the follow year, would become the first nuclear row-charge experiment. With the information gained from these blasts, Carryall would follow in 1967. Yet under federal legislation the California Department of Highways had to have I-40 finished by 1972. To meet that deadline the state wanted to complete any nuclear excavation by the autumn of 1966, thereby permitting time for the radioactivity to dissipate and conventional equipment to finish the work. The AEC was "hopeful" that California would accept a delay of a year "if they were given reasonable assurance in the near future that the Carryall demonstration project would be conducted on the schedule" the agency had suggested.[44]

The Canal versus the LTBT

The United States thus appeared on the verge of a major excavation project (Carryall), with an even bigger one (the canal) it hoped would follow several years later. Yet both, and possibly even the tests to precede them (such as Schooner), would certainly violate the test ban treaty. Gerald Johnson himself complained in June 1965, "It is now beginning to appear unless the ground rules are changed that we will not be able to fire Schooner as desired this year."[45] Because of the uncertainty over what was permissible under the LTBT, within months of that treaty's ratification U.S. officials had begun to debate whether the Soviet Union would accept an amendment allowing peaceful-use explosions. The general consensus was that it was unlikely; rather Washington should seek Moscow's assent to specific tests.[46] Even so, in July President Johnson accepted a State Department recommendation to feel out the Soviets on the subject of altering the test ban treaty to permit large excavation projects. With that authority Secretary of State Rusk and former U.S. ambassador to the Soviet Union Llewellyn Thompson met with Foreign Minister Andrei Gromyko and Moscow's ambassador to the United States, Anatoly Dobrynin, on December 21. The two Americans explained that while the United States would not be in a position for several years to put nuclear explosives to use in Panama—neither made mention of Carryall— the atom could help curb construction costs, particularly on large projects. Rusk then "inquired whether the Soviet Union had any projects in mind for peaceful nuclear explosives." Though "he had no information as to whether such plans existed," Gromyko said he had no opposition to using atomic devices as long as they were employed "only for peaceful purposes." He said nothing, though, about amending the LTBT.[47]

For Seaborg, the test ban treaty did not matter, at least for the moment. Testifying before the JCAE on January 5, 1965, the AEC chair contended that it would take about five years before Plowshare scientists were in a position to start moving dirt for a canal. Interestingly this was half as long as he had estimated ten months earlier. He believed that Plowshare had made progress during 1964, and he may have recalled the angry response he got when he told senators previously that it could take up to a decade for his agency to give the go-ahead to start digging. Still, it would take five years, he pointed out, because the AEC had to create the necessary explosives, produce them in the proper number, and conduct more tests to develop a better understanding of "the whole phenomenology of cratering."[48] By that time maybe Washington would have obtained a modification of the test ban treaty.

If Seaborg assumed his new estimate for canal construction would please lawmakers, he was wrong. Senator Clinton Anderson, who had long questioned the accuracy of the statements given to him by the AEC, went on the attack. "Some years ago," he began, "we talked about the great possibilities of Plowshare to use it to build harbors. Now, you have a good answer why you can't build harbors. To use it to dig canals. Now we find many years before we can do that. . . . I am just wondering where Plowshare is going or whether it is going backward." Senator John Pastore (D-Rhode Island) also was dissatisfied. Aside from the time factor, there was the possibility that the AEC might decide nuclear excavation of a canal was impossible. He asked, "Would we have wasted a lot of money, then? Wouldn't we have wasted a lot of money in these experiments that we are not going to end up using?" Seaborg rejected the assertion, explaining, "There are so many other applications where excavation—nuclear excavation—technology might be applicable." Here Representative Hosmer jumped in, pointing to highway construction—a clear allusion to Project Carryall. Representative Chester Holifield (D-California), another of Plowshare's champions, also came to the rescue. The AEC had to conduct further experiments to create the clean explosives needed for the canal or any other excavation project. Pastore was unconvinced: "I am one who feels that I am perfectly willing to double, treble, or quadruple the appropriation if we are going to use nuclear devices for the building of a canal. If we are not, I would like to take a second look at the size of the budget."[49]

The members of the JCAE had good reason to question where Plowshare was going. Aside from the money spent and the time needed for the AEC to be in a position to start construction, breaking dirt in Panama could be delayed further if the Johnson and Robles governments were unable to find common ground on the terms of the Panama Canal treaties. On January 8 the president formally authorized the State Department to open discussions with Panama, Costa Rica, Colombia, and Nicaragua on a sea-level waterway and the right to survey possible routes. According to his instructions, based on his December 18 speech, the United States would build the waterway and retain the right to defend it, while the nation in which the canal was dug would retain sovereignty over it. With regard to Panama specifically, Johnson stated that the United States would agree to negotiate a new treaty that would replace the treaty of 1903 and would turn over the existing canal to Panama once the new waterway opened. Cognizant of how much Panama relied on the lock waterway, the United States would seek to help Panama offset any economic loss it might face when the sea-level route began operations.[50] To make the U.S. position clear and further assess possibilities for digging the waterway, the president selected Mann and Ailes to lead a mission to the countries in question.

While publicly pleased with Johnson's speech, the Robles government privately was not happy with his willingness to consult other nations about canal construction. Panama's new foreign minister, Fernando Eleta Almaran, called it a "transparent U.S. effort [to] blackmail [the Government of Panama] into [a] more submissive posture on canal issues generally." Vaughn "expressed surprise," for Robles himself had "publicly welcomed" Johnson's comments. Writing Rusk afterward, Vaughn concluded that Panama honestly feared the United States might accept spending more money on a waterway in another nation if it meant avoiding the problems it had faced a year earlier. Robles would find himself trapped between standing up to the United States and jeopardizing bilateral relations, or backing down and risking a political crisis that could bring down his government. Vaughn wrote, "We see no harm and some possible good in attempting [to] accommodate them to extent hearing them out prior to start of Mann-Ailes trip," as long as Panama understood that the United States still planned to consult with other countries.[51]

In an attempt to calm down the Panamanians, Rusk asked Vaughn to inform Eleta that, of the possible choices, the United States favored Panama for the new waterway, and Robles could explain as much to his country's people. At the same time the United States had every intention of visiting the other nations on the list. "To delay approaching other interested governments on this," the secretary wrote, "would serve no good purpose as far as we can see but would obviously delay entire program."[52]

On January 21 the United States announced the Ailes-Mann trip, and the two men departed at the end of the month. Their first stops were Nicaragua and Costa Rica. While not prepared to rule out a canal, neither country seemed enthusiastic. President René Schick of Nicaragua believed "the canal should be constructed in Panama since the Panamanian economy depended upon the operation of the present canal," and his Costa Rican counterpart, Francisco Orlich Bolmarcich, cited the lower price tag associated with a waterway in Panama compared to one along the Nicaraguan–Costa Rican border.[53]

Ailes and Mann likely anticipated the testiness they encountered at their next destination, Panama. The two sides could not come to terms on such issues as tolls on the new canal or whether the United States, Panama, or a bilateral U.S.-Panamanian commission would oversee the waterway. Eleta again expressed his irritation with the United States holding talks with other nations about a new canal and asserted that building it required Panamanian approval. Mann rejected that argument: "The United States does not agree that it has any legal or moral obligation to consult with Panama before a canal is constructed in another country." Washington, however, "would wish to be as helpful as possible in assisting Panama to meet its economic problems, most of which are not the proximate cause of the existence of the present canal or its abandonment."[54]

In Colombia both Foreign Minister Fernando Gómez Martínez and President Guillermo León Valencia expressed an interest in seeing the canal built there and granted permission to have a more extensive survey begin along the Atrato-Truando route. Mann conveyed his appreciation, commenting that the United States wanted to avoid problems similar to those it had had in Panama in 1964. At the same time, and in what was a lie, he told his hosts that U.S. surveys in nations other than Panama were in no way designed to put pressure on the Robles government.[55]

Though Mann's and Ailes's reports to Washington were secret, the U.S. media had a good sense which nations most wanted the canal and the full pretext for the two officials' trip. Journeying to the same countries visited by Mann and Ailes, *Washington Post* reporter George Natanson found most people in Costa Rica "indifferent" to the waterway, while many Nicaraguans "don't even want the canal." Based on its joint survey with the United States, Colombia believed the Atrato-Truando route offered the best option for construction. Panama, for its part, was "desperate" to have the canal. Additionally Natanson correctly gathered that the aim of Mann and Ailes was more than simply to consider possible sites for the new waterway. It was also "to exert some pressure on Panama and let that country's government know that the United States was serious when it proposed alternate routes through Colombia and Nicaragua-Costa-Rica."[56]

The Panamanians continued to express resentment at their treatment. Meeting in Washington with Edward W. Clark of the State Department's Office of Panamanian Affairs on March 5, Special Panamanian Representative Diógenes de la Rosa used the word *blackmail* to describe Washington's Panama policy. He expressed his frustration again in a meeting the next month with John N. Irwin II, whom Johnson had recently appointed as Robert Anderson's deputy. Whether Panama liked it or not, Irwin responded, the United States intended to follow the negotiating position set out by President Johnson in December. Furthermore it would prove difficult to convince the U.S. Senate to approve a treaty replacing that of 1903 without simultaneously presenting to the Upper House a sea-level canal agreement. In an attempt to assuage his Panamanian colleagues, he expressed his belief that the United States would indeed build the canal in Panama.

Only if engineering studies found it infeasible or if there was renewed unrest in Panama would Washington turn elsewhere.[57]

From Mississippi to Nevada

As the negotiations continued, the AEC began looking at four other experiments, all with a clear connection to an isthmian canal: the Tennessee-Tombigbee Waterway and Projects Phaeton, Dogsled, and Palanquin. The Army Corps of Engineers, which had established a Nuclear Cratering Group within the LRL-Livermore laboratory, had initiated its own investigation into nuclear excavation. Among several possibilities, one that gained the Corps' attention was a canal through Tennessee, Mississippi, and Alabama to connect the Tennessee and Tombigbee rivers. The region had seen growth in chemical manufacturing, and the proposed canal would connect some ten thousand miles of inland waterways to the Gulf of Mexico.[58]

Believing LRL's promise that clean explosives would curtail fallout, by 1960 the governments of all three interested states had endorsed the idea of the canal project and established the Tennessee-Tombigbee Waterway Development Authority. That same year Governor Ross Barnett of Mississippi asked his state's Industrial and Technological Research Commission to raise the project with LRL-L. Enthused, Livermore sent Johnson and Edward Teller to Mississippi to discuss the project further. The two scientists encouraged Mississippi to undertake a feasibility study. The Houston-based engineering firm Brown and Root, alongside the Corps of Engineers, determined in September 1960 that nuclear excavation would cut only $400,000 off the estimated $227 million price tag. Yet the project had cultivated national interest, with the magazine *U.S. News and World Report* commenting in 1963, "The first use of a nuclear explosion for peacetime construction may be to help build a canal in the U.S. South, instead of a harbor in Alaska or another Panama Canal."[59]

In addition to rather than *instead of* would have been a more appropriate phrase. Just as Plowshare's defenders linked Carryall and the Central American canal, so both state and federal officials tied together the Tennessee-Tombigbee and Panama waterways. Glover Wilkins, the Development Authority's administrator, wrote Seaborg in the winter of 1964, "The potential study of using nuclear devices on the divide cut of the Tennessee Tombigbee Waterway is particularly appropriate at this time due to consideration being given to building a new canal across the isthmus in Central America." The cut to which Wilkins referred was a small stretch of the canal. While the feasibility study envisioned the use of conventional methods to complete much of the 253-mile, six-lock waterway, it called for eighty-one nuclear explosives, totaling 1.9 megatons, to blast through about three miles of hills.[60]

There was the rub. About 1,500 residents lived within five miles of ground zero, and more than 340,000 within fifty. One Sandia engineer commented, "There are so very many people nearby." Having seen the study, Johnson estimated the fallout zone would range forty to fifty miles downwind and cover a swath about sixty to seventy degrees in width, requiring evacuation of everyone in the area "for an unspecified time." For this reason he now considered the plan impractical. The AEC, at first enticed by the project, also began to reconsider. It determined that iodine-131 could affect the environment for some two hundred miles downwind. It had little knowledge of how nuclear explosions would act when set off in limestone, one of the media through which the canal would have to travel, and the blasts would contaminate aquifers in portions of Alabama and Mississippi. To conduct safety studies alone would cost $20 million, plus about another $10 million for postshot analyses. Finally, in June 1965 the Commission pointed out that it would have to spend an enormous amount of time and resources trying to convince residents who had left that they could "return to their homes if the area ha[d] been contaminated by fallout." The Commission thus joined with Livermore against the waterway,[61] and the proposal died.

Project Phaeton appeared headed for a similar fate. Conceived at least as far back as 1962, this one-megaton explosion had the purposes of learning more about cratering and trapping radioactivity from large explosions. As the plans for the sea-level canal called for using megaton-size devices, such data were important. By late FY 1964, however, the Commission had proven unable to locate a site for the blast, and it was put on the shelf.[62]

Shelved as well was Project Dogsled. Also designed in 1962, it envisioned using a device of about 100 kilotons to learn more about cratering, ground shock, and entrapment in limestone or sandstone. By late 1963 the U.S. Geological Survey had identified almost a dozen possible sites in Utah and Arizona. But for reasons that remain uncertain, discussion of Dogsled came to an end after September 1964.[63]

This left Project Palanquin. Having realized from Sulky that placing a nuclear explosive at more than optimal depth produced an undesirable result, the AEC adopted a new approach, proposing to bury a four-kiloton device 210 to 260 feet underground. In so doing it hoped to make progress in developing a cleaner explosive and determining the best depth at which to place it, as well as to test a new "'debris entrapment' technique." The agency anticipated a release of radioactivity similar to that of Sulky, but if the entrapment technique failed, the fallout would approach that of Danny Boy, or "an amount appreciably larger than that predicted for Sulky."[64]

Because it posed a greater likelihood than Sulky of violating the LTBT, Palanquin generated an even more intense intra-administration debate. On February 24
the Review Committee on Underground Nuclear Tests approved the shot in principle, pending coordination with both the State Department and ACDA. ACDA
director William Foster argued against proceeding, for at the time Washington
had yet to receive a response to an inquiry regarding a recent Soviet test.[65]

Foster's reference was to a blast that had taken place a month earlier. Although
Soviet officials claimed in 1949 that they had used the atom for peaceful purposes, it was not until the mid-1960s that they began their own version of Plowshare, called "Program Number 7—Nuclear Explosions for the National Economy." Why the Kremlin decided to wait to follow the U.S. lead is not clear. Maybe
it feared that if the Plowshare program worked, it would increase U.S. prestige
worldwide. Another possibility is that the Soviet Union had seen no reason beforehand to apply the atom to civilian projects. It is known that the person who
pushed the Kremlin to begin its own version of Plowshare was Efrim P. Slavskiy,
formerly the minister of the Medium Machine Building Ministry, who report-
edly was inspired by the American peaceful-use program. On January 15, 1965,
the Soviet Union tested its first civilian atomic explosive, a 140-kiloton cratering
shot in Kazakhstan that created a lake.[66]

The blast, though, also produced fallout, a significant amount of which landed
on Japan. Secretary Rusk immediately demanded that Dobrynin tell him what
had happened. As far as Palanquin was concerned, Foster deemed it inappropri-
ate to hold "a cratering experiment while we are still pressing the Soviets for an
explanation of their last event." It is also likely the ACDA head judged that justifying Palanquin on the results of the Soviet experiment might cause the Kremlin
to respond in kind. If Palanquin then vented, it could lead the superpowers down
a slippery slope of tests that generated ever more fallout. When Dobrynin replied
to Rusk, he insisted theirs was an underground test that had vented an "insignifi-
cant" amount of radioactivity. Washington at first did not buy the explanation
but later decided the amount of fallout generated did not constitute a treaty violation. Even so, a voice of caution persisted, with Brown, who had previously
endorsed Sulky, now raising a red flag. During preparations for Palanquin, the
explosive the AEC had hoped to use did not work, forcing it to turn to "another
device with different characteristics." Brown worried that "the proposed alternative nuclear device" and the "'debris entrapment' technique" might fail, causing a violation of the LTBT.[67]

To address such concerns, the AEC deepened the hole to 280 feet. Seaborg admitted that this meant the scale depth of burial was equivalent to Sulky's, thereby
reducing the chances of creating a crater. "We are doing this," the AEC chair wrote,
"so as to provide additional assurance that the Palanquin experiment can be

conducted in a manner consistent with the Limited Test Ban Treaty." With that alteration, the full Review Committee approved Palanquin for execution in April.[68]

Exploded on April 14, Palanquin did not act like Sulky. When a nuclear explosive is buried underground, it is "stemmed," meaning concrete and backfill are put into the hole to keep the radioactivity from entering the atmosphere. In the case of Palanquin, a "stemming failure" caused the entrapment procedure to fail. Instead of keeping the radioactivity trapped underground, the gas blasted through the four-foot-wide emplacement hole and left behind a crater 350 feet across and 100 feet deep. Worse, Seaborg informed the president, the shot generated a cloud of dust that rose to eight thousand feet, inside of which the level of radioactivity, though "well below any possible health hazard," was "higher than expected." The AEC head realized the test posed possible trouble for the United States. "PALANQUIN shot, which was fired yesterday, is giving rise to large amounts of air borne debris which may cause difficulty in connection with possible violation of Test Ban Treaty," he wrote in his journal. The AEC quickly informed the media that though there had been a release of radioactivity, it had "no evidence this experiment caused radioactive debris to be present outside the territorial limits of the United States." That was not the case. The U.S. Air Force recorded "measured concentration of PALANQUIN debris" over the U.S. East Coast and Bermuda; it was likely therefore that the Soviet Union would detect it. The only consolation was that Moscow would have a hard time trying "to date this debris."[69]

On April 29 Dobrynin demanded more information about the test and expressed the Kremlin's doubts that the fallout had remained within U.S. borders. Determined not to admit to a violation of the LTBT, the United States replied simply that the AEC had taken the necessary precautions to prevent venting, and even though the blast did send radioactivity into the atmosphere, it had remained within the United States. In an attempt to take the high ground, the administration also made sure to reference the Soviet blast of January 15. Despite this, Palanquin was an embarrassment to Plowshare scientists, one that, according to a later report, set the entire program back by two years.[70]

If there was any consolation, it was that the negotiations with Panama had begun to show signs of real progress. In May the Johnson administration decided to move from two treaties to three: one on canal defense, a second regarding a sea-level waterway, and a third to replace the agreement of 1903. Once the drafts of the treaties were completed, the chief executives of both nations would submit them as a package for ratification by their respective legislatures. The United States also made official Irwin's idea of completing the negotiations with Panama before considering other countries. By late June the Panamanian negotiators had adopted this strategy. Three months later Presidents Johnson and Robles publicly announced this agreement.[71]

The next step was getting the surveys under way. The Canal Commission felt no pressure to seek approval for a survey along the Costa Rica–Nicaragua border, as the Inter-American Geodetic Survey had already begun to map that region. Colombia and Panama were different stories. The Canal Commission originally hoped to begin surveying route 17 in November 1965 and route 25 in early 1966. Yet signing and ratifying a treaty with either Panama or Colombia before then appeared impossible. Therefore Robert Anderson asked Rusk to seek an executive agreement permitting the surveys. The U.S. embassy in Panama made a similar suggestion to the Robles government. Desirous to have the canal, the two nations exchanged notes in February 1966 authorizing the studies.[72] Finally, the United States and Panama appeared on the road toward construction of a sea-level waterway.

Plowshare, Vietnam, and Ecology

In March 1965, while the talks with Panama continued and the AEC made final preparations for Palanquin, President Johnson escalated the war in Vietnam. A month earlier communist insurgents had attacked a U.S. Army base in the South Vietnamese village of Pleiku, killing nine servicemen. The president retaliated with what became a sustained bombing campaign against North Vietnam and, on March 8, had 3,500 U.S. Marines land at the U.S. airbase at Danang, South Vietnam. In April the White House authorized the deployment of another forty thousand ground troops.[73] Thus began a commitment to a war that would see as many as 550,000 U.S. soldiers, sailors, and airmen in and around South Vietnam at any one time, divide Americans, sap billions of dollars out of the U.S. Treasury, and cost some fifty-eight thousand American lives.

As the conflict in Vietnam intensified, biologist Ira Rubinoff published an article in the August–September issue of *Natural History*. Repeating a warning first raised at the 1959 Second Plowshare Symposium, he wrote that a sea-level canal would result in intermingling of Atlantic and Pacific marine life, something that had not happened since the "isthmian landbridge" had closed some five million years earlier. Consequently some species might interbreed, while others might disappear in the face of more aggressive fauna. Plants also would be affected. Though not opposed to construction of a sea-level waterway, Rubinoff called for a "complete and thorough pre-canal survey," which "would make it possible to evaluate properly the changes in the physical and biological environment that are produced by the canal."[74]

Rubinoff's article received little notice, but it and the Vietnam War both could complicate the digging of a sea-level canal. The environmental aspects of construction clearly had to address more than seismic shock, ground motion, or fallout; they also had to take into account the waterway's impact on species migration. The escalating U.S. commitment to Vietnam offered to cut even more into Plowshare's budget, which already had to compete with such initiatives as the war on poverty. Longer, more costly surveys and a Plowshare program that lacked full funding could delay even longer the tests the AEC wanted to conduct before canal construction began.

While the budget was arguably beyond the control of the AEC and LRL, the two had not helped their cause. To Plowshare's defenders within and outside of Washington, Carryall and the Tennessee-Tombigbee Waterway would improve the nation's transportation infrastructure, demonstrate to the world the safety of nuclear excavation, and provide data for the all-important sea-level isthmian waterway. Yet Plowshare's champions knew that a sizable number of the blasts used in such construction projects would be cratering shots similar to Sedan, which, by their nature, caused fallout. This necessitated developing cleaner explosives and conducting shots that released a minimal amount of radioactivity into the atmosphere. Here the two most important tests the AEC conducted during 1964 and 1965 were Sulky and Palanquin, both of which failed to act as intended, embarrassed Plowshare scientists, forced them to recalibrate their assumptions, and slowed down the progress of the nuclear cratering program. Carryall and the Tennessee-Tombigbee Waterway were either in serious trouble or canceled. Most serious, lawmakers, including members of the Joint Committee on Atomic Energy, had begun to express aggravation with the program's pace. How long their patience would last was not clear.

Still the AEC remained wedded to the idea that it could move humans down the road of progress. "Although it took nearly 400 years for the chemical 'black powder' explosives to be adapted from military purposes to mining," declared the authors of a 1966 AEC report, "the imaginative mind of man is already defining— with the atomic age only two decades old—an array of peaceful wonders and benefits from nuclear explosives." Plowshare's purpose was "to develop, within years, a technology for using nuclear explosives peacefully comparable to that developed for conventional explosives over a span of centuries." The peaceful-use program was "an ambitious undertaking," but it was "one in which the rewards are commensurate with the effort."[75]

Nuclear Testing, Nonproliferation, and Plowshare

Speaking before the United Nations General Assembly in September 1958, Ireland's minister for external affairs, Frank Aiken, asked for help in halting the growth of the "nuclear club," made up of the United States, the Soviet Union, the United Kingdom, and France. He further appealed to those countries with atomic technology not to pass it on to others and for nonnuclear states not to acquire it. "Try to imagine," he asked those present, "whether, if nuclear war broke out, we would not then regret having failed to make the sacrifices which might have helped to avoid it." The next month he submitted to the General Assembly a draft resolution aimed at stopping nuclear proliferation. Though he did not get the endorsement he desired, Aiken each year afterward presented a similar document, gathering ever more backing. Finally, in 1961 the Assembly unanimously adopted Resolution 1665, calling on all nations to work toward an international agreement barring the dissemination of nuclear technology and prohibiting those countries without such know-how from obtaining it.[1]

Adoption of Resolution 1665 demonstrated international recognition of the danger posed by the spread of nuclear technology, a danger acknowledged by President Johnson. France had joined the "nuclear club" in 1960, and there was no telling how many others might follow suit in the near term. In his first National Security Council (NSC) meeting after assuming the presidency, Johnson told his top aides, "The greatest single requirement is that we find a way to ensure the survival of civilization in the nuclear age. A nuclear war would be the death of all our hopes and it is our task to see that it does not happen."[2]

A nonproliferation agreement offered one method of preventing the dissemination of atomic technology. Another was a comprehensive test ban treaty (CTBT) that would eliminate the provision in the LTBT permitting underground tests. Whether through a nonproliferation treaty (NPT) or a CTBT, Plowshare certainly would be affected. Already facing restrictions to the peaceful-use program as a result of the LTBT, Plowshare's defenders wanted to make sure that program did not suffer further. They insisted that neither the NPT nor the CTBT discussions interfere with PNEs. Further, they desired that an NPT specifically permit offering nuclear technology to nonnuclear states for nonmilitary projects. Indeed, contended Plowshare's defenders, if countries without atomic bombs knew they could turn to the nuclear club for help with civilian enterprises, the have-nots would have much less reason to develop their own nuclear explosives, thereby protecting U.S. security. Opponents rejected all of these arguments. Conducting Plowshare tests during the nonproliferation or comprehensive test ban talks could open the United States to charges that it was not serious about stopping the spread of nuclear technology. Moreover to offer such know-how to others for civilian projects would only serve to accelerate rather than check its dissemination, which could pose a far greater threat to U.S. defense than Plowshare's defenders were willing to admit. While this debate did not stop Johnson from authorizing Plowshare tests, by the summer of 1967 it had placed in jeopardy the program's centerpiece: the construction of a sea-level isthmian canal.

Nonproliferation versus Plowshare

After World War II the United States had given consideration to halting the spread of nuclear technology. The 1946 Baruch Plan, which proposed an international organization to regulate atomic energy and would have retained America's monopoly on nuclear weapons, was an early example. In his Atoms for Peace speech of 1953, President Eisenhower had issued a call for an international body to make sure atomic technology was employed for peaceful purposes. Four years later the world community established the IAEA, but it had only a limited ability to stop nuclear proliferation.

There were various reasons for renewed attention to nonproliferation by the mid-1960s. For one, it seemed the logical next step toward a general disarmament agreement. From approximately 1957 to 1963 the focus of much of the world, including that of the superpowers, was on the negotiations leading up to the LTBT. With that treaty, after 1963 arms control efforts could turn to making sure that those nations that did not already have the atom did not get it.[3]

Then there were intertwined military and diplomatic considerations. The nuclear club seemed about to explode in size. France had developed an independent atomic deterrent both as a means of retaining its great power status and to meet a criticism it shared with other members of NATO, among them West Germany, that they had to rely on the U.S. nuclear arsenal for their protection. Bonn indicated a preparedness to go the way of Paris. Communist China, long a Soviet ally but now viewing both Moscow and Washington as threats, also appeared on the verge of joining the nuclear club, while India, Sweden, and Israel "were potential candidates."[4]

The thought of other nations acquiring the power of the atom was something neither of the superpowers could ignore. Having been attacked by Germany in both world wars, the Soviet Union viewed a nuclear West Germany, on top of an atomic China, as a serious menace. Sino-Soviet relations had soured by 1965, and Beijing posed a threat both to U.S. allies in East Asia and the U.S. effort in Vietnam; both Moscow and Washington thus worried about a nuclearized China. An atomic West Germany also proffered trouble for the United States. Rather than see Bonn follow Paris, at the end of the Eisenhower administration Washington proposed establishing a multilateral force (MLF) by which multinational crews from NATO would man atomic-armed warships. This would give West Germany a sense of actively participating in its own defense and deflect it from seeking an independent nuclear stockpile. If Bonn, however, went the way of Paris, then the MLF would die, other NATO members might decide as well to develop atomic bombs, and Western unity could suffer.[5]

To complete a nonproliferation treaty, talks opened between the United States and the Soviet Union in February 1964. The MLF became a sticking point. In October China successfully tested an atomic bomb, and the United States believed that that event could open the floodgates to acquisition of atomic bombs by other countries, among them India, Japan, Pakistan, and Israel. "As additional nations obtained nuclear weapons," commented a 1965 U.S. report, "our diplomatic and military influence would wane, and strong pressure would arise to retreat to isolation to avoid the risk of involvement in nuclear war." Yet even then the United States could find itself facing "nuclear powers—perhaps some in this hemisphere—individually possessing the capability of destroying millions of American lives." Hence it was critical to achieve passage of an internationally supported nuclear nonproliferation agreement. While the Kremlin shared that goal, it saw an inconsistency in the White House's promoting arms control while offering West German membership in the MLF. Until Washington addressed that discrepancy, it could not anticipate Moscow's willingness to join a nonproliferation pact. As Foreign Minister Andrei Gromyko told Rusk in December 1964, "The Soviet Union could not ignore the fact that Germany had unleashed two world wars within the span of one generation." For this reason "a non-dissemination agreement was obstructed by the MLF plans. If that obstacle were removed, a broad non-dissemination agreement could be concluded which would be in the interests of both the U.S. and the U.S.S.R., and of the world at large."[6]

By early 1965 the United States had scuttled the MLF in favor of a British proposal to create an Atlantic Nuclear Force (ANF). Loosely affiliated with NATO but led by its own command structure, the ANF would include some elements of the U.S. and British nuclear arsenals (as well as France's, if it decided to join). West Germany would also receive an invitation to take part. All ANF members would have veto power in the Force's employment. And any nonnuclear ANF partners (meaning West Germany) would have to promise not to develop their own atomic weapons. The ANF, however, was no more acceptable to the Soviets than the MLF.[7]

In an attempt to make progress on nonproliferation, the United Nations Disarmament Committee in June submitted a resolution calling for the "early resumption" of the ENDC negotiations, which had recessed the previous September. Following overwhelming passage by the General Assembly, with the United States voting in favor and the Soviet Union abstaining, the ENDC delegates returned to work in late July. President Johnson expressed his hope for forward movement on nonproliferation, and as part of that effort the United States submitted a draft nonproliferation treaty in August that would prohibit states with nuclear arms from giving such technology to nations without them, and for nonweapons countries not to try to acquire atomic devices. But the ANF continued to divide the superpowers.[8]

It was not until the fall of 1966 that a breakthrough occurred. In part this was the result of the United Kingdom's deciding to give up the ANF. Within the British Foreign Office it had become apparent that the ANF stood in the way of the NPT, and Whitehall decided it made sense to forgo the Atlantic Force if it would open the way to a nonproliferation treaty. It was also in part because of negotiations between Rusk and Gromyko through which the Americans and Soviets worked out compromise language barring the transfer or control of nuclear weapons to any other state. With that, a nonproliferation agreement seemed well on its way to becoming reality.[9]

Passage of a comprehensive test ban treaty seemed far less likely. By its very name the Limited Test Ban Treaty of 1963 did not bar all nuclear tests; underground testing could continue. Nonnuclear states had an opportunity not just to acquire the power of the atom but to conduct experiments to improve the capabilities of the nuclear weapons they developed. The comprehensive test ban, however, appeared for the time being dead in the water. In this case the problem was not the MLF or ANF, but verification. Since it was possible to decouple nuclear tests, Washington considered verification of any comprehensive ban requiring on-site inspections, though it was prepared to accept a "minimum number," defined as seven annually. The Soviets contended that was too many. At first the Kremlin asserted its long-held stance that it would accept no more than three. But by early 1965 it had taken the position that the state of scientific advancement meant that verification could take place without any inspections. Furthermore inspection would permit the West to spy on the Soviet Union. From the U.S. point of view, it was possible for the Soviets, if they took precautions, to avoid detection of tests smaller than two kilotons,[10] thus making on-site checks necessary.

The fact remained, however, that both a nonproliferation and comprehensive test ban agreement were on the table, and the question was whether either was compatible with Plowshare, let alone U.S. security. Speaking for the AEC, John G. Palfrey commented that his agency had neither the "intention" nor, under the Atomic Energy Act, the legal right to provide "to other countries information concerning Plowshare device design or manufacture." In fact, he declared, providing PNE services to other nations was consistent with nonproliferation. With peaceful-use explosives for civilian projects available at a cheap price, other countries would find it economically inexpedient to develop their own nuclear capability. A comprehensive test ban was a bit trickier. Even Palfrey himself commented, "Under a comprehensive test ban treaty . . . [Plowshare] probably will have to be scrapped." The answer to this potential conundrum was to add an annex to a CTBT that made special provision for peaceful-use blasts.[11]

Others rejected such suggestions. In November 1964 Spurgeon Keeny, a member of the NSC, told the attendees at a State Department meeting that Plowshare would undermine a nonproliferation agreement, for it "might provide just the rationale that India, Japan, and others might need to start their own weapons programs." The Gilpatric Committee reached a similar conclusion. Established by President Johnson in November 1964, the Task Force on Nuclear Proliferation, better known as the Gilpatric Committee after its chair, former deputy secretary of defense Roswell Gilpatric, had the job of studying ways to curb the spread of atomic weapons technology. In January 1965 the Committee concluded, "[Although Plowshare] may have long-term economic importance, we do not believe that the program should be allowed to jeopardize a comprehensive test ban treaty or to encourage interest in nuclear weapons." Plowshare made "nuclear explosives appear desirable, necessary and acceptable for countries presently considering undertaking nuclear weapons programs." Nor was it a good idea to permit an exception for Plowshare tests within a comprehensive ban, for it would offer "a loophole under which nuclear weapons could be developed."[12]

Canal Options

For the time being AEC Chair Glenn Seaborg and his allies did not have to worry about trying to get a "loophole" for Plowshare, as a comprehensive test ban, let alone a nonproliferation treaty, appeared unlikely in the near term. The LTBT, however, was on the books, and it continued to place a pall over plans for nuclear excavation of a canal. "What is needed," Seaborg said in the spring of 1966, "is a criterion of good sense on permissible levels of radioactivity." The problem was that the United States and the Soviet Union had yet to come to terms on what that criterion was, and that same spring Seaborg foresaw consensus as unlikely in the near term.[13]

If anything, use of the atom appeared even further off than before. Of the five top options for a sea-level canal, nuclear excavation could not take place along one of them, the existing lock canal. Of the remaining four, Mexico was all but out of the running, both because of the cost involved and its determination to run the canal itself. In early 1967 the Atlantic-Pacific Interoceanic Canal Commission decided against the Nicaraguan–Costa Rican route (route 8). Using the information from the Inter-American Geodetic Survey, the U.S. Army Corps of Engineers, AEC, and the Panama Canal Company issued a joint report in March establishing that building a canal along route 8 required 718 nuclear explosives, totaling 692.7 megatons. This was more than 2.5 times as much explosive power as required for Atrato-Truando in Colombia (route 25) and nearly four times that needed for the Sasardi-Morti in Panama (route 17). The anticipated time of completion was three to four years, assuming two detonations took place each month. The study expected air blast damage to occur to parts of the cities of San Jose, Costa Rica, and Managua, Nicaragua, which had a combined population of about 450,000 people. The exclusion area, where those persons living would have to be relocated for the duration of the blasting, if not permanently, encompassed "approximately 50 percent of the land area of Costa Rica." This totaled about 1,170,000 people, plus another 175,000 who, while living outside the exclusion zone, resided "within the range of potential air blast damage." Not only would moving so many residents prove extremely costly, but it would wreak havoc on the economies of the two nations. After reading the report, the Canal Commission concluded that route 8 "[did] not merit further investigation."[14]

This left what were from the beginning the two top choices for nuclear excavation: the Sasardi-Morti and Atrato-Truando. Starting the surveys along both had taken far longer than anticipated. Robert Anderson, the head of the Atlantic-Pacific Interoceanic Canal Commission, had hoped to put survey teams into the field as early as the 1965 dry season. That proved impossible. The Commission had wanted to borrow "helicopters and other equipment" from the U.S. military, only to have most of these diverted to the war in Vietnam. Then there were the delays caused by the negotiations with Panama and Colombia. It was not until February 1966 that Panama and the United States had exchanged notes formally giving Washington permission to survey the Sasardi-Morti route. It took an additional eight months for such an exchange to take place with Colombia. Not until January 1967 did the surveys actually begin, and by then Anderson was pessimistic about meeting the June 1968 reporting deadline. Even before those surveys got under way, he suggested to lawmakers that he would ask for $4 million more in appropriations so the Canal Commission could complete its work by the middle of 1969.[15]

There was more disconcerting news. Ira Rubinoff's warning in 1965 that a sea-level canal could have destructive consequences for the regional ecology had started to gain traction. In August the *Christian Science Monitor* reported that the President's Science Advisory Committee wanted closer study of Atlantic and Pacific marine life should the two intermix as a result of a sea-level canal. The next month scientists at a conference in Tokyo also warned about what might happen should the two oceans' fauna intermingle.[16]

Then there were the treaty negotiations, which continued at their plodding pace. In August 1966 Panama's delegation asked to know within a certain period of time whether the United States would build a sea-level canal and continued to insist on a promise that Washington not negotiate construction of a waterway with another country. John N. Irwin II, Anderson's deputy, refused both requests. The United States, he said, could not insist on an indefinite period of time to decide whether to construct a sea-level waterway, but it also could not set a deadline for such a decision, for it was unclear when the Canal Commission would complete its work. In May 1967 the Panamanians tried a new tactic, offering to add to "the lock canal treaty a provision that Panama would not give any other country the right to build a sea level canal in Panama if the U.S." promised not to construct such a waterway outside of Panama. Anderson said no. Such a quid pro quo "could result in a Congressional resolution to the effect that the U.S. would never build a sea level canal in Panama." If Panama wanted any chance of the Senate's agreeing to turn the lock canal over to it, then it had to acquiesce to a sea-level canal option that allowed the United States to choose the place for its construction.[17]

Conflict over Cabriolet

Assuming the United States and Panama could work through their differences and come to terms by the time the Canal Commission had finished its work, the

AEC wanted to have completed its experiments that would prove whether nuclear excavation of a canal was possible. In congressional testimony in March 1966 the AEC's John Kelly estimated that through the end of fiscal year 1967 his agency needed to conduct six more excavation experiments, none of which had yet received White House approval but one of which was then under consideration.[18] Kelly did not provide the name of the blast, but Cabriolet became the focus of the most intense intra-administration debate in Plowshare's history.

Seaborg had first proposed Cabriolet in 1965. It called for a two-kiloton explosive emplaced 170 feet underground at the NTS, about six-tenths of a mile from where Palanquin had taken place and in a hard rock similar to that planned for Project Schooner (which the agency had pushed back to 1967). The AEC head expressed his desire to begin preparation for Cabriolet so that the AEC would be in a position to set it off by March 1, 1966. The AEC could then use the data from Cabriolet to conduct the other tests it believed necessary to provide a recommendation prior to the Canal Commission's June 30, 1968, reporting deadline. By having the option of nuclear excavation of a canal, the United States would be in a better position to negotiate favorable terms with whatever nation in which it chose to construct the waterway.[19]

Embarrassed by the stemming failure that had caused radioactivity to vent from the Palanquin blast, the AEC reassured the White House that it had taken steps to prevent a repeat. Though admitting that there was the possibility of as much as 20 percent of the radioactivity from Cabriolet escaping, the AEC anticipated "only one-fifth to one-seventh of that produced by Palanquin." With so little fallout, Seaborg expected no violation of the LTBT.[20]

Still the possibility of a treaty violation existed, and so Johnson refused to authorize Cabriolet prior to its consideration by the Review Committee on Underground Nuclear Tests. It was not until March 4 that the Committee met, and there was virtually unanimous opposition. Deputy Secretary of Defense Cyrus Vance and William Foster, the head of the ACDA, warned that the blast risked an LTBT violation. Moreover, said Foster, there were indications that the Soviet Union was willing to discuss a peaceful-use exception to the limited test ban. He probably had in mind an approach by Vasily S. Emelyanov, a Soviet representative to the 1964 Geneva Conference on the Peaceful Uses of Atomic Energy, who had raised with the Plowshare scientist, Gerald Johnson, the possibility of superpower cooperation on PNEs. Emelyanov's motion had made the State Department wonder if Plowshare offered "an opportunity for cooperation and a relaxation of tensions," particularly at a time when the Vietnam War continued to offer an impediment to better superpower ties. From Foster's point of view, "a venting incident at this time could prejudice" any chance of amending the test ban treaty.

In an attempt to avoid trouble with the Kremlin, Leonard Meeker, a legal adviser at the State Department, suggested using a "cleaner device," but, Seaborg explained, such an explosive would not be available for "a couple of years." As it stood, Cabriolet was "about the smallest shot from the standpoint of fallout that we can do."[21]

Seaborg felt the pressure. Canceling Cabriolet would hurt the AEC's partner laboratories, which had devoted enormous time and resources to seeing Plowshare succeed. Morale at places like LRL and Sandia would flag, to the detriment of the peaceful-use program. The AEC head also had to contend with pressures from the Canal Commission and lawmakers. The former considered Cabriolet "crucial to their assignment." Some members of the Senate Appropriations Committee had threatened to withhold funding for the Canal Commission for fiscal year 1967 if Cabriolet did not receive the green light. The JCAE also threatened the AEC's pocketbook; when the AEC asked for $3.6 million for FY 1966 to conduct Schooner in early 1967 the JCAE had refused. Hesitant to authorize so much money for a blast that the AEC had continually delayed, and with the AEC now giving priority to Cabriolet, the JCAE offered only $300,000 for Schooner, with another $1.68 million to go to Cabriolet. Expressing the JCAE's frustration, Representative Chester Holifield (D-California) commented, "The committee has no basis for believing that project Schooner will be executed in fiscal year 1967 if Cabriolet is not carried out in fiscal year 1966." He then warned that if the White House refused to authorize peaceful-use tests, "the entire Plowshare program will have to be reevaluated."[22] Coming from one of Plowshare's most zealous advocates, those words must have made a strong impression on Seaborg.

Determined to break through the resistance from the executive branch, Seaborg pressed his case. Meeting with Walt Rostow, the head of the NSC, he again pointed to the importance of Cabriolet to the labs as well as the entire Plowshare program. To pause in the hopes Moscow might accept a peaceful-use exception to the LTBT meant delaying Plowshare indefinitely, with no guarantee the superpowers could come to terms. As the United States waited, the Soviets, who had no compunction to follow suit and who were "far ahead of [the United States] with 10–14 experiments already conducted," would have an opportunity to proceed with and refine their version of Plowshare, boosting Moscow's worldwide prestige in the process. Writing Rusk that same day, Seaborg cautioned that without Cabriolet U.S. nonproliferation policy would suffer a setback, for if Washington could not offer peaceful-use services to other countries, those countries might see no alternative to developing their own. Last, the United States would lose the leverage over Panama of having the option of a nuclear-excavated canal elsewhere. As it stood, Seaborg wrote, "99% of all

Panamanians feel in their hearts that this (locations outside of the Canal Zone) is just a gimmick."[23]

Opponents fought back. "We may seem overly touchy on this subject," Keeny wrote Rostow, "but our annoyance has built up over a long period during which the AEC has repeatedly used and abused intelligence for self-serving purposes." President Johnson's special assistant for science and technology, Donald Hornig, joined the chorus. He acknowledged that Cabriolet's postponement would cause difficulties for the Canal Commission, but added, "I do not believe that the exact timing of this particular test or the precise pace of the Plowshare project is of critical importance to our national interests." He rejected Seaborg's claim of ten to fourteen Soviet Plowshare-style tests, calling such a number "misleading." To accept Seaborg's statistics would "attribute to Plowshare ½ to ⅔rds of the entire Soviet nuclear test program since the Limited Test Ban Treaty." It appeared to the science adviser that Seaborg had failed to consider the Soviets' "interest in nuclear testing for military purposes." Likely recalling that John F. Kennedy had used claims of a "missile gap" to convince Americans to vote for him rather than the Republican candidate in the 1960 presidential election, Hornig wrote, "I hope that the thinking on this already difficult problem will not be confused by the introduction of a non-existent 'Plowshare gap.'"[24]

Possibly unsure whether he had made a convincing case, Hornig then appealed to Johnson's highly attuned political antennae. Cabriolet, he warned, would mean a short but noticeable increase in iodine-131 levels in milk: "[While iodine] in itself is probably not really dangerous, it is a very touchy subject at the moment in Colorado, Arizona, and Utah since there is local concern about the unusually high incidence of abnormal thyroids in school children throughout the area." Seaborg's only response was, "The domestic issue posed by radioactive iodine in milk will ultimately have to be faced if we are going to conduct PLOWSHARE tests."[25]

Rusk, whose recommendation carried a great deal of weight with the president, had yet to choose sides. Still hoping to persuade the secretary, on May 1 Seaborg repeated many of his earlier arguments and then offered to postpone Cabriolet to November. Doing so would permit the grazing season to end, thereby eliminating concerns about iodine-131 getting into milk. Despite his own doubts about success, he proposed that the State Department open negotiations with the Soviets prior to Cabriolet's detonation to establish a common interpretation of shots allowable under the LTBT. Rusk accepted the recommendation, suggesting two to three months of discussions with Moscow: "We would then be in a position to give the President an evaluation of this key alternative." Seaborg was pleased. He asked, though, to have a presidential decision "in principle" by August 1, which would give the AEC time to prepare the shot for execution in November. Since the Canal Commission needed to know what was happening, AEC Commissioner Kelly informed it of the delay.[26]

The August 1 deadline came and went with no word. After waiting for several more weeks, Seaborg wrote Rusk, who promised to look into it. Another week passed, and the AEC chair's frustration grew. "The Cabriolet decision hasn't been made yet," Seaborg confided to his journal on September 1, "[and] if this is delayed much longer, perhaps we should give up the excavation part of the Plowshare program and emphasize the development of cleaner explosives and underground engineering and scientific experiments."[27]

Maintaining a Balanced Program

Seaborg's comment pointed to the effort of the AEC and LRL to maintain a balanced Plowshare program, one that gave weight not just to excavation but to other possible uses for PNEs, among them element generation, mining, resource stimulation, and storage. Confirmation of success in one or more of these areas offered numerous potential rewards. One was greater political and financial support for Plowshare at home and abroad. Another was the opportunity to defend U.S. economic and military security. Finally, the more uses for the peaceful atom Plowshare's champions were able to sale, the closer they could come to creating the better, brighter future they envisioned for the peoples of the world. Once again the AEC and LRL perceived no inconsistency with nonproliferation, for by obtaining peaceful-use services for nonexcavation projects, foreign countries would have fewer reasons to acquire nuclear explosives of their own. A comprehensive test ban was another matter, but maybe the superpowers would adopt a Plowshare annex.

Creating new elements and isotopes, which had both civilian and military applications, continued to pose problems. In June 1966 the AEC conducted Project Vulcan and during the year also collected data from two non-Plowshare tests, Duryea and Kankakee. The AEC assumed that a higher neutron flux—increasing the number of neutrons passing over an area within a certain period of time—would create new heavy elements. The results were not encouraging: "Existing theoretical models of heavy nuclides, particularly regarding their stability, are inadequate."[28]

Mining seemed to offer more promise. In 1959 the Utah-based mining company, Kennecott Copper, bought a sizable deposit of low-grade copper ore nine miles northeast of Safford, Arizona. Copper was (and is) a strategically important ore, for in addition to such uses as roofing and coinage, its conductivity makes it a vital component in wiring for vehicles and appliances. Between 1960 and 1966 America's use of copper rose from 1.35 million tons to 2.35 million, while the availability of mined copper grew by only 10 percent during that same period. Hence Kennecott saw dollar signs in accessing its newly purchased ore deposits. Unfortunately for the company, getting at even the higher grade ore was too expensive using the normal methods of underground or open-pit mining. "As the future reserves will be found to lie deeper beneath the surface and the metal content of the ores probably will be lower," commented James Boyd, Kennecott's vice president for exploration, in 1960, "the cost of mining must inevitably increase unless we find less expensive ways of doing it." Nuclear explosives offered such an approach, and in 1963 Kennecott began looking into their use. Having determined from drilling that there was no water nearby that an atomic device might contaminate, the company presented its proposal to the AEC in 1965. The Commission assigned the project the name Sloop.[29]

In March 1965 the AEC, Kennecott, and the U.S. Bureau of Mines proposed a feasibility study for Sloop. It called for burying a twenty-six-kiloton explosive into the company's low-grade copper deposit. After the explosive blasted a chimney some 200 feet wide and nearly 450 feet high and broke up an estimated 10 million pounds of copper, Kennecott would insert a leaching agent to dissolve the ore, bring the solution to the surface via wells, and then separate the copper from the liquid. Of course, the blast would contaminate the copper with radioactivity. But the study concluded that most of the radioactivity would be safely deposited in the bottom of the cavity created by the blast, leaving the isotopes that came to the surface at such a low level as not to pose a health hazard.[30] It was now a matter of waiting for Kennecott and the state of Arizona to decide whether to proceed.

Even more encouraging, despite some frustrations along the way, were efforts to meet the nation's ever-growing demand for energy. With the demise of Oilsands, it was not until late 1963 that the AEC again took a look at this application for the atom. Engineers at the U.S. Bureau of Mines' research station at Bartlesville, Oklahoma, urged officials at Texas-based El Paso Natural Gas Company (EPNG) to consider using the atom to increase gas production. It did not take much to convince El Paso. The company had made over $40 million during 1965 "on record operating revenue of about $540 million," and it wanted to continue that trend. Within the Rocky Mountains was an estimated 317 trillion cubic feet of natural gas—over 35 trillion cubic feet more than the nation's proven reserves. "At an average wellhead price of 11 cents per thousand cubic feet in the Rocky Mountains," explained the Bureau of Mines' director, Walter Hibbard, "317 trillion cubic feet of natural gas has a potential value of about $35 billion." Hibbard made sure to highlight the benefits for the U.S. government as well.

Since getting at all of that gas required leasing federal land, Washington would obtain some $4 billion in revenue.[31]

The next step was to bring LRL and the AEC on board, which too did not prove difficult. Calling the experiment Gasbuggy, the parties proposed a PNE in land owned by El Paso in the San Juan Basin, an area of some two thousand square miles in northwestern New Mexico. The Bureau of Mines' deputy director, Frank C. Memmott, wrote AEC General Manager Robert E. Hollingsworth that of the nation's proven reserves, about 64 trillion cubic feet lay in the San Juan Basin. Yet conventional extraction techniques, such as the use of nitroglycerin to fracture the hard rock surrounding the gas, permitted access to only about 10 percent of those reserves. "We think the proposed project is a particularly timely one," Memmott wrote. Not only was a corporation again showing an interest in Plowshare, but natural gas production was barely keeping up with consumption. In 1964 the nation used just over 15 trillion cubic feet of natural gas, which was about the same amount produced. Exploding a nuclear device in a low-producing or deeply buried natural gas reservoir would create a chimney and do a much better job than conventional methods in fracturing the surrounding rock. Large quantities of gas would then flow upward into the chimney—44 trillion feet of it, by Memmott's calculations, enough to feed the nation's demand for "more than two years." The *Christian Science Monitor*'s Neal Stanford was just as enthusiastic, reporting that Gasbuggy could "make possible recovering 5, 10, even 15 times as much gas as now is possible or feasible."[32]

Making so much gas available was important not just for the corporate or governmental bottom line but for national security. "U.S. economic and defense planners have expressed concern over growing dependence on imported oil (now one-fifth of annual consumption)," commented *Rotarian*'s Alfred Balk in January 1965. Particularly alarming was ongoing tension between Israel, a close U.S. ally, and Israel's Arab neighbors, which offered an opportunity for the Soviet Union to increase its influence in the strategically important Middle East. Granted, Gasbuggy's purpose was to expand natural gas production, but, commented Memmott, it had applications to oil consumption. While the nation's known reserves of natural gas had increased each year, its known petroleum reserves had "decreased four of the last eight years. . . . In the event of a National emergency and the unavailability of foreign crude oils, the importance of appreciable increases in our proved reserves of all hydrocarbon fuels can hardly be overemphasized."[33] Hence Gasbuggy could allow Americans to curtail their dependence on foreign sources of crude and more ably handle any decision by the petroleum-rich nations of the Middle East, either on their own or at the behest of the Soviet Union, to curtail or embargo oil shipments to the United States.

By early 1966 the AEC had selected a site some fifty-five miles east of the town of Farmington, New Mexico. Within the area was some 5.3 billion cubic feet of gas, of which about 70 percent, scientists believed, would be freed by the blast. But there was a problem: lack of money. In January 1966 President Johnson had proposed a national budget for FY 1967 of $112.8 billion. This included $600 million additional for the Great Society and, more significantly, a $12.8 billion supplemental request for Vietnam. Since all of this spending risked a large deficit, some of Johnson's aides suggested he raise taxes, but the president refused. With the war in Vietnam and the Great Society sapping ever more of the administration's budget, other initiatives had to take a backseat, and Gasbuggy was among them. Testifying before the JCAE on March 11, Kelly explained that the administration's Bureau of the Budget did not like the fact that EPNG offered to cover only about $1 million of the approximately $4.7 million project. That comment did not please Senator Clinton Anderson, a member of the JCAE and a supporter of Plowshare in whose home state Gasbuggy was to take place. What right, he queried, did Budget have to cancel a project about which it lacked the expertise to understand; in which energy companies other than El Paso had shown an interest; and which, if successful, might convince those other firms to follow suit as well, thus helping the nation meet its ever-growing need for gas? Did Budget even ask the AEC, Department of Interior, or the Bureau of Mines about Gasbuggy, he wanted to know. It did, Kelly replied, and the AEC had not only given its opinion on the project but had provided Budget information from Interior and the Bureau of Mines. Anderson's aggravation grew. "I don't want to appear critical of your part in [Gasbuggy]," he told Kelly, "because I know you folks believe it should be done. I have criticism toward the Bureau of the Budget because I don't think they gave it much consideration."[34]

Knowing they had little chance of forcing Budget's hand, Anderson and Holifield decided to approach the matter from the industry side, believing that a greater contribution by industry could convince Congress to open its wallet a little more. When EPNG's chairman of the board, Howard Boyd, appeared before the JCAE, Holifield, pointing to the profits made by El Paso and other gas companies, inquired whether they might foot more of the bill. When Boyd did not count out that possibility, Anderson pressed the point, observing that El Paso stood the chance of huge monetary gain if gas stimulation succeeded. Boyd rejected the assertion. "That might be true if we were an unregulated company, but we are a fully regulated company, regulated by the Federal Power Commission." This meant that El Paso could make money only off the "production properties"; the greatest benefit, he continued, would go to the consumer, not his company.[35]

Still, Boyd had shown openness to allocating more dollars to Gasbuggy, and so Holifield approached another JCAE witness that day, H. F. Coffer, the vice president of CER Geonuclear Corporation. Founded in 1965 by Reynolds Electrical and Engineering Company, Edgerton Germeshauseum & Grier, and Continental Oil Company (CONOCO), and based in Las Vegas, CER represented eighteen oil and gas firms. Not wanting to see Gasbuggy go under because of lack of funding, Holifield asked Coffer to approach others in the industry about earmarking additional funds. "I may be a little previous," Coffer responded. "Last night we had a meeting in Las Vegas of all the research managers of the major oil companies," during which he had raised with them the very possibility of a request for dollars.[36]

The pressure on El Paso and CER Geonuclear was only partially successful. On the one hand, EPNG boosted its offer to $1.5 million. Its confidence buoyed, the JCAE submitted to the full Congress legislation asking for $17.7 million for Plowshare for FY 1967, including $1.5 million for Gasbuggy. This would not be enough to pay for the full cost of the experiment, but the Joint Committee anticipated covering the remainder for FY 1968, thereby allowing the shot to take place at that time. The bill passed both houses of Congress later that month.[37]

On the other hand, El Paso's fellow energy companies, reluctant to fund a project that might not work, continued to stand on the sidelines, prompting President Johnson to remove money for Gasbuggy from the administration's 1968 budget. Deeply disheartened, Seaborg asked Boyd about EPNG's augmenting its offer again. Though he was reluctant, Boyd asked what the AEC had in mind. A sixty-forty split of the total cost, answered Seaborg, which would constitute El Paso's raising its contribution to $1.88 million. Boyd immediately offered the extra funds.[38]

Just how important Gasbuggy was to the AEC became clear in discussions the following month. The Commission had in mind two other gas stimulation experiments, called Dragon Trail and Rulison, Seaborg explained to Coffer, but it had no intention of proceeding with either until Gasbuggy's completion and assessment. Coffer "expressed his regret that the entire nuclear underground engineering program might rest solely on the success or failure of Project Gasbuggy."[39]

With the creation of new elements having gotten nowhere, uncertainty surrounding application of the atom to mining, and the excavation program's future in doubt, Plowshare's defenders did not want to see resource stimulation fail. Plus there was the possibility that the necessary appropriations for Gasbuggy, whether from industry or government, might still come through. Accordingly on January 31, 1967, the AEC, Interior Department, and El Paso signed an agreement to proceed with the shot. The Southwest Radiological Health Laboratory (SWRHL), based in Las Vegas, now entered the picture, contacting officials at New Mexico's Health Department. Working together, SWRHL and New Mexico state health officers took a census of people, "domestic livestock, wildlife, and other environmental media necessary to develop a comprehensive program." This allowed for the creation of an evacuation plan for certain areas around the blast site, just in case.[40]

The release of radioactivity into the atmosphere that might necessitate local evacuation was one concern of the AEC. The others were contamination of underground water supplies and damage to nearby dams and gas-producing wells. The AEC considered none of these events likely. The plan for Gasbuggy called for burying a twenty-kiloton explosive at a depth of 4,240 feet, while calculations determined that burial at 1,200 feet was enough to guarantee complete containment. Indeed, argued the AEC, in September 1963 it had conducted a shot called Bilby, which, though two hundred kilotons in size and buried only 2,400 feet underground, released no radioactivity into the atmosphere. The nearest aquifer to Gasbuggy was 560 feet above the proposed blast, far enough away, calculated the Commission, to make unlikely any contamination. Two dams, the Navajo and the El Vado, were also considered too distant to be endangered. Though believing Gasbuggy would not impact any gas-producing wells in the area, the AEC would make sure that just prior to the blast, "all producing wells within a five-mile radius of ground zero were physically separated from the gas transmission system."[41]

During the summer SWRHL and New Mexico Health Department officers began an environmental sampling program to determine normal levels of radioactivity. Thus they could ascertain if the explosion had caused any contamination and, if so, how much. Natural gas sampling also took place. There was some thought that the shock waves from Gasbuggy might increase the amount of radon-222, a short-lived, radioactive gas, in the natural gas, and so it was important to know what the existing level of radon was.[42] The AEC wanted to make sure there was no repeat of Gnome by demonstrating that it had taken every possible measure to ensure public safety.

In addition to increasing gas production, Gasbuggy offered an opportunity to demonstrate U.S. technological know-how and to develop cordial ties with the Soviet Union. Despite disagreements over the war in Vietnam, superpower relations after the Cuban missile crisis had continued to improve, and the Johnson administration hoped to maintain that progress. One of those potential "areas of cooperation" was Plowshare. In July 1966 President Johnson signed a national security directive that called for cultivating "areas of peaceful cooperation with the nations of Eastern Europe and the Soviet Union." To help this process along, the AEC invited hundreds of people, including Soviet officials, to witness the Gasbuggy shot.[43]

Yet even if successful, there were questions about Gasbuggy that remained unanswered. What would the blast do to the gas? That question could have an impact on other proposed projects. "Gas Buggy will answer some of the questions still unanswered about Project Ketch," the *Washington Post* pointed out in March. "For instance, will radioactivity contaminate the natural gas stirred in the cavern and transmit it in the homes served by the Columbia firm? The AEC hopes to find out whether the gas needs to be or can be 'scrubbed clean of contamination.' "[44]

The relationship between Projects Gasbuggy and Ketch was that while Gasbuggy's purpose was to stimulate production of natural gas, Ketch's was to provide a place to store it. In 1964 Columbia Gas Company had contacted the AEC about using an underground blast to create a storage facility for natural gas where one did not exist. Underground storage was cheaper than surface storage, and having the gas immediately available in the area would allow Columbia to provide gas to its customers more efficiently and reduce utility bills. By April 1965 the company had picked a location in central Pennsylvania's Sproul State Forest, about twelve miles southwest of the town of Renovo. Columbia then asked the AEC to join it in a feasibility study, which got under way in September. Even before completing the study, the AEC proposed using an explosive about the same size as that called for by Sloop, but burying it at a depth of 3,300 feet. The expectation was that the blast would create a cavity 180 feet wide and 300 feet high and provide as much as a half-billion cubic feet of storage space. Columbia believed that over a thirty-five-year period it would recoup Ketch's $6 million price tag and save itself nearly $700,000 by using nuclear excavation over conventional methods. Of course, such profits assumed a willingness by the public to use gas laden with radioactivity. Whether it was possible to reduce the radioactivity in the gas "[could not] be fully answered except by performing the experiment."[45]

In addition to providing the region with a storage facility, the AEC determined that the location for Ketch made sense because of the sparse population. The fact was that there were people who lived nearby who did not like the idea of a nuclear explosion in the immediate vicinity, but AEC investigators who surveyed the region gave them little recognition. In what amounted to a replay of their treatment of the Eskimos, AEC officials admitted to "very limited contact" with the locals—or "natives," as they again called them—but determined that many of those living nearby resided in " 'rickety' dwellings" and showed an unwillingness to accept "change or progress."[46]

More important to Ketch's proponents was state approval. Both Columbia Gas and the AEC made their first approaches to Pennsylvania officials in early

1966. "My first reaction, and I think the reaction of many state officials," recalled Thomas Geursky of the Pennsylvania Department of Health, "was one of disbelief. A nuclear device being exploded in our backyard? Unbelievable! Nevada, with its sparse population and open spaces, was a far cry from the populated Northeast." The initial reaction of people like Geursky did not mean rejection of the proposal, and so in addition to the Department of Health, AEC officers met with members of the state's Departments of Forest and Waters, Mines and Mineral Industries, and Commerce, the State Fish and Game Commission, and other agencies, all of which in one way or another would play a part in Ketch if approved. Also involved was a Ketch subcommittee established in 1966 by Governor William W. Scranton that advised the state's Departments of Health and Commerce on matters related to atomic energy and radioactivity. Its nine members, who included experts in education, labor, and science, had the job of giving the project a further going-over.[47]

Throughout these discussions the AEC emphasized the economic value of Ketch to Pennsylvania. State officials, however, were not fully convinced. The Ketch subcommittee agreed to permit the AEC and Columbia to proceed with the first phase of Ketch, in which they would assess the feasibility of the chosen location for the shot. However, before allowing Ketch to proceed beyond that, the state demanded that the AEC conduct a full safety review for Harrisburg's perusal. The purpose of the safety review was to demonstrate that Ketch could occur without harming people or the environment or damaging "natural and man-made structures." Moreover the state insisted that if Ketch received the go-ahead, the AEC would promise monetary compensation for damage to property or personal injury.[48] With that tacit approval, the AEC had reason to press on with Ketch.

There was yet another storage project that had caught the AEC's attention, this one in Arizona. As early as 1959 scientists had raised the possibility of using the atom for water resource projects. Building dams and creating cavities for aquifers were among those considered. In 1966 Arizona became the focus of such possibilities when its state AEC approached the U.S. AEC about applying the atom to the Central Arizona Water Project. As part of that larger effort, the Arizona AEC inquired about creating an "aquifer storage for water runoff." Soon thereafter an investigation got under way.[49]

The Debate Rages On

More than anything, the AEC wanted to see the isthmian canal become reality. As the debate over Cabriolet continued, the president told Congress that the

Canal Commission likely would ask for an extension of its reporting deadline. He also authorized several Plowshare blasts. Between March and November 1966 the AEC conducted three underground experiments aimed at developing cleaner explosives for use in excavation projects: Templar, Saxon, and Simms.[50] There is no indication any of them generated controversy, nor does it appear that they received consideration by the Review Committee. They were all deeply buried, thereby promising full containment and no risk of a test ban treaty violation.

Cleaner explosives, however, meant nothing if the AEC could not put them to use. That was possible only if Cabriolet got beyond the drawing board. Rusk had promised to bring the blast to the president's attention in August, but he did not do so until mid-September. Calling his decision a "51/49 vote," the secretary recommended giving it the green light. There were dangers in such a course. The United States risked a violation of the LTBT, and the ACDA had charged that Cabriolet would "prejudice" America's nonproliferation efforts. However, the secretary saw "no health hazard involved." Additionally Cabriolet would allow the United States to improve its peaceful-use technology, provide the data the Canal Commission needed, and "maintain the credibility of the nuclear excavation option," thereby giving the United States leverage in its negotiations with the Panamanians. Convinced, Johnson authorized the shot.[51]

Johnson's decision fomented another intra-administration row. The President's Science Advisory Committee, the ACDA, and most officials in the State Department called for postponement. Cabriolet, they stressed, threatened an LTBT violation and was too small to provide the data the Canal Commission needed; that data could come only through additional and much larger shots, which had an even greater likelihood of detection. Hornig even went so far as to suggest not just a delay but "an immediate study . . . of the entire nuclear excavation program." Rostow fought back. He found convincing AEC Commissioner Gerald Tape's contention that Cabriolet could "reduce venting by as much as a factor of ten," thereby opening the door to the other experiments the AEC wanted to conduct. Furthermore, wrote the NSC adviser, to "call off" the blast would mean Plowshare's indefinite postponement, if not death, and the waste of the money already spent to prepare for Cabriolet.[52]

Feeling a renewed sense of uncertainty, in early October Johnson turned to Nicholas Katzenbach, formerly his attorney general but now serving as undersecretary of state, to act as arbiter. "Until we know that the political risks are worth taking," Katzenbach replied a few days later, "I opt for not taking them." Domestically, a sizable release of fallout by Cabriolet would generate a strong public reaction. The international ramifications were even greater. At the time, the United States and Soviet Union were on the verge of entreating all UN members to stop the spread of atomic technology. If radioactivity released from Cabriolet crossed U.S. borders, Washington might find itself charged with a test ban treaty violation. "Our problems would be compounded if this happened while the General Assembly was still sitting in New York in December," asserted the undersecretary. If Cabriolet violated the LTBT, any appeal by the superpowers on nondissemination "would be lost in the noise." Based on these considerations, Katzenbach favored canceling Cabriolet or, at the very least, deferring it until January 1967.[53]

The continued holdup in a decision added to the level of frustration at the AEC. On the afternoon of November 14, Seaborg and Tape met with Rostow and Keeny and urged a decision by the next day to start preparations for Buggy—a nuclear "row charge" experiment which the AEC had planned to conduct after Cabriolet—and, by November 22, authority to carry out Cabriolet so that the experiment could take place in December. "Otherwise," they cautioned, "for operational and meteorological reasons it will slip to January or February 1967."[54]

No matter what, the AEC knew it could not meet its test schedule. In March 1966 Kelly had stated that by the end of FY 1967 his agency wanted to complete the six experiments necessary to determine if nuclear excavation of a canal was possible. Now the AEC pushed the last of those blasts to FY 1969, with Cabriolet and Buggy to take place in FY 1967, Buggy II and Schooner the following year, and Galley and an unnamed experiment in 1969. Yet as before, Plowshare had to compete with other initiatives. Spending on the war in Vietnam absorbed ever more appropriations, so the Bureau of the Budget saw no reason to authorize the funding the AEC desired for Plowshare. Instead it provided only enough money to conduct Cabriolet in FY 1967, Buggy in FY 1968, and two unnamed experiments in FY 1969. Further complicating matters for the AEC was the lack of an agreed interpretation with the Soviets on the LTBT. While the president had authorized seeking common ground with the Soviets on Plowshare, it was not until October that Moscow showed a willingness to open discussions, and another month before the U.S. ambassador, Llewellyn Thompson, received White House authorization to meet with Kremlin officials.[55]

Seaborg was of no mind to wait for the Soviets to come around. Hearing nothing from the Oval Office in November, he complained to Katzenbach that the AEC did not have time to prepare for a December Cabriolet blast. It also appears he approached Rostow, for on December 10 the presidential assistant urged Johnson to give the go-ahead. Without Cabriolet, he stated, Anderson could anticipate an angry congressional reaction when he had to tell lawmakers the Canal Commission was unable to complete its work because the AEC had yet to conduct the requisite experiments. Even Katzenbach had shown a change of heart. He was still unconvinced that PNEs had much of a future. For Plowshare to realize its full potential required amending the LTBT, something Katzenbach believed "would be unfortunate." Additionally, to pursue peaceful-use blasts "at a time when [the United States was] attempting to prevent non-proliferation" made little sense to him, especially considering that the explosives used for Plowshare and the military were little different. But he had reached the conclusion that Cabriolet should proceed. First, the White House could not ignore that the Soviet Union had begun its own peaceful-use program. While he did not say so, he likely understood that stopping Plowshare in its tracks would upset peaceful-use advocates in Congress, who would charge the White House with allowing the Kremlin to gain an advantage over the United States in that area of research. Second, Katzenbach apparently had grown frustrated with the pace of the Panama Canal negotiations; to proceed with Cabriolet, he wrote, would prove "useful" in those talks. Hornig remained the one significant holdout. He was still certain that Cabriolet risked transgressing the LTBT. When Rostow raised with Hornig the Canal Commission's need for nuclear excavation data, the latter replied, "Getting into a debate about a Test Ban Treaty violation is more important than Bob Anderson's problem with the Congress."[56]

Finally, on the afternoon of December 20, Seaborg received the news for which he had long been waiting when Rostow told him that Johnson had approved Cabriolet. "There is one caveat," Seaborg wrote in his diary: "a prior announcement of what we propose to do," including an assurance that the shot would take place within the limits of the LTBT. The administration, however, gave the AEC some leeway insofar as having the announcement state that an experiment would take place and lead to some venting but not specifying the date or time.[57]

The public statement went out in January, with an added note that no observers would be permitted to witness the blast. That did not sit well with all of Nevada's congressional lawmakers, Senators Alan Bible and Harold Cannon and Representative Walter Baring, who charged that the failure to permit observers violated the AEC's stated desire to help Americans better understand the power of the atom. They urged the AEC to permit newsmen to witness the blast. Seaborg refused. With weapons testing also occurring at the NTS, the AEC did not want people without proper clearance to potentially gather information on secret technology. Instead he promised "to release to the media complete information, including still and motion pictures shortly after the test is conducted." Doing so, he contended, would fulfill the AEC's desire to improve public awareness of nuclear excavation. In his journal he confided that he had not told the senators the full story: "Actually an additional reason, which we can't disclose, is the potential problem of venting to extent of debris crossing U.S. borders."[58]

The AEC had intended to hold the blast later that month, only to face disappointment once again. The wind kept blowing from the wrong direction, risking the possibility of radioactive fallout over populated areas. After several days of such meteorological activity, Johnson withdrew his approval. There were several reasons for his decision. One was preparations for the signing of the Treaty of Tlatelolco. To avoid a repeat of the Cuban missile crisis, in April 1963 five Latin American nations had called for a regional agreement not "to manufacture, store, or test nuclear weapons or devices for launching nuclear weapons." After several years of negotiations the treaty was ready for signing on February 14, 1967. Its provisions followed the lines of the 1963 joint declaration, though it established arrangements for peaceful-use tests. Johnson judged that if Cabriolet triggered significant fallout, it might cause potential signatories to rethink Tlatelolco's PNE provisions.[59]

The Vietnam War also encouraged the president to call for a delay. By early 1967 that conflict had begun to take its toll, not just monetarily but emotionally and politically. Despite having over 385,000 troops in Vietnam, the fighting showed no sign of ending. An antiwar movement had developed at home, marked by teach-ins and ever larger street protests. The White House faced growing pressure, not just domestically but internationally, to find a negotiated solution aimed at ending the conflict. To authorize Cabriolet, only to have it vent, would add to the public outcry Johnson already faced as a result of Vietnam.[60]

Finally, there were the ongoing nonproliferation talks. With the resolution of the dispute over the MLF and ANF, indications pointed to a successful outcome in Geneva. In mid-October 1966 Moscow and Washington had issued their call at the UN to stop nuclear proliferation. The next month the UN General Assembly overwhelmingly sanctioned a treaty to prevent the dissemination of atomic technology. By January 1967 the superpowers appeared to be moving steadily toward a nonproliferation agreement. There were issues that still required resolution, such as the matter of inspections to guarantee compliance, but newspaper reports suggested positive movement. A repeat of Palanquin could create a backlash that would encumber the progress taking place. For all of these reasons, the president concluded that "the risk of an incident with Cabriolet at this time was too great to take."[61]

Seaborg had no intention of accepting an indefinite deferral. By late February the considerations that earlier had moved the White House to postpone Cabriolet seemed no longer in effect, at least to the AEC head and those of like mind. In early February Johnson had accepted an offer by the British and Soviets to mediate an end to the war in Vietnam, asked North Vietnamese leader Ho Chi Minh to join him in finding a solution to the conflict, and, as a further inducement to the North Vietnamese, ordered a one-week pause in the bombing of the North, to begin February 6. Ho's reply was a diatribe against the U.S. government. He refused to discuss a cessation of hostilities until the United States permanently stopped the bombing of the North and removed all troops from the South. To

Johnson, these conditions were nonstarters. Meanwhile the Treaty of Tlatelolco had been completed and opened for signature on February 14. Seaborg could argue that there was no longer any reason to worry about Cabriolet's affecting Tlatelolco. As for Vietnam, Johnson could take the moral high ground, asserting that he had attempted to seek the peace his critics had demanded, only to have North Vietnam throw his effort back in his face. Accordingly the president could anticipate far less of a backlash if he green-lighted Cabriolet. And there was one other consideration: the grazing season fast approached.[62] If the AEC did not set off the blast soon, it would have to postpone it until the fall, when the grazing season ended.

On February 28, therefore, Seaborg and Tape approached Rostow, asking for presidential authorization by March 10. They commented that when the AEC had earlier received approval for the blast, it had emplaced the Cabriolet explosive in the ground; if the AEC was forced to postpone the explosion until the following fall, it would have to destroy the device, for the existing one would not be reliable after sitting underground for so long, and leaving it "in place might well compromise the radiochemical determination of the yield of a new experiment when fired." Creating and emplacing a new device would add another $1.4 million to the price tag. Rostow brought the matter to Johnson's attention the next day. He explained that in addition to the cost, another deferral of Cabriolet would set back the schedule of tests the AEC hoped to conduct, raise questions in the minds of the Panamanians whether the United States was truly serious about nuclear excavation in another country, and reduce U.S. leverage over Panama. He saw reason, though, to accept postponement. The United States had announced a deferral earlier in the month in part because of the ongoing nonproliferation talks. To suddenly announce Cabriolet's approval "would be interpreted as reflecting a basic change in our views concerning the prospects for the Non-Proliferation Treaty." After considering both sides, Rostow recommended "taking no action at this time" and then, in the spring, announcing that Cabriolet and Buggy would occur in fiscal year 1968. Katzenbach shared Rostow's recommendation, while ACDA opposed "rescheduling CABRIOLET at this time." Johnson sided with Rostow and Katzenbach and asked Rusk and Seaborg to let him know by mid-April whether Cabriolet could be held in the fall of 1967. Moreover he wanted to have funding for both Cabriolet and Buggy available for the "1967 and 1968 budgets to protect the option of conducting both tests during FY-1968."[63]

Responding a few days later, the secretary of state and the AEC chair accepted the idea of holding Cabriolet in the fall of 1967, followed by Buggy the following spring. Designing and burying the new device, wrote Seaborg, would in fact cost $1.7 million, money the AEC had not budgeted. On top of that was the need to fabricate the explosives for Buggy. To conduct Cabriolet and Buggy on the new schedule would require carrying over $2.365 million from the FY 1967 budget into 1968. The Bureau of the Budget approved a reprogramming of this money. This pleased Seaborg, but he was obviously discouraged by the constant delays. The next time he wanted "a reasonably high probability of execution," for another deferral or cancellation "would be neither prudent nor fair to the highly skilled scientific and technical manpower engaged in these programs."[64]

Discouragement or Hope?

If the news surrounding the excavation program was not bad enough, the storage program suddenly encountered unanticipated resistance. Having apparently learned from its experience in Alaska, the AEC, in conjunction with Columbia Gas, hoped to preempt any opposition to Ketch through a large-scale public relations campaign. The federal government oversaw or owned large portions of the land in America's eleven westernmost states, where almost every nuclear blast up to this point had taken place. Hence, the AEC commented, people out west had come to view such explosions "as almost routine." The AEC had conducted an underground nuclear blast in Mississippi in 1964 called Project Salmon, the purpose of which was to gain information for the Vela program. But this did not mean that easterners would accept Ketch as did their western counterparts.[65]

Before the AEC and Columbia Gas could get their public relations program under way, the *Pittsburgh Press* leaked the plans behind Ketch to the people of Pennsylvania. Voices of outrage were heard in Renovo, followed by State College, the home of Pennsylvania State University and only thirty miles south of the blast site. Those against the shot rejected the AEC's promises that it could take place safely and raised doubts about whether it would offer any economic benefit to their state. The AEC and Columbia Gas Company made matters worse by claiming that the land around the blast site was "marginal" and sparsely populated. The truth was that there were several hundred hunting cabins in the immediate vicinity, and campers and hikers, in addition to hunters, frequented the area. People from central Pennsylvania sent letters of protest and anti-Ketch petitions to state officials, the media, the AEC, and Columbia Gas, pointing to the region's "unspoiled mountain land" and "undisturbed forest reserve." Deduced the *Washington Post*, "Seemingly the Keystone State isn't yet ready to challenge Nevada as a nuclear testing site, even for peaceful purposes."[66]

The sudden controversy surrounding Ketch only added to the dejection felt by Seaborg, Tape, and others who wanted to see Plowshare create the wonderful world they visualized. Funding for the peaceful-use program continued to suffer as the White House sought to fund the Great Society and Vietnam War without raising taxes. Fears about disrupting the NPT negotiations and violating the LTBT had repeatedly delayed Cabriolet, thereby placing in doubt the entire excavation program and plans to build the strategically and economically important sea-level isthmian canal. Attempts to use the atom to generate new elements had seen yet more failures. Now it appeared that Ketch faced the same kind of grassroots opposition that had doomed Chariot.

Yet for all the bad omens, there were reasons for hope. Despite the setbacks for Plowshare, the very idea of nuclear engineering seemed to be gaining strength. By 1967 over a dozen universities around the nation offered courses in the subject, and more had plans to do so.[67] It was not yet clear if the outburst against Ketch was a temporary phenomenon, and by all appearances the Pennsylvania state government remained supportive of that blast. Cabriolet had been delayed, not canceled. Anderson had hinted to lawmakers he might ask for more money, and the president had told Congress to expect a request to give the Canal Commission more time. If the Canal Commission got additional appropriations and a deadline extension, and if the AEC received the funding it desired, then it might yet complete the experiments needed to prove whether nuclear excavation of a canal was possible. Through these projects, along with Sloop, Aquarius, and Gasbuggy, all of which were in varying states of readiness, Plowshare could prove its value to America's economic and strategic well-being, if not to the welfare of the entire planet.

Maybe the best news of all, ironically enough, was the NPT. The draft nonproliferation treaty the United States had submitted to the ENDC in August 1965 said nothing about offering peaceful-use services to other countries because the AEC and ACDA disagreed over whether to do so. After a year of wrestling the AEC emerged victorious. In August 1966 Adrian Fisher, ACDA's deputy director and the U.S. representative to the ENDC, announced, "If and when peaceful applications of nuclear explosives that are permissible under the test ban treaty limitations prove technically and economically feasible, nuclear-weapons states should make available to other states nuclear explosives for peaceful applications." Adopting language similar to that of the AEC, Fisher continued that offering such services would give those nations without nuclear bombs a reason not to develop them.[68] For the AEC, LRL, and their allies, Aquarius, Sloop, Gasbuggy, and the canal project, combined with international endorsement of providing peaceful-use services to other countries, could finally make the vision offered by Plowshare a reality.

Making Headway?

It had become clear to Robert Anderson, the head of the Atlantic-Pacific Inter-oceanic Canal Commission, that his agency simply could not finish its work in time and with the appropriations it had received. On March 6, 1967, he wrote Vice President Hubert Humphrey, asking for another $6.5 million and an extension of his agency's reporting deadline from June 30, 1968, to December 1, 1970. Delays in getting the necessary surveys under way, a lack of equipment, the slow progress of the Plowshare nuclear excavation program, and "more realistic cost estimates based upon actual field conditions" had moved him to make the request. In June the Senate gave Anderson most of what he wanted, approving $4.5 million in additional monies and the deadline extension.[1] The House of Representatives had yet to give its opinion, but Anderson hoped it would follow suit.

That same month President Johnson and President Robles of Panama announced that they had reached agreement on three treaties related to the Panama Canal. The first two detailed arrangements for the neutrality, defense, and operation of the existing lock waterway. Panama received sovereignty over the canal and more revenue from the tolls. In return the United States made up the majority of a nine-person commission to operate the Zone and received the right to operate military bases there. The third treaty permitted Washington to build a sea-level waterway in Panama. If the U.S. government selected Panama for such a canal, Panama had the right to reject use of the atom as a means of construction and would help run the waterway. Control over the Canal Zone would revert from the United States to Panama in 1999 or, if the United States chose to build a sea-level waterway in Panama, a year after the new canal began operations.[2]

This was all terrific news to the AEC, LRL, and others involved in the Plow-share program. Assuming the House followed the Senate's lead, an extension of the Canal Commission's reporting deadline meant more time for the AEC to complete the list of experiments it believed necessary to demonstrate whether nuclear excavation of a canal was possible. While the Panama Canal treaties still required ratification, they formalized the determination by both countries to see a sea-level waterway, possibly built with the help of the atom, become a reality.

The next eighteen months gave Plowshare's defenders additional reasons for optimism. After an extended debate the AEC finally set off Cabriolet in 1968 and followed it up with two more excavation blasts later that year, Buggy and Schoo-ner. Use of the atom to stimulate the production of natural gas appeared to get off to a good start in 1967 with the detonation of Gasbuggy. Meanwhile prepara-tions continued for both Projects Sloop and Aquarius. The NPT, which included an article favored by the AEC that permitted states with nuclear weapons to offer PNEs to nonnuclear countries, opened for signature in the middle of 1968. Fi-nally, the House accepted giving the Atlantic-Pacific Interoceanic Canal Study Commission until December 1970 to finish its work.

But there was also reason for pessimism. As he increased spending on the Vietnam War, Johnson sought to avoid raising taxes while simultaneously hold-ing down the deficit. Something had to give. The Great Society suffered, but so did other programs, among them Plowshare. Compounding the problems of the peaceful-use program was an increasingly vocal outcry against Ketch. Gasbuggy, though considered a success by the AEC, left serious questions about the safety of nuclear stimulation of natural gas. Consequently by the end of Johnson's term in office, the excavation program had yet to prove the viability of canal construc-tion, Ketch had been canceled, and the AEC and LRL had to wonder if the pro-gram to which they had devoted so much time, money, and emotion might be on its last legs.

The Canal and Cabriolet

Two months after Johnson and Robles made their announcement, news of prog-ress came out of Geneva. At the ENDC the United States and the Soviet Union appeared to have found a way around a disagreement over Article III of a draft NPT. The purpose of that article was to provide safeguards aimed at preventing nondissemination of nuclear technology. The controversy was over whether nu-clear power plants located in the European Atomic Energy Community (Eura-tom), a coalition of Western European states founded in 1958, should be subject to Euratom or IAEA safeguards. The Soviet Union wanted only the IAEA to conduct inspections to make sure the safeguards were being upheld. The United States and Euratom believed that Euratom officials could carry out those examinations; to the Kremlin, that amounted to "self-inspection."[3]

Then, on June 17, communist China announced it had successfully tested a hydrogen bomb. The sudden advancement in China's nuclear capabilities frightened both Washington and Moscow and added to their eagerness to complete the NPT as quickly as possible. Unable to resolve their differences on Article III, the superpowers decided on August 24 to submit to the ENDC identical drafts of their proposed treaties, leaving Article III blank. Articles I and II required nuclear signatories not to provide atomic weapons or explosives to nonnuclear states or to help countries without the atom "to manufacture or acquire nuclear weapons or other nuclear devices," and for nonnuclear nations not to try to acquire or manufacture the same. Article IV permitted all states the right to develop "nuclear energy for peaceful purposes." Aside from a blank Article III, there was still much to work out. Nothing in the treaty committed nuclear states to make peaceful-use technology available to nonnuclear parties. Nonnuclear countries like Brazil and India complained that, as written, the NPT limited their ability to create and use their own atomic devices for peaceful purposes, and they wanted to make sure that any safeguards applied not just to nonnuclear but also to nuclear countries. Yet the draft treaties marked a milestone. Commented the *New York Times*, "American-Soviet agreement on even an incomplete treaty constitutes evidence that the world's two nuclear super-powers can recognize a powerful common interest despite their bitter and perilous disagreements."[4]

With the Panama Canal treaties signed, with the positive signals coming out of Geneva, with Cabriolet in the midst of another delay, and with the Canal Commission's deadline on his mind, Anderson decided on July 25 to take up matters with the president. The House of Representatives had not yet given its opinion on money or a deadline extension, so he intended to ask again for pushing back the Canal Commission's reporting date to December 1, 1970. Yet for his agency to decide whether nuclear excavation of a canal was feasible, the AEC had to finish its list of experiments. "Another postponement," Anderson wrote, "will eliminate the possibility that we will be able to determine the feasibility of nuclear canal excavation during our investigation." He also raised the specter of U.S. security. If the Soviet Union or another nation proved the utility of nuclear excavation before the United States did, Washington might find itself in a disadvantageous position in future negotiations with Panama or Colombia over construction of a new canal. Impressed by Anderson's argument, in early August Johnson requested the House to grant the Canal Commission both the 1970 reporting deadline and the $6.5 million for which Anderson had originally applied.[5]

Anderson's efforts certainly encouraged AEC Chair Glenn Seaborg, and there was more heartening news. During the summer of 1967 the White House authorized two more blasts at the NTS. On June 22 the AEC set off Switch, a 3.1-kiloton device buried almost a thousand feet underground, designed to create a cleaner explosive. The AEC determined the device worked well, "keeping fission product and induced radioactivity to a low level." Marvel followed in September 21. A 2.2-kiloton device set 572 feet below the surface, its purpose was to improve means of trapping radioactivity generated by cratering explosions.[6] As with Templar, Saxon, and Simms, there is no evidence either of these shots received consideration by the Review Committee on Underground Nuclear Tests or caused any uproar.

Also heartening was the AEC's calculation that it could drill down to the Cabriolet explosive and recover it, allowing use of the same hole for the new device. The cost was still about the same as to destroy the old bomb and dig a new hole, but at least the AEC would save the old explosive. After salvaging the device in October, Seaborg asked for authority to proceed with Cabriolet the following month. Once again the president sent the request to the Review Committee.[7]

Despite all of the auspicious indicators from the previous few months, the Review Committee's meeting came at a difficult time for the White House. The war in Vietnam, of course, remained a problem. In October Euratom offered some concessions regarding inspection, but it was not clear how the Soviets might react to them. Although Moscow had indicated its preparedness to discuss a common interpretation of the LTBT, it did not want to commence such talks until after the nuclear nonproliferation treaty negotiations had come to an end. On top of all of this, ratification of the Panama Canal treaties was at best uncertain. In the Senate Strom Thurmond (D-South Carolina) insisted on U.S. retention of the waterway: "The property that now would be abandoned is federal property as sure as any national park or military reservation." The House of Representatives, which would appropriate funding to put the new treaties into effect, also expressed anger. Daniel Flood (D-Pennsylvania) led the charge, stating that the treaties would permit a communist takeover of Panama. About 150 members of the House joined Flood, submitting a resolution critical of the treaties and demanding the addition of reservations. Nor was the situation in Panama free of roadblocks. There a struggle for power brewed between Robles's party and nearly twenty other political parties, all of which had their own agenda regarding the canal. Moreover presidential elections were scheduled for May, and it seemed unlikely that Panama would act on the treaties until after voters had gone to the polls.[8]

All of these considerations played their part in another round of intense administration debate over Cabriolet. Most voices opposed giving the green light.

Leonard Meeker, the State Department's legal adviser, warned that Cabriolet would foment charges of an LTBT violation and inflame opinion in the UN General Assembly at the same time the United States sought to convince nonnuclear states to sign the NPT. "The domestic political repercussions could be substantial," he added. Nicholas Katzenbach, who had recently left the Justice Department to become undersecretary of state, Presidential Science Adviser Donald Hornig, Ambassador to the United Nations Arthur Goldberg, and Bureau of the Budget Assistant Director Charles Schultze seconded Meeker. Katzenbach realized another postponement would displease the JCAE, likely kill any possibility of a nuclear-excavated canal, and reduce what leverage the United States had over Panama in the canal negotiations—leverage Katzenbach considered minimal. But Cabriolet risked an LTBT violation, and Katzenbach said, "I am persuaded that the possible dangers to the NPT—which is vital to the President—and the hell we would probably catch in the UN (and at home) if we went through with the test, are simply not worth the price." Hornig and Goldberg too pointed to Cabriolet's potential impact on the General Assembly. "I think," Hornig wrote, "consideration should also be given to deferring a greater part of the nuclear cratering program until we have an acceptable political base on which to proceed." Schultze raised financial considerations. The White House had refused to increase taxes while it simultaneously sought to wage a war in Vietnam and a war on poverty. In light of "the current budgetary situation—under which, without a tax increase, substantial reductions in budgeted expenditures will have to be made," it made sense to defer the entire Plowshare program.[9]

Some took the opposing viewpoint. Seeing a close connection between Plowshare and the U.S. military's efforts to improve its own technology, the Joint Chiefs of Staff urged authorization. Herman Pollack, director of the State Department's Office of International Science and Technology Affairs, contended that rather than inhibiting the NPT discussions, Cabriolet would move them forward. Using the language of progress and modernity, he asserted that the blast would prove the United States was "seriously proceeding with . . . plans for learning all that is necessary about the yet untested technology in order to make its benefits eventually available to the rest of the world." Director of Central Intelligence Richard Helms pointed to Soviet advances in their version of Plowshare (though he did not say what those advances were). Anderson, who also wanted to see Cabriolet take place but was cognizant of the weight of opinion against doing so, urged NSC adviser Walt Rostow to let him speak with the president before Johnson made any decision.[10]

Wanting to give Cabriolet's defenders time to build their case and change dissenters' minds, John Kelly, the head of the AEC's Division of Peaceful Nuclear Explosives, informed the White House that his agency could wait until December 2 for a decision, with execution to take place on December 19. The General Assembly would have adjourned prior to then, meaning a UN outburst would no longer be an issue. Postponement to December 19 also permitted the Plowshare excavation program to remain on schedule. Meanwhile Anderson did his part. Meeting with the president, he warned that another postponement of Cabriolet would kill any chance of the AEC getting "additional time and money from the Congress to enable it to determine the feasibility of nuclear canal excavation." In that case the United States would lose the option of building a canal outside the Canal Zone at a time when the talks with Panama over ratification of the treaties were "at a critical stage." Unwilling to override majority opinion, Johnson asked Anderson to raise these points with the cabinet.[11]

That cabinet meeting, which took place on November 28, saw all sides sticking to their guns. Anderson and Seaborg emphasized the cleanness of the blast, the risk of losing congressional support, and the positive impact Cabriolet could have on the NPT discussions. Hornig, Schultze, and Katzenbach warned that the political and economic risks were simply too great. While still noncommittal, Rusk himself evinced doubts. He had found that scientists were not always correct with regard to their estimates of fallout and wondered if it made sense first to reach an agreement with the Soviets on an interpretation of the LTBT before proceeding with Cabriolet. Replied Seaborg, "We've tried to talk to the Soviets for two years and we haven't gotten anywhere."[12]

With the passage of the December 2 deadline and still no response from the White House, Seaborg asked Rostow to remind the president of the need for an answer. Rostow did so, but Johnson, still wavering, asked his NSC adviser for an opinion. "On balance we should go forward," Rostow wrote. The White House could not permit the Soviet Union to outstrip the United States in peaceful use technology; Cabriolet posed no threat to public health; without proving the utility of nuclear excavation, Washington had no hope of offering Plowshare services through an NPT; in all likelihood the discussants involved in the NPT talks would pass the treaty even if Cabriolet took place; and based on the venting of their own blasts, such as that of January 1965, the Soviet Union had accepted a "de minimis interpretation of the limited test ban treaty." If the president sanctioned Cabriolet, Rostow suggested a series of steps to avoid a backlash. He proposed holding the shot in "late January . . . after the state of the Union speech and the resumption of the ENDC," the latter of which was to take place on January 18. The White House would begin "some low-key press discussion of the de minimis interpretation of the LTBT," pointing out that Soviet tests had caused fallout beyond Soviet borders. Then the AEC would "make a low-key announcement of the test as close to the event as possible." Meanwhile William Foster, director of the Arms Control and Disarmament Agency, would tell the ENDC how the United States could offer Plowshare devices to other nations under an NPT. To avoid any protests from them, the United States might quietly inform both Mexico and Canada of the shot in advance, giving special emphasis to the small amount of radioactivity that might cross their borders. Finally, if the Kremlin did issue a protest, the White House could, as it had done previously, point to past Soviet violations of the LTBT.[13]

It was not until December 19 that Johnson finally gave the green light for Cabriolet—as long as Rusk agreed to it as well—but he refused to endorse any further experiments until the completion of an assessment of that shot. While this meant abandoning Buggy for the time being, Seaborg had determined beforehand that the delay in approving Cabriolet would have pushed Buggy back into the grazing season. As the AEC did not want to risk fallout at that time, Buggy had to wait until the fall. Furthermore Seaborg accepted the White House's desire to keep the shot "low key" so as to avoid political repercussions.[14]

Assuming Rusk would endorse the test, the AEC began preparations for a January 24 detonation. However, this left the problem of justifying Cabriolet under the LTBT. Spurgeon Keeny, a member of the NSC who had previously opposed Cabriolet but had changed his mind, engaged in intense lobbying to bring ACDA and the State Department around to the idea that the explosion posed no treaty violation. With all parties in agreement, Rusk, who "didn't understand why he was given the 'veto' over Cabriolet," agreed to the date. With that, the AEC began to emplace the device. The delays, removal of the explosive, and reemplacement had turned an experiment originally estimated at about $2.7 million to one that cost the AEC $5 million.[15]

Detonated on January 26 at a depth of 170 feet, Cabriolet threw debris nearly two thousand feet into the air and left behind a crater about 360 feet wide and 120 feet deep. To the AEC's delight, about 95 percent of the radioactivity was trapped inside the crater, while the greatest amount of fallout reported was well below danger levels. Seaborg commented that the wind that day was "perfect," while "a snowstorm in northern Nevada apparently brought much of the debris down." Though scientists following the radioactive cloud believed it crossed from North Dakota into Canada about thirty-two hours after the test, there was no evidence that the Canadians, who had received advance word of the shot, could demonstrate that any radioactivity they detected conclusively came from Cabriolet. Iodine-131 appeared in only "trace amounts," and there was no way to prove that what iodine did exist was a result of Cabriolet.[16] For the AEC, the test was a complete success and proof of its ability to conduct nuclear excavation with fallout so small that no one could accuse the United States of violating the test ban treaty. The AEC now hoped for quick authorization of Project Buggy.

Project Buggy

Project Buggy was a row-charge experiment, in which the AEC would set off five 1.1-kiloton nuclear explosives placed in a line and in close proximity to one another. The AEC anticipated the result would be a channel. Apparently this blast traced back to Sedan, from which the AEC concluded that nuclear excavation, whether individually or in a row, could work. It would be safe to assume, however, that the AEC also relied on its planning for Chariot, which itself had called for creation of a channel using a queue of explosives. Assuming Buggy took place without incident, the Commission planned to follow it with the 100-kiloton Schooner experiment; Buggy II, another row-charge test using explosives in the ten- to twenty-kiloton range that, if all went well, would link up to the channel Buggy was to create; Galley, yet another row-charge shot using five to ten explosives of an even larger size; and then an unnamed experiment. Thus each blast would be progressively larger than the one before it. What the final experiment might entail was not clear. Since the early 1960s, though, the AEC had been planning a shot called Phaeton, which would extend cratering data to the megaton range.[17] As the canal construction program called for megaton-size devices, this experiment certainly was one possibility for that last test.

In October 1966, as planning for Cabriolet continued, Seaborg asked for authorization to begin "non-committal preparatory work" on Buggy, but Rostow did not believe Johnson would give consideration to any shots beyond Cabriolet. And there was the matter of cost. The AEC chair tried to allay the latter concern, pointing out that his agency had already appropriated the necessary $2.4 million. He desired a positive decision by November 15, thereby allowing the AEC to make the necessary preparations for a March 1967 blast. Instead he heard nothing. Disappointed, he wrote in his journal on November 21 that Buggy had been "disapproved for execution next spring by default." As the shot now could not take place until the coming fall to avoid the grazing season, Keeny told the Bureau of the Budget not to allocate any money for Buggy until Cabriolet's results became known.[18]

Cabriolet became the catch for Buggy. Since Toboggan in 1958 the AEC had conducted other row-charge experiments using high-explosive charges, among them Pre-Buggy I and II and Dugout. Those tests had convinced the AEC it could indeed build a ditch using nuclear explosives. There was an important difference, though: high-explosive devices did not release radioactivity or risk a violation of the test ban treaty. The president had asked lawmakers to retain money in the FY 1967 and 1968 budgets for both Cabriolet and Buggy, but without proof provided by Cabriolet that it was possible to conduct a nuclear excavation experiment without causing the international repercussions of Palanquin, there was little chance of White House approval for Buggy. As Foster and the ACDA explained in April 1967, "Since BUGGY will involve several times as much venting as CABRIOLET, it raises the same problems in more acute form."[19]

After Cabriolet occurred without a hitch, the AEC asked for the right to proceed with Buggy. "It is the AEC's judgment," W. E. Johnson, the Commission's acting chair, wrote, "that the probability of Buggy-I behaving like Palanquin is extremely low." As with Cabriolet, the AEC warned that as much as 20 percent of the radioactivity produced could return as fallout, but, and again as before, it regarded that estimate as high. Still, the agency felt it wise to err on the side of caution "because there has been no previous experience with row craters." Nor did the AEC anticipate problems with milk contamination. "Assuming cows are not foraging, iodine in milk at the nearest ranches" would fall within safe levels.[20]

Charles Weaver warned that the AEC's assumption was just that. The director of the Department of Health, Education, and Welfare's Environmental Surveillance and Control Program, Weaver pointed out that "under certain meteorological conditions, it is possible that a situation could occur that would require some degree of protective action with regard to iodine levels in milk at nearby ranches." That admonition caused yet another intra-administration dispute. Both the Environmental Science Services Administration—a body created in 1965 that combined the Weather Bureau and the Coast and Geodetic Survey—and the Air Force Technical Applications Center disagreed with "the AEC's meteorological analysis." With the apparent lack of consensus among Washington officials and with the AEC desirous to conduct the experiment prior to the grazing season, the president again asked for the views of State, Defense, ACDA, and the Canal Commission.[21]

As had happened with Cabriolet, outside considerations became apparent. Key was the NPT negotiations. On January 18 the superpowers presented to the ENDC matching drafts of a revised NPT. Article III was no longer blank; it made the IAEA the ultimate guarantor of upholding the treaty's provisions, but to please Euratom it called on the IAEA "to negotiate agreements with individual states or groups of states in order to satisfy itself that agreed safeguards are effective." The treaty included as well three new articles. Nonnuclear states had complained that the previous draft had unfairly denied them "the benefits of peaceful nuclear explosions." That accusation, combined with the AEC's long-standing desire to offer peaceful atomic services, had led to Article V. It exhorted countries with nuclear devices to provide, "under appropriate international observation and through international procedures, potential benefits from any peaceful applications of nuclear explosions . . . to non-nuclear weapon States Party to the Treaty on a non-discriminatory basis." Article VI called on signatories to continue efforts at disarmament, and Article VII urged nations to come together and establish nuclear-free zones.[22]

While many countries regarded the revised draft as a step forward, it was not good enough for others. Brazil, India, and Sweden charged that Article III was still discriminatory, for it targeted only nonnuclear powers. Brazil and India also disparaged Article V, for if they signed the treaty, they would not have the right to develop their own nuclear explosives for peaceful purposes. Canada and Sweden, while less critical of Article V, wanted the IAEA to oversee any agreement by a nuclear state to provide peaceful-use services to a nonnuclear country.[23]

Looking at this situation, Foster argued against approving Buggy. Just because Cabriolet had not vented much radiation, Buggy might, especially considering that Buggy proposed using not one but five explosives, each of them of greater power than employed in Cabriolet. The consequence would be detectable fallout over Canada and accusations that the United States had violated the LTBT. "Such charges would, among other consequences," he insisted, "have a decidedly adverse impact on our efforts to secure acceptance of a non-proliferation treaty."[24]

Unlike Cabriolet, Buggy received support from most of President Johnson's top aides. Deputy Secretary of Defense Cyrus Vance's successor, Paul Nitze, believed Cabriolet demonstrated that Buggy could take place safely. Katzenbach acknowledged the possibility of an angry Canadian response but asserted, "The timing from an international standpoint is about as good as we expect to have." The expectation was for the draft NPT to reach the UN General Assembly shortly after it began deliberations in April, so if the United States could hold the shot before then, it would "have breathing space before the debate begins." For Anderson, Buggy was necessary for the Canal Commission to determine the feasibility of nuclear excavation of a sea-level waterway. Additionally it would assist his effort to get Congress to extend his reporting deadline. After considering the various points of view, Johnson approved the shot.[25]

Following a delay because of "unfavorable weather," Buggy took place on March 12 in an area made of basalt. Coincidentally this was a day after Washington and Moscow submitted their joint treaty to the ENDC. The five explosives, buried 135 feet underground at 150-foot intervals, left a channel 75 feet deep, just over 300 feet wide, and 930 feet long, or approximately what the AEC had predicted. The Commission learned from the test that it could space explosives farther apart than originally believed, which meant using fewer devices in the building of a canal and a lower construction cost. In other good news, only about 1 percent of the radioactivity was released as fallout. However, because of unforeseen meteorological conditions, the wind blew the radioactive cloud produced by the blast in a more northerly direction than had been anticipated. Less than four days after the explosion, the cloud crossed into Canada from Michigan, though by then the amount of radioactivity had dissipated to some extent. "We plan to await a Canadian response—if any," Rostow told the president, "and play it cool." Once again nothing came from Ottawa. "This is a very successful shot," Seaborg wrote in his journal ten days after Buggy, "and gave no test ban problems, despite the almost endless concern about it and Cabriolet in ACDA and State Department."[26]

Stimulation

The international quiescence experienced after Cabriolet and Buggy matched a lack of domestic reaction to Gasbuggy and gave the AEC, LRL, and their allies all the more reason to believe the Plowshare program might yet prove its value. The biggest concern with Gasbuggy was not that it might release radioactivity, for the device would be buried deep underground, thereby containing the explosion. Rather it was whether the blast might make the gas radioactive. If the AEC could not guarantee the gas was 100 percent free of radioactivity, would homeowners accept the idea of using it, no matter how cheap it was?

Norman and Jon Carlisle, writing for the monthly magazine *Popular Mechanics*, believed they had the answer. Thirty-nine million homes in the nation used natural gas, they wrote, and the gas stimulated by a nuclear explosive (or NE, as they put it), was far cheaper than that stimulated using conventional methods. "NE offers a bigger bang for the buck. . . . Producing one million B.T.U. with TNT costs $250. A giant economy size NE blast (bigger than Gasbuggy) can produce the same amount of energy for as little as 75 cents!" But what about radioactivity? "The experts say there's no chance of any radioactive gas reaching your furnace," the Carlisles argued. Yet other media outlets had quoted officials from LRL admitting that the blast would contaminate the gas with tritium, a radioactive hydrogen isotope with a half-life of about twelve years that is easily ingested into the body through water or air and can cause cancer. The nuclear explosive would also produce krypton-85, a radioactive gas with a half-life of almost eleven years. It is possible that the Carlisles had such reports in mind, for in the same article they qualified themselves: The experts "estimate that half of the remaining activity will be drawn off when they extract the first chimney full of gas," and that level of radioactivity would be further reduced by mixing the nuclear-stimulated gas with gas not produced by atomic blasting.[27] In other words, rather than guaranteeing "no chance," the Carlisles admitted that some radioactivity might enter a person's home. Would even a minute amount of radioactivity be too much for the average consumer? This the authors did not address.

Glenn Werth, the associate director of LRL-L, had answered this question, or so he thought. "Gas stimulation continues to be a promising application of nuclear explosives," he wrote Kelly in February 1967, "but the tritium contamination produced by thermonuclear explosives remains a problem with respect to household consumption, even with drying, dilution with other gas, and allowing for dilution from burning." The only options, he concluded, were either "all fission systems"—for fission produced less tritium than fusion—"or the use of existing thermonuclear explosives with utilization of the gas in central power or other industrial plans until the radioactivity has dropped to satisfactory levels."[28] But here was the rub: what constituted a "satisfactory" level to the AEC might not for the public.

And there was a final question. Even if Gasbuggy proved completely successful, including a public willingness to use the gas produced, was it economical? The Carlisles said it was; others were not so sure. To get access to the entire 317 trillion cubic feet of reserves in question required some "44,400 U.S. wells similar to Gasbuggy," observed *U.S. News and World Report*. "To be commercially profitable," though, "atomic shots would have to cost not more than a half million dollars each, industry experts say," or one-ninth the price of Gasbuggy.[29] This, of course, did not take into account other potential costs, such as damage caused by seismic shock or, worse, the impact of fallout in the event of accidental venting.

In September the AEC led a symposium in Farmington, New Mexico, on Gasbuggy attended by about 550 locals and visitors, including Vladimir Shmelev of the Soviet Union. The plan was to hold the shot the next month. However, a delay moved the blast date from mid-October to mid-November. Then leakage of water into the emplacement hole moved the AEC to push the execution date back again, this time to December 6. But on December 3 an electrical short "put a refrigeration unit in the bomb canister out of commission"; as a result the heat in the canister rose, which threatened to cause the explosive to act differently than anticipated. Not until December 10 did the shot, equivalent to twenty-six kilotons of TNT, take place. Watching from nearly six miles to the north, the invited observers felt two shock waves, at least one of which was strong enough to cut a phone line to a trailer six miles south of the shot's epicenter. In Farmington, located fifty-five miles away, residents noticed windows shaking in homes and buildings.[30]

It appeared that all had gone as planned, and in essence it had. EPNG workers had "physically cut apart all gas pipelines within a five-mile radius" of the blast site, preventing any possibility of a leak or explosion. Though "a shower of rocks fell from the ceiling of the Anvil Points oil-shale mine near Rifle, Colorado," some two hundred miles away from ground zero, it was not clear whether the two events were related. More ominous, and unbeknown to the observers and

Figure 6. Emplacement of the Gasbuggy device. Photo courtesy of Los Alamos National Laboratory.

the media, was that the test had nearly released radioactivity into the air. Eight hours after the shot took place the AEC detected radioactive xenon and krypton gas at the surface. The insulation in one of the holes containing an electric cable had failed to provide a solid seal. AEC officials had to cut the cable and seal the hole. There were four other holes that the AEC believed might pose a similar problem, so they were closed as well.[31]

Not only had the AEC prevented any significant release of radioactivity, but all of the initial results of Gasbuggy looked promising. The blast had created a chimney just over 150 feet in diameter and 333 feet high and fractured rock some 440 feet from the epicenter, or about what the scientists had predicted, creating approximately 2 million cubic feet of space for the gas to enter. Samples of the gas sent to LRL-L found that "concentrations of radioactivity measured . . . were lower than anticipated." Impressed with the results, a number of companies, including Holmes and Narver, Gulf General Atomics, and Du Pont, contacted the AEC about using Plowshare for their own projects. A proud Gerald Johnson wrote the AEC's Willard Libby, "I believe it is obvious that Gasbuggy established an important precedent for industrial leadership for Plowshare."[32]

But the initial findings proved misleading. A month after the test scientists drilled into the cavity to take another gas sample, in the process releasing a significant amount of radioactivity into the atmosphere. The state of the gas itself was not promising. Whereas normal natural gas is 99 percent hydrocarbon, which allows it to burn easily, the explosion had changed its composition, reducing it to just over 41 percent hydrocarbon. Much of the remainder was noncombustible carbon dioxide. This meant that the heat generated by one gallon of Gasbuggy gas was far less than from one gallon of normal gas. Even more alarming, the gas was radioactive. Fusion explosives create tritium, which, because it is a form of hydrogen, easily bonds with natural gas. The *Washington Post* reported in November 1968 that rather than containing a small amount of radioactivity, the gas was "contaminated with so much radioactive tritium that it is not commercially saleable." It was "more tritium than you'd want to breathe," Kelly admitted, and making the gas usable would require "expensive treatment." Kelly considered it possible to find a cheaper solution, but Sam Smith of EPNG was more doubtful: "I think it will take four or five more experiments, or at least two or three, to establish [the] feasibility [of nuclear stimulation]." But that would require at the very least the development of cleaner nuclear explosives, an expensive proposition in itself.[33]

Another problem, which Kelly failed to mention, concerned flaring. To get rid of the tritium required burning off the radioactive gas. This had three results. First, it wasted gas that might otherwise have been used had it not been contaminated. Second, even after months of flaring, the gas had reached only 75 percent hydrocarbon. Third, the burning process turned the gas into radioactive water, which could enter the environment. A U.S. Public Health Service report concluded that "radioactivity in vegetation downwind from Gasbuggy was increased by 10 times" as a result of the flaring.[34]

Despite the clear problems with Gasbuggy, the AEC and its allies sought to justify their work. It was true, Kelly conceded, that even if EPNG could have sold the gas produced by the blast, it could not have recouped the money spent. Gasbuggy, though, "was purely an experiment," one designed to see if it was possible to stimulate gas production in an effort to meet the nation's energy needs rather than actually sell it, so the cost was justifiable. The American Gas Association also emphasized the positive, pointing out in May 1969 that the well at the Gasbuggy site had produced gas for a period of two weeks in July 1968 and continuously since November of that year. During that period, "231 million cubic feet of gas have been produced and flared," which was "more gas than was recovered from five of the eight wells within 1¼ miles of Gasbuggy during their production history of 8 to 11 years."[35]

If anything, it appeared for the moment that luck was on the side of Plowshare. The national media, apparently finding underground nuclear tests so commonplace as to lack newsworthiness, took virtually no interest in the shot. Even locally there had been little public outcry. Downwind from Gasbuggy were no watersheds or milk-producing sites and very few people, so there was little reason to anticipate complaints. The only damage definitely attributable to Gasbuggy was "a few minor cracks in the dirt access road, a bent axle to a cable reel, and modest damage to some electrical equipment at the control point." Gas wells in the area came away unscathed. Simply put, the AEC could sell Gasbuggy as a significant achievement. This was vital, commented the *Wall Street Journal's* Herbert Lawson, for congressional support for other Plowshare projects, among them Bronco, Dragon Trail, Sloop, and Ketch, "hinges a great deal upon Gasbuggy's success."[36]

Like Gasbuggy, Bronco was a stimulation project but one aimed in this case at oil shale. The AEC's determination to prove the atom's ability to increase oil supplies dated back to the collapse of Project Oilsands. Since then the Commission had searched for a similar project and came to focus on the Green River Formation, which bordered western Colorado and Wyoming and eastern Utah. Estimates placed the amount of oil shale there at some 480 billion barrels. In 1964 the AEC began to search for a site and in October 1967, in conjunction with CER Geonuclear, settled on a plot of land near the town of Rifle, Colorado. By burying a fifty-kiloton explosive 3,350 feet underground, the Commission anticipated creation of a chimney 230 feet across and over 500 feet high that could hold about 1.3 million tons of shale, the equivalent of approximately 750,000 barrels of oil.[37]

In July 1968 CER Geonuclear, the AEC, and the Department of Interior accepted a draft contract by which the oil companies involved would pay for the entire $18 million price tag, minus the cost of the explosive. The firms involved did not like the terms and began withdrawing their support. Marathon Oil's W. H. Barlow, for instance, concluded that the recent discovery of promising reserves in Alaska offered greater financial returns, and H. Pforzheimer of Sohio Petroleum called the price tag "six times as much as we had expected."[38] Lacking the necessary industrial support, the AEC gave up on Bronco.

Nor did the Commission have any luck with Dragon Trail. First proposed by CONOCO in July 1966, Dragon Trail called for setting off a twenty-six-kiloton device about 2,700 feet underground in the Douglas Creek Gas Field, located about fifty miles north of Grand Junction, Colorado. This time industry would assume about 60 percent of the shot's $2.5 million cost. A lack of government funding, combined with a desire to assess the Gasbuggy experiment, continued to push back Dragon Trail's execution. Finally, in May 1969, CONOCO withdrew from the project because of the cost of drilling, a determination that the reserves in the area were smaller than anticipated, and a feeling that Gasbuggy and a shot then under preparation, called Rulison, could answer any questions Dragon Trail might have provided.[39]

Storage

The negative turn of events for the gas- and oil-stimulation program matched that for Project Ketch. One concern for the AEC was funding. The Vietnam War had begun to take so much money out of the U.S. Treasury that the Commission wondered if it could appropriate any dollars to Ketch. It hoped for a more favorable turn in the conflict in Southeast Asia, which "might allow for the reallocation for funds for this item. Funds might also become available from related activities such as the Appalachian Region Development Act and from the Federal Power Commission."[40]

Then there was the response to the feasibility study, which Columbia Gas Company and the AEC completed in July 1967. Because of the remote location, they did not anticipate any serious problems from seismic shock. The explosive would be placed "2,000 feet below the depth of the nearest known aquifer," making contamination of groundwater unlikely. Nor was atmospheric contamination a worry because of the depth of burial. This left radioactivity in the gas placed within the storage facility, but that too was discounted, for diluting the contaminated gas with radioactive-free gas would bring the radioactivity down to a safe level prior to use by consumers.[41]

The feasibility study also made clear that the AEC and Columbia envisioned Ketch as the first of many such explosions: "Assuming the average nuclear reservoir to be one produced by a 50-kiloton detonation with a capacity to handle 875 million cubic feet of annual turnover gas, this would indicate a need for 1,115 new nuclear storage reservoirs," most of them in Pennsylvania. "In the seven years through 1975, if full saturation were attempted, an average of about 160 nuclear storage fields per year would be required, provided suitable locations could be found."[42]

What made this study important was not that it determined the project was feasible. It was its emphasis. When it first proposed Ketch to Pennsylvania state officials, the AEC had pointed to the economic value offered by the project. But in January 1967, prior to the leak by the *Pittsburgh Press*, the Commission had decided instead to focus "on the technical feasibility aspects rather than the economic aspects." Pennsylvanians had to wonder therefore why they should endorse a project that offered them no benefit.[43]

That the Commission seemed unable to settle on Ketch's purpose only intensified the grassroots campaign against it. The environmental movement, now in full swing, had made Americans all the more sensitive to the long-standing warnings about fallout. "These people are crazy," commented Ernest Sternglass, a professor of radiological physics at the University of Pittsburgh, on learning about Ketch. Despite promises of safety, he pointed out, there was always the possibility of an accident. "This is the heart of dairy country. Millions of curies of radioactive iodine would poison the milk all the way up to New England, all the way to New York, Washington, down to Philadelphia. This is madness."[44]

A month before the release of their feasibility study, and in an attempt to convince dissenters, the AEC and Columbia held a public meeting in Harrisburg that state officials also attended. The Commission assured those present that it had ample experience in safely conducting underground nuclear blasts. State authorities, including Governor Raymond P. Shafer, offered to permit the first phase of the project, which entailed an evaluation of the site, to continue. However, Shafer insisted on having the right to veto the project prior to execution if his aides determined it unsafe. Whether in fact the state could put a stop to the project was questionable, at least from the viewpoint of the AEC. Following a meeting with Commission authorities, a state legal aide wrote, "The AEC desired no restrictions upon their operations; particularly, those pertaining to conservation and pollution, save what they themselves would impose."[45]

To state residents, it did not matter whether Harrisburg could put a stop to Ketch. The number of protesters grew. With 1968 being an election year, a group formed in the state called "People against Ketch." Claiming over a hundred members, this organization sent letters and petitions to lawmakers and newspaper editors, gave speeches, and provided testimony to Pennsylvania and U.S. governmental officers. Though Shafer, a Republican, was not up for reelection until 1970, Democrats saw Ketch as an opportunity to gain political points. Milton Shapp, the Democratic candidate for governor in 1966, publicly spoke out against the blast, as did the party's state congressional candidate for the district that included Centre County, the home of State College and Penn State. This is not to say that Republicans supported Ketch. Many Pennsylvanians in the region had personal reasons for seeking the blast's cancellation, and so opponents included people from all political orientations. The coal industry, not wanting to compete against natural gas, let alone gas paid for in part with taxpayer funds, joined the chorus.[46]

The AEC took notice. "At present," Kelly wrote the AEC's commissioners in June, "there is a very vocal and somewhat organized opposition to Project Ketch being expressed through some local central Pennsylvania news media and in correspondence and petitions to State officials." Even so, "Columbia Gas officials have assured us that the company is resolute in its decision to conduct Phase I with full awareness of the possibility that the Governor may disapprove Phase II." The company's vice president for engineering and research, Sy Orlofsky, tried to restore public confidence in the project by returning to the theme of economic benefit. Speaking before an audience at Lock Haven State College in February, he explained that a growing U.S. population meant a greater demand for energy. Ketch could help meet that need in the region while simultaneously bringing jobs and millions of dollars in investment to Pennsylvania. In a further effort to stress the shot's economic worth, Columbia paid for an advertisement entitled "Dress Mom with the Money You Save with Gas." In cartoon-like drawings the company proclaimed that "by using gas instead of electricity," a woman could save enough money to purchase a new hat, coat, dress, and shoes.[47] The campaign to change opinions failed. Many Pennsylvanians, already worried about the possibility of fallout, saw little reason to trust an agency and a company that seemed to change their story as to whom the blast would help. In the face of such strong opposition, Columbia's resolution buckled, and in July 1968 it withdrew its request to proceed with Ketch in Pennsylvania.[48]

This was not the final nail in Ketch's coffin, for Columbia Gas and the AEC hoped to find another locale for the shot. Both Kentucky and West Virginia showed an interest, and planning for the blast continued. It also appears that Ketch became entwined with Election Day, for in October the AEC instructed its Nevada Operations Office as well as LRL not to "participate or encourage visits to potential Ketch sites until November 5, 1968," which was that month's first Tuesday. Yet after Election Day no takers made themselves apparent.[49]

This left Sloop and Aquarius. Here the AEC could point to progress, albeit slow. With the feasibility study concluding that Sloop was both possible and safe, the Commission led a public hearing on October 1, 1967, near the proposed blast site, in Safford, Arizona, where it reassured residents who raised concerns regarding damage to buildings by seismic shock and contamination of local water supplies. The AEC, the U.S. Bureau of Mines, and Livermore spent the following year

developing a technical plan for the blast and made a number of recommendations, such as the need for comprehensive hydrological studies. To conduct such
studies, the AEC decided the postpone Sloop to fiscal year 1970.[50]

Arizona was also the state where Aquarius was to take place. Interested in applying Plowshare technology to water storage, that state's Atomic Energy Commission funded research at the University of Arizona to identify specific projects. In October 1967 the university researchers presented their findings to LRL,
the AEC's San Francisco Office, and the Nevada Operations Office. They suggested two types of projects: surface reservoirs and underground aquifers. While
the state preferred the latter, viewing it as compatible with the Central Arizona
Water Project, LRL preferred the former, regarding it as "most practical."[51] It is
significant that Livermore suggested a surface reservoir, which risked a release of
radioactivity into the atmosphere and a violation of the LTBT. The likely explanation is that LRL believed such a project was legal under a liberal interpretation
of the test ban treaty.

Impressed by the report, in May 1968 Governor Jack R. Williams of Arizona
contacted Seaborg and Secretary of the Interior Stewart Udall and expressed his
interest in Aquarius. The following month federal and state officials, including
representatives from the AEC, the Arizona AEC, LRL, the U.S. Geological Survey, and U.S. Public Health Service, gathered in Phoenix. It was here that Aquarius got its name from the mythological water-bearer. The attendees agreed to
begin a study to consider the feasibility of the project, its cost as compared to
using conventional methods, and possible locations where the blast might take
place. The intention was to complete the study by the middle of 1969.[52]

The NPT, the Canal, and Schooner

Much faster progress took place in Geneva. In an attempt to guarantee passage
of their draft NPT by the UN, the Soviet Union and the United States made further changes to it. On March 11, 1968, they resubmitted it to the ENDC, which,
on April 24, sent it to the UN General Assembly. Despite criticism from India,
Brazil, Pakistan, South Africa, and others, the treaty received a largely positive
response. Seeking as wide support as possible, Mexico proposed revising Article
V to read that nuclear states had to offer to nonnuclear states " 'under appropriate international observation and through appropriate international procedures,' the potential benefits from any peaceful nuclear explosion." Nonnuclear
nations would receive "such benefits, pursuant to a special international agreement or agreements [and] through an appropriate international body with adequate representation of non-nuclear-weapon States." The wording pleased most

countries, and on June 12 the General Assembly voted ninety-five to four, with twenty-one abstentions, in favor of the NPT.[53] When opened for signature on July 1, over sixty nations, including the United States, promised to adhere to its provisions.

For the Atomic Energy Commission, passage of the NPT by the majority of the nations of the world offered a boon for Plowshare. The Commission had argued for years that providing peaceful-use services to nonnuclear nations might convince them not to try to develop their own atomic explosives, thereby benefiting nonproliferation efforts and protecting U.S. security. Now it had an international agreement obliging the United States to offer those very services to other countries. Of course, what would help even more was some kind of project that might prove Plowshare's usefulness. The Commission had several on the books, but none was more important than the isthmian canal. Completing the requisite experiments to determine the feasibility of nuclear excavation of such a waterway had just achieved a new level of urgency.

Indeed the canal had become so central to the work of the AEC and its attendant labs that they all but ignored reports suggesting that even if a sea-level canal received the necessary approvals, constructing it was far more problematic than originally anticipated. Major William Wray of the Army Corps of Engineers warned that the field studies along the Sasardi-Morti (route 17) found the clay so unstable that megaton-size blasts would cause already completed portions of the channel to collapse. The yearly monsoon season would only add to the waterway's instability. Furthermore the Canal Study Commission found evidence that air blast along the Darien route would break windows in Costa Rica and Colombia, and the seismic shock from the explosions would create earthquakes comparable to an 8 on the Richter scale, damage buildings in countries as distant as Ecuador, and add nearly $220 million to the total cost of excavation.[54] The Canal Commission could look toward Colombia as an alternative, but U.S. officials had already told Panama that they wanted to see the canal built in Panama. Moreover constructing a canal in Colombia raised similar problems, such as air blast and seismic shock. Myopically focused on the canal and the program to which they had devoted so much time and resources, however, Plowshare scientists cared only about completing the requisite experiments. For them, June brought more good news. Since 1967 Senator Anderson had tried to get the House to accept the Senate's offer to give the Canal Commission more money and until December 1970 to issue its report. In June 1968 lawmakers approved the reporting date and an additional $6.5 million.[55]

Having additional appropriations and time to complete its list of experiments, the AEC turned its attention to Schooner. The project had undergone changes since first proposed several years earlier. Originally it was to be a 100-kiloton explosion in Idaho. By 1968 the AEC had redesigned it as a forty-kiloton test set for execution at the NTS. Moving the shot farther south made sense, as there was general agreement that it would vent, with some of the radioactivity crossing the U.S.-Canadian border and risking an LTBT violation. The farther south the shot, the more time for any fallout to dissipate before it reached Canada. Another reason for relocating the blast was to avoid radioactivity falling on area ranches and causing a spike in iodine-131 levels in milk.[56]

In June Seaborg requested presidential approval of Bowline I, a series of blasts that included Schooner and another project named Stoddard. The latter, a thirty-one-kiloton explosive the AEC planned to bury 1,535 feet underground at the NTS had, like Switch, the purpose of creating a cleaner explosive. Assuming Stoddard worked, the AEC could then use the device in Schooner. As a result Schooner would release less radioactivity than previous blasts and limit the likelihood of international or domestic repercussions. Proceeding with Schooner, commented Seaborg, was essential. It would add to the AEC's knowledge on cratering experiments, in this case, experiments in hard rock at a magnitude higher than Cabriolet. Such data were "of particular importance to the Atlantic-Pacific Interoceanic Canal Study Commission since construction of a sea-level transisthmian canal by nuclear means would require higher yields." It would also prove useful should a harbor project be proposed in another nation. "Schooner, in extending nuclear excavation technology to higher yields, would thus also be in keeping with U.S. policy supporting the Non-Proliferation Treaty."[57]

Conducting Stoddard, which by all expectations would be fully contained, was one thing. Schooner, which by its nature would release radioactivity into the environment, was another. President Johnson, whose popularity had plummeted because of the war in Vietnam, had decided not to run for reelection. Vice President Humphrey therefore stepped into the ring and ran for the Democratic Party's nomination. Rostow, realizing that Schooner "might cause domestic problems" for the administration and Humphrey's bid, told Seaborg not to include Schooner in Bowline I but to request approval for that blast separately. On receiving the requests, President Johnson authorized Stoddard but not Schooner.[58]

Stoddard successfully took place on September 17. With proof that the clean Stoddard device worked, Seaborg requested presidential approval for another series of tests, called Bowline II, which included Schooner. Realizing the risk of radioactivity falling on Canadian soil, the AEC said it would wait to hold the blast until favorable meteorological conditions presented themselves and cattle were not grazing to avoid iodine-131 contamination of milk. Yet on the latter score the AEC admitted, "Under certain meteorological conditions it is possible that a situation could occur that would require some degree of protective action." Despite the risks, Rostow recommended green-lighting the blast. Foster resisted, fearing a possible LTBT violation. Johnson sided with his ACDA head.[59] He did not want to authorize a shot that might infuriate Canada, contaminate milk supplies, and cost Democrats in the upcoming election.

On October 16 Seaborg made still another approach. The deadline for the Canal Commission report was two years away, he emphasized. "Conduct of Schooner in the November–December 1968 time is necessary to maintain the schedule established for the [canal] program and the necessary tests." The AEC had tentatively set the experiment for November 21, weather conditions permitting. It had the necessary funding to cover the cost of the shot. What it needed was "execution authority about two weeks in advance."[60]

For the most part, key administration figures backed Seaborg. Katzenbach concluded that although there was a possibility of detection by Canada, the AEC planned to take precautions to prevent that from happening. He pointed out as well the importance of Schooner to the Canal Commission's work. Hornig seconded Katzenbach. "I am informed," he wrote, "that there has been some relaxation in the reporting standards of the U.S. and Canadian Public Health Services so that compared to previous tests the net probability of reported detection of low levels of radioactivity has been reduced." Granted, it was hard to ensure the weather conditions on the day of execution would be such to eliminate the possibility of detection. Further, the AEC still had tests to conduct after Schooner, "including much larger ones," prior to presenting its findings to the Canal Commission. Despite these issues, Hornig concluded, "[Finding] no new basis to question the desirability of proceeding with Project SCHOONER, I would recommend approval of the blast." The Department of Defense, the Joint Chiefs of Staff, and the Bureau of the Budget either registered approval or did not object. The one significant dissenter was Foster, who concluded that despite the promised precautions, Schooner still offered too great a risk that the United States would be charged with violating the LTBT: "Such charges would, among other consequences, have a decidedly adverse impact on our efforts to secure adherence to the Non-Proliferation Treaty." Based on the response, Rostow recommended on November 16 that Johnson approve the blast, which the president did that same day.[61] Unstated was that the presidential election was over, thereby eliminating it as a consideration.

Postponed for several days because of the weather, the AEC set off Schooner on December 8. Exploding with a force of thirty-five kilotons, it shot a cloud of radioactive dust twenty thousand feet into the air and left behind a crater 725 feet wide and 250 feet deep, making it second only to Sedan in size. The AEC declared that most of the radioactivity fell within the blast site. While aircraft following the dust cloud as it headed over Utah, Idaho, Wyoming, and southern Montana found radioactivity seventy miles from ground zero, the U.S. Air Force and U.S. Public Health Service officials onboard the planes concluded it was "far below 'tolerable levels.'" Moreover most of the radioactivity consisted of tungsten-187, an isotope with a half-life of only one day. While Canadian authorities detected an increase in radioactivity, there was not enough evidence to ascribe it to the blast. Wrote Seaborg in his journal, "[Schooner] was very successful and there seems to be no danger of violating the Limited Test Ban Treaty."[62]

Or so Seaborg believed. On January 21, 1969, the Soviets' acting chargé d'affaires, Yuri Chernyakov, delivered to the U.S. government an aide-mémoire citing a "2 to fivefold increase in . . . fallout" in portions of the Soviet Union and charging that Schooner possibly had violated the LTBT. While the United States denied any violation, Seaborg explained to Robert Ellsworth, aide to the recently elected president, Richard Nixon, that the amount cited by the Soviets was "absurdly small . . . and one that in [his] opinion was never intended to represent a violation of the Test Ban Treaty." Assuming that the Soviets' "detection techniques" were similar to those of the United States, what Moscow charged as a violation was about "0.1 picocuries per cubic meter," far less than "the hundreds of picocuries per cubic meter" normally found in the air. Moscow had also conducted tests that Washington could charge as LTBT violations. The problem was that the United States announced its tests in advance, giving the Soviet Union time to set up equipment to detect any increase in radioactivity. What was needed, said Seaborg, was to develop with the Soviets a more reasonable "interpretation of the Limited Test Ban Treaty with respect to Plowshare excavation experiments."[63]

The fact was that the superpowers had yet to agree on such an interpretation, and in that respect the Soviets' response should have been a warning. The AEC had to complete more experiments to obtain all of the data it needed for the Canal Commission. Those tests would include larger explosives, certain to release even more radioactivity and to generate additional, if not more vehement, charges of LTBT violations. If the AEC somehow avoided that minefield of troubles, there were still the multiple blasts needed for construction of a canal, assuming the Canal Commission approved that option. In this respect Seaborg's argument that nuclear excavation of an isthmian waterway was an unlikely proposition under the test ban treaty remained as valid in 1969 as it had in 1963.

Yet Another Setback?

Complicating matters was a change of government in Panama. In May 1968 Arnulfo Arias emerged as the victor of that nation's election, only to find himself overthrown in October by his military. The new ruling junta, led by Lieutenant Colonel Omar Torrijos, promised elections in 1970. The White House could do little. Nixon's accession to the presidency created an administration with its own priorities. It was not likely the new government in Panama intended to ratify the existing treaties. Assuming that Nixon sought to negotiate a new agreement, it was questionable whether Torrijos wanted to do so. The best advice the outgoing Johnson administration could suggest to its successor was to "leave to Panama the initiative in seeking new treaty talks and enter into such talks only with the understanding that they are preliminary in nature, pending the 1970 elections promised by the junta."[64]

The uncertainty surrounding U.S.-Panamanian relations only added to the existing uncertainty encompassing the Plowshare program. Gasbuggy had shown promise for atomically stimulating natural gas production, but it was not clear whether customers would purchase a product that was even slightly radioactive. Sloop and Aquarius were under way, yet neither was close to the execution stage. While the Nuclear Nonproliferation Treaty had formally countenanced the idea of offering peaceful-use services to nonnuclear countries, the Limited Test Ban Treaty made the AEC wonder if it could meet the Canal Commission's looming 1970 deadline.

The AEC, though, had a potential ace up its sleeve. Seaborg had mentioned that Schooner's data could prove useful should another nation request help in constructing a harbor. In fact just before 1968 came to an end, the AEC received a request from Australia to consider nuclear excavation of a harbor. The construction of a usable port Down Under might just prove to Plowshare's doubters the potential of the peaceful atom and give the AEC the data it needed for the canal project.

Plowshare Goes Down Under

"What specific potential applications of nuclear excavation technology have been identified?" asked an internal AEC memorandum in the fall of 1966. The answer included projects of various sizes, among them Carryall and the sea-level isthmian waterway. Yet the number of projects for which the AEC considered use of the atom was incredible. The memorandum listed more than 110 possibilities, over half of them outside the United States, ranging from building canals in Canada and Malaysia, harbors and dams in the Somali Republic and India, and roads in Colombia and Chile to eliminating a waterfall in Bolivia, removing rapids from a river in Brazil, and draining swamps in South Korea.[1]

The AEC had reason to conjure up such an enormous list. It was not just because the Commission and its attendant labs believed so strongly in the better world the peaceful atom could create. In the years after Plowshare's inception officials from France, the United Kingdom, Israel, Romania, Thailand, the United Arab Republic (UAR), and Indonesia all had expressed interest in Plowshare. France, for instance, had suggested construction of a harbor in northern Africa, the UAR had asked about building a ditch between the Qattara Depression in northwestern Egypt and the Mediterranean Sea to produce power, and Thailand's minister for national development Pote Sarasin had proposed using nuclear explosives to mine lignite. During discussions at the ENDC, India, Sweden, Mexico, and the United Kingdom all had indicated their support for the peaceful use of nuclear explosives. Attendees at a March 1967 Plowshare meeting at LRL saw an opportunity to use that sentiment to gain worldwide support for their program. Their conclusion: "We had better get an international project."[2]

That was easier said than done. Some of the projects were comparable to building an isthmian canal, making them impossible under the provisions of the LTBT. The plans for the Qattara Depression, for example, called for using a minimum of 181 explosives ranging in size from 150 to 500 kilotons. Funding was another matter. Again the Qattara project is a good illustration; its cost estimates ranged from $510 million to $820 million. How much of a share the AEC, Egypt, and other parties might assume was an issue. Finally, aside from Panama, India, and Thailand, there was little evidence that anyone at the highest levels of government had an interest in Plowshare. And in the case of India, the main protagonist, the influential physicist Homi J. Bhabha,[3] passed away in 1966.

Beyond the problems of fallout, ground shock, and air bursts, Plowshare projects in India and Israel would have posed an additional complication, for both countries refused to sign the NPT. How could the United States guarantee that neither would use Plowshare technology for weapons? Knowing the tense relationship between Israel and its Arab neighbors, as well as the fact that the Soviet Union had a close relationship with some of those Arab countries, the White House refused to give Plowshare technology to Israel. The State Department's William Y. Elliott wrote in 1959, "Nothing should be done that might lead the Israelis to infer that we were stimulating their interest in this project, [for] there is probably no area more sensitive about a Plowshare experiment than the Middle East." India, which had remained neutral through the cold war and which some U.S. officials hoped to draw toward the West, was another matter. The AEC saw several reasons for offering peaceful-use technology to India: it would no longer have reason to develop its own nuclear explosives; offering Plowshare services would "provide a significant prestige program to help the Indians counter the impact" of the 1964 Chinese atomic bomb test; and "Indian participation in Plowshare would help obtain international acceptance of Plowshare and willingness to modify the Limited Test Ban Treaty in such a way as to permit the Panama Canal project."[4]

Spurgeon Keeny of the NSC found none of these rationales convincing. Even with Plowshare assistance, India might still seek to develop its own nuclear weapons. The AEC had "exaggerated the value of Plowshare with U.S. devices as an Indian prestige item," he wrote. To conduct nuclear explosions on Indian soil would foment charges of an American violation of the LTBT. And if Plowshare gained domestic and international support, it would be harder to get a comprehensive test ban adopted by the world community. Summing up, Keeny wrote, "I think it is clear that a cooperative U.S.-Indian Plowshare program would further complicate the already worldwide problem of nuclear proliferation and that such a program is not [of] very great value to Indian prestige or to our Panama

Canal policy." ACDA joined Keeny in opposition, and the White House rejected giving such technology to New Delhi.[5]

As it turned out, the debate over offering Plowshare services to India set a precedent. During the second half of the 1960s, officials from Western Australia, the Australian Atomic Energy Commission (AAEC), and private industry approached LRL and the AEC, asking for their help in building a harbor on Australian soil. To their American counterparts, the Australian harbor not only offered a way to prove the economic value of Plowshare but would provide information relevant to the all-important isthmian canal. The Australian requests, though, fed into the existing debate within the United States over Plowshare and generated arguments in Australia similar to those seen during planning for Chariot. Unfortunately for Plowshare's proponents on both sides of the Pacific, the outcome of the debate in both countries was not what they had wanted. With the collapse in 1969 of the Australian harbor project and continued lack of support within the U.S. government for conducting excavation experiments on U.S. soil, hope of atomic construction of an isthmian canal faltered.

Australia Comes Calling

Australian interest in Plowshare appeared as early as the summer of 1960. Despite setbacks for the proposed Chariot experiment, the apparent success of Rainier and the possibility that the Alaska harbor project might yet take place drew the attention of the Australian physicist Sir Mark Oliphant. He endorsed the peaceful use of the atom, and it was during a visit to Livermore in August 1960 that he became acquainted with America's peaceful-use program. Enticed, he wrote Maurice Timbs, an AAEC commissioner and first assistant secretary in the Prime Minister's Department, that in light of the low level of radioactivity produced by the Rainier shot, the likelihood that Chariot would pose little risk to the local biology in Alaska, and the possible financial savings compared to using conventional explosives, Australia should consider applying the atom to mining and water storage projects. Indeed, he asserted, Australia was a perfect location for a Plowshare test, for its population was small, "and the hazards therefore are also small."[6]

Harold Raggatt, who had gotten wind of Oliphant's recommendations, gave them cautious consideration. A veteran of World War I who held a degree in geology, he became director of Australia's Bureau of Mineral Resources after World War II. In 1951 he assumed the secretaryship of the Department of National Development and, six years later, joined the AAEC as its deputy director. While accepting that the atom offered promise for Australia's economic interests, he was a bit wary: "At this stage I have considerable reservations about the possible use of the Plowshare technique in mining operations, particularly if expert opinion is that the radiation hazard cannot be eliminated. . . . I do not have the same reservations with respect to the method for water storage or civil engineering works."[7]

There was a distinction, though, between simply gathering more information and actually partaking in a nuclear experiment. In November 1960 Oliphant discussed what he regarded as Plowshare's promise with the prime minister, Sir Robert Menzies. Menzies found the Plowshare program interesting and had Raggatt convene an informal meeting in March 1961 that included Oliphant and Timbs. The purpose of the gathering was twofold: to consider establishing a liaison with scientists at both LRL and the AEC and to examine whether there were any projects in Australia to which Plowshare technology might be applied. In the course of their discussions the participants decided to ask Ian Bisset of the Australian embassy in Washington to invite LRL's Gerald Johnson to Australia to discuss the program further. They also agreed to form a Plowshare study group, chaired by Raggatt, to consider additional steps. Bisset passed on the invitation to AEC Chairman Glenn Seaborg and John Kelly, the head of the AEC's Peaceful Nuclear Explosives Branch. "Kelly was delighted at the possibility of Johnson going to Australia," Bisset wrote. Furthermore Livermore was willing to host Bisset or anyone from the AAEC who wanted to learn more about the lab and Plowshare.[8]

At the time of the invitation to Johnson, the test ban treaty negotiations were under way. Just as discussion of Plowshare shots pitted the AEC and the U.S. State Department against one another, so the AAEC and the Australian Department of External Affairs found themselves in opposing corners. It was bad enough, wrote M. J. Cook of External Affairs' UN Political Section, that his department had not received notice of the March meeting. But a nuclear blast, even discussion of one, "could easily be seized on by the USSR no matter how much we protested that the explosion was peaceful, distant and undecided." Timbs rejected such concerns. Because Johnson's visit was "not, repeat not, related to any specific proposals for nuclear explosions in Australia," there was no reason to consult External Affairs. Rather the purpose was simply to promote cooperation between the two nations and to learn more about Plowshare testing in the United States.[9] With interest in Plowshare at the highest levels in Canberra, it was Timbs and his allies who won the day. Because Johnson's duties prevented him from coming to Australia, Gary Higgins, the director of LRL-L's recently established Plowshare Division, was invited instead.[10]

Higgins's visit took place in the spring of 1962. The intervening months had proven troublesome for the peaceful-use program. Opposition to Chariot had increased because of concerns over the possible environmental impact of that shot, and the unexpected venting of Gnome added to questions about Plowshare's feasibility. Despite such setbacks, Higgins, who met with officials from the Australian government, mining and engineering groups, and the AAEC, received an enthusiastic response. Even Raggatt began to reconsider. "I think the next move should be for a group of us to talk about this matter, informally in the first place, with a view to seeing whether there is a locality in Australia suitable for recommendation to the Plowshare Group." However, if or when Canberra approached Washington, Australia had to make clear that its interest was strictly "exploratory and contain[ed] no commitment for an experiment or project in Australia."[11]

As Australian officials pondered possible projects to which to apply the atom,[12] Seaborg learned about the results of Higgins's visit. What he heard left him confident that he might find Down Under a blast to replace Chariot. In October 1962 he informed Howard Beale, Australia's ambassador to the United States, that based on discussions between Australian and U.S. officials, "particularly those with Dr. Gary Higgins . . . we have the preliminary impression that there may be projects in Australia that could be conducted in a manner to provide valuable technical data and at the same time accomplish excavation which might have potential value to Australia." Intrigued, in May 1963 the Australian cabinet decided to send a letter expressing interest in Plowshare but, before taking any action, to ask Seaborg if the AEC might host three Australian scientists who would learn more about the Plowshare program. Seaborg happily offered his agency's services.[13]

Over the next several weeks, the Menzies government selected its delegates: Alan R. W. Wilson, the head of the AAEC's Technical Policy Section; E. B. Pender, an engineer with the Snowy Mountains Hydro-Electric Authority; and Edwin K. Carter, a geologist who worked for the Bureau of Mineral Resources. A month before their departure, the United States, the United Kingdom, and the Soviet Union signed the LTBT. Within days Australia had signed on as well. Bisset approached Kelly to find out if the new treaty might restrict Plowshare's continuation. Kelly replied that it was a matter of interpretation, and he made clear he favored a liberal one that would permit the peaceful-use program. External Affairs First Assistant Secretary Patrick Shaw passed this on to the three Australian delegates. But, he added, there was the need to keep in mind a Soviet government that was "deeply suspicious of the possibility of peaceful explosions being used for military purposes."[14]

The Australians arrived in the United States on September 1 and stayed until October 26. They found a warm reception. Johnson and the AEC's John Philip suggested a "continuing association" on Plowshare between the two nations, with "Australian scientists and engineers working within the Plowshare group at Livermore." The AEC also apparently hoped that their guests might "discuss specific projects which could be tackled in Australia" and was disappointed that the latter had no authority to do so.[15]

Following their return, Wilson, Pender, and Carter spent several months putting together their findings, which they issued in March of the following year. The Wilson report, as it became known, made no definite recommendations. The authors believed Australia offered a good locale for Plowshare blasts because it had a sparse population, unexploited mineral resources, and "the resources of technologists, the engineering capacity, and the financial and management skills needed to carry out major projects involving the use of nuclear explosives." Even so they acknowledged the possible hazards that might result from Plowshare shots, including unanticipated fallout patterns, inhalation of radioactive isotopes, contamination of milk, and ground and air blast. They cited the need for more experimental data and "refinements in ability to predict ground shock and air blast hazards" before Australia committed itself to a Plowshare explosion on its soil.[16]

In fact Pender had misgivings about the report's findings, and when he learned that the AAEC had liked what it read, he was concerned that this "may lead to some reliance on the Report." He warned, "I believe it is desirable that the limitations of this Report be brought to notice." There were still far too many unknowns and dangers involved in Plowshare explosions. "There are over 700 man-made isotopes of the natural elements and many more of artificial elements," yet few had received detailed study. These included strontium and cesium, both of which could get into the soil and then into crops eaten by animals or humans. "The report is, I understand, to be circulated widely, and if this is so, there is a risk that non-engineering readers, being unaware of its incompleteness, may be led to believe that the risks and problems involved are much less than they actually are."[17]

A Western Australia Port, Round 1

If Pender was cautious about permitting Plowshare blasts on his country's soil, the same was not the case for Western Australia's territorial premier, Sir David Brand, and his minister for industrial development, Charles W. Court. Brand had previously served as minister for works, water supply, and housing, during which he promoted a number of industrial projects. Court regarded his post as an opportunity to develop Australia's industry, particularly iron ore. Both saw great promise in the peaceful atom, and in April 1964 Court opened preliminary discussions with the Pittsburgh-based engineering firm Palmer and Baker.[18]

Another person who took an interest in nuclear excavation was Ian McLennan of Broken Hill Proprietary (BHP), headquartered in Melbourne. BHP and U.S.-based Cleveland Cliffs were in the process of developing iron ore for export near the Robe River in Western Australia, about 550 miles north of Geraldton, but they could not locate a suitable site to create a harbor using conventional means. McLennan evidently had explained BHP's problems to Raggatt, who contacted Timbs; together Raggatt and Timbs sent McLennan information on nuclear excavation. McLennan admitted that he did not understand much about the process involved, but he found it enticing enough to offer to take part in a feasibility study. Raggatt, who had largely tossed aside his earlier cautiousness about Plowshare, grabbed the opportunity. He wrote McLennan in September, "Wilson says that the United States Atomic Energy Commission and the U.S. foreign office are fairly confident that if they had a specific proposal to put before the signatories to the nuclear test ban treaty they would be able to get permission to go ahead with it."[19]

The possibility of a Plowshare project in Australia gained steam over the next several months. On his way back from a meeting of IAEA in Vienna, Wilson made stops in the United States, where he spoke with officials at the AEC and LRL. He discovered "new-found confidence" among the Plowshare scientists that they could continue nuclear excavation experiments: Sulky had demonstrated that the AEC could reduce the amount of radioactivity released in cratering experiments, Soviet officials who recently had held talks with their U.S. counterparts in Geneva on the peaceful use of nuclear explosives had shown an interest in Plowshare, and the Japanese had not strongly demonstrated against fallout over their nation generated by a Soviet test in January 1965. Granted, "a full-scale demonstration," such as creating a harbor, would require amending the test ban treaty, but U.S. officials were "hopeful that such arrangements could be readily concluded." Wilson moreover determined that the Johnson administration would heartily endorse a Plowshare project in Australia, to the point of even offering and emplacing the explosives "free of charge." Such a project "would provide a valuable endorsement of the safety of the technique by an independent government." Additionally the White House had recently established the Atlantic-Pacific Interoceanic Canal Study Commission. Given that one of the jobs of the Canal Commission was to consider the feasibility of the atomic construction of a sea-level waterway, creating a harbor in Australia using nuclear explosives could provide vital information. In fact LRL favored building the harbor in Australia before building the canal. As participants at a meeting at Livermore commented, "[The] best way of stating we can make the Transisthmian Canal is to say we made this harbor."[20]

The Brand government took another step toward a harbor in March, when it invited officers from Palmer and Baker for further discussion. Company president Wayne Palmer and his managing director, Hamilton Reese, traveled to Perth shortly thereafter. Brand considered building a harbor at Geraldton unrealistic because it was a populated area. Instead he proposed constructing one about six hundred miles to the north and much closer to the BHP–Cleveland Cliff operations. Sold, on their return Palmer and Reese met with representatives from LRL and the AEC, as well as the Australian embassy's atomic energy attaché, Frank Bett, and suggested a site slightly south of the Robe River. Aside from its nearness to the BHP–Cleveland Cliffs mines, the area was largely devoid of people; Onslow, the nearest populated center, had only about two hundred residents and was seventy miles away. The LTBT remained a hurdle, as both Johnson and Kelly admitted. But they repeated the AEC's earlier contention that the Soviets appeared willing to make an accommodation. Also promising was Australia's isolated geographic location, which increased the likelihood that Moscow would accept modifying the treaty.[21]

With everyone on the same page, Court received an invitation to come to New York to join Palmer, Reese, Raggatt, Gerald Johnson, and Kelly. In their meeting at the end of April, Johnson and Kelly assured the others, " 'Clean' nuclear systems are immediately available." With Palmer, Reese, and the two Australians reassured, the group developed a plan of attack. Palmer and Baker would contact BHP, which would then approach Cleveland Cliffs to determine what type of harbor facilities the two mining firms would need. Assuming all went well between the two companies, Palmer and Baker and BHP would each offer $200,000 for a feasibility study, which they would submit to the Western Australia government. If Perth approved the study, it would send it to Canberra and recommend the establishment of "a Commonwealth-State Committee to make a critical appraisal of the proposal." The Menzies government meanwhile would address such matters as possible violation of the LTBT. Once again the Americans drew a connection between the harbor and the isthmian canal project. "If the proposed harbor were to be excavated in 2–3 years time," Gerald Johnson pointed out, "it could almost certainly substitute for planned U.S. 'Plowshare' experimental work, when probably all aspects of the nuclear explosion could be funded by the U.S. government." He made specific reference to a two- to three-year time frame "because the harbor excavation would be in the experimental program for the sea-level Transisthmian canal program which would require the work to be done at this time."[22]

At this point the harbor project began to break down. "I have been assured by Mr. John S. Kelly, Director of the Division of Peaceful Nuclear Explosives,

USAEC," Bett wrote Timbs in July, "that the present U.S. Administration would be very much in favour of participation in the proposed Palmer and Baker design study of a North Western Australian harbor." But getting an American commitment to participate in the nuclear excavation of the anchorage was another matter. "Kelly made it quite clear that if the design study were completed," if the study found the explosion would release little radioactivity, if Canberra believed the project was in Australia's "best interests," if Australia submitted "a comprehensive proposal to the U.S. government based on the results of the design study," and if it appeared possible to find a negotiated settlement that would permit excavation under the test ban treaty, then Washington would "agree in principle" to participate in the project. Furthermore the United States would not actually proceed with building the harbor until the discussions regarding the test ban had reached a "successful conclusion." A "successful conclusion" meant some form of amendment to the LTBT, for it was almost certain that the harbor project, which of necessity would call for sizable blasts, would release radioactivity beyond Australia's borders. This was recognized on both sides of the Pacific. Seaborg had noted in congressional testimony the unlikelihood of constructing a canal under the LTBT. Likewise Australia's minister for national development David Fairbairn told Menzies that everyone involved in the discussions regarding the harbor, both Australian and American, "acknowledge[d] that the Nuclear Test Ban Treaty could prevent the project going ahead."[23]

There were the snags. BHP was reluctant to offer $200,000 because it doubted nuclear excavation was possible in the face of the LTBT. This left Australia with no firm data to present to the AEC or the U.S. government regarding the harbor project. Amending the LTBT required the United States to approach the Soviet Union. The AEC, which previously had expressed optimism about reaching an accommodation with the Kremlin, and the State Department both showed little willingness to talk with their Soviet counterparts. Kelly mentioned to Bett on November 3 that Moscow "stood to lose by agreeing to accommodations," for any amendment "could only serve to allow demonstrations of U.S. superiority in the field" of peaceful explosions. Furthermore there were political considerations, on which the State Department's Scott George elaborated the following day in a meeting with Bett and R. W. Furlonger of the Australian embassy. In particular was the Vietnam War, which had begun to escalate and which "made it impolitic for the U.S. to raise such an issue unilaterally at this time." And anyway the AEC had no plans for conducting experiments in the short term that necessitated amending the LTBT. What if a harbor project would benefit both the United States and Australia, Furlonger queried, "and would deposit such small quantities of radioactive debris outside Australian boundaries that an accommodation could reasonably be requested?" In that case, replied George, the White House might approach the Kremlin, but only under two conditions: first, that the Johnson administration agree with a feasibility study finding that such "an accommodation could be reasonably requested"; second—and in a clear reference to the Vietnam War—"that the political situation had not deteriorated to such a point that the request would be impolitic." In light of the U.S. position, Furlonger notified Minister for External Affairs Paul Hasluck that any hope of amending the LTBT required first the completion of the feasibility study.[24]

Meeting that first condition appeared ever more unlikely. After discussions between them, BHP decided to join Cleveland Cliffs in developing a harbor at Cape Preston, about ninety miles northeast of Onslow. Both companies had iron ore deposits nearby, and Cleveland Cliffs had signed a contract to start shipping iron ore pellets to Japan in April 1969. The plans they developed called for construction of a railway to the coast, a causeway to an offshore island, and then a jetty alongside which ships could load and unload. "It is clear," commented the AAEC's R. K. Warner, "that existing commitments depending on the development of Cape Preston would preclude the use of nuclear explosives to form the port initially, and of course subsequent deepening would not be possible by this means."[25] With that, the harbor project ended up on the back burner.

A Western Australia Port, Round 2

For approximately the next three years Australian officials made few comments about Plowshare. This is not to say that they had given up on use of the peaceful atom. During a visit to Australia in January 1967, Seaborg found government and media representatives interested in applying Plowshare technology to harbor construction, water storage, natural gas stimulation, and mining projects. Nevertheless Australia did not go beyond expressions of interest. Seaborg discerned a disinclination Down Under to be the first nation "to formally suggest the use of nuclear explosives in such a manner as to necessitate the modification of the Test Ban Treaty." Moreover, Australian officials concluded that in some cases, such as water storage, the application of Plowshare technology made little sense because of the lack of "rainfall and high evaporation rates." Still, Seaborg remained confident: "If the treaty questions can be reconciled, I am certain that the U.S. will receive firm requests from Australia to proceed with several of these projects."[26]

Seaborg may have been aware of an approach made by National Bulk Carriers, based in New York City, to Holmes and Narver, the engineering firm that had contracted with Livermore. Sentinel Mining Company, a subsidiary of National Bulk, had an agreement with the government of Western Australia to exploit iron ore at Nimingarra, about seventy-five miles east of the town of Port

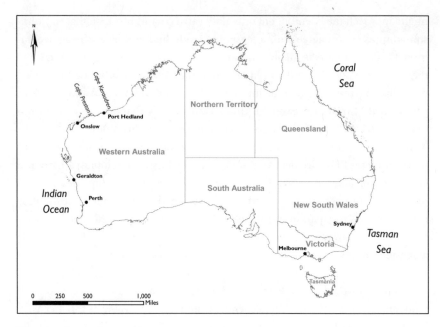

Map 3. Australia.

Hedland and eight hundred miles north-northeast of Perth. Port Hedland appeared headed toward exceeding its capacity, so National Bulk had asked about the possibility of using nuclear excavation to create a harbor at Cape Keraudren, approximately a hundred miles up the coastline from Port Hedland. The site was one of the few in the region where the population was sparse enough to permit nuclear excavation; the nearest town was over twenty miles from ground zero. Holmes and Narver calculated that using the atom to construct a harbor at least 200 feet wide, 1,200 feet long, and 50 feet deep would cost between $6 million and $7 million. Additionally, based on past experiments by the AEC using both conventional and nuclear explosives, Holmes and Narver considered the technique feasible and, with proper precautions, safe. But the engineering company recommended against employing the atom. The possibility of an accidental release of radioactivity, the restrictions imposed by the LTBT, the time it might take to get that treaty amended, and the relatively small amount of dirt that had to be removed made conventional excavation quicker, safer, and more economical.[27]

Using conventional methods entailed dredging a channel approximately five hundred feet wide, followed by construction of a wharf and a 7,500-foot-long jetty. Commented Timbs, "This was a first stage operation and it would be necessary to build a much larger harbor in a short time." Understanding all that was involved in conventional excavation, Sentinel Mining sought a second opinion and held preliminary discussions with the AEC and LRL. Not surprisingly both endorsed the nuclear option. Rather than building a harbor over a two-stage process, they offered to do it all at once: using five 200-kiloton explosives placed 800 feet deep and about 1,100 feet from one another, they could create a crater with a width of about 1,300 to 1,600 feet, a length of 5,000 feet, and a depth of 200 to 400 feet in the center. Once the radioactivity died down, conventional equipment could finish the process. Their reassurances to Sentinel "encouraged" it to approach the government of Western Australia.[28]

As had been the case with the earlier harbor proposal, Court fully endorsed the Cape Keraudren project and, assuming it proved both feasible and safe, encouraged Brand to approve it. Brand and his cabinet shared Court's sentiment, but the Western Australian premier knew that any such project required the endorsement of the government in Canberra. Writing the new prime minister, John Gorton, a few days later, Brand urged a quick decision. Not only did Sentinel have a timetable to keep, but development in Western Australia had reduced the number of possible locations for nuclear excavation. Before replying, Gorton asked the advice of the AAEC. Timbs recommended moving the project forward. He admitted that the LTBT might prohibit nuclear excavation, yet Kelly had concluded that the AEC and Sentinel would pay for its entire cost, and Kelly also believed the project could take place within the confines of the test ban treaty. For these reasons Timbs suggested that Gorton accept the idea of a feasibility study and ask the AEC to participate in it. Gorton regarded these recommendations as sensible and contacted Brand along those lines. On January 22 Canberra requested AEC participation in the feasibility study.[29]

For the AEC, the timing could not have been better. Carryall had collapsed because the state of California concluded that waiting to proceed with the blast would violate a state mandate to begin construction of I-40 in time to complete it by 1972. Now the AEC had a new opportunity to prove Plowshare's worth, not only experimentally but economically. Even better, Sentinel wanted to have the port available for use by the end of 1970. That schedule would work well for the AEC and LRL, as it would allow them to replace Project Galley, obtain vital data, and, if all went well, meet the December 1970 reporting deadline of the Atlantic-Pacific Interoceanic Canal Commission. As an added benefit, pointed out Livermore scientist Milo Nordyke, the Cape Keraudren project might illustrate "the practicality of the nuclear approach" to canal construction and consequently lead to "the acceptance of nuclear excavation as a viable engineering tool by the governments of the United States, Panama, Colombia, and their peoples."[30]

If the AEC was to pay for a portion of the harbor project, it needed an increase in appropriations. For fiscal year 1969, it had requested from the Bureau of the Budget $26.6 million for the peaceful-use program, only to have that cut to

$14.5 million. Assuming it would not get more than that, the AEC originally requested that amount for its FY 1970 budget, with about $6.7 million of that going to excavation experiments. With the Australian harbor now a possibility, and determined to meet the deadlines for both that project and the isthmian canal, Seaborg asked the White House to increase the FY 1970 budget by about $15 million, bringing the total to approximately $29 million. The AEC head had allies in this endeavor, among them Representatives Craig Hosmer (R-California) and Chester Holifield (D-California), two of Plowshare's strongest defenders on the JCAE. Both offered their assistance, which Seaborg gladly accepted. "I said [to Hosmer] we will probably need some help," he recalled. "Our budget isn't the best. The new President may have to do something about that."[31]

That new president was Richard Nixon. The increasingly unpopular war in Vietnam and unrest at home had taken its toll on President Johnson's approval rating, and in March 1968 he had withdrawn from the presidential race. Nixon, the Republican candidate, who had promised to end the war in Vietnam and to restore domestic order, defeated his Democratic contender, Hubert Humphrey.

Like Johnson, Nixon was an exceedingly complex personality. Highly intelligent and politically ambitious, he was also very distrustful of others, insecure, shy, proud, easily offended, and manipulative. He had developed a reputation as a staunch anticommunist, gaining national fame for almost singlehandedly bringing former State Department assistant secretary and Soviet spy Alger Hiss to justice. His notoriety and his ability to draw votes both from California and his party's right wing convinced Eisenhower to make Nixon his vice president, where he would remain during Eisenhower's two terms in office. After losing a bid for the presidency in 1960, he returned to private life, only to come back to politics eight years later as president.

As vice president Nixon had sat in on some meetings where Plowshare was discussed and had expressed intense interest in the program.[32] As president his sentiment toward Plowshare appeared unchanged. Seaborg wanted a quick decision on the Cape Keraudren project and met with Nixon eight days after the inauguration. The AEC head recorded in his journal that the president "wanted [Plowshare] to have a high priority in his administration; in fact, he said he has a special prejudice for this program." When Nixon asked Seaborg what he needed to "get on with" the Cape Keraudren project, the AEC chair asked for additional funding and "a more realistic interpretation of the test ban treaty." In his view the LTBT permitted the harbor project, but the Johnson White House had shared the view of the State Department and ACDA that "any amount of radioactivity, no matter how small, might be a violation . . . if it were detectable beyond the borders of the country where the excavation experiment had been performed." While State and ACDA had hampered America's peaceful-use program, added Seaborg, the Soviet Union, which had adopted "a realistic interpretation of the test ban treaty," was continuing its own Plowshare program and had conducted "at least ten underground weapons tests or excavation experiments, and possibly as many as 15, 20, or 25, in which debris was readily detectable outsider their borders." As an additional incentive to get presidential approval, Seaborg pointed to Article V of the NPT, under which the United States and other nuclear nations had promised to render peaceful-use technology to nonnuclear countries.[33]

Congressman Hosmer tried to help Seaborg. He pointed out to Nixon that the harbor project offered numerous potential rewards. Bestowing Plowshare services on Australia might convince those countries that had yet to sign the NPT to do so in the hopes of receiving similar assistance. The project would take only about a year to complete and "at [a] relatively modest cost" of about $12 million to $14 million, and "benefit directly in a technical way the Inter-American canal project." To make sure that the harbor was ready by Sentinel's deadline, the nuclear excavation would have to take place in "December, 1969 or January, 1970." What the AEC needed immediately was $300,000 to begin its work and another $2.5 million for FY 1969, the latter of which could be obtained through reprogramming of funds.[34]

Requesting presidential help was one thing; getting it was another. Not until late in his administration did Johnson accept a tax surcharge to pay for the Vietnam War and the Great Society. But the surcharge was not enough to cover the cost for both as well as other government expenditures, bequeathing to Nixon a $25 billion deficit, nearly three times what it was the year before. All of that spending had also pushed up the rate of inflation to 5 percent, the highest in nearly two decades.[35] In an effort to curb spending as well as meet his promise to end the war in Vietnam, Nixon began the process of withdrawing U.S. troops from Southeast Asia and reduced funding for a number of antipoverty programs. It was not clear if he could give Plowshare what it needed and still hold down the deficit.

The LTBT also potentially stood in the way of the harbor. Article I prohibited signatories from conducting an explosion underwater. The question was whether the Cape Keraudren project risked a violation. The AEC argued that since the explosives would be buried in the seabed, it constituted an underground explosion and hence was legal. The State Department demurred, contending a device emplaced in the seabed was underwater and therefore prohibited. Soviet questioning of the legality of the blast only added to State's cautiousness. The State Department's worries about an LTBT violation explained why it was "dragging its feet," according to Seaborg, and gave him an additional reason to meet with Nixon on January 28. His conversation with the president worked. Nixon ordered State to issue a reply, which it did on February 3: "The United States

Government agrees that it would be desirable, and most expeditious, to have this study performed by the United States Atomic Energy Commission, the Australian Atomic Energy Commission, and other interested organizations in Australia and the United States." Washington was "prepared to begin the feasibility study as soon as possible." Encouraged, the AAEC established the Australian Plowshare Committee and the Cape Keraudren Project Committee to coordinate with the U.S. AEC.[36]

Even if the United States and Australia found a way around the LTBT, there was yet another hurdle: the NPT. By the end of 1968 over seventy-five nations had signed the NPT. Australia was not among them. This was largely the result of a fight between the AAEC and the Australian Department of External Affairs, as well as their allies, over Australian nuclear policy. The AAEC's chair, Sir Philip Baxter, believed that no one but he should determine the future of Australia's nuclear policy. He further claimed that the treaty would not stop the proliferation of nuclear technology and, more important, would prevent Australia from developing its own atomic weapons. Finally, while Australia had no nuclear power plants, the treaty's provisions would allow inspectors, including possibly communist ones, to gather information on Australian industrial and defense facilities.[37]

Baxter had powerful associates. One was Timbs, himself an outspoken member of the AAEC. Others were Fairbairn, Minister for Supply Kenneth Anderson, and Minister of Defense Allen Fairhall. Most significant, however, was Prime Minister Gorton himself.[38] Known for his "larrikin personality," Gorton was also highly nationalistic. Under the Australia, New Zealand, United States Security Treaty of 1951, Washington had promised to help defend its two allies, including with the use of nuclear weapons, if necessary. But Gorton believed that Australia had relied too much on the United States for its defense and instead should look toward augmenting its own technological and industrial power, including "nuclear options."[39]

The Department of External Affairs, which wanted to see Australia sign the NPT, did not have such potent friends. Paul Hasluck, Gorton's foreign minister and himself a commanding presence in the Liberal Party, took little interest in the debate over the NPT that had emerged between his agency and the AAEC. This is not to say External Affairs lacked a voice. Malcolm Booker, first assistant secretary of Division II, was a vocal advocate for Australia to become a party to the NPT.[40] But with Hasluck disengaged and Gorton backing the AAEC, Booker had little hope of convincing Canberra to sign the treaty. Not until 1970 did Australia become a signatory.

Australia's decision to withhold its endorsement of the NPT posed a dilemma for U.S. officials. On the one hand, Articles III and IV of the treaty permitted signatories to engage in the peaceful use of nuclear technology. On the other, Article I declared they would not help nonnuclear states "manufacture or otherwise acquire nuclear weapons or other nuclear explosive devices, or control over such weapons or explosive devices." While Article V allowed nations with nuclear technology to make it available to nonnuclear countries, it made specific reference to states that had signed the NPT. As Canberra was not a party to the agreement, could Washington legally conduct a nuclear excavation in Australia? Seaborg believed the United States could, as the treaty did not outright prohibit a signatory from providing nuclear technology to a nonsignatory for use in a peaceful nuclear experiment. The U.S. Senate Foreign Relations Committee and its powerful chair, J. William Fulbright (D-Arkansas), objected. "By any standard," the committee stated in a report in early 1969, "it would be consistent with the intent of the treaty to be more willing to provide . . . assistance in the nuclear excavation field to a signatory country . . . than to a non-signatory." Australian officials recognized the quandary they faced. "There has been speculation in Canberra," commented Perth's daily newspaper, the *West Australian*, "that the Australian government might have to sign the nuclear non-proliferation treaty before the U.S. would provide peaceful nuclear devices."[41]

The Gorton government attempted to find a way around the NPT. In its note of February 3 the State Department had referenced America's decision to sign the nonproliferation pact and its preparedness under Article V to offer Plowshare services to other countries; Australia asked for removal of that language, regarding it as an attempt to pressure it to sign. The request bred anger in the White House. Citing a recent U.S. decision to limit the importation of meat from Australia, Walter Rice, the U.S. ambassador to Australia, warned Laurence McIntyre, Australia's deputy secretary for external affairs, that Canberra's petition "was causing some irritation in the State Department in Washington— coming as it did on top of our recent pressures over United States import restrictions, meat in particular." If the Gorton government kept up the pressure, Rice continued, the White House might end up turning to one of several other countries that had also requested U.S. help in the field of peaceful explosions. The ambassador urged Canberra to "remember that there was a completely new administration in Washington which had no particular sense of past affiliations with Australia and which would be more responsive, for the time being at least, to sounds of co-operation rather than of protest."[42]

Even assuming all of these hurdles were overcome and the harbor was built, there was no guarantee the iron ore might find a market. Sentinel had yet to sign an agreement to ship its ore to Japan, and it was likely the Japanese would wait to do so "until they [saw] the results of the nuclear blast." Even then, Japan, sensitive about nuclear matters as a consequence of its World War II experience, might decide it was not "expedient to accept shipments from a nuclear blasted harbor." If that happened, Sentinel could find itself without a buyer for its product.[43]

Of the roadblocks the Cape Keraudren project faced, however, possibly the least expected was that posed by Sentinel Mining itself. In the first meeting between company and Australian government officials, Sentinel declared that the idea of excavating a harbor at Cape Keraudren was the AEC's. While Sentinel offered to allow atomic blasting at the site, it wanted the harbor completed and radiation-free by its declared March 1970 deadline. Furthermore it would accept financial responsibility only for building the harbor out of the craters created by the explosives; it would not pay for the atomic devices nor for the feasibility study, except for the salaries of company officials who took part in that investigation. Sentinel's position caught Canberra off guard. It was not clear whether March 1970 was time enough to conduct the feasibility study and the blast itself, commented Robert W. Boswell, Gorton's secretary of the Department of National Development and a member of the AAEC. He added, "We do not know whether the U.S.A.E.C. is prepared to carry the full cost of the feasibility study and we do not know whether they have even contemplated carrying the full cost of the nuclear blast operation."[44]

The news only got worse for the harbor project's champions. On February 19 M. Reed of Sentinel Mining informed the AEC's Kelly that his company was having second thoughts about participating in the feasibility study because it was not sure of the quality of the ore at Nimingarra. The sudden uncertainty prompted Kelly to suggest that Timbs contact Reed, which Timbs did on February 21. When Reed stated that his company wanted more time to assess the ore before proceeding with the feasibility study, Timbs got angry. "I said I found this attitude extremely difficult to understand. It was Sentinel which had first raised the idea of developing Cape Keraudren," and the company had "had plenty of time to think about the consequences." Both the Australian and U.S. governments had publicly stated their desire to proceed with nuclear excavation at Cape Keraudren, "and, if it did not go ahead at a reasonable rate, it would be embarrassing, particularly as in the United States the President himself was involved." Whether building the anchorage could proceed became even more unlikely when, according to Seaborg, the Bureau of the Budget "clobbered" the AEC's funding request. Rather than increase appropriations for Plowshare for FY 1970, Budget cut them to $13.7 million, less than half of what the AEC had wanted and $800,000 less than in 1969.[45]

Matters began to reach a head. The U.S. and Australian governments had expected Sentinel to offer $200,000 toward the feasibility study, which would cover the cost of seismic and hydraulic studies as well as, if necessary, an "exploratory drill hole." In mid-March Peter Stork, Sentinel's Perth-based manager, announced that his company disagreed with expending so much on "a project of uncertain value." This was because the Japanese wanted a quality guarantee for any ore they purchased, and accepting such a requirement, said Stork, "would set a dangerous precedent" for his and other companies.[46]

Based on the number of hurdles involved, it appeared unlikely the Cape Keraudren project would get off the ground. Had the parties involved overcome these difficulties, however, one must wonder whether blasting would have occurred. Anyone who remembered Chariot certainly would have had a case of déjà vu, for just as in Alaska, the Cape Keraudren project aroused in Australia an increasingly intense public debate, which pitted the media, government officials, and scientists against one another.

As with Chariot, the regional press tended to favor the harbor. Cape Keraudren, commented Perth's *West Australian*, "would put [Western Australia] at the centre of world-wide interest in the U.S. Plowshare programme." The site itself was perfect for nuclear excavation, the blast would not violate the LTBT because of the depth of burial of the explosives, and the harbor would reaffirm the obligation of nuclear states to offer peaceful-use services to those without nuclear technology. The *Kalgoorlie Miner* seconded the *West Australian*. "There is no logical reason," it insisted, "why anyone should recoil at the idea providing it can be done safely." Even newspapers on the other side of the continent were disposed toward the shot. The *Melbourne Age* excitedly noted that the project would "spotlight the nation as few other events could," and the *Sydney Sun-Herald* commented, "Because it is an experiment never before attempted by man . . . [it] is being likened to the historic Apollo 8 mission around the moon last Christmas." Just as in the case of Alaska, the Australian press focused on the uninhabited nature of the Cape Keraudren region, failing to note the presence of nomadic Aborigines who, like the Eskimos, exhibited a greater presence of radioactive isotopes in their bodies than whites.[47]

The Aborigines' experience was a result of British nuclear tests at Woomera in Western Australia in the 1950s. That history also played into increasingly vocal opposition within Australia against testing. Whereas a 1952 opinion poll found that 58 percent of Australians favored atomic tests, by 1957 66 percent wanted an international pact to halt them. In 1960 the Campaign for Nuclear Disarmament, which had begun three years earlier in the United Kingdom, spread to Australia. While Australia did not witness the intensity of protests against testing seen in the United Kingdom,[48] it was obvious that Australians were less than keen on seeing nuclear weapons exploded on their soil.

As in the case of Chariot, among the first to raise red flags about Cape Keraudren were scientists. One of the earliest was David Ride, a zoologist and director of the Western Australian Museum in Perth. In an interview with the Australian Broadcasting Company in mid-February he commented that little was known of the biology in the region around ground zero. He then questioned the AEC's timetable. It was possible to conduct a feasibility study in a few months if the purpose was simply "to collect samples in order to test whether the fauna [was] locally unique": "But to cover a study of, say, food chain and the biology and ecology of organisms, I would think several years would be an extremely conservative estimate." Furthermore he warned that the blast could cause harm to the pearl industry, which conducted operations not far from the blast site. Even Wilson, who headed the Cape Keraudren Project Committee, acknowledged that the three months permitted by the AEC and AAEC was not enough time.[49]

In March three University of Sydney scientists, physical chemist A. E. Alexander and biologists N. A. Walker and L. C. Birch, joined the critics. Aware of the dispute over Chariot, they had obtained the June 1961 issue of *Nuclear Information* that warned of the dangers of that shot. Alarmed, they put together a petition critical of the Cape Keraudren project and sent it to five hundred Australian colleagues. Eventually signed by over 250 scientists and published in the *Australian* newspaper in 1969, the petition made six demands, including "a full ecological study of any land and sea areas to be affected," publication of those findings, disclosure of the radioactive isotopes the blast would release, and the appointment of "an independent committee to decide on the safety aspects of [the] project."[50]

The domestic uproar soon encompassed members of the opposition Labour Party. Fred Collard, who represented Kalgoorlie, questioned the need to move so quickly toward construction of the harbor, especially if there was the possibility of fallout. Gough Whitlam, quoting the 1964 Wilson report, pointed out that an "'ecology study should cover at least the complete seasonal cycle,' that is, at least one year." Yet the AEC and AAEC expected to complete it by early June at the latest. "Why," he asked, "is it now believed that it is no longer essential to extend the study over at least one year?" Fairbairn attempted to assure Collard that the blast would not take place unless there was no chance of fallout. He was less able to answer Whitlam's question, but assumed that the study would take "rather longer than . . . originally expected."[51]

The debate became moot at the end of March. Unsure it could profit from the harbor, Sentinel decided not to fund the feasibility study. In a scathing editorial, the *Sydney Morning Herald* laid much of the blame at the feet of "Fairbairn and his advisers" who had "clearly acted much too hastily in pushing the proposal." But the editors also saved some criticism for the rest of the government, which "seemed to be swept along by the excitement of the idea of being the first to use atomic devices for such a purpose." They concluded, "Clearly enough, in the future we must approach projects of this kind much more warily. We must satisfy ourselves that the use of nuclear explosives is absolutely necessary and that they will be absolutely safe."[52]

Third Time Is the Charm?

What the *Morning Herald* did not know was that Cape Preston was once again in play. A couple of weeks prior to Sentinel's decision to withdraw from the feasibility study, the AAEC sought to redirect Gorton's attention back to Cape Preston, citing the need for deep water ports in that region of Australia if the country was to exploit nearby natural resources. Gorton found the suggestion worthy of consideration, though he was not yet ready to openly commit himself to the idea. Rather, he asked Fairbairn to instruct a delegation of Australian officials on its way to Washington to "encourage" the United States to suggest alternatives to Cape Keraudren, should Sentinel pull out.[53]

That strategy began to bear fruit. Meeting with the Australians on March 27, Tape asked if Australia had any ideas for a project to replace Cape Keraudren, "for example Cape Preston." Foreign Minister Gordon Freeth immediately instructed his ambassador to the United States, Sir Keith Waller, to "keep all options open." However, he made clear that there was not at present any formal proposal to use nuclear excavation at Cape Preston, and so "any exercise there would have to be viewed at this stage as primarily an American requirement in which Australia had a sympathetic, but not a specific commercial interest." Furthermore Australia intended to make no financial commitment to such a project beyond the feasibility study stage. Waller questioned this strategy. The reason the United States had taken such an interest in Cape Keraudren, he commented, was that it provided "evidence of foreign interest and confiden[ce] in the technique" offered by Plowshare. "To stress at this stage that any exercise would have to be viewed as an American requirement might well reduce the chances of any American initiative emerging."[54]

The following month officials from the Australian National Development Department, the AAEC, the Prime Minister's Department, External Affairs, the Department of the Treasury, and the Attorney General's Department gathered to decide whether Australia or the United States should take the next step. The attendees shared Waller's opinion that it made sense for Canberra to indicate its desire to make another attempt at harbor construction. However, before actually proceeding they agreed they should first obtain a corporate commitment, and one that involved the company paying for a sizable portion of the construction costs. With that, Timbs wrote Seaborg asking if the AEC would consider "possible sites" for an atomically constructed harbor. "We will be happy to participate," replied the AEC head.[55]

For the Australian Plowshare Committee, the most logical site was Cape Preston. BHP had reached the conclusion that nuclear excavation of that harbor made sense, but it did not want to commit itself until it knew whether the ore nearby was of quality. Just in case, the Plowshare Committee had a team led by Wilson conduct a preliminary survey of Cape Preston, which it completed in July. Wilson and his colleagues concluded that the site offered a perfect place for nuclear excavation in all respects: the types of rock were suitable, ground shock or air blast posed little danger, and the population in the region was sparse. There were two caveats. First, BHP believed using conventional methods to build the port and facilities would take two years; hence it wanted evidence that nuclear excavation would take less time. Second, the LTBT, depending on how it was interpreted, might prohibit use of the atom. That said, the Australian Plowshare Committee decided to send the report to the AEC and write up by September, "by which time B.H.P. should have the results of its current tests of Robe River ore," a "pre-feasibility study." Using that data, the Australian, Western Australian, and U.S. governments, along with BHP, could decide whether to proceed with "a full scale feasibility study."[56]

This was as far as the planning got. In September, F. L. McCay, chair of the Plowshare Committee, commented that BHP had "entered into an arrangement with the Cliffs Company and it is now considered unlikely that Cape Preston will be developed as a port site for the nuclear experiment in which the USAEC is particularly interested." BHP had been part of a consortium of companies that had offered $245 million to develop iron ore in the Robe River region, but for reasons that its president, Daniel K. Ludwig, refused to divulge, his company withdrew.[57] That decision marked the end of any serious planning for a harbor in Australia.

The Canal Collapses

Ludwig's announcement also proved to be one of the last nails in the coffin of the already embattled sea-level isthmian canal project. Scientists had continued to point to the potential harm caused by an intermingling of Atlantic and Pacific species. Writing in *Science* magazine in August 1968, Ira Rubinoff again warned that a sea-level canal might result in hybridization of Atlantic and Pacific marine species or even extinction of some. Seconding Rubinoff were Robert Topp, a marine biologist at the Florida Department of Natural Resources; John C. Briggs, a zoologist at the University of Florida; and Lamont Cole, an ecologist at Cornell

University. To try to assess what a sea-level canal might mean for the life in the region, the Smithsonian Tropical Research Institute had begun a limited study, and the Canal Commission asked the Battelle Memorial Institute to undertake its own modest survey. Sidney Galler, the Smithsonian's assistant secretary, estimated that a full study, one of a much greater scale than the Smithsonian's or the Battelle Institute's, would run anywhere from $25 million to $50 million and take fifteen to twenty-five years.[58]

The AEC did not have that much time. Nor did it have the money necessary to conduct the requisite experiments. Seaborg and Kelly testified to Congress in April 1969 that their agency needed to conduct four more cratering blasts, including the Australian harbor project, to have the information it needed for the Canal Commission but had only enough money in the FY 1970 budget for one. What about using tunnels and shafts already at the NTS as a way of saving time and money, Hosmer asked during a hearing the following month. Kelly said that was not possible, for those already used could not be reused, and those set aside "for weapons tests are used for weapon tests and so they are not available for Plowshare use." How about trying "to piggyback some Plowshare experiments onto some weapons events?" Kelly again shot down that suggestion. "We already do as much of that as we think is technically reasonable," he commented. The situation left Robert Anderson, chairman of the Canal Commission, dejected. He wrote in June that there was no way to prove by December 1970 whether it was possible to conduct the nuclear excavation of a canal.[59]

The AEC remained determined. With the Australian harbor likely out of the question, it had put Galley back on the books and had changed its proposed list of blasts. Buggy II was out; Phaeton was back in. These two explosions would join two recently proposed experiments, Sturtevant and Yawl. The former, at 170 kilotons, would test a new type of device; the latter, originally planned at 100 kilotons but now envisioned at six times that size, would put the Sturtevant device to use in an excavation experiment in "an area of water-saturated soil" similar to that found on canal routes 17 and 25. As the type of soil necessary did not exist on the NTS, the AEC planned for it to take place just outside the Test Site, on the Nellis Air Force range. The one-megaton Phaeton blast would come next, followed by Galley, a row experiment involving five to seven devices of one hundred to two hundred kilotons each. Seaborg anticipated no problems with Sturtevant, despite the fact that it was six times bigger than Schooner. In addition to testing excavation techniques using larger yield explosives, Sturtevant would also employ cleaner technology. Consequently though Sturtevant would initially produce more fallout than Schooner, it would entail shorter-lived isotopes. Thus within fifty hours of detonation, the radioactivity would largely mimic that of Schooner.[60]

Unfortunately for Seaborg, the cards had turned against him. In April 1969 the United States and the Soviet Union finally opened negotiations that the AEC hoped would lead to a common interpretation of the LTBT, but the two sides proved unable to find a meeting of the minds. Meanwhile the State Department had reached the conclusion that a sea-level canal, even if it generated only a small amount of fallout, would increase anti-American sentiment in Central America. The Army Corps of Engineers, long an ally of the Plowshare program, defected. General R. H. Groves, the Canal Study Commission's engineering agent, told attendees at the January 1970 Symposium on Nuclear Explosives that he could not endorse nuclear excavation of a canal, in part because it would require the forcible removal of as many as twenty-five thousand people from their homes. Then came what *Washington Post* reporter Victor Cohn called "a severe blow." Shortly after its establishment, the Canal Commission had asked the National Academy of Sciences to establish a committee to advise it on environmental matters related to canal construction. That body, headed by Harvard University zoologist Ernst Mayr, became known as the Committee on Ecological Research for the Inter-Oceanic Canal. In April it determined that a nuclear-excavated waterway posed numerous hazards: it would release radioactivity, endanger nearby population centers, cause harmful intermingling of oceanic species, and generate seismic shock. Commented Mayr, "It's been established just for one thing that the world's tritium level would go up by about 50 per cent."[61]

In May the AEC conducted Project Flask at the NTS. The origin of this experiment is not clear, but its purpose was to test a new, cleaner explosive. Consisting of three separate explosions of 105 kilotons, 90 tons, and 40 tons buried at depths ranging from 500 to just over 1,700 feet, the AEC found the results promising. It "provided a proven explosive design in the 100 kt yield range producing four times less radioactivity than the previous design."[62]

Although Flask was another step toward proving nuclear excavation of a canal possible, Seaborg had come to realize there was no way he could finish the remaining experiments in time. The same month as Flask, the AEC chair withdrew Sturtevant. At about the same time, Yawl joined Sturtevant in the trash heap. As Phaeton relied on the data obtained from Sturtevant and Yawl, it too was discarded. With that, Seaborg formally informed Anderson in July that the AEC could not complete the requisite experiments in time for the Canal Commission's December 1970 deadline.[63]

On December 1 the Canal Commission formally recommended against the atomic option. "One provision of the law required us to determine the practicability of nuclear canal excavation," the commission members wrote Nixon. "Unfortunately, neither the technical feasibility nor the international acceptability of such an application of nuclear excavation technology has been established at this date." The Commission accordingly endorsed building a new canal along route 10, the existing lock canal, which it considered "physically feasible" and would run about "$2.88 billion at 1970 price levels."[64]

The End of Nuclear Excavation

After spending $21.4 million of its $24 million in appropriations, the Canal Study Commission had proven unable to complete it task. Representative Daniel Flood (D-Pennsylvania) was furious, calling it a waste of money and promising to fight any treaty that might turn the canal over to Panama.[65] It is questionable whether Flood had reason for such anger, for even at the time it was obvious the canal project faced tremendous obstacles, among them the danger posed by fallout on humans and the environment, a lack of funding for the necessary experiments, and a risk of violating the LTBT. It was for these reasons that the AEC put so much energy into the Australian harbor project. It offered not only to replace Project Galley but to act as an end and a means: an end in the sense of proving that the peaceful atom could serve humankind, and a means both for gathering data for the isthmian canal and convincing opinion within the United States and abroad that additional projects, also aimed at creating a better world, could take place safely.

There is no doubt the nuclear excavation program suffered from bad luck. It had to compete for funding with other White House initiatives, divisions within the Australian and U.S. governments over its legality and safety continued to dog it, and the desired industry support failed to materialize. But the AEC and LRL were also at fault. They talked about having clean explosives even though, as they both admitted, their cleanest devices would generate fallout. They minimized the danger posed by nuclear excavation of a canal, despite the fact that such a project would require numerous explosives, some of them of a megaton or more. With their record of accidental and unexpected results, their efforts to reassure the peaceful-use program's many doubters that success was around the corner not surprisingly fell on deaf ears.

Although Plowshare scientists had called for a balanced peaceful-use program, one that gave largely equal emphasis to excavation and nonexcavation projects, the isthmian canal had been their primary focus. The demise of the waterway, however, did not mean the death of Plowshare. Gasbuggy's apparent success had given Plowshare scientists hope that they could send their program in a new direction, which, like the canal, had a direct relation to U.S. security and creating a better future for all, but for which the LTBT would not prove a hindrance: the stimulation of natural gas and oil production.

Dead as a Doornail

"The American Gas Association reported over the weekend that proved reserves of natural gas decreased by almost 2 per cent in 1968," wrote *New York Times* reporter Gene Smith in April 1969. "The trade association stated that a major factor in the decrease of 5.5 trillion cubic feet in reserves was 'the continuing decline in exploratory wells drilled in the search for oil and natural gas.'" The year also had seen a reduction in the country's petroleum reserves. Although at this time the cost of oil and natural gas remained low, numbers such as those quoted by Smith could not but put U.S. officials on notice. The nation was increasingly dependent on imported oil, with one quarter of the petroleum coming from foreign sources by 1970. Of that, up to half came from the Middle East. That too was reason for concern. The Soviet Union maintained close ties with Arab countries and might try to manipulate if not take control of their oil export policies. Commented Richard Nixon early in his presidency, "The difference between our goal and the Soviet goal in the Mideast is very simple but fundamental. We want peace. They want the Middle East." Additionally, following the Arab-Israeli war of 1967, Arab nations implemented an embargo on oil exports to three nations, including the United States. Although the embargo lasted only three months and had little impact on gas prices, it made Washington realize the danger posed by relying heavily on petroleum from the Middle East.[1] Finally, even without an embargo, the possibility of Americans' ever increasing demand for fuel threatened to diminish U.S. reserves, meaning higher prices. The question therefore was whether it was possible to increase those reserves, which might simultaneously curb dependence on foreign energy sources and hold down domestic gas and oil prices.

The AEC, Lawrence Radiation Laboratory (renamed Lawrence Livermore National Laboratory [LLNL] in 1971), and their friends believed they had the answer: the stimulation of natural gas and petroleum production. By the middle of 1969 atomic construction of a canal or any other project appeared highly unlikely, and storage, mining, and isotope and heat generation were in no better shape. Gasbuggy, however, had shown promise. By shifting the focus of Plowshare to resource stimulation, particularly after the rejection in December 1970 of nuclear excavation of a canal, defenders of the peaceful-use program could continue to claim they were protecting U.S. security and trying to create a better world, in this case by demonstrating they could get at heretofore inaccessible reserves of oil and gas. Senator Clifford Hansen (R-Wyoming) testified in March 1971, "We are too reliant on foreign sources of oil." His solution: "The plowshare program . . . offers one of the quickest and surest solutions to our gas and energy shortage problems."[2] Because these explosions would take place underground, there was a high likelihood of containing the radioactivity, thereby preventing an outcry over fallout or an LTBT violation. By proving Plowshare was safe, utilitarian, and legal, the program's champions might finally convince those in the legislative and executive branches of government to stop cutting funding for it.

Plowshare's proponents, however, had not prepared themselves for vocal and determined political, environmental, and even industrial opponents who resisted the idea of explosions that could unleash damaging seismic shocks underground or radioactivity into the atmosphere. Nor did they anticipate the unwillingness of consumers to use natural gas tainted with what the AEC and LLNL regarded as a safe level of radioactivity. On top of all of this was a White House that, even more than in the past, saw Plowshare as unworthy of the appropriations the program's defenders believed it deserved. By the mid-1970s Plowshare had come to an ignominious end.[3]

Environmentalism Ascendant, Credibility in Decline

The environmental movement that Plowshare had helped engender with the bioenvironmental studies that began in 1959 had, a decade later, become both powerful and influential. Through her book *Silent Spring*, Rachel Carson had brought attention to the danger posed by pesticides to both animals and humans. A year later environmentalists joined opponents of nuclear testing to get the LTBT passed. Lady Bird Johnson, President Johnson's wife, made preservation of the nation's natural beauty one of her key agenda items. In 1968 Ralph Nader, famous for championing auto safety, formed the Center for Study of Responsive Law to suggest new regulations aimed at curbing pollution and protecting the environment.[4]

The work of activists such as Mrs. Johnson and Nader helped generate passage of numerous pieces of environmental legislation. The Highway Beautification Act of 1965 regulated the construction of billboards along the federal highway system and called for making those roads more scenic. The Endangered Species Act, passed a year later and amended in 1969, gave protection to certain types of fish and wildlife. The Air Quality Act of 1967 altered the 1963 Clean Air Act and had the purpose of reducing air pollution. And the National Wild and Scenic Rivers Act of 1968 prohibited development on or near rivers regarded as particularly beautiful or wild or of historical, geologic, or cultural significance.

Yet with the possible exception of 1962, when Carson's book appeared, no year brought more attention to environmentalism than 1969. An article in the January issue of *Sports Illustrated* asserted that nuclear power plants had created thermal pollution harmful to marine life. That same year saw the publication of two books, both of which pointed to the potential danger posed by nuclear power. In *The Careless Atom*, Sheldon Novick addressed what might happen in the event of a meltdown at a nuclear power plant, and in *Perils of the Peaceful Atom*, Richard Curtis and Elizabeth Hogan contended that the use of the atom for electricity offered so many threats that humans had to consider alternatives.[5]

For others, the problem was not nuclear but conventional fuel. In January a blowout occurred on a Union Oil Company petroleum platform off the coast of Santa Barbara, California. About 235,000 gallons of oil covered thirty miles of the state's beaches. That same month the Cuyahoga River literally caught on fire after years of having oil dumped into it. What happened on the Cuyahoga drew attention to the waste cities such as Buffalo, Detroit, and Cleveland had dumped into Lake Erie over the years. "Of 62 beaches along its shores," commented *Time* magazine, "only three are rated completely safe for swimming. Even wading is unpleasant; as many as 30,000 sludge worms carpet each square yard of lake bottom."[6] If books like Novick's warned of the environmental harm that *could* happen because of a failure to adequately check the atom, the events of January proved that it *would*.

The power of environmentalism coincided with a loss of faith in the government's trustworthiness. Early on many Americans had questioned what government officials, such as those at the AEC, told them about the safety of nuclear testing. The Vietnam War had greatly intensified that lack of trust as the seemingly never-ending conflict belied repeated White House promises that the war would be over soon.[7] The "credibility gap," as it became known, made Americans wonder why they should trust anything officials in Washington said.

Project Rulison

The AEC's desire to defend the nation's security and promote progress by meeting the nation's energy needs and, in the process, protect Plowshare clashed with the environmental movement and the credibility gap as the Commission turned its attention to Project Rulison. Rulison's life had begun two years before Gasbuggy took place, when the Houston-based Austral Oil Company and CER Geonuclear approached the AEC about using a nuclear device to stimulate production in the Rulison gas field, located near the town of Rulison, Colorado, about fifty miles northeast of Grand Junction. The specific site chosen was not company or government property but owned by a private citizen, Claude Hayward. In his seventies, with an eighth-grade education, Hayward apparently received more than one visit from interested officials to permit the blast. Though urged by his family not to accept, one day, "over a bottle of whiskey" and a promise of $100 a month if Austral generated a profit from the blast, Hayward granted the company use of his property.[8]

Originally Rulison called for the simultaneous detonation of two fifty-kiloton explosives, but concluding that was too complex, the AEC changed it to a single fifty-kiloton device buried eight thousand feet underground. This made Rulison the deepest explosion ever to take place on U.S. soil. Furthermore since one of the byproducts of fusion is a large amount of tritium, the planners turned to fission, which generated less tritium. As the device selected for Rulison was larger than that for Gasbuggy, it would break up more rock and liberate a greater amount of gas than its predecessor. Even so the AEC determined the blast posed little seismic threat, while the nearest sources of water were too far away to risk contamination. There remained issues to work out, such as drilling so far down and providing refrigeration at that depth to keep the explosive cool,[9] but if successful Rulison would guarantee more bang for the buck.

Determining the shot feasible, the AEC, the Department of Interior, and Austral signed a contract in March 1969 to conduct the blast, with industry covering 90 percent of the $6.5 million cost. It is important to note that the document did not include the signature of the governor or anyone representing his office. Because Rulison was to take place on private land within the state of Colorado as opposed to federally owned property, no law required the AEC and its corporate sponsors to obtain state authorization in advance of the blast. Not until years later did Coloradans establish a legal mechanism aimed at regulating nuclear blasts in their state. Significant as well was the determination by the AEC and Austral that if Rulison proved successful, over a hundred additional blasts, each of about two hundred kilotons, would follow, with the purpose of stimulating the entire gas field.[10] It was around this time that the public learned of the proposal. The response was much different from that for Gasbuggy: for the most part loud and angry.

Among the first to raise red flags about Rulison were about twenty academics and professors who formed a group called the Colorado Committee for Environmental Information. In May they sent a petition to the state legislature urging disapproval of the blast. Students on the University of Colorado's main campus at Boulder joined the cause. While many students in Boulder had become politicized because of the war in Vietnam, others had taken up the cause of environmentalism and formed the Anti-Pollution Committee. Joining forces with the Colorado Committee, these students wrote articles about the test for the university's newspaper and sent reprints of those stories to people living near ground zero.[11]

By August three people had emerged as the leaders of the anti-Rulison movement: Peter Metzger, a research scientist and the president of the Colorado Committee; Robert H. Williams, a physicist at the University of Colorado; and Edward Martell, a radio chemist at the National Center for Atmospheric Research. Rulison posed numerous dangers, they argued. The fission device produced about 25 percent of the tritium of Gasbuggy, but this still meant there would be tritium in the gas. The blast also would generate a large amount of krypton-85. That the AEC hoped to follow Rulison with additional blasts would increase the radioactivity exponentially. Not only would so many explosions cause widespread damage from seismic shock, but the flaring would affect farmland and water supplies, including those that served the people of Denver. The result would be "a rather larger effect on our environment than the tenfold increase in the radioactivity in the vegetation downwind from Gasbuggy."[12]

Nor were Rulison's opponents assuaged by the AEC's assurances of safety. Metzger recalled that prior to the blast, the AEC held public hearings—a step not required by law—during which the agency's David Miller compared the threat posed by radioactivity "to iodine": although unsafe if drunk "straight from the bottle . . . one drop diluted in a glass of water is harmless" and "even kills germs." Metzger deemed Miller's statement "misleading." For one, no federal body, including the AEC, had determined the maximum amount of radioactivity permissible in any gas sold to the public, yet the AEC claimed to know when diluted radioactivity was safe. Additionally the AEC had "ignored the well-known mechanisms," such as those demonstrated in the Chariot bioenvironmental studies, "by which radioactive fallout is concentrated by the food chain, thus reversing the effects of dilution."[13]

Metzger was not alone. Lieutenant Governor Mark Hogan was not fully convinced, asking that someone other than AEC officials decide whether the shot posed any danger. Sharing Hogan's reservations, the Aspen City Council voted unanimously against the shot, charging there were "too many unknowns" about it. Fred Smith, who lived about thirty miles from Rulison, went even further: "The leaders of the Uranium Capital of the World had sold our body and soul to the AEC many years ago, and the manager of the Chamber of Commerce saw this event as merely something that was good for the restaurant and hotel business." Such outcry against the shot was, recalled Seaborg, "something that the Plowshare program had not previously encountered and something that had probably not entered sufficiently into our planning."[14]

Not everyone accepted such admonitions and assertions. Governor John A. Love, despite his own doubts, accepted the AEC's reassurances of safety. Far more favorable toward the explosion was Representative Wayne Aspinall (D-Colorado), the chair of the Committee on Interior and Insular Affairs and a member of the JCAE. A long-time advocate of resource development—which did little to please environmentalists—Aspinall relied heavily on the support of both the oil-shale and uranium industries, which "had a considerable presence in" his district. He charged "preservationists and the professors, most of them now wearing long hair," along with "some of the livestock people" for worrying too much "about environmental quality." If anything, Aspinall wanted to move faster on Rulison than did the AEC. The original plan was to hold Rulison on May 22, but the AEC decided to delay execution until September so it could study whether a dam about twenty-five miles away might be damaged by the shock waves and determine whether it was necessary to lower the water level in the dam, wait until the tourist season had ended, and avoid spring thaws that made mountain slopes unstable, thereby increasing the chance of landslides. Quizzing the AEC's John Kelly, Aspinall asked how the Commission could plan a shot only to delay it for reasons of which it should have been aware before setting an execution date. "Due to administrative constraints placed upon us," Kelly replied, "we were not allowed to spend money on the Rulison project until we had a contract with the interested industrial group." Until then the AEC had not had anyone in the area; afterward, he said, the Commission had the money necessary to go to the site and determine the difficulties of proceeding.[15]

Aspinall was dumbfounded. "Who in the name of commonsense ever advised you that this was an area where the tourists went? This is one of the four reasons which have been given, been publicized, for the postponement?" he asked. The advice came from Colorado state officials and the U.S. Public Health Service," rejoined Robert Miller, manager of the AEC's Nevada Operations Office. Aspinall found that answer unsatisfactory. "Now you suggest that September and October would be a better time in which to hold the shot and you know that the cattle will be there and you know that the deer hunters and the elk hunters will be in there in much greater numbers than any other recreation group that you could possibly think of." It did not make sense, he continued, for the AEC to plan a shot and delay it, at the cost of "at least $100,000 and maybe twice that much" to Austral.[16]

With Rulison scheduled for September 6, the Colorado Open Space Coordinating Council, an alliance of conservation organizations, and the American Civil Liberties Union brought suit in U.S. district court, seeking an injunction to halt the shot on the grounds that it would create radioactive fallout, contaminate water supplies, and damage property. On August 26 District Court Judge Alfred A. Arraj ruled against the plaintiffs, deciding that the AEC had taken all of the steps required by law to ensure the blast would not pose a threat to lives or property. The plaintiffs immediately turned to the Tenth Circuit Court of Appeals, which also ruled against them, and then to the U.S. Supreme Court, which on September 3 denied their request for a restraining order.[17] All the legal avenues now closed, there was nothing to prevent the blast from taking place.

Nothing except weather. With the wind coming from the wrong direction, the AEC put the detonation on hold once again, followed by yet more delays— again because of the weather—on September 7 and 8. "The whole situation is completely absurd," Seymour Shwiller, a member of the JCAE staff, complained. Austral had to spend between $30,000 and $33,000 every day the experiment languished. "If the circumstances which can prevent the detonation of deeply buried Plowshare devices . . . are not reexamined and developed independently of weapons testing rules, there may not be another joint government-industry sponsored experiment." He suggested that it was time to examine each shot "on its own merits" rather than apply the same standards to all of them.[18] No doubt to Shwiller this meant permitting underground shots, which stood little chance of releasing radioactivity, no matter what the meteorological conditions.

On September 10 the AEC set off the 1,200-pound device, which measured only fifteen feet in length and nine inches in diameter. It created a chimney about 150 feet wide and fractured the rock for a radius of some two hundred feet. Approximately three dozen families living within a five-mile radius of ground zero had been paid to evacuate their homes for safety reasons. Some of them joined scientists, journalists, and businesspersons who had stationed themselves six miles from the blast site. About fifty others, carrying signs reading "Downwind from Rulison, ruin in 15 years" and "No contamination without represen-

Figure 7. Protest outside of the Rulison blast site. Photo courtesy of Los Alamos National Laboratory.

tation," quietly joined those at the observation tent. Another dozen opponents, led by antinuclear activist, Chester McQueary, successfully evaded security personnel, made it to ground zero, and, in plain view of those at the observation tent, laid down on top of the 10,000-foot-high mesa in which the Rulison device had been placed. "We guess that we were lifted six, seven inches off the ground," McQueary remembered of the explosion's impact. Some locals, who believed that Rulison would bring economic benefits to the region, made clear that they would have had no problem with the blast killing McQueary and his group. "To hell with them," said one farmer, John C. Clem.[19]

Rulison was even more successful than Gasbuggy, as there was no release of radioactive gas and the AEC found no indication of damage to buildings, mines, dams, or roads near the test site. Within four hours of the explosion, all of the evacuated families had returned home. Seaborg later wrote that the AEC received about a hundred claims for damage totaling some $19,000, far less than the $235,000 it had estimated. (In fact it received just over 170, at a cost of $122,000.) Promising too was the pressure in the wellhead, which by the end of the year measured better than 2,510 pounds per square inch. This was more than six times what it had been before the explosion took place and suggested that Austral could expect a nice flow of gas once scientists opened the wellhead.[20]

But what happened when the wellhead was opened? The AEC planned to wait six months before doing so to allow gas to flow into the cavity and permit shorter lived isotopes, such as iodine-131, to dissipate. Yet once it did open the wellhead, radioactivity would certainly enter the atmosphere, just as it had with Gasbuggy. It was with that concern in mind that in January 1970 the ACLU filed suit to prevent the flaring of gas. In mid-March Judge Arraj rejected the complaint, arguing that the level of tritium and krypton-85 generated by the blast was within safe limits and that the AEC had taken adequate measures to guarantee life, health, and property. There was a catch, however: Arraj made clear that his decision applied only to the Rulison well; he did not approve additional explosions or flaring from those shots.[21] Arraj's judgment was significant. While he had not denied the AEC or Austral the right to follow Rulison with other detonations designed to stimulate the entire gas field, he had left the door open to lawsuits aimed at stopping those same explosions. Austral could thus anticipate, in addition to the expense of those blasts, the cost of fighting future cases in court.

The flaring began in April, and the news for Austral and the AEC was mixed. On the one hand, the well produced 210 million cubic feet of gas in one month, equivalent to six years' worth of production from a conventional well in that region. Moreover the AEC determined that the level of tritium "in the gas [was] lower than expected and four to five times less than that from Gasbuggy." On the other hand, there *was* tritium in the gas. Arthur Tamplin, who worked in LRL-L's Biomedical Division, asserted, "There is no justification for exposing anyone to any amount of radiation—no matter how small—as a result of Project Rulison." Seaborg realized that Tamplin was not alone, and the fear of radiation exposure would make Americans unwilling to purchase Rulison-generated gas, no matter how well treated it was. When the Biomedical Division prepared a report in mid-1970 for release to the public attesting to the existence of tritium-laden gas, Seaborg wrote in his diary, "This will surely lead to adverse public reaction when it is issued." With Americans ever more sensitive about environmental protection, the AEC decided not to sell the Rulison gas. In December Governor Love, having become aware of the strength of opinion against nuclear blasting in his state, asked Seaborg to conduct no more such experiments in Colorado "without official sanction." As an indication of his seriousness, in 1971 he established an eighteen-person advisory committee to review any future AEC requests.[22]

Not surprisingly Austral officers were irate. The company's president, C. Wardell Leisk, complained to the JCAE in March 1971 that when the AEC proposed Rulison, it anticipated the shot would cost about $6 million, with the government assuming 10 percent of that amount. But because of delays and legal fees, Austral had spent closer to $11 million and "probably will never recover one penny." Then there was the way the government conducted business. Rather than guaranteeing funding over a long period, said Leisk, the government could offer appropriations only on a yearly basis; this meant that there was no guarantee a project given financial support in one year would receive it in the next. It was for this reason that Washington had consistently asked the corporate sector to assume part of the cost of nuclear stimulation experiments. "Industry can't work like this," Leisk grumbled. "I can't commit to another $10 million experiment unless I know in what period of time it will be spent, because I have to budget my funds. But our partner—the Government, in this instance—is not doing this."[23]

Even had Rulison been totally clean, it is questionable whether it would have generated the profit Austral and the AEC had anticipated. According to figures released by the AEC and industrial officials, the Rulison explosive cost $750,000, emplacing the device and cementing the well was another $750,000, drilling into the cavity following the blast added $230,000, and paying for property damages totaled $62,000. Add in the cost of interest, and a decade-long investment in Rulison would run about $3 million. In 1970 500 million cubic feet of gas had a value of $75,000. Metzger calculated that, "to be economic," Rulison would have to generate approximately "a hundredfold increase in gas production,"[24] which the AEC in its best estimates had not suggested.

Joining the voices of dissent was Representative Teno Roncalio (D-Wyoming). In addition to the damage caused by shock waves and harm to the environment, he maintained, nuclear stimulation of natural gas had actually harmed the security of the nation by unnecessarily wasting a much needed source of energy. "Natural gas is a depletable resource; it is estimated that we will run out of it in the next 50 to 150 years," he explained in June 1972 during a debate over the AEC's appropriations for the next fiscal year. "No thought is given to the fact that natural gas is also a unique and extremely important chemical resource, and that by burning more than 97 percent of our production each year, we are literally throwing away a vital resource, a resource that once it is gone, can never be replaced." He proposed an amendment that would place a twelve-month freeze on further appropriations for Plowshare. The House rejected his amendment,[25] but Roncalio had no intention of giving up his fight.

Changes at the Top

Within a year of Rulison, atomic stimulation of natural gas had emerged as the new focus of the Plowshare program. The AEC had been unable to finish the experiments needed to determine the feasibility of nuclear excavation of a canal. Generation of heat had proven a nonstarter. Isotope and element generation had made little progress, and in 1969 the AEC gave up on this aspect of the program. Ketch had found no takers, prompting the Commission to deactivate that project and abandon utilization of Plowshare technology for gas storage. The Aquarius feasibility study, issued in 1969, found conventional methods of creating water storage facilities cheaper than nuclear and without the danger of tritium contamination; after 1970 that project too received no further consideration.[26]

Use of the atom for mining suffered a similar fate. Nixon had promised to withdraw U.S. forces from Vietnam, and by late 1970 that process was well under way. Even so the Vietnam War continued to strain the nation's monetary resources. Worse, a recession had begun in 1970, marked by a rise in both unemployment and inflation rates to 6 percent, a three-month strike by workers at General Motors, and a decline in business confidence. Nixon met the economic slowdown with voluntary, and then mandatory wage and price controls, as well as cuts in government spending. Again Plowshare was one of the initiatives to take a hit. For fiscal year 1971 the AEC had requested $23 million, only to have the Bureau of the Budget cut the amount to $7.4 million. The next year Budget reduced it by another $500,000, and the AEC asked Kennecott Copper to absorb more of the expense for Sloop, but Kennecott received information that the cost of using nuclear explosives to get at the ore was little different from using conventional means and decided not to proceed with the project.[27]

The budget cuts and their effect on Plowshare took their toll on Seaborg. Reappointed in 1963 to a full five-year term by President Kennedy, he had requested to remain at his post for only two years when President Johnson asked him to stay on. He had then planned to resign, but in 1970 Nixon too asked him to stay. Seaborg agreed to do so, but only for an additional year. During that time his impression of Nixon changed. Whereas he originally believed Nixon was a defender of Plowshare, he came to view the president as holding "an antiscience or antiscientist bias." He found that prejudice shared by Nixon's influential national security adviser, Henry Kissinger. For his part Kissinger saw in Seaborg—and many others in the administration, such as Secretary of State William Rogers—a competitor for influence over presidential decision making and successfully took steps to limit the AEC chair's access to the Oval Office. "My distance from the White House—and the distance between my relationship with Lyndon Johnson and that with Richard Nixon—was never clearer than when budget time arrived," Seaborg later wrote. On the only occasion when he met with Nixon in person to discuss the AEC budget, he found the president unimpressed. After that the White House asked him to present his appropriations requests "through the Budget Director, who had already ruled against [the AEC]." Fed up with the situation in Washington and wanting to return to private life, he held to his promise and "eagerly" resigned in July 1971.[28]

James Schlesinger replaced Seaborg as the AEC's chairperson. Schlesinger had earned a Ph.D. in economics from Harvard University and taught at the University of Virginia before joining the RAND Corporation as director of strategic studies. In 1969 he joined the Nixon administration as the Bureau of the Budget's assistant director before moving to the AEC. He was hard-nosed and outspoken, and observers found him much more interested in the "internal administration" of the AEC than Seaborg had been and less concerned about what Schlesinger considered the AEC's heretofore "single-minded preoccupation with nuclear technology." Their leadership styles were also different. Seaborg ran the AEC like a seminar, "presiding but not dominating." Schlesinger considered himself more of a manager, giving each commissioner certain assignments and ensuring that "their meeting agendas [were] more tightly circumscribed."[29] Yet this managerial style and lessened focus on nuclear technology did not mean Schlesinger planned to give up on Plowshare. As head of the AEC, it was his job to defend the program, and his later comments demonstrated his intention to do just that.

Schlesinger stayed at the AEC for about eighteen months, after which Nixon shifted him to the directorship of the Central Intelligence Agency. The president then turned to Dixy Lee Ray. She had received her Ph.D. from Stanford University in marine biology and could not understand why the administration wanted someone with no training in physics, atomic technology, or defense matters. There apparently were several reasons for her selection. John Ehrlichman, Nixon's assistant for domestic affairs and a close adviser and friend of the president's, was originally from Washington State, as was Ray. Also the White House sought to appoint women to high posts in the federal government, and it had gathered information on a number of women throughout the country who might be qualified; Ray was among them. In light of the fact that the AEC had been a "men's club," the administration wanted one of its members to be a woman. Hence giving Ray the AEC chair would fulfill the call not only for a more diverse Commission but for giving women important jobs in the capital. Attracted by the post's salary and advised by both friends and coworkers not to pass up the opportunity, Ray accepted.[30]

It is likely that the White House also picked Ray because of her politics. One might naturally conclude that as a marine biologist, she would be a strong champion for the environmental movement. There is no doubt the media and public viewed her this way, which would permit the administration to answer the challenges it faced from environmentalists. But Ray was in fact not a member of the movement. "I'm for preservation and conservation," she once stated, "but I wouldn't be caught dead with a membership card. I wish more people in the sciences felt that way and stuck by it."[31] Impressed by her credentials, the Senate approved her nomination.

Project Rio Blanco

Schlesinger had reached the conclusion that Plowshare should emphasize energy stimulation, but moving that program forward proved challenging. Between 1969 and 1971 at least three stimulation experiments disappeared from the AEC's list. Project Thunderbird, first proposed in either 1966 or 1967, called for burying a nuclear explosive in northeastern Wyoming to increase coal production. Yet sometime after June 1969 the Commission gave up on it. Project Utah, suggested by Western Oil Shale Corporation and CER Geonuclear in 1968 or early the following year, foresaw using a buried atomic device to fracture oil shale near the town of Ouray, Utah. Based on a meeting held in 1971 with numerous parties, including about a dozen oil companies, it appeared there was widespread interest in the project, yet there was no indication Utah went any further. That same year Edward Teller attempted a new twist on the underground blast. He had spent much of the previous decade establishing and chairing the Department of Applied Science, a partnership between the University of California at Davis and UCRL. But his beloved Plowshare program had never been far from his mind. He proposed seting off a nuclear device in a cavity filled partway with water. Companies could capture the steam generated by the explosion to provide power. Although the JCAE favored appropriating $500,000 for this project, the AEC, already short of funding, considered the proposal a waste of money and refused to designate funds for it.[32]

This left Rio Blanco. Like Project Rulison, Rio Blanco was a cooperative effort between the AEC and CER Geonuclear. In December 1970 they began to study a site near Rifle, Colorado, about ten miles east of Rulison. Unlike Gasbuggy and Rulison, Rio Blanco would use three explosives, each of thirty-three kilotons and placed vertically at depths of 5,840, 6,230, and 6,690 feet, which the AEC would set off in staggered blasts. In so doing it could avoid the shock waves a single large explosion would generate, fracture more rock than in previous shots, and hopefully see a much greater increase in gas production. Because of continued cuts in its funding, the AEC asked for and received an industry promise to pay 85 percent of Rio Blanco's $8.9 million price tag.[33]

Rio Blanco faced the most roadblocks yet to realization. In January 1970, a couple of months after the Rulison blast, Nixon signed into law the National Environmental Policy Act (NEPA). The president himself was ambivalent when it come to protecting the environment, but polls showed that "environmental concern had tripled since 1965"; both Senators Edmund Muskie of Maine and Henry Jackson of Washington, two potential Democratic nominees for president in 1972, called for doing more to stop environmental degradation; and Ehrlichman had a strong interest in the subject. Signing the law, the president declared, "The 1970s absolutely must be the years when America pays its debts to the past by reclaiming the purity of its air, its water, and our living environment. It is literally now or never."[34]

In addition to establishing the President's Council on Environmental Quality, NEPA requires all agencies of government to prepare environmental assessments and environmental impact statements. The assessment determines whether the proposed activity will have an effect on the environment. If the government entity involved finds that the impact on the environment will be significant, it must fill out an impact statement, for which it must seek comment from the public, other government agencies, and outside parties before proceeding. (The agency involved may sometimes move directly to an impact statement before filling out an assessment.) Following comments, that agency then must submit a final impact statement detailing how the comments on the earlier draft affected its ultimate decision on the project in question. Simply put, NEPA not only added one more step to completion of any peaceful atomic-use project, but its requirement for public commentary ensured Plowshare opponents a voice in governmental decision making.

About four months after Nixon signed NEPA into law, the first Earth Day was celebrated. Inspired by the teach-ins that took place on college and university campuses in opposition to the Vietnam War, Senator Gaylord Nelson (D-Wisconsin) proposed a similar movement, but one aimed at protecting the environment. Though the Nixon administration did not favor the idea, pressure brought on the White House prompted the Interior Department and other federal agencies to lend their support. When it took place on April 22, Earth Day attracted some 20 million participants throughout the nation.[35] More aware than ever before of the interest in protecting the environment, Nixon later that year established the EPA to coordinate the administration's environmental programs. Consequently the AEC had to add the EPA to the list of those whose approval it needed to meet NEPA requirements.

The voices given a chance to express themselves through NEPA made themselves heard. CER Geonuclear proposed that Rio Blanco constitute the first in a three-phase program to demonstrate the feasibility of gas stimulation. If Rio Blanco proved successful, then in late 1973 or 1974 CER Geonuclear and the AEC would use the atom to stimulate four to six wells on one day. If that went without incident, phase 3 would start around late 1974 and involve between twenty and sixty well stimulations. A single shot involving three explosives was worrisome enough to Rio Blanco's opponents, but the idea of potentially dozens of such blasts was far more frightening. Critics once again pointed to the danger posed by radioactive gas, seismic shocks, or water contamination. Some scientists argued that the radioactivity generated by Rio Bravo would serve to increase cancer. The Oil Shale Corporation, a company founded in California in 1955, charged that the shaking caused by Rio Blanco would damage its nearby mining operations. "We have conservatively calculated the value of the recoverable oil shale alone to be 100 times greater than the value of the gas which the Rio Blanco project seeks to produce," commented Louis H. Yardumian, vice president of the corporation. David Evans of the Colorado Open Spaces Council attested that the AEC itself had admitted that an underground weapons test in Alaska in 1971 would contaminate groundwater, and there was no guarantee the same would not happen as a result of Rio Blanco. And even if the shot went off without a hitch, the casings that held the explosives would eventually deteriorate, leaking radioactivity into the Colorado River.[36]

Rio Blanco's defenders rejected such charges. In July 1971 the AEC had conducted Project Miniata at the NTS. An eighty-three-kiloton blast, Miniata used a new type of fission explosive, called Diamond. It was smaller and designed "with a shield to absorb the small quantities of tritium that would be produced." Rio Blanco would also use the Diamond explosive, and, asserted the test's defenders, any radioactivity that might enter the atmosphere would be less than that a person would receive flying from the East to West Coast. The Oil Shale Corporation had nothing to fear, pledged Kelly, because the explosives were placed too far from the oil shale to cause any damage. Even some locals were prepared to allow the blast to take place. Said William Brennan, a rancher, "Most people here will go along with this first shot and then evaluate its effects."[37]

Supportive voices notwithstanding, Seaborg had learned from Rulison that the AEC could not ignore opponents. Based on its past experience, it is surprising the Commission took so long to realize the difference between conducting tests at the NTS and off-site. For tests taking place at the NTS, all the AEC needed was executive approval; it did not have to take into account local or state reaction to the blast. In fact it could keep those tests secret if it so chose. This did not hold for off-site explosions. In those cases the Commission had to make local and state officials aware of its plans. Yet it had assumed that it could treat those tests the same way it did blasts at the NTS. Maybe because of the lack of reaction to Gasbuggy, the AEC had presumed little public outcry as it prepared Rulison. Still Chariot and Ketch should have taught it not to make such an assumption. In those two instances the Commission did not realize its error until the opposition had become overwhelming, and by then it was too late.

This time the AEC took no chances. In early 1971 it joined a new body called the Ad Hoc Committee on Project Rio Blanco. Consisting of representatives from the AEC, LLNL, CER Geonuclear, and a variety of local environmental organizations, it had several purposes, including liaison with Coloradoans, "encouraging public-participation in the decision-making process at the earliest possible stages of planning," and "establishing criteria for adequate environmental impact statements," as required by NEPA.[38]

In January 1972 the AEC submitted an environmental statement for review by federal and state agencies, among them Governor Love's advisory committee, the Colorado Water Pollution Control Commission, the U.S. Department of Interior, and the EPA. The AEC followed up with public hearings two months later in Meeker—the nearest town, located thirty miles from ground zero—and Denver. Though the commission tried to assuage public concerns over safety, the outcry continued. Morey Wolfson, the director of Environmental Action of Colorado and a member of the Rio Blanco Committee, told an audience in Denver that the AEC's narrow focus on economic gain made it oblivious to the potential danger posed by fallout. In that respect claims by Plowshare's defenders that they were trying to create a better world was nothing more than talk. "The A.E.C.," he proclaimed, "seems to be bent on a course of threatening the health and welfare of the public by clinging to 1945 technology—fission—instead of researching and developing the energy sources of the future—fusion and solar." He reminded his audience that Rio Blanco was planned as the first of many such blasts that threatened the region's environmental well-being.[39]

Floyd Haskell, one of Colorado's two Democratic U.S. senators, also found fault with the impact statement. "My conclusion, based upon the available data and conferences with informed individuals, is that full field development of the project is out of the question," he wrote Secretary of the Interior C. B. Morton. "The number of atomic blasts involved would result in unacceptably high levels of radioactivity and, of course, there are other obvious dangers endemic to nuclear explosions." He argued that since Rio Blanco was the first of a multiphase nuclear stimulation program, the AEC needed to submit a revised environmental impact statement regarding the entire program. Until then he wanted to see Rio Blanco deferred. Taking into account such criticism, the Commission submitted an addendum to its impact statement in March 1973, though it still concluded the shot was safe. As far as the AEC was concerned, it had "met all of the legal requirements" and had "taken every means to assure the public that the safety of this project [was] its utmost concern." With that, the Commission requested the Bureau of Land Management to transfer into its hands "360 acres of public land" so that it could proceed with the shot.[40]

With the AEC having taken another step toward holding Rio Blanco, the debate over the blast intensified. Speaking for the Federation of American Scientists, Gordon J. F. McDonald, Herbert Scoville Jr., and Edward L. Tatum pointed out that the three-phase program proposed by the AEC meant, "300 nuclear explosions with yields of 30 KT are proposed to be detonated just to determine the feasibility of this technique. Full-field development may require about a thousand underground nuclear explosions." What would be the results? Considering that "more than 20 U.S. nuclear tests at the Nevada test site including those in the lower yield ranges" had vented accidentally, there was the likelihood of similar incidents during the entire Rio Blanco program. "Flaring of the gas will automatically place large quantities of radioactive nuclides, particularly Tritium Carbon 14, Argon and Krypton, into the atmosphere." There was every chance of radioactive contamination of water. Furthermore, even when completed, the full Rio Blanco program would "only produce approximately one trillion cubic feet per year, about 2–3% of the total U.S. estimated 1985 gas requirements."[41]

Local, state, and industrial officials, as well as conservationists, joined the chorus and urged the Bureau of Land Management not to turn the land in question over to the AEC. The Aspen City Council unanimously voted not to accept gas that was any more radioactive than that which the city currently used. The Pitkin County Commission, which represented Aspen, protested that the county might suffer fallout, water contamination, and reduced tourist business. Glenn E. Keller Jr., the president of the Colorado State Board of Health, expressed concern that flaring of the gas "could result in downwind contamination of vegetation and population." Governor Love, who had shown a willingness to permit Project Rulison, seemed more concerned than ever about nuclear stimulation, commenting, "I can't personally imagine a time, a society, in which several hundred shots would be acceptable." Evans of the Colorado Open Spaces Council observed that extrapolating the findings of the Federation of American Scientists with regard to stimulating the Rio Blanco field meant thirteen thousand nuclear-stimulated wells would be needed to get at all of the gas in the Green River region of Colorado and Wyoming. Just the damage from the seismicity would cost in the millions of dollars, making the project economically untenable. Oil Shale Corporation continued to express its objections, and the Sierra Club's Lee Dodge charged, "We are the nation's guinea pigs in an insane experiment for a few dollars for a few corporate enterprises which includes the AEC."[42]

Haskell, fellow Colorado representative Pat Schroeder, and Senator Gale Mc-Gee (D-Wyoming) added legal, bureaucratic, and resource concerns to those of seismic and environmental damage. Haskell indicted the AEC for not permitting public comment on the addendum to the environmental impact statement because "for some reasons" that even AEC Chair Ray did not know, "it was prohibited by the Department of Defense." Schroeder accused the AEC of breaking the law by not submitting an environmental impact statement to cover the entire Rio Blanco program, and McGee argued that with their calendars already full, lawmakers did not have time to fully assess the addendum prior to the blast. Even Senator Hansen had begun to backtrack from his earlier endorsement of nuclear stimulation of energy sources. Although he acknowledged that the atom could help "in making other more conventional sources of energy available to man," he added a caveat: "This is unproved. No one knows what will happen. And obviously, because [the AEC] does propose to move the atom into a new and relatively untried realm, we are greatly concerned."[43]

The most strident congressional commentary, though, came from Congressman Teno Roncalio. Now in his second term, Roncalio had obtained a seat on the JCAE and clearly intended to use it to try to convince his colleagues not to conduct the blast. Aside from the danger Rio Blanco posed to the environment and humans, it was, he proclaimed, an unnecessary waste of the nation's uranium. The energy released by each blast could have been put toward producing electricity rather than squandered in gas stimulation. As it was, the amount of uranium available in the country was not enough to fulfill the requirements of the AEC's nuclear reactor program; to use that uranium for Plowshare would mean even less for nuclear power. "It is clear that we have to accelerate exploration and extraction and guard against inefficient use—such as Plowshare could represent."[44]

Citizens in the area had their own concerns. "I don't mind a single shot, but if they knock the house down 200 or 300 times, that gets kind of old," commented J. O. Welland, who owned a ranch not far from the blast site. Elfred Morlan, manager of a liquor store near the Meeker Hotel, declared, "I'm about as scared as I can get," and John Hughes, the hotel's manager, believed that Rio Blanco would not "do any good": "And the way the Government is, I wish they'd shoot it off in Washington, D.C."[45]

The Federation of American Scientists, Haskell, McGee, Roncalio, and others believed there was an alternative to nuclear stimulation, known as hydraulic fracturing. Developed after World War II, hydraulic fracturing uses a fluid to break up the rock around deposits of oil, gas, or water. Advances in the technology had demonstrated its potential, fracturing advocates insisted, and it did not offer the danger posed by radioactivity. It was also relatively cheap. Roncalio contended that at a total cost of about $11 million—the same amount of money Austral Oil Company had spent on Rulison—hydraulic tests at the Rulison field had produced 450 million cubic feet of gas. Fracturing had been used at twenty-nine well sites near Rio Blanco "at an average cost per well of only $14,000, with comparable average gas flow."[46]

Rio Blanco's defenders rebuffed every one of these arguments. Assistant Secretary of the Interior Stephen A. Wakefield, the AEC's Gerald Johnson, and Paul M. Dougan of Equity Oil Company—one of the firms represented by CER Geonuclear—agreed that hydraulic fracturing could work in media that was porous and therefore easy for the fluid to break up. But the permeability of the gas formations at Rio Blanco was "almost a hundred times less than those in which successful hydraulic fracturing techniques have been applied."[47]

Furthermore the AEC and its allies believed that the shot's critics had placed too much emphasis on the thousands of blasts potentially required to develop the full gas field. When Governor Love wrote Schlesinger in December 1972 regarding his concerns about Rio Blanco, the AEC chair replied that the blast did not in any way "prepose or commit to a production campaign." Johnson seconded him. "As the Rio Blanco Environmental Statement specifies no commitment has been made by the AEC to any future use of nuclear explosives for natural gas stimulation beyond Rio Blanco." To take that step, Johnson continued, would require the AEC to submit a new environmental impact statement and to amend the 1954 Atomic Energy Act to allow the AEC to provide nuclear explosives "to industry on a commercial basis." Even if Rio Blanco proved successful and the AEC and interested firms decided to press on with developing the entire gas field, there was no reason to believe that the country would use up its uranium reserves. Roncalio had based his findings on a report that focused only on uranium of a certain price, charged LLNL's Gary Higgins; there was in fact additional, though more expensive, uranium available. If nuclear stimulation worked as well as planned and proved as profitable as the AEC believed it would, then the AEC could use the more expensive uranium for stimulation projects, leaving the lower priced ore for other purposes.[48]

Nor was seismic damage an issue, asserted Rio Blanco's defenders. The land around the blast zone was sparsely populated, and staggering the explosives would further limit any destruction to nearby buildings. The AEC and CER Geonuclear anticipated the total cost of the damage would be no more than $64,000, and CER Geonuclear had taken steps to cover any claims.[49]

As for the potential environmental impact from Rio Blanco, scientists at Oak Ridge National Laboratory studying gas from the Rulison test reported that the annual increase in radioactivity a person would receive from using that gas was less than that person would get from the sun if he or she moved to an elevation about five feet higher. One could anticipate that gas produced by the much cleaner Diamond explosive would prove even less radioactive. Nor was there any reason to worry about water, for the nearest aquifer was 3,500 feet above the blast zone. "We can envision no possible mechanism of transport of the radioactivity through these nonwater-bearing formations to the aquifers above," maintained Johnson. Indeed Rio Blanco and the Plowshare program writ large were environmentally friendly. Stated Robert C. McHugh, the president of Colorado Interstate Gas Company, "The role of natural gas in alleviating air pollution in our major consuming centers is acknowledged by industry and by all levels of government."[50]

In case these assertions in favor of Rio Blanco were not enough, maybe cold war security concerns would be. Between April 1969 and July 1971 the United States and the Soviet Union held three series of meetings to discuss the peaceful use of nuclear explosives. At those talks U.S. officials began to get a clearer idea of the extent of the Kremlin's program, which included not just activities similar to that of the U.S. Plowshare program, such as mining, storage, and canal construction, but also stimulating oil production and stopping gas well fires. Johnson pointed out that during just 1971 and 1972 the Soviet Union had conducted sixteen experiments: "[Thus] the Soviet Union is today in a more favorable position to utilize nuclear explosions for peaceful purposes and in a broader range of applications than is the United States."[51] If Washington did not develop an effective peaceful-uses program of its own, one that it could offer to other nations as required by the Nuclear Nonproliferation Treaty, then Moscow would step in, gaining prestige and, possibly, allies as a result.

Some local officials and residents also took the AEC's side. The Mesa County Board of Commissioners and the mayor of Grand Junction, the largest city in Mesa County, endorsed the blast because it would allow for the development of resources in the region. A survey of residents in Rifle ascertained that 59 percent wanted to see Rio Blanco proceed. *New York Times* reporter James P. Sterba concluded that the most "common view" was one held by dude rancher James Fox, who had lived in the area for four decades: "It doesn't interest me a damn bit."[52]

Those locals who endorsed the blast tended to place their trust in the AEC and CER Geonuclear that nothing harmful would occur. But the AEC and CER Geonuclear admitted that there was always the possibility of an accident that could generate a "minor" leak of radioactivity into the atmosphere. Additionally, as in the case of Gasbuggy and Rulison, the flaring of the gas would mean "a measurable increase in radioactivity in air, soil, plants or animals." In fact CER Geonuclear had taken out insurance to cover up to $11 million in claims to provide further protection in the event of a mistake. For these reasons a group of Colorado environmental organizations on May 12 attempted to convince a state district court to halt the blast, only to have the judge in the case, Henry E. Santo, throw out their suit. He determined that the AEC had taken the required steps under NEPA by informing federal and state authorities of the planned explosion and holding public hearings on the shot. He also found that the evidence submitted showed that Rio Blanco would not permit the escape of dangerous amounts of radioactivity to enter the atmosphere.[53]

Although they could have pursued the case in appellate court, the plaintiffs lacked the money to do so. Nor was it likely Governor Love could have stopped the blast, even had he shown a willingness to do so. Said Schlesinger in January, "The Federal Government has the authority to proceed with such a test on Federal lands. . . . Thus, cancellation of the Rio Blanco test would reflect intergovernmental consultation rather than exercise of State authority."[54]

Nixon authorized Rio Blanco on May 11. Six days later the AEC exploded the three devices, each measuring only seven inches across. Ray and Love watched it from a helicopter flying over the site, while just over a dozen protestors ensconced themselves at the Rio Blanco general store, about eighteen miles distant. It went "perfectly," Ray proudly declared afterward. There was no release of radioactivity, and local residents felt virtually nothing. "I thought I'd be rocking around like a drunk," said one person who had come to Meeker to witness the blast. Nor was the damage that significant. The AEC ended up paying only $60,000 in claims.[55] At issue now was to gauge how much gas the explosion had stimulated and the level of radioactivity in it. That assessment certainly might affect two other shots the Commission had in mind: the Wyoming Area Stimulation Project (WASP) and Project Wagon Wheel.

Projects WASP and Wagon Wheel

A joint venture of the AEC and about six oil companies that owned nearly 300,000 acres in the Green River Basin in southwestern Wyoming, WASP was first proposed in 1967 and focused on a reservoir of gas 10,000 to 18,000 feet underground. The project involved only a single explosive, but it was unique in two respects. First, the depth of burial would be ten thousand feet, deeper than any test up to that point. Second, the 100-kiloton device would be the largest yet.[56]

WASP never reached the execution phase. In August 1968 Robert McDonald of the International Nuclear Group—which represented the companies—complained that for the shot to proceed, its corporate participants needed the information then being gathered from Gasbuggy. No one, however, was prepared to give his clients what they needed. Yet it appears that the companies involved finally received the requisite information, for in 1969 the AEC and the companies signed a "project definition agreement," and a survey began to look for a site. In January 1971 Seaborg wrote that WASP was in the planning stage, but there is no evidence that the project received any further consideration.[57]

Wagon Wheel got much further and consequently provoked far more controversy than WASP. A joint effort of the AEC and EPNG, its focus was a site in Sublette County, Wyoming, located in the southwestern part of the state and not far from the area proposed for WASP. Ground zero sat over the Pinedale Unit, an area of about ninety thousand acres of land owned by the U.S. and Wyoming governments, EPNG, and two other gas companies. EPNG had approached the AEC as early as 1958, but because of the lack of necessary technology, nothing further took place until after Gasbuggy. Encouraged by Gasbuggy, on Christmas Eve 1968 the AEC, Interior Department, and EPNG signed a contract to proceed with a feasibility study.[58]

Following investigations in 1969–70, the AEC put together a design concept for the blast, which built on the proposal it had developed for Rio Blanco. Instead of three devices of about thirty kilotons each, Wagon Wheel would use five 100-kiloton explosives stacked vertically between 9,220 and 11,570 feet underground. Like Rio Blanco, the explosions would be staggered. If the shot, planned for fiscal year 1974, worked, then the AEC and EPNG called for developing the entire field, with the blasting of ten wells to take place in 1977 and adding ten per year, reaching fifty annually starting in 1981. Pointing to Wagon Wheel's economic value, the Commission contended that full field development would employ as many as twenty thousand people "and involve investment at a rate of about 200 million dollars per year." In January of the following year the AEC submitted a draft environmental impact statement, which, as in the case of Rio Blanco, anticipated damage from seismic shock and the release of radioactivity from flaring but concluded that restitution would not prove exorbitant and that the radiation would pose no environmental hazard. Just in case, it had set aside $65,000 for any damages.[59]

The environmental impact statement did not reassure Roncalio. "I am personally concerned about the possibility of flaring gas during production testing, and I'm not certain this is in the best interests of public safety," he declared. He acknowledged that it was important to meet the nation's demand for energy, but added, "I still believe these material values have to be balanced with human values, and unless these questions are resolved, then Project Wagon Wheel ought not to proceed at this time."[60]

Many locals felt similarly. Within twenty miles of ground zero lay the towns of Pinedale, Big Piney, Marbeton, and Boulder, with a combined population of just over 1,800. Pinedale, the largest of the four communities, became the locus of the resistance. Mary Ann Steele, a retired science teacher who knew about the impact of Bravo and Linus Pauling's work, called the draft environmental impact statement "a flimsy little piece of garbage." She warned Hansen, who was up for reelection, that his bid for another term could flounder if Wagon Wheel proceeded. Another local, rancher Floyd Bousman, became furious when he learned the AEC had priced a recently completed "dam at Boulder Lake" at $150,000, when "it cost in excess of a half a million dollars. Then we became aware of the Price-Anderson Act, which limits the liability for any atomic incident to $5,000." There was simply no way, he said, that $65,000 would cover the cost of the damage caused by Wagon Wheel. Determined to stop the blast, Steele, Bousman, and other locals formed the Wagon Wheel Information Committee (WWIC). "I would say there were probably twelve people who came together as a group," recollected Steele. But each had a specialty that proved highly useful. Bousman was "a natural fine public speaker. Ken Perry was a geologist that knew his stuff and had taught in the university." Sally Mackey, a librarian, "kept the records," and Mackey's daughter, who "had a little bit of journalism experience . . . was getting out press releases." Fred Smith, one of Rulison's opponents, helped out as well. "Nothing but knowledge could prevent kids from enjoying plutonium candy," he wrote friends, and so he provided the WWIC with advice and the "names of folks shook up by Rulison."[61]

The AEC had its defenders, however. For the moment Governor Stan Hathaway stood behind the Commission, believing the environmental impact statement had proven both that hydraulic fracturing would not work and that Wagon Wheel would lead to only a minimal release of radioactivity. Comparing these potential costs to the benefits the blast offered in terms of meeting the nation's demand for energy, he saw no reason to veto the experiment. The council of Big Piney, the closest populated area to the blast and the home of a large number of people who had made money from the gas companies, voted unanimously in support of the experiment. The editors of the Casper, Wyoming's Star Tribune wrote, "It is heartening to find some support for scientific endeavor to unlock new reserves of natural gas—the cleanest burning fuel we have."[62]

The AEC tried to calm the brewing storm by holding public hearings in both Meeker and Denver in late March. It also took into account commentary given it by the EPA on such matters as other possible sources of energy and the risks versus benefits of selling radioactive gas. It then issued a final environmental impact statement in April, reasserting the blast's safety and utility. These efforts backfired. An angered Steele wrote EPA Administrator William Ruckelshaus, asking if there was anything more his agency could do to prohibit the blast. Answering for Ruckelshaus, Donald Dubois, the EPA's deputy regional administrator, explained that under NEPA the AEC assumed the power of "lead agency" for Wagon Wheel, and therefore all the EPA could do was to act as "reviewer." Perry, who taught at the University of Wyoming, declared that the region could "be-come the earthquake center of the world," a warning that probably explained an advertisement by a local insurance company. Putting the word *Wagonwheel* in bold letters at the top, the ad declared, "THERE, WE'VE CAUGHT YOUR ATTENTION. Why not drop in to discuss your insurance?"[63]

Joining the WWIC were state officials and the media. Roncalio and McGee continued to resist the AEC, the latter charging that the impact statement "was premature, failed to cover the overall impact, and failed to comply with some criteria laid out for the preparation of such reports." Hathaway, though not up for reelection, demonstrated a change of heart. Along with the reelection-minded Hansen, he concluded that the final environmental impact statement left too many questions unanswered and asked the AEC to hold another public hearing on the blast before committing themselves. Even the *Star Tribune* now admitted to "some second thoughts on proceeding at full speed." The paper questioned the blast's "economic feasibility." It also took note that ranchers in Big Piney and Pinedale, most of whom neither "enjoy[ed] the convenience of pipeline gas" nor wanted a bunch of outsiders coming to their communities, lacked the enthusi-asm exhibited by the Pig Piney town council. Concluded the *Star-Tribune*, "Wagon Wheel can wait for more convincing evidence."[64]

Adding to the troubles faced by Wagon Wheel was funding. For fiscal year 1973, Plowshare's budget was $6.8 million, of which $2.7 million was slated for a test shot for Wagon Wheel; Livermore's Glenn Werth wanted another $1 million to guarantee enough money for the five explosives required for the project. Con-gressman Craig Hosmer of California, cognizant of the Nixon administration's determination to cut costs, and likely desirous to wait until the results of Rio Blanco came out, was reluctant to recommend such a large appropriation. He wondered if the AEC was saving money by ordering five devices instead of just one or two. Furthermore, if Congress did approve the $1 million, would the AEC actually use the devices within that fiscal year? Otherwise, it would turn out to be a waste of money. "I would not want to give you a million dollars if you could not tell me that you are going to save anything," he explained during a hearing of the JCAE.[65] Roncalio was even more adamant. His desire to see Plowshare fund-ing completely cut for fiscal year 1973 resulted from his determination to see Wagon Wheel killed.

Roncalio's failure to kill Plowshare gave the program's defenders some hope they might yet save it and Wagon Wheel. Among them was Teller. Stopping in Sheridan, Wyoming, in September, he attacked Wagon Wheel's opponents, fo-cusing his vituperation against not Roncalio but McGee: "By exploiting this scare, and behaving like a Democrat, McGee makes it difficult for us to go ahead with it." He implied that the Wyoming lawmaker was antiprogress, for Wagon

Wheel was "underground mining, without the miners going underground." He then pulled out his well-worn cold war card, asserting that the Soviets had progressed much further than the United States in their peaceful-use program. "The Russians don't let their Senator McGees write idiotic letters," he declared. "I don't like Sen. McGee, but I vastly prefer him to the USSR."[66]

EPNG also went on the offensive. In August it announced it had hired two scientists, Keith Schiager, a radiation ecologist from Colorado State University, and H. G. Fisser, a plant scientist from the University of Wyoming, to gather data to augment the final environmental impact statement and prove Wagon Wheel's innocuousness. EPNG director Philip Randolph, possibly hoping to prove his company had the interests of the locals in mind, promised that if the people living nearby did not want Wagon Wheel, his company would not pursue it.[67]

The effort to change minds had little effect. Teller's comments angered Sylvia Freeman, the chairperson of Sheridan County's Democratic Central Committee, who termed the physicist's remarks "particularly disturbing, coming from someone who is supposed to be motivated by the standards of scientific objectivity": "Teller's position seems to be that since he, personally, is in favor of Wagon Wheel, no one should question it." The two scientists hired by EPNG had previously spoken in favor of Wagon Wheel, the *High Country News* pointed out. "With men like Schiager and Fisser, why even have a study? It's like having Lyndon Johnson do an independent evaluation of our involvement in the Vietnam War."[68]

The tension between the two sides increased in November when the WWIC held a straw poll on election day. Of the 1,230 who participated, an overwhelming 71 percent expressed opposition. EPNG rejected the results. Randolph charged that the WWIC "distributed large amounts of misleading and erroneous information even before the current studies [were] concluded." Calling the survey "premature," he added, "Under these conditions we do not feel the poll accurately reflects the feeling that the citizens of Sublette County will have after consideration of factual and unbiased information." When reminded that EPNG had promised not to conduct Wagon Wheel if local residents did not want it, Randolph remained unmoved. His company had not yet made up its mind on whether to conduct the blast; only if EPNG decided to proceed would public opinion matter.[69]

Randolph's remarks left the WWIC indignant. The recently reelected Hansen met with the group a few days later and accepted a suggestion that he set up a meeting in Washington between Wyoming's congressional delegation, Schlesinger, EPNG representatives, and the WWIC. Paying either out of pocket or with the help of donations, eleven WWIC delegates went to the capital in February 1973, where they held discussions with Roncalio, McGee, Hansen, and representatives from the AEC, EPA, and EPNG. Bousman also took the opportunity to appear on NBC's *Today* show, where he used the forum to express the WWIC's opposition to the blast. By the time they left, whatever goodwill existed between the WWIC and its allies on the one hand and the AEC and EPNG on the other was gone. The WWIC delegates had assumed Schlesinger would meet with them only to have someone else from the AEC do so. Meanwhile officials from EPNG, recalled Bousman, "did a lot of quibbling over semantics." He admitted, "The attitude of the AEC and El Paso officials at this February 7 meeting in Washington destroyed for us what little credibility they had left."[70]

McGee, himself incensed, sent a formal letter of protest later that month to Ray, who had just been made chair of the AEC, no doubt hoping that he would find a more receptive ear. Ray made clear that the fiscal year 1974 budget approved by Congress in late January 1973 contained "no funds . . . for the Wagon Wheel Project or any preparatory development and testing of explosives capable of sequential detonation." And even if funding became available in FY 1975, there was no way for Wagon Wheel to take place prior to 1977. That Wagon Wheel would receive no such funding became clear during discussions over the FY 1975 budget. The proposal, Ray stated, was "dead as a doornail." Realizing the death of Wagon Wheel almost certainly meant the death of the entire Plowshare program, a dejected Hosmer told her, "You are talking about the project I love."[71]

Plowshare's Slow Demise

On March 29, 1974, the *Wall Street Journal* reported that the AEC had granted CER Geonuclear a contract valued at up to $3 million to test hydraulic fracturing as a method of stimulating natural gas production. "Generally," the newspaper reported, "nuclear stimulation has thus far disappointed its backers because it has released smaller amounts of gas than had been hoped."[72] The *Journal*'s report was most telling, for it was an indictment of the entire resource stimulation program.

Indictment did not mean death, however. Despite Ray's remarks and the *Journal*'s report, Plowshare's demise was not immediate. Indeed Ray explained before the JCAE that Wagon Wheel was "dead" only for the present. "By 1977, however, things may have changed." Key was the final report from Rio Blanco, and in the event those findings proved propitious, then similar experiments, including Wagon Wheel, might follow. For that reason Ray asked for $107 million in early 1974 to cover gas and oil shale stimulation projects over the next five years.[73]

Rio Blanco did not achieve the intended results. The AEC had assumed the individual explosives would form a single, large chimney; instead they created three separate cavities. The AEC found no gas in the top cavity and was unable to get a drill into the middle one. It found no tritium, but it did discover cesium-137, which immediately brought a stop to the flaring. Adding to the AEC's woes was the discovery by Colorado health officials of strontium-90 in the well. Already skeptical that the AEC could remove the cesium, the Nuclear Regulatory Commission prohibited sale of the fuel when it learned of the presence of the strontium, and the oil companies involved in the project withdrew their support. With that, Rio Blanco, Wagon Wheel, the gas stimulation program, and Plowshare all came to an end. Yet in a move analogous to putting a wooden stake in the heart of a vampire, Colorado voters, through their own initiative in November 1974, amended their state's constitution to prohibit any nuclear explosions without their approval. Two years later the AEC sealed the Rio Blanco cavity and gave up on any plan to develop the Green River field. After spending a combined $80 million on nuclear stimulation technology and tests between 1966 and 1973, the AEC and corporate sponsors had come up empty-handed.[74]

As had proven true with excavation, other aspects of the Plowshare program, including isotope and heat production and storage, mining, and stimulation of natural gas, were in part the victims of forces beyond their control. In some cases, such as isotope and heat production, the explosives simply did not act as hoped, and the AEC decided to give up on what it concluded was a lost cause. With regard to mining, cuts in federal appropriations and a lack of corporate interest had the greatest impact. Even when industry or a state took notice, as in the cases of Ketch and Aquarius, the financial cost, resistance from some firms, powerful grassroots opposition, and political considerations all took their toll. Nowhere, however, did a lack of federal funding and the coalition of local, state, federal, environmental, and corporate opponents merge as they did with regard to stimulation of oil and natural gas. The AEC no longer had the support it needed to overcome such resistance.

Yet the AEC was again in part responsible for the difficulties it faced. It was notoriously slow in learning lessons. Chariot, Ketch, and the Panama Canal project should have taught the AEC that conducting tests at the NTS, which required only White House approval, was far different from explosions held outside of the test site. Seaborg stated that, as a result of Rulison, the AEC had understood its mistakes, and it did make an extra effort to convince residents in Colorado and Wyoming that both Rio Blanco and Wagon Wheel could take place safely. Even then, though, it remained myopically focused on seeing those blasts through. Plowshare's defenders continued to use the language of progress and security by pointing to economic benefits offered by their program or the need to stay ahead of the Soviet Union in peaceful-use technology. In a world where trust in government had fallen precipitously and in which U.S.-Soviet relations had shown significant improvement, such words carried little weight, and the preparedness of Plowshare's corporate allies to ignore voices of dissent did not help matters. While it is unlikely the AEC could have convinced interested parties that nuclear stimulation or the gas it produced was safe, the Commission had done itself no favors.

Back from the Dead?

The Erie Canal, Edward Teller told an audience in Tokyo in 1973, "played a great role in opening up the Middle West, which at that time was a wilderness." Begun in 1817, that waterway commenced operations in 1826, "and within a few years paid for itself." Now, said Teller, there was an opportunity to achieve a similar feat using nuclear explosives.[1]

The subject about which Teller spoke was not a new isthmian canal. Rather he hoped to sell the audience on the construction of a waterway across the Kra Isthmus in Thailand, the narrow strip of land that connects mainland Asia to the Malay Peninsula. Thailand's prime minister, Thanom Kittikachorn, had first raised this project in 1967 during a visit by Glenn Seaborg, chairman of the AEC. "The Kra canal," wrote Seaborg, "would cut off almost a thousand miles of transport by sea from Bangkok to the west and even more should the Straits of Malacca be closed due to international tensions." Now, in 1973, Teller hoped to see the proposal become reality. Some had estimated the cost of construction at $800 million, but he insisted it was lower. While there remained the need to develop clean nuclear devices for such a project, he believed they would be available "in the not too distant future." "This would serve to reduce people's fears which they show today."[2]

At the time of Teller's visit, Plowshare was in the process of its slow death. All aspects of the peaceful-use program, save stimulation of natural gas, had perished. Despite that, Teller still hoped to save it. Unfortunately for him and other Plowshare proponents, the Kra Canal never got beyond a concept. The project called for using 139 explosives totaling over forty-one megatons, which required evacuating 200,000 people. Thanom had become increasingly unpopular as he seized ever more authority at the expense of the nation's democratic system, and moving so many people would have added to the growing restlessness among the population. That restlessness became violent in October 1973. After three days of mayhem Thanom left his country. With that, wrote physicist Milo Nordyke of LLNL, Thailand "put this project on hold and it joined the many other Plowshare projects that were studied, judged technically feasible, but never realized."[3]

Plowshare's End

Teller's commentary was revealing in two respects. First, it represented the devotion to Plowshare displayed by those involved in or supportive of the program and their conviction that it could create a better world. Those at the AEC, Seaborg wrote years later, "truly believed that the program could lead to enormous and otherwise unobtainable benefits for mankind." Even the names of the various Plowshare projects hint at such a vision. While some, like Rulison and Rio Blanco, took their names from people and population centers, and others, such as Gnome and Aquarius, came from mythical creatures, most got their designation from modes of transportation: Chariot, Wagon, Wagon Wheel, Carryall, Gondola, Coach, Buggy, and Cabriolet.[4] Plowshare was a program constantly on the move, conveying humankind toward a happier future.

Teller's comments also illustrated a conviction that the program was essential to national security. To Plowshare's proponents, national security was simultaneously economic, geopolitical, and military in nature. Economically a Kra Canal and similar waterways, alongside roads, railroads, and harbors, would permit industry more efficient, cheaper methods of getting their goods to market, thereby maximizing profits while at the same time reducing costs for the consumer. By stimulating the production of natural gas and oil (and providing places to store it) the United States could simultaneously meet the growing domestic demand for energy and reduce its dependence on imported fuel. Accordingly, should countries in the Middle East, many of which had close relations with the Soviet Union, decide to curtail or embargo oil shipments, the economic impact on the U.S. economy would not be nearly as severe. The threat posed by the Kremlin was tied as well to geopolitical concerns. In a world where the Soviet bloc posed an omnipresent threat to the United States and its interests a peaceful-use program would demonstrate U.S. technological prowess, thereby enhancing Washington's worldwide prestige and credibility. Plowshare could serve the nation militarily in several respects. Offering peaceful-use services to countries without atomic explosives might halt the proliferation of atomic weaponry. With fewer nations having the power of the atom, there would be less chance of a rogue state getting it or of regional conflicts going nuclear. Plowshare tests might develop new isotopes or elements with military applications. Moreover it might be possible to build a sea-level isthmian canal with the atom, one less vulnerable to sabotage or conventional or nuclear attack than the existing lock waterway.

In trying to move humankind down the path of progress while simultaneously protecting U.S. security, Plowshare's champions advanced what they said was a balanced program, one that did not seek to emphasize any one use for the atom. The truth was that nuclear excavation received the most attention. Between 1964 and 1971 two-thirds of Plowshare funding went to cratering and excavation experiments. Of those projects, the centerpiece was the sea-level isthmian canal. It was not just that the waterway offered a demonstration of Plowshare's potential and a means of protecting U.S. interests. It was the possibility of that project achieving fruition that, more than anything else, gave lawmakers a reason to authorize funding for the peaceful-use program. Senator John Pastore, who for a time served as chair of the JCAE, made this clear in testimony in 1965. He said, "[It is the canal] that has given this thing life and the one thing that has more or less enthused this committee to provide the money for Plowshare. Once you have ruled that out, I am afraid interest is going to drop off." It is thus understandable why every excavation test and every proposed excavation project, including those that had what Chariot's creators called "utilitarian value"—such as Chariot, Carryall, and the Australian harbor—were directly related to the isthmian canal. Of the twenty-seven nuclear Plowshare tests conducted between 1961 and 1973, eighteen had some relevance to a sea-level waterway.[5]

Unfortunately for Plowshare's defenders, the excavation program never got beyond the experimental stage. Nor did they have much luck in proving the peaceful-use program's potential for nonexcavation projects. Mining ore, producing heat or new isotopes and elements, and creating storage facilities never proved themselves. This left stimulation of energy resources, but here too the hopes of Plowshare's proponents failed to achieve fruition. After spending at least $180 million on their tests, the peaceful-use program came to an end.[6]

There were many reasons for Plowshare's lack of accomplishment, but they fall under two categories. One was that it was a victim of forces beyond the control of its champions. The peaceful-use program had numerous allies, including scientists in the AEC, at Livermore, and in both the Pentagon and Congress. Members of the executive branch, among them Eisenhower, Kennedy, Johnson, and Nixon, as well as officials in the State Department, offered varying levels of support. The key phrase, however, is *varying levels*. No matter how much Plowshare might intrigue them, those with the highest positions in government had no intention of allowing it to interfere with what they regarded as more important priorities. International and domestic opinion, reassurances from his scientific experts that it was possible to detect clandestine Soviet tests, and Secretary of State Dulles's contention that a moratorium offered political benefit to the United States moved Eisenhower to suspend atomic tests, which he considered a first step toward a more comprehensive test ban agreement. Kennedy continued that policy, permitting what became the first two Plowshare experiments, Gnome and Sedan, only after the Soviets resumed testing. But Kennedy remained wedded to achieving a test ban agreement, and in 1963 he secured his goal with the signing and ratification of the LTBT.

Both Johnson and Nixon appeared more amenable to peaceful-use experiments, yet again Plowshare was not a top priority. For Johnson and the majority of his advisers, an NPT was important, and they did not want to permit blasts that might prevent the treaty from becoming reality. Even more central to Johnson was the Great Society and, as time went on, the Vietnam War. Extricating the United States from Southeast Asia and confronting an economy in recession became essential for Nixon.

Prioritization did more than draw White House attention away from Plowshare. It also sapped much-needed funding. During the moratorium the AEC restricted its budget requests, knowing that it could not ask for money for blasts the White House certainly would not authorize. The Johnson administration wanted to pay for both the Great Society and the war in Vietnam without raising taxes and still avoid a sizable deficit. This meant something had to give. Hence the Bureau of the Budget consistently approved less funding for Plowshare than the AEC wanted. Likewise the war in Vietnam and the desire to curb the deficit convinced the Nixon White House to reduce government spending, including that for PNEs.

Priorities and funding tied in with a third difficulty beyond the control of Plowshare's defenders, that of interpretation of international law. It was not clear whether the United States could legally offer Plowshare services to nations that had failed to sign the NPT, such as Australia. An even greater impediment, though, was the Limited Test Ban Treaty. To Seaborg, John Kelly, Gerald Johnson, and others at the AEC and Livermore, the LTBT permitted explosions that caused fallout, even at a detectable level, as long as it did not pose a threat to humans. To William Foster and his subordinates at the ACDA, such a de minimis interpretation was far too liberal and threatened to strain relations with the Soviet Union, if not undermine the LTBT itself. Nor were U.S. and Soviet officials able to come to a meeting of the minds over how to interpret the LTBT or whether to amend it..

The Soviet Union was not the only nation that stood in the way of Plowshare's progress. In December 1970 the United States conducted the Baneberry weapons test at the NTS. Designed to remain contained, a stemming failure permitted a large amount of radioactivity to enter the atmosphere, some of which crossed the border into Canada and prompted a protest from Ottawa. Spurgeon Keeny, who now was a member of ACDA, pointed out that this was "the first time a foreign government, other than the USSR, ha[d] officially approached the U.S. government concerning the detection beyond U.S. borders of radioactivity debris from a U.S. nuclear test." As a result Washington temporarily halted further testing at the NTS.[7] While by this time the Plowshare excavation program had come to an end, the Baneberry accident proved that the United States could not expect even friendly nations to acquiesce to an initiative that dropped significant amounts of radioactivity on their soil.

The Canadian reaction was significant as well in that Plowshare scientists regarded it as important to find an international project that would prove what their program could accomplish and with little to no threat to plant, animal, or human life. While some nations, among them the United Arab Republic, India, Australia, Panama, Thailand, and Canada, all demonstrated interest in Plowshare, much of that interest came from people below the policymaking level. Even when support did exist at the top, it was cautious. Canada did not want to approve any explosions that might interfere with the test ban talks. Panamanian officials had concerns about the impact of multiple blasts on their nation's environment and people, and Australian leaders had to contend with an increasingly vocal movement opposed to testing Down Under as well as restrictions they might face as a result of the LTBT and their refusal to sign the NPT. Political instability took its toll on Plowshare as well, as seen in the overthrow of governments in Panama and Thailand that had been willing to give consideration to explosions on their soil.

Yet another problem beyond the control of Plowshare's defenders was the relationship between their program and private industry. From Plowshare's beginning, the AEC had wanted to garner corporate support, not only to give the program legitimacy but to defray costs. Though a variety of firms expressed interest, it was not until fairly late in the program's life that private firms opened their wallets. Even then industrial sponsors faced numerous hurdles. For one, Plowshare tests sometimes pitted corporations against one another. The coal industry and Columbia Natural Gas had taken opposing sides during planning for Project Ketch. Similarly CER Geonuclear and the Oil Shale Corporation did not agree on Project Rio Blanco. Even in cases where there was not a corporate sponsor, such as Project Gnome, there existed industrial opposition, in that case from International Minerals and Chemicals Company.

Cost posed an additional difficulty. The AEC never proved able to do more than offer estimates for each shot, meaning the corporate sponsor might have to spend more than originally anticipated. Further adding to those industrial costs was the fact that the AEC had to rely on government appropriations; should that year's funding decline, the Commission had no choice but to ask sometimes reluctant firms to dedicate more money to the project in question. In some cases, such as Rulison, the corporation involved complained about how much it had been forced to spend. In others, among them Dragon Trail, Bronco, and Sloop, the price tag played a role in the refusal of industry to appropriate funding. Another cost consideration was whether conventional technology, which did not offer the environmental or public relations drawbacks raised by the atom, could do the same job for about the same number of, or fewer, dollars.

Then there were the devices themselves. It was to the military weapons program that Plowshare traced its origins, and the explosives employed for PNEs were little different from those used by the armed forces. Consequently, from start to finish, the scientists involved in Plowshare maintained a close relationship with the military. Stated Seaborg, "Development of Plowshare devices . . . was so intertwined with weapons work that this activity could not very well be transferred [to other parties]." In the name of protecting government secrets, the Atomic Energy Act prohibited companies from developing or testing their own nuclear explosives, and Washington from giving such technology to those corporate entities. Bills introduced in Congress between 1968 and 1972 to allow the AEC to offer "nuclear detonation services to private firms" never passed. Thus to conduct a PNE the firm in question had to go through numerous bureaucratic hoops. A 1975 U.S. government study pointed out that "in some cases almost 300 separate agencies, bodies or groups could be involved in the regulatory and public decision processes." Getting approval from so many parties proved laborious and only added to any individual experiment's overall cost.[8]

A final impediment to the relationship with industry was specific to the energy stimulation program. In 1969 EPNG had halted production tests at the Gasbuggy well to permit dilution of the gas and resumed them in May 1973. By that time EPNG had determined the radioactivity in the gas was so low as to be "of marketable quality." The problem was that "standards and regulations permitting the sale of gas from nuclearly stimulated wells ha[d] not as yet been adopted" by the government.[9] As a result there was no way the AEC or industry legally could sell the gas to consumers.

Plowshare, however, was not just a victim of forces beyond its control. It also failed because of mistakes made by the scientists, politicians, and businesspersons involved in or supportive of the program. The industrial response is one example. While acknowledging the need for corporate help, the AEC believed that the private sector lacked the expertise necessary "to assess and plan its own nuclear detonations." Hence the Commission intended to make those determinations. Kelly, who headed the AEC's Division of Peaceful Nuclear Explosions, commented in 1964, "Hopefully, as industry or other government agencies acquire the capability to judge the feasibility of the various applications for nuclear explosives, it will not be necessary for us to be so intimately involved in the early stages of project development."[10]

While it made sense for the AEC to oversee the nuclear aspects of any Plowshare project, the Commission could not decide which individual test deserved priority. This was especially problematic in light of government funding limits. In 1967, as the AEC considered Project Dragon Trail, Livermore's associate director for Plowshare, Glenn Werth, wrote, "Should funding be available for Ketch and not Sloop, or Dragon Trail and not Ketch or Sloop, we would proceed without waiting for Sloop." He added, "The relative priorities of Dragon Trail and Rulison depend in fair measure on the relative interest of the sponsoring industrial partners." Yet knowing they did not have the AEC's full support gave companies little reason to appropriate large sums of money to a project that might ultimately end up low on the Commission's list of proposals. This was indeed one of the justifications given by Dragon Trail's corporate partners to withdraw from that project. It was also why Kelly called for a "streamlined operational system" when "consider[ing] future joint ventures."[11]

Furthermore there was what Gerald Johnson cited in 1969 as "the greatest problem in the Plowshare program—that of establishing public confidence and acceptance."[12] Plowshare scientists and officials lost in the court of public opinion in three ways. One was the close relationship between the peaceful-use and military weapons programs. It was not until 1961 that the AEC established a separate Division for Peaceful Nuclear Explosives. Even then Plowshare scientists shared their findings with the armed forces (and vice versa), which made it all the more difficult for observers to tell the two apart. Commented Nordyke, "Any explosion, peaceful or weapon, will kill people. The difference, basically, is that peaceful nuclear explosions are designed physically and chemically so that they are optimized for the peaceful nuclear explosion use. . . . But there's nothing to keep them from being used as weapons."[13]

Second, Plowshare's defenders were never able to prove their program was innocuous. They avoided direct answers to key questions, such as the amount of radioactivity that could harmlessly enter the atmosphere or gas used by consumers. Nor could they assure Americans of their ability to conduct explosions safely. After Baneberry the AEC temporarily suspended its tests at the NTS; after deciding that it had done everything correctly prior to Baneberry, the Commission held another test, only to see it release radioactivity beyond the NTS. Observing the AEC's troubles, the U.S. comptroller general commented, "The safety of the underground nuclear weapons testing program has been impressive . . . [but] the risks are probably larger for the 1900 explosives required for [a limited commercial development program] *and certainly far larger for the 30,000 explosives required for the release of the 300 trillion cubic feet of gas.*"[14]

The most significant reason why those involved in Plowshare failed to garner public acceptance was how they treated opponents. The AEC and its contracting laboratories had available to them the Nevada Test Site, where they needed only White House authorization to hold tests they could conduct in secret. Building harbors, canals, or storage facilities or stimulating gas or petroleum production, however, necessitated leaving the NTS and going to the site of the project in question. Plowshare's defenders suddenly found themselves facing the scrutiny of laypersons, scientists, journalists, state officials, environmentalists, and industrialists who contested the purpose or impact of the blasts in question and insisted on studying those experiments further or canceling them outright. Rather than attempt to co-opt such grassroots resistance, champions of the peaceful-use program ignored or demonized detractors. During the debate over Chariot they denounced the Committee for Nuclear Information, snubbed businesspersons who contended a harbor at Cape Thompson made no sense, and refused to talk with the Eskimos until very late in the game. They failed to consider the possibility that Carryall might deposit fallout on populated areas, forcing them to conduct further studies. They rejected open discussions over Ketch and strongly suggested that they would override any veto by Pennsylvania's governor. They repeatedly attempted to use the language of the cold war, charging detractors as being communists or communist dupes. Or they took the position that opponents were simple-minded, ignorant "natives" who stood in the way of progress. None of these tactics was likely to garner public goodwill.

The AEC did not help itself by changing the rationale for at least two of these tests. Chariot, originally designed as a harbor to benefit the state of Alaska, became instead an experiment aimed at providing data for Plowshare. At first emphasizing Ketch as good for Pennsylvania's economy, the AEC and Columbia Gas shifted their attention to that blast's feasibility. When that did not work, they returned to the argument of economic benefit. The constantly adjusted explanation confused the public and made Pennsylvanians wonder if the AEC and its friends were more interested in helping themselves than the American people.

By disregarding or attacking their opponents, Plowshare's defenders helped sow the seeds of their beloved program's destruction. Most significantly, they assisted in establishing the foundation for the modern environmental movement. It was that environmental movement that played a part in bringing down Chariot, in drawing attention to the dangerous intermixing of species an isthmian canal might cause, and in raising criticism of Ketch. It was that same movement that added a new legal hurdle to Plowshare tests in the form of the National Environmental Policy Act.

Only slowly did the AEC realize its mistakes, yet neither it nor its partners gave up the old ways easily. The lack of a backlash against Gasbuggy apparently made the AEC believe it could proceed with stimulation of gas and energy without having to seek public support. The agency thus was not prepared when residents in Colorado protested Rulison. The AEC and its corporate sponsors tried to get ahead of the game in the cases of Rio Blanco and Wagon Wheel by offering to hold public hearings early on and liaise with environmentalists and other opposition groups. When efforts at co-optation failed, however, Plowshare's proponents denounced the opposition, claiming detractors overestimated the environmental danger, exaggerated the possibilities offered by hydraulic fracturing, held premature polls, and unknowingly abetted the Soviet Union.

None of this is to suggest that Plowshare's opponents would have cooperated with those involved in the program. Americans had long had concerns about the danger posed by fallout, and the environmental movement made them all the more sensitive to any policies or actions that threatened the planet's well-being. Moreover their lack of faith in government as a result of the Vietnam War made them question what came out of the mouths of officials in Washington. In this respect it is possible that no matter how many concessions the AEC made, it would have faced intense resistance to its endeavors. Seaborg perceptively wrote, "Plowshare could not survive the increased scrutiny; the benefits thought to be obtainable from peaceful nuclear explosions did not appear to be of sufficient magnitude or certainty to overmatch the potential hazards."[15] The point is that only when it was too late did the AEC try to convince detractors that the hazards were not that great, and even then its effort came across as half-hearted.

When Plowshare officially died is a matter of debate. The last time the program received mention was in the AEC's 1974 report to Congress. The Commission itself had come under enough criticism that that same year Congress passed the Energy Reorganization Act, which abolished the AEC and separated its functions into the Nuclear Regulatory Commission and the Energy Research and Development Administration. Yet some funding for PNEs continued. Not until 1978 did the federal government eliminate all funding for the peaceful-use program.[16]

Although Plowshare had come to an end in the United States, the Soviet Union continued its version of the program. According to recent scholarship, between 1965 and 1988 Moscow conducted 122 separate experiments. The actual number could be greater, for some smaller explosions may not have been recorded, while others possibly were confused with earthquakes. It is known that the Soviet program surpassed that of America's in scope, for while the Kremlin too sought to create storage facilities, mine ore, stimulate the production of natural gas, and excavate, it also conducted seismic sounding to learn more about the planet's geology and even claimed to have used the power of the atom to stamp out oil and gas well fires. Not all went according to plan. A Siberian explosion in 1978 called Kraton-3 "vented so much radioactive steam . . . that the Soviets had to declare a two-kilometer exclusion zone around the site." Physicist Viktor Mikhailov, whom General Secretary Mikhail Gorbachev appointed minister of atomic power and industry in 1989, commented, "I ended the program because I knew how worthless this all was. Radioactive material was still seeping through cracks in the ground and spreading into the air. It wasn't worth it."[17]

But the end of the Soviet version of Plowshare did not kill interest in that country to apply the atom to civilian projects. As the Soviet economy, weakened by mismanagement and excessive spending on the military sector, collapsed in the 1980s and early 1990s, officials in that nation looked for a way to acquire needed capital. In November 1991 the *New York Times* reported that International Chetek Corporation, a private company based in Moscow with ties to the Soviet armed forces, had offered to use underground blasts to destroy "toxic wastes": "But the company says it will eventually try to do whatever the customer wants, as long as it is commercial and peaceful in nature, including conducting nuclear explosions in other countries." The proposal came under criticism for opening the door to the proliferation of nuclear technology. Ultimately no one accepted Chetek's offer.[18]

Back from the Dead?

Plowshare also continued to draw interest in the United States. The environmental studies conducted in relation to Chariot, the isthmian canal, and other projects gave scientists valuable data on the flora, fauna, and people of the regions in question. Astronauts in the Apollo 14, 16, and 17 missions conducted training in and near the Schooner crater because it had "features common on the moon." The Sedan crater is the largest of all those at the Nevada Test Site and is now open to the public,[19] who can view it during scheduled monthly tours.

Yet there was, and is, a much more ominous side to the attention Plowshare has received in the United States. In 1992 Daniel T. O'Neill, a researcher at the University of Alaska at Fairbanks, discovered that thirty years earlier the AEC and U.S. Geological Survey had buried radioactive dirt near Ogotoruk Creek— the site selected for Chariot—to see how rain dispersed radioactive elements. Afterward they buried 7.5 tons of contaminated dirt at the site. O'Neill's findings generated international notice and outrage within Alaska. Governor Walter Hickel and U.S. Senator Frank Murkowski demanded the federal government clean up the site. Over the next year, and at a cost of $6 million, Washington moved the dirt to the NTS. For the people of Point Hope, who had witnessed an inordinately high number of cancer-related deaths, the entire affair left them angry. Said Mayor David Stone, "We feel betrayed. The people have lost trust in the Federal Government."[20]

Prior to 1992 only a few people knew where the U.S. government had buried the radioactive soil at Cape Thompson. Anyone, however, could find the location of the four Plowshare blasts that took place on U.S. soil—Projects Gnome, Gasbuggy, Rulison, and Rio Blanco—for each is marked by a plaque. All of them continue to have an impact, some more significant than others.

Following further tests, EPNG sealed the Gasbuggy hole in 1978, cleaned up the surface around the site, and sent some radioactive dirt to the NTS for burial. In the 1980s the Department of Energy tested samples at the Gasbuggy site and found no significant ground-level radioactivity. Gasbuggy had contaminated water in a sandstone formation with tritium, strontium-90, and cesium-137. But because of the slow rate at which water would penetrate the sandstone, the Energy Department estimated it would take many years before that water reached the San Juan River, about fifty miles distant. The Energy Department anticipated that by that time, the radioactivity would fall well within federal guidelines.[21]

In 1977 the U.S. government began an extensive cleanup at the Gnome site. While the levels of tritium and cesium trapped underground remain dangerous, the Energy Department decided in 1980 that radioactivity at the surface was safe enough to permit unrestricted use. Nor was there any indication that the blast had affected groundwater. However, some doctors blame Gnome for a high level of physical ailments among locals, including heart disease and liver defects.[22] While there is no conclusive evidence of such a link, it is known that radioactivity can harm the body, so it is possible the connection exists.

People living near the Rulison and Rio Blanco blast sites have begun to raise concerns of their own. In the 1970s the U.S. government conducted cleanup operations at both locations and sent any contaminated soil to the NTS. The Department of Energy admits, though, that surface contamination persists at Rulison, while the cleanup effort at Rio Blanco "was not well documented and may not meet today's standards." Because radioactivity remains trapped underground, the Energy Department presently prohibits any drilling in a forty-acre radius around both sites. Colorado state officials extended the restricted area to a half-mile around ground zero. Both the U.S. and Colorado governments began easing those restrictions around 2004. In 2009 the Energy Department announced a draft plan that would permit gas companies to conduct hydraulic fracturing within the half-mile restricted zone until either radioactivity appeared at the surface or the drilling reached the forty-acre area around each blast site. Marion Wells, who lived about ten miles from Rulison, charged the federal government with "playing roulette with [his] life and the lives of [his] neighbors."[23]

In fact one must wonder if a Plowshare-like program could reappear in the future. Although the Obama administration denounced CNN anchor John Roberts's impromptu comment to use atomic explosives to stop the Deepwater Horizon oil spill of 2010, the president did meet with nuclear experts to discuss methods of stopping the flow of petroleum into the Gulf of Mexico. While there is no evidence that the specialists with whom Obama met advanced the atomic option, Nordyke argued that the atom deserved consideration. So did Matthew Simmons, who had served as energy adviser to President George W. Bush.[24] It is obvious that faith in the peaceful atom remains alive in some quarters.

Other developments also raise the possibility of Plowshare's revival. Advocates of hydraulic fracturing maintained it was safer than atomic stimulation of natural gas, yet recent reports have found that fracturing has similar shortcomings, including environmental degradation and the release of radioactive elements buried deep underground. Scientists are in the process of developing a new generation of atomic explosives that do not require fission to set off the thermonuclear detonation and, despite their tiny size, have the firepower equivalent to tons of TNT. Because they release virtually no radioactivity, these new nuclear devices may not violate the CTBT, which over 150 nations have ratified since the United Nations opened it for signature in 1996.[25] If these new nuclear explosives do indeed prove to be clean, then it is not beyond the realm of imagination to assert that others may join Nordyke and Simmons in advancing the civilian use of atomic explosives. As implausible as it may sound, it is possible Dixy Lee Ray's declaration that Plowshare was "dead as a doornail" was premature.

Notes

ABBREVIATIONS USED IN NOTES

AHC American Heritage Center, University of Wyoming, Laramie
AWF Ann Whitman File
DDEL Dwight D. Eisenhower Library, Abilene, Kansas
DOE Department of Energy Archive, Germantown, Maryland
FMA-P Foreign Ministry Archive, Panama City, Panama
FRUS *Foreign Relations of the United States*
JFKL John F. Kennedy Library, Boston, Massachusetts
LBJL Lyndon B. Johnson Library, Austin, Texas
LLNL Lawrence Livermore National Laboratory, Livermore, California
NA-A National Archives, Pacific Alaska Region, Anchorage, Alaska
NA-CP National Archives II, College Park, Maryland
NA-SB National Archives, Pacific Region, San Bruno, California
NAA-C National Archives of Australia, Canberra
NAA-M National Archives of Australia, Melbourne
NAA-S National Archives of Australia, Sydney
NPMP Nixon Presidential Materials Project
NSF National Security File
NTSOHP Nevada Test Site Oral History Project
OFACJEO Office Files of Associate Commissioner James E. Officer
OSS Office of the Staff Secretary
PACS Papers of the Alaska Conservation Society
PBSL Papers of Benjamin S. Loeb
PCP Project Chariot Papers
PCPA Papers of Clinton P. Anderson
PDCF Papers of Don C. Foote
PDTO Papers of Daniel T. O'Neill
PET Papers of Edward Teller
PGJ Papers of Gerald Johnson
PGTS Papers of Glenn T. Seaborg
PJBK Papers of John B. Krygier
PJGP Papers of John G. Palfrey
PLLS Papers of Lewis L. Strauss
PLV Papers of Leslie Viereck
PMW Papers of Morey Wolfson
PPPUS *Public Papers of the Presidents of the United States* Washington, D.C.:
   Government Printing Office, 1957–
PRBA Papers of Robert B. Anderson
PTR Papers of Teno Roncalio
PWAH Papers of W. Averell Harriman
PWOP Papers of William O. Pruitt
RG 57 Records of the U.S. Geological Survey

RG 59   General Records of the Department of State
RG 75   Records of the Bureau of Indian Affairs
RG 77   Records of the Office of the chief of Engineers
RG 185.8   Records of the Canal Zone Government and the Panama Canal Company
RG 326   Records of the Atomic Energy Commission
RJCAE   Records of the Joint Committee on Atomic Energy
SASEOS   Special Assistant to the Secretary for Energy and Outer Space
SROWA   State Record Office of Western Australia, Perth
UAF   University of Alaska, Fairbanks
WHCF   White House Central File
WHO   White House Office

INTRODUCTION

1. William J. Broad, "Nuclear Option on Oil Spill? No Way, U.S. Says," *New York Times*, June 3, 2010.

2. Brands, "Testing Massive Retaliation," 142.

3. "Remarks Prepared by Dr. Willard P. Libby, Commissioner United States Atomic Energy Commission for Delivery before a Colloquium at the California Institute of Technology Pasadena, California, May 26, 1958," Libby, Willard F., 1958, May–Dec., Atomic Energy Commission Series, Box 60, PLLS.

4. Teller, *Legacy of Hiroshima*, 87.

5. *PPPUS, Lyndon Johnson*, 1967, 1:213.

6. Hietala, *Manifest Design*, 71; Wilson quoted in Bromley, *William Howard Taft and the First Motoring Presidency*, 361–62.

7. *PPPUS, Dwight D. Eisenhower*, 1957, 581–82.

8. Gladwin Hill, "Atomic Excavations Are Planned by the A.E.C.," *New York Times*, June 25, 1964; "Administrative History of the Atomic Energy Commission," undated, vol. 1, Administrative History, pt. 1, chaps. 1–7, Administrative Histories, no box number, LBJL.

CHAPTER 1

1. U.S. Congress, Senate, Subcommittee of the Committee on Foreign Relations, *Control and Reduction of Armaments*, 1366; "Remarks Prepared by Dr. Willard P. Libby, Commissioner United States Atomic Energy Commission for Delivery before a Colloquium at the California Institute of Technology Pasadena, California, May 26, 1958," Libby, Willard F., 1958, May–Dec., Atomic Energy Commission Series, Box 60, PLLS; Miller, *Under the Cloud*, 291.

2. O'Neill, *Firecracker Boys*, 14.

3. Kirsch, *Proving Grounds*, 9; Sylves, *The Nuclear Oracles*, 16, 17, 27, 105; Seaborg with Loeb, *Stemming the Tide*, 321n.

4. Gaddis, *Strategies of Containment*, 80; Skartvedt, "Plowshare Program," 141–42; Wasserman, Solomon, Alvarez, and Walters, *Killing Our Own*, 58.

5. Blumberg and Panos, *Edward Teller*, 115; O'Neill, *Project Chariot*, 201; "The Atomic Future," *Time*, Aug. 22, 1955, 65.

6. "Text of Dulles' Statement on Foreign Policy of Eisenhower Administration," *New York Times*, Jan. 13, 1954.

7. Divine, *Blowing on the Wind*, 17.

8. Teller, *Memoirs*, 225.

9. Herbert York, interviewed by Mary Palevsky, Jan. 16, 2004, transcript, NTSOHP.

10. York interview; Koop, "Plowshare and the Nonproliferation Treaty," 794–95.

11. Reines, "Are There Peaceful Engineering Uses of Atomic Explosives?," 171–72; York interview; Gerber, Hamburger, and Hull, *Plowshare*, 22.

12. Chernus, *Eisenhower's Atoms for Peace*, 80; Divine, *Eisenhower and the Cold War*, 111.

13. Gosnell, *Truman's Crises*, 306.

14. Strong, "Eisenhower and Arms Control," 246–47; Ambrose, *Eisenhower*, 2:147; Chernus, *Eisenhower's Atoms for Peace*, 32–33.

15. *PPPUS, Dwight Eisenhower*, 1953, 815, 817, 820, 821; Strong, "Eisenhower and Arms Control," 247.

16. O'Neill, *Firecracker Boys*, 14–15; Atomic Energy Act of 1954, PL 83-703.

17. Smith, *Morality, Reason, and Power*, 45; Weizman, *Battle for Peace*, 239.

18. Gerber et al., *Plowshare*, 23.

19. York to Starbird, Oct. 15, 1956, AEC Meetings—1956–1958a, Box 3, PDTO.

20. Milo D. Nordyke, "Plowshare and Edward Teller," Jan. 14, 1993, no folder title, Box 386, PET; "Plowshare Program—Executive Summary," undated, Plowshare Program, Executive Summary, 1973, no box number, LLNL.

21. York interview; author e-mail correspondence with Harold Brown, Dec. 12, 2009; Teller with Brown, *Legacy of Hiroshima*, 82; Teller, *Memoirs*, 449.

22. *Engineering with Nuclear Explosives: Proceedings of the Third Plowshare Symposium*, Apr. 21–23, 1964, Engineering with Nuclear Explosives, Proceedings of the Third Plowshare Symposium, no box number, LLNL; J. Foote, "Project Chariot," Mar. 1, 1961, A.E.C. Project Chariot: Foote, Joe—Outline of Events, Box 10, PDCF.

23. Bupp, *Priorities in Nuclear Technology*, 182–83.

24. "Executive Summary, Plowshare Program," undated, https://www.osti.gov/opennet /reports/plowshar.pdf, accessed June 9, 2009; AEC 811/6, "Non-Military Uses of Explosive Nuclear Devices," June 13, 1957, Military Research Applications Non-Military Use of Atomic Weapons," RG 326, Office of the Secretary, Box 184, NA-CP.

25. "Non-Military Uses of Explosive Nuclear Devices"; "Executive Summary."

26. Jolly, "Linus Pauling," 149.

27. Egan, *Barry Commoner and the Science of Survival*, 51–52.

28. Pfau, *No Sacrifice Too Great*, 163.

29. Divine, *Blowing on the Wind*, 3–4, 5.

30. Ibid., 7–8, 12; Tal, *American Nuclear Disarmament Dilemma*, 64–65.

31. Pfau, *No Sacrifice Too Great*, 166, 168.

32. Wasserman et al., *Killing Our Own*, 92, 94–95; Pfau, *No Sacrifice Too Great*, 192–93; "Atomic Future"; "Happy Ending," *Time*, Aug. 29, 1955, 40–41.

33. Kreith and Wrenn, *Nuclear Impact*, 40–41.

34. Eisenbud and Gesell, *Environmental Radioactivity*, 48. For changes in the allowable annual dose, see North Carolina State University, "Radiation Safety and Regulatory Compliance," www.ncsu.edu/ehs/radiation/forms/RegComp.pdf, accessed Oct. 10, 2010.

35. Divine, *Blowing on the Wind*, 78–81.

36. Goertzel and Goertzel, *Linus Pauling*, 8, 109–10, 113–15, 122–26.

37. Ibid., 143–44; Divine, *Blowing on the Wind*, 41, 123; Hager, *Force of Nature*, 477; Greene, *Eisenhower, Science Advice, and the Nuclear Test-Ban Debate*, 123.

38. Divine, *Blowing on the Wind*, 72, 88–89, 94; Egan, *Barry Commoner and the Science of Survival*, 52.

39. Ambrose, *Eisenhower*, 2:153; Divine, *Blowing on the Wind*, 60; Tal, *American Nuclear Disarmament Dilemma*, 63.

40. Divine, *Blowing on the Wind*, 87–88, 90.

41. Ibid., 128; Serafini, *Linus Pauling*, 178.

42. Seife, *Sun in a Bottle*, 59; Smith, "Advertising the Atom," 220; Zoellner, *Uranium*, 100.

43. Sylves, *Nuclear Oracles*, 59, 60; Divine, *Blowing on the Wind*, 14.

44. Divine, *Blowing on the Wind*, 105–6; "Teller Pessimistic on Arms Accord," *New York Times*, Mar. 3, 1958; Teller, *Memoirs*, 438.

45. Hager, *Force of Nature*, 471.

46. AEC Meeting No. 1484, Mar. 10, 1959, vol. 22, RG 326, Minutes of the Meetings of the AEC, Box 12, NA-CP; Anderson to McCone, Mar. 11, 1959, Joint Committee on Atomic Energy–Project Plowshare, Box 817, PCPA.

47. Gallup, *Gallup Poll*, 1229, 1452, 1488.

48. Johnson, *Unfinished Business*, 11–12; Wasserman et al., *Killing Our Own*, 99.

49. Although released in Japan in 1954, *Godzilla* (called *Gojira* in Japan) did not see its American debut until 1956. Renamed *Godzilla, King of the Monsters!* and starring Raymond Burr, it gave far less attention to the danger posed by the atom than did the original. See Tsutsui, *Godzilla on My Mind*, 38–42.

50. Greene, *Eisenhower, Science Advice, and the Nuclear Test-Ban Debate*, 118, 120–22, 130.

51. *Engineering with Nuclear Explosives*; Nordyke, "Plowshare and Edward Teller"; Miller, *Under the Cloud*, 291; "Remarks Prepared by Dr. Willard P. Libby."

52. Gladwin Hill, "Still-Warm Cavern Yields Secrets of '57 Atom Blast," *New York Times*, July 10, 1961; Divine, *Blowing on the Wind*, 157–58; Miller, *Under the Cloud*, 291; Gerald W. Johnson et al., "The Underground Nuclear Detonation of September 19, 1957: Rainier, Operation Plumbbob," Apr. 17, 1958, interview before Humphrey Senate Subcommittee, Speech file, Box 13, PLLS; U.S. Congress, *Control and Reduction of Armaments*, 1366, 1368; Ray Hebert, "Newsmen See Site of Subsurface Atom Test," *Los Angeles Times*, Mar. 7, 1958, I, 2; "Remarks Prepared by Dr. Willard P. Libby"; "Atomic Test Detection," *New York Times*, Mar. 13, 1958.

53. Miller, *Under the Cloud*, 291; U.S. Congress, *Control and Reduction of Armaments*, 1367.

54. U.S. Congress, *Control and Reduction of Armaments*, 1368–69, 1380.

55. Teller, Talley, Higgins, and Johnson, *Constructive Uses of Nuclear Explosives*, 251; Boyd to Strauss, Apr. 15, 1958, Atomic Energy Commission, Miscellaneous, 1968, Atomic Energy Commission Series, Box 5, PLLS; "Plowshare Program—Executive Summary."

56. Memo, Larson to Strauss, Oct. 15, 1957, Fallout, Correspondence, 1957, Atomic Energy Commission Series, Box 26G, PLLS; Libby to the Chairman, Oct. 14, 1957, Libby, Willard F., 1957, July–Dec., Atomic Energy Commission Series, Box 60, PLLS; Starbird to Chairman, Military Liaison Committee, Dec. 12, 1957, and McCool to Files, Dec. 20, 1957, Non-Military Uses of Atomic Weapons, RG 326, Office of the Secretary, Box 117, NA-CP.

57. Larson to Strauss.

58. Pfau, *No Sacrifice Too Great*, 76, 83, 84, 179–80; Divine, *Blowing on the Wind*, 10–11; Alden Whitman, "Lewis Strauss Dies; Ex-Head of A.E.C.," *New York Times*, Jan. 22, 1974.

59. Pfau, *No Sacrifice Too Great*, 52–53; Smith, "Advertising the Atom," 213; Seife, *Sun in a Bottle*, 60.

60. "Notes for Briefing the Legislative Leaders at the White House, 3 December 1957," Speech file, Box 3, PLLS.

CHAPTER 2

1. Donald L. Vandegraft, "Project Chariot: Nuclear Legacy of Cape Thompson," http://arcticcircle.uconn.edu/VirtualClassroom/Chariot/vandegraft.html, accessed Mar. 19, 2009; Don C. Foote, notes, undated, A.E.C. Project Chariot: History Notes A, Box 11, PDCF; O'Neill, *Firecracker Boys*, 29–30.

2. "Plowshare Program: Fact Sheet on Project Chariot," undated, AT Atomic Energy 1961 Executive, WHCF, Subject File, Box 10, JFKL; O'Neill, *Firecracker Boys*, 28, 29; O'Neill, *Project Chariot*, 219, 221.

3. Skartvedt, "Plowshare Program," 179; Memorandum for the Record, Assistant Chief, Military Geology Branch, Feb. 5, 1958, Project Plowshare, Phase I, Correspondence, RG 57, U.S. Geological Survey, Project Chariot Files, 1958–63, Box 2, NA-A; Kirsch, *Proving Grounds*, 46.

4. Gates to Page, Feb. 26, 1958, Project Plowshare, Phase I, Correspondence, RG 57, Project Chariot Files, 1958–63, Box 3, NA-A.

5. O'Neill, *Firecracker Boys*, 28–29; O'Neill, *Project Chariot*, 225, 227.

6. Chairman, AEC, to Gates, Feb. 27, 1958, and Gates to Strauss, Mar. 24, 1958, Non-Military Use of Atomic Weapons, RG 326, Office of the Secretary, Box 117, NA-CP.

7. Divine, *Blowing on the Wind*, 60; Greene, *Eisenhower, Science Advice, and the Nuclear Test-Ban Debate*, 116; Bupp, *Priorities in Nuclear Technology*, 187–89.

8. "Project Chariot: A Summary," Sept. 28, 1960, C-T, D. Foote, 1960, Box 1, PLV; O'Neill, *Firecracker Boys*, 29.

9. E. J. Longyear Company, "Report to University of California Radiation Laboratory on the Mineral Potential and Proposed Harbor Locations in Northwestern Alaska," Apr. 18, 1958, 12H Peaceful Uses Subject File: 17b, Project Plowshare, 1959, RG 59, SASEOS, Records Related to Atomic Energy Matters, 1944–63, Box 217, NA-CP.

10. J. Foote, "Project Chariot," Mar. 1, 1961, A.E.C. Project Chariot: Foote, Joe— Outline of Events, Box 10, PDCF; O'Neill, *Firecracker Boys*, 41; Walter Sullivan, "H-Bombs May Dig Harbor in Alaska," *New York Times*, June 5, 1959. It is unclear when Chariot received its name, though it likely took place at this meeting. By the end of May officials were referring to the blast as "Project Chariot." See, for instance, Gates to Péwé, May 28, 1958, Project Plowshare, Phase I, Correspondence, RG 57, Project Chariot Files, 1958–63, Box 2, NA-A.

11. O'Neill, *Firecracker Boys*, 44.

12. Foote, "Project Chariot."

13. "AEC Plans for Harbor Discussed," *Fairbanks News-Miner*, July 15, 1958; O'Neill, *Firecracker Boys*, 31–32; J. Foote, "Report from Tigara," Apr. 1961, A.E.C. Project Chariot: Foote, Joe—"Report from Tigara," Box 11, PDCF; O'Neill, *Project Chariot*, 654–55.

14. O'Neill, *Project Chariot*, 242.

15. "Japanese Interested in Coal," *Fairbanks Daily Miner*, July 16, 1958; "AEC Plans for Harbor Discussed"; "Atom Scientists Here Tell Plans to Blast Harbor," *Anchorage Daily Times*, July 15, 1958; Ray Moholt, "Consent of Alaskans Sought for A-Blast," *Anchorage Daily News*, July 16, 1958.

16. O'Neill, *Firecracker Boys*, 35–36; "Alaska Can Have Massive Nuclear Engineering Job," *Fairbanks Daily Miner*, July 17, 1958; Al to Les, Feb. 21, 1961, D. C. Foote Collection Documents, and Patty to Atomic Energy Commission, Sept. 19, 1958, Box 10, PDTO; Morgan, *Art and Eskimo Power*, 166–67.

17. "Nuclear Engineering in Alaska," *Fairbanks Daily Miner*, July 24, 1958; O'Neill, *Firecracker Boys*, 37.

18. Albert Johnson, "Science, Society and Academic Freedom," undated, Albert Johnson Correspondence File, Box 9, PDTO; Foote, "Project Chariot"; "Project Chariot—An

Artificial Harbor to Be Excavated by Nuclear Explosives," Feb. 23, 1960, Alaska Briefing Book, Papers of Fred A. Seaton, Interior Series, State Briefing Book Subseries, Box 1, DDEL; O'Neill, *Firecracker Boys*, 38; Gates to Péwé, May 28, 1958, Gates to Page, June 3, 1958, and Eberlein to Thilleur, July 2, 1958, Project Plowshare, Phase I, Correspondence, RG 57, Project Chariot Files, 1958–63, Box 2, NA-A.

19. Péwé to Eberlein, July 22, 1958, and Rube to Gates, July 23, 1958, Project Plowshare, Phase I, Correspondence, RG 57, Project Chariot Files, 1958–63, Box 2, NA-A; Foote, "Project Chariot"; O'Neill, *Firecracker Boys*, 45–46; Teller to Starbird, Aug. 15, 1958, Project Chariot, Box 386, PET.

20. Teller to Starbird, Aug. 15, 1958; Teller to Jackson, Sept. 22, 1958, and Memo, "Plans for the Peaceful Use of Thermonuclear Explosives (Plowshare) in Alaska and Elsewhere," undated, Plowshare, vol. 1 General, General Correspondence, Box 504, RJCAE.

21. "Construction of a Trans-Isthmian Sea Level Canal," Dec. 2, 1959, 12H P.U. Subj. File: 27 Trans-Isthmian Canal, 1959, RG 59, SASEOS, Records Related to Atomic Energy Matters, 1944–63, Box 225, NA-CP; O'Neill, *Project Chariot*, 221.

22. *Engineering with Nuclear Explosives: Proceedings of the Third Plowshare Symposium,* Apr. 21–23, 1964, Engineering with Nuclear Explosives, Proceedings of the Third Plowshare Symposium, no box number, LLNL.

23. Froehle, "Backdrop," 15; Frenkel, "A Hot Idea?," 304.

24. "Isthmian Canal Plans: 1960," Feb. 11, 1960, Cabinet Meeting of April 29, 1960, Cabinet Series, Box 16, AWF; "The Atlantic-Pacific Interoceanic Canal Study Commission during the Administration of President Lyndon B. Johnson," undated, Administrative History of the Atlantic-Pacific Interoceanic Canal Study Commission, Administrative Histories, LBJL; Frenkel, "Hot Idea?," 304.

25. LaFeber, *Panama Canal*, 87–88, 117–19; Eisenhower to Wilson, July 25, 1956, *FRUS, 1955–1957*, 7:281.

26. "Construction of a Trans-Isthmian Sea Level Canal."

27. Lindsay-Poland, *Emperors in the Jungle*, 78; Heath to Potter, Mar. 4, 1958, Improvement Studies and Planning of PC-US Policy and Present Isthmian Canal, RG 185.8, Box 3, and Memorandum for the Files, Sept. 4, 1958, 12H Peaceful Uses Subject File: 17b, Project Plowshare, 1958, RG 59, SASEOS, Records Related to Atomic Energy Matters, 1944–63, Box 217, NA-CP.

28. "Report on Remote Sea Level Canal," Sept. 1959, 12H P. U. Sub. File: 27. Trans-Isthmian Canal, 1959, RG 59, SASEOS, Records Related to Atomic Energy Matters, 1944–63, Box 224, NA-CP.

29. "Construction of a Trans-Isthmian Sea Level Canal"; "Report on Remote Sea Level Canal"; "Section VI of Canal Report," undated, 12H P. U. Sub. File: 27, Trans-Isthmian Canal, 1959, RG 59, SASEOS, Records Related to Atomic Energy Matters, 1944–63, Box 224, NA-CP.

30. Divine, *Blowing on the Wind*, 200–201.

31. Jolly, "Linus Pauling," 150–51.

32. Memorandum of Conversation, June 5, 1958, and untitled, undated (Sept. 15, 1958) statement, 12H Peaceful Uses Subject File: 17b, Project Plowshare, 1959, RG 59 SASEOS, Records Related to Atomic Energy Matters, 1944–63, Box 217, and AEC Press Release, "Atomic Energy Commission to Investigate Practicality of Harbor Excavation by Nuclear Detonation," June 9, 1958, Military Research Applications: Non Military Use of Atomic Weapons, RG 326, Office of the Secretary, Box 184, NA-CP.

33. Pfau, *No Sacrifice Too Great*, 213; Divine, *Blowing on the Wind*, 206–7, 209–10.

34. For more on Strauss's loss of influence see Greene, *Eisenhower, Science Advice, and the Nuclear Test-Ban Debate*, especially chaps. 6–7.

35. Divine, *Blowing on the Wind*, 208, 210–11.

36. "Strauss Now at Odds with Many in Capital," *New York Times*, May 11, 1958.

37. Anderson with Viorst, *Outsider in the Senate*, 202–3, 204–5, 211.

38. Strauss to the President, May 17, 1957, Gruenther, Alfred M., 1947–58, Atomic Energy Commission Series, Box 37, and unsent draft letter, Strauss to the President, May 23, 1957, Adams, Sherman, 1956–60, Atomic Energy Commission Series, Box 1, PLLS.

39. Strauss to the President, Mar. 31, 1958, and Memorandum for the Files of Lewis L. Strauss, Apr. 7, 1958, Eisenhower, Dwight D., Jan.–Apr. 1958, and Strauss to Eisenhower, and Eisenhower to Strauss, June 5, 1958, Eisenhower, Dwight D., May–June 1958, Atomic Energy Commission Series, Box 26E, PLLS.

40. Divine, *Blowing on the Wind*, 218–19; Moore to Strauss, July 7, 1959, Dulles, John Foster, 1958–59, Atomic Energy Commission Series, Box 26A, PLLS.

41. Divine, *Blowing on the* Wind, 219; Record of Meeting, Aug. 18, 1958, *FRUS, 1958–1960*, 3:644–46; Dokos, *Negotiations for a CTBT*, 6–7.

42. Telephone calls, Aug. 19, 1958, Christian A. Herter Telephone Calls July 1–Sept. 30, 1958, Papers of Christian A. Herter, Box 11, DDEL; telegram, New York to Secretary of State, No. Secto. 13, Aug. 21, 1958, 12H Peaceful Uses Subject File: 17b, Project Plowshare, 1958, RG 59 SASEOS, Records Related to Atomic Energy Matters, 1944–63, Box 217, NA-CP; Fetter, *Toward a Comprehensive Test Ban*, 4–5.

43. *PPPUS, Dwight D. Eisenhower*, 1958, 635–36.

44. Ambrose, *Eisenhower*, 2:480.

45. Starbird to Fields, Apr. 28, 1958, RG 326, Military Research Applications: Non-Military Use of Atomic Weapons, Box 184, NA-CP; "AEC Report of the Oil Shale Meeting of January 6 and 7, 1959," Plowshare, vol. 1—General, General Correspondence, Box 504, RJCAE; Ankeny to Sunkel, Dec. 3, 1959, Joint Committee on Atomic Energy—Project Plowshare, Box 817, PCPA.

46. U.S. Congress, Subcommittee on Research and Development of the Joint Committee on Atomic Energy, *Frontiers in Atomic Energy Research*, 32.

47. Memorandum for the Files, Sept. 4, 1958, 12H Peaceful Uses Subject Files: 17b, Project Plowshare, 1958, RG 59, SASEOS, Records Relating to Atomic Energy Matters, 1944–63, Box 217, NA-CP; Johnson, "Nuclear Explosions in Science and Technology," 159.

48. Ambrose, *Eisenhower*, 2:446; Memoranda for the Files, Sept. 4 and 26 and Oct. 21, 1958, and Draft Memo by Kelly, "Program for Peaceful Applications of Nuclear Explosives," Oct. 10, 1958, 12H Peaceful Uses Subject Files: 17b, Project Plowshare, 1958, RG 59, SASEOS, Records Relating to Atomic Energy Matters, 1944–63, Box 217, NA-CP.

49. Memoranda for the Files, Sept. 4 and 26, 1958; U.S. Congress, *Frontiers in Atomic Energy Research*, 32, 33, 34.

50. Memoranda for the Files, Sept. 4 and 26, 1958; Memorandum for the Record, Dec. 10, 1959, 12H Peaceful Uses Subject Files: 17b, Project Plowshare, 1958, RG 59, SASEOS, Records Relating to Atomic Energy Matters, 1944–63, Box 218, NA-CP; Kramish, *Peaceful Atom in Foreign Policy*, 120.

51. Skartvedt, "The Plowshare Program," 203, 205; U.S. Atomic Energy Commission, "Plowshare Program," undated [ca. 1958], Atomic Energy Commission, Papers of Fred A. Seaton, Subject Series, Box 4, DDEL; AEC 811/61, "The Plowshare Program," Dec. 17, 1959, AEC Meetings—1959b, Box 3, PDTO; Sylves, *Nuclear Oracles*, 201. Tuff is a rock made up of volcanic ash.

52. See, for instance, John W. Finney, "Kennedy Approves 5-Kiloton Cave Test of Atom for Peace," *New York Times*, Oct. 26, 1961; "Peace Bomb to Be Set Off in Tunnel Today," *Los Angeles Times*, Dec. 10, 1961.

53. "For the Record: A History of the Nuclear Test Personnel Review Program, 1978–1986," Aug. 1, 1986, https://www.osti.gov/opennet/servlets/purl/16389340-T673cu/

16389340.pdf, accessed Feb. 1, 2009; "11-4.1 Program Letters" folder, undated, https://www.osti.gov/opennet/servlets/purl/16022924-fu54Y8/16022924.pdf, accessed Jan. 27, 2009; Szasz, "New Mexico's Forgotten Nuclear Tests," 352.

54. Raymond Harbert, interviewed by Mary Palevsky, Apr. 3, 2006, transcript, NTSOHP; Starbird to Anderson, Feb. 25, 1959, Joint Committee on Atomic Energy–Project Gnome, Box 817, PCPA.

55. Harbert interview; Gladwin Hill, "U.S. Is Host to 200 at Atom Test Site," *New York Times*, Nov. 26, 1961; AEC 811/27, "Plowshare Program," Oct. 14, 1958, AEC Meetings—1958b, Box 3, PDTO; AEC Memorandum of Conversation, Jan. 12, 1960, and AEC Meeting No. 1583, Jan. 22, 1960, vol. 24, RG 326, Office of the Secretary, Minutes of the Meetings of the AEC, Box 13, NA-CP; Beers et al. to Reeves, July 22, 1959, Joint Committee on Atomic Energy—Project Gnome, Box 817, PCPA; Szasz, "New Mexico's Forgotten Nuclear Tests," 353–54.

56. AEC Memorandum of Conversation, Jan. 12, 1960; AEC Meeting No. 1583; AEC Meeting No. 1660, Oct. 7, 1960, vol. 25, RG 326, Office of the Secretary, Minutes of the Meetings of the AEC, Box 14, NA-CP.

57. Eisenhower to Teller, Aug. 22, 1958, Atomic Weapons, WHCF, Confidential File, Subject Series, Box 9, DDEL; O'Neill, *Firecracker Boys*, 52.

58. Memorandum of Conference with the President, Mar. 10, 1960, Atomic Energy Commission, vol. 3, WHO, OSS, Subject Series, Alphabetical Subseries, Box 3, DDEL; Memorandum for the Files, Sept. 4, 1958, 12H Peaceful Uses Subject File: 17b, Project Plowshare, 1958, RG 59, SASEOS, Records Related to Atomic Energy Matters, 1944–63, Box 217, NA-CP.

59. O'Neill, *Firecracker Boys*, 55–56; Teller to Shute, Jan. 26, 1959, AEC Meetings—1959a, Box 3, PDTO; Teller et al., *Constructive Uses of Nuclear Explosives*, 205–7.

60. O'Neill, *Firecracker Boys*, 56–57.

61. Bernie Morris, "Cape Thompson Nuclear Harbor Blast Now under Consideration on Smaller Scale," *Daily Alaska Empire* (Juneau), Feb. 26, 1959.

62. Memorandum for Files, May 25, 1959, 12H Peaceful Uses Subject File: 17b, Project Plowshare, 1959, RG 59, SASEOS, Records Related to Atomic Energy Matters, 1944–63, Box 218, NA-CP; Teller to Shute, Jan. 26, 1959; Morris, "Cape Thompson Nuclear Harbor Blast Site."

63. Robinson to Eberlein, Jan. 10, 1959, Project Plowshare, Phase I, Correspondence, RG 57, Project Chariot Files, 1958–63, Box 2, NA-A; O'Neill, *Project Chariot*, 297; "Scientists Give Data on Devices," *Fairbanks Daily Miner*, Jan. 10, 1959; Foote, "Project Chariot."

64. Robinson to Eberlein, Jan. 10, 1959; Al to Les, Feb. 21, 1961; O'Neill, *Firecracker Boys*, 63–68.

65. "Executive Summary, Plowshare Program," undated, https://www.osti.gov/opennet/reports/plowshar.pdf, accessed June 9, 2009; Bupp, *Priorities in Nuclear Technology*, 189–90; Teller to Shute, Jan. 26, 1959; "Plowshare Program: Fact Sheet on Project Chariot," AT Atomic Energy 1961 Executive, WHCF, Subject File, Box 10, JFKL; O'Neill, *Firecracker Boys*, 76–77, 80–81; Foote, "Project Chariot."

66. O'Neill, *Firecracker Boys*, 81–85.

67. O'Neill, *Project Chariot*, 347–48.

68. "Project Plowshare," 416; Smith, "Advertising the Atom," 62–63.

69. Teller Commencement Address, May 18, 1959, Transcription by Philip Munger, Oct. 1993, Oral History Section, UAF.

70. Ibid.

CHAPTER 3

1. O'Neill, *Firecracker Boys*, 85–87; Johnson to Viereck, Mar. 24, 1959, Atomic Energy Commission, Correspondence, 1959–60, Box 1, PCP.

2. J. Foote, "Project Chariot," Mar. 1, 1961, A.E.C. Project Chariot: Foote, Joe— Outline of Events, Box 10, PDCF; O'Neill, *Firecracker Boys*, 87, 93.

3. "Science, Society and Academic Freedom," undated, Albert Johnson's Correspondence File, Box 9, PDTO; AEC, "Chariot Environmental Program," July 1959, Project Chariot, Environmental Program, RG 57, Project Chariot Files, 1958–63, Box 6, NA-A; O'Neill, *Firecracker Boys*, 99–100; Hedman and Diters, *The Legacy of Project Chariot*, 4.

4. O'Neill, *Firecracker Boys*, 84; "Chariot Environmental Program"; "LASL Report Library, Readiness Report, 1 April 1959," AEC Meetings, memo, letter, reports, etc., dated from 1959, Conrad-Ogle Collection, https://www.osti.gov/opennet/servlets/purl/16023064 -xBbqNF/16023064.pdf, accessed Jan. 28, 2009; AEC 811/42, "Plowshare—Alaska Harbor Project," May 18, 1959, AEC Meetings—1959a, Box 3, PDTO.

5. "Project Chariot: A Summary," Sept. 28, 1960, C-T, D. Foote, 1960, Box 1, PLV.

6. O'Neill, *Firecracker Boys*, 91.

7. Ibid., 91–93.

8. Foote, "Project Chariot"; "Wade Asking More Contact with AEC," *Anchorage Daily Times*, Aug. 27, 1959; Egan to Durham, Aug. 19, 1959, Project Chariot, RJCAE, General Correspondence, Box 506, NA; McCone to Egan, Oct. 19, 1959, Correspondence: A.E.C. Project Chariot, Box 11, PDCF.

9. Foote, "Project Chariot"; Eberlein Memo for Chariot Phase II file, Aug. 19, 1959, Plowshare—Program Chariot, RG 59, Theoretical Geophysical Branch, Records concerning Projects, 1942–62, Box 4, NA-CP; O'Neill, *Firecracker Boys*, 96–97.

10. Rennie Taylor, "Cape Thompson Blast Preparations Entail Census of Wilderness Area," *Fairbanks Daily News-Miner*, Dec. 5, 1960; O'Neill, *Firecracker Boys*, 105–6.

11. Minutes of Special Meeting, Point Hope Village Council, Nov. 28, 1959, and Petition, Point Hope Village Council to AEC, Nov. 30, 1959, Point Hope Protest Letters, Box 11, and Campbell to Foote, Nov. 17, 1959, and Foote to Campbell, Nov. 26 and 29, 1959, D. C. Foote Collection Documents, Box 10, PDTO.

12. AEC press release, Nov. 12, 1959, Joint Committee on Atomic Energy—Project Plowshare, Box 817, PCPA; AEC 811/61, "The Plowshare Program," Dec. 17, 1959, AEC Meetings—1959b, Box 3, PDTO. Teller himself drew the connection between Ditchdigger and the isthmian waterway. See Teller to the President, May 11, 1960, Coordination: Information Center Documents, Box 10, PDTO.

13. "Statement of Committee on Environmental Studies for Project Chariot," Jan. 7, 1960, A.E.C. Project Chariot: Memorandums and Press Releases, Box 11, PDCF; Johnson et al. to Committee on Environmental Studies, Project Chariot, undated, C-T, Correspondence, 1959–60, Box 1, PLV; O'Neill, *Firecracker Boys*, 163–64.

14. Kirsch, *Proving Grounds*, 218n3; Hewlett and Holl, *Atoms for Peace and War*, 529.

15. AEC 811/12, "Non-Military Uses of Nuclear Explosive Devices," June 6, 1958, AEC Meetings—1956–58a, Box 3, PDTO; AEC Meeting No. 1437, Dec. 4, 1958, and No. 1438, Dec. 5, 1958, vol. 21, RG 326, Minutes of the Meetings of the AEC, Box 12, NA-CP; Bupp, *Priorities in Nuclear Technology*, 187–88.

16. Johnson to Shute, July 1, 1960, AEC—Meetings, Box 3, PDTO; Eberlein to Klepper, Jan. 7, 1960, Kachadoorian to Chariot File, Jan. 26, 1960, and Kachdoorian to Chariot File, Jan. 28, 1960, Plowshare, Phase III, Correspondence, RG 57, Project Chariot Files, 1958–63, Box 3, NA-A.

17. "Executive Summary, Plowshare Program," undated, https://www.osti.gov/opennet /reports/plowshar.pdf, accessed June 9, 2009; Reuben Kachadoorian, "Geologic Aspects

of the November 1960 High-Explosive Test at the Project Chariot Test Site, Northwestern Alaska," May 1961, www.dggs.alaska.gov/webpubs/usgs/of/text/of61-0081.PDF, accessed Aug. 2, 2010.

18. O'Neill, *Firecracker Boys*, 113.

19. Ibid.; "Executive Summary, Plowshare Program"; Chariot Meeting, Mar. 9, 1960, D. C. Foote Collection Documents, Box 10, PDTO; "Isthmian Canal Plans—1960," Feb. 11, 1960, Cabinet Meeting of Apr. 29, 1960, AWF, Cabinet Series, Box 16, DDEL.

20. O'Neill, *Firecracker Boys*, 114–16.

21. Ibid., 112, 117, 137.

22. Meeting at Alaska Episcopal Mission, Point Hope, Mar. 14, 1960, AEC Meeting at Point Hope, Box 11, PDTO.

23. Glasstone, *Effects of Nuclear Weapons*, 481.

24. O'Neill, *Firecracker Boys*, 140–42.

25. Ibid., 146–47. A curie is the amount of radioactivity in one gram of the element radium. The number of curies produced by a gram of another radioactive element, such as uranium or plutonium, is different from that of radium.

26. Meeting at Alaska Episcopal Mission, Point Hope, Mar. 14, 1960.

27. Ibid.; O'Neill, *Firecracker Boys*, 129.

28. Teller to McCone, Nov. 13, 1959, 12H Peaceful Uses Subject File: 17b, Project Plowshare, 1959, RG 59, SASEOS, Records Related to Atomic Energy Matters, 1944–63, Box 218, NA-CP; Sullivan to Acting Secretary, Apr. 28, 1960, 1960 [Cabinet], Papers of Christian A. Herter, Box 19, DDEL; AEC Meeting No. 1597, Mar. 2, 1960, AEC Meetings—1960a, Box 3, PDTO; "A.E.C. Is Pursuing Harbor Project," *New York Times*, Mar. 13, 1960; "Project Chariot Harbor Blast Slated for '62," *Nome Nugget*, Apr. 29, 1960; Kistiakowsky, *Scientist in the White House*, 365.

29. Greene, *Eisenhower, Science Advice, and the Nuclear Test-Ban Debate*, 170–71, 182–87.

30. Ibid., 189, 195, 209–10; Dokos, *Negotiations for a CTBT*, 13–14.

31. Administrative History, Atlantic-Pacific Interoceanic Canal Study Commission, undated, Administrative Histories, no box number, LBJL; "Annex VI: Engineering Plan for Construction of a Sea Level Canal by Nuclear Methods," Jan. 1960, Department of the Army, WHCF, Confidential File, Subject Series, Box 6, DDEL; "Isthmian Canal Plans—1960," Cabinet Meeting of Apr. 29, 1960, Cabinet Series, Box 16, AWF.

32. "Engineering Plan for Construction of a Sea Level Canal by Nuclear Methods"; "Annex VII: Nuclear Construction of a Sea Level Canal and Cost of Nuclear Excavation," Jan. 1960, Department of the Army, WHCF, Confidential File, Subject Series, Box 6, DDEL. For knowledge of cesium's potential threat, see "Radioactivity in Milk Measured by Detection," *Popular Mechanics* 112 (Sept. 1959): 112. Teller was aware of the danger posed by cesium. See Edward Teller and Albert Latter, "The Compelling Need for Nuclear Tests," *Life*, Feb. 10, 1958, 64.

33. "Annex VII: Nuclear Construction of a Sea Level Canal and Cost of Nuclear Excavation."

34. Ibid.

35. Smith, *Rogue Tory*, 353; AEC 811/59, June 13, 1960, AEC Meetings—1960b, Box 3, PDTO.

36. "Underground Atom Blast Planned by U.S. for 1961," *New York Times*, Mar. 17, 1960; "Going Underground," *Newsweek*, Mar. 28, 1960, 58; Gerber et al., *Plowshare*, 27–28.

37. Seaborg, *Kennedy, Khrushchev, and the Test Ban*, 24–25.

38. Foote to Johnson, May 5, 1960, and Foote to Wolfe, June 17, 1960, D. C. Foote Collection Documents, Box 10, PDTO; Foote to Pruitt, May 5, 1960, Correspondence: Pruitt, William Jr., Box 11, PDCF; Les to Lois, Mar. 15, 1960, Correspondence—Leslie

Viereck, 1960–61, PACS, Box 13, and Wolfe to Johnson et al., July 11, 1960, Atomic Energy Commission, Correspondence, Div. Bio & Med., 1959–66, Box 1, PCP; Viereck to Wood, Dec. 29, 1960, C-T, Correspondence, 1961, Box, 1, PLV.

39. O'Neill, *Firecracker Boys*, 206–7.

40. Ibid., 207; Egan, *Barry Commoner and the Science of Survival*, 60–61.

41. "A Baby Is Born," *Time*, 70, no. 22 (1957): 112; "Model of Atom Car Displayed by Ford," *New York Times*, Feb. 14, 1958; John A. Osmundsen, "U.S. Plans A-Bomb as a Space Engine," *New York Times*, Aug. 16, 1959.

42. Gallup, *Gallup Poll*, 1553; Murray Illson, "Rise in Strontium Noted in Humans," *New York Times*, Feb. 7, 1958.

43. "Unarmed Atom Bomb Hits Carolina Home, Hurting 6," *New York Times*, Mar. 12, 1958; "No Radiation Noted at Atom Bomb Scene," *New York Times*, Mar. 13, 1958. The crater, though somewhat filled, remains to this day.

44. Egan, *Barry Commoner and the Science of Survival*, 63–64.

45. Ibid., 64; O'Neill, *Project Chariot*, 278, 279; O'Neill, *Firecracker Boys*, 208.

46. *Nuclear Information*, June 1960, Committee for Nuclear Information—Newsletter, Box 1, PWOP.

47. Lawrence E. Davies, "Proposed Atomic Blast in Arctic Is Called Safe," *New York Times*, Aug. 17, 1960; O'Neill, *Firecracker Boys*, 171.

48. Higgins to Wolfe, Sept. 7, 1960, Project Chariot, Box 386, PET.

49. Davies, "Proposed Atomic Blast in Arctic Is Called Safe."

50. Les to Al, Aug. 20, 1960, and Don to Les, Oct. 9, 1960, Albert Johnson's Correspondence File, Box 9, PDTO; Les Viereck to Don, Aug. 27, 1960, C-T, D. Foote, 1960, Box 1, PLV; Les to Celia, Ginny, and Woody, Aug. 27, 1960, Correspondence—Leslie Viereck, 1960–61, PACS, Box 13, and Pruitt to Foote, Sept. 5, 1960, D. C. Foote Collection Documents, Box 10, PDTO. Foote's emphasis.

51. Kessel to Wolfe, Apr. 19, 1960, Atomic Energy Commission, Correspondence, Div. Bio & Med., 1960–61, Box 1, and Brina to Al, Oct. 10, 1960, Correspondence—Albert Johnson, 1958–60, Box 2, PCP.

52. O'Neill, *Firecracker Boys*, 173–76.

53. Brina to Al, Nov. 5, 1960, Correspondence—Albert Johnson, 1958–60, Box 2, PCP.

54. O'Neill, *Project Chariot*, 311, 315, 371; Brina to Al, Dec. 3, 1960, Correspondence—Albert Johnson, 1958–60, Box 2, PCP.

55. Foote to Haddock, Nov. 18, 1960, C-T, Correspondence, 1959–60, Box 1, PLV.

56. Viereck to Wood, Dec. 29, 1960.

57. "Alaska Area Eyes All Forms of Life," *New York Times*, Dec. 4, 1960.

58. Bupp, *Priorities in Nuclear Technology*, 197.

59. Kline, *First along the River*, 70–73.

60. Carson, *Silent Spring*, 6.

61. See, for instance, Dunlap, *DDT*, 102–4; Lutts, "Chemical Fallout," 211–25; Worster, *Nature's Economy*, 340; Strong, *Dreamers and Defenders*, 185–86, 224–26.

62. Teller, *Memoirs*, 451; O'Neill, *Project Chariot*, 284.

CHAPTER 4

1. Sorensen, *Kennedy*, 617; Seaborg, *Kennedy, Khrushchev, and the Test Ban*, 32–33; "Tabulation Shows How Kennedy Has Voted Since Election to the Senate in 1952," *New York Times*, July 16, 1960; "Kennedy Widens Atomic Lexicon," *New York Times*, Apr. 14, 1959; "Kennedy Opposes U.S. Resumption of Nuclear Tests," *New York Times*, Oct. 10, 1960; "Text of Kennedy's Letter Giving Stand on Resumption of Nuclear Testing," *New York Times*, Oct. 10, 1960.

2. Dokos, *Negotiations for a CTBT* 15, 34; Greene, *Eisenhower, Science Advice, and the Nuclear Test Ban Debate*, 236–37.

3. Meeting of Principals, Mar. 2 1961, ACDA, Disarmament, Committee of Principals, Memos of Conversation, 3/61-11/63, NSF, Departments and Agencies, Box 267, JFKL.

4. Foster to Committee of Principals, Apr. 15, 1963, Peaceful Nuclear Explosions and Plowshare Programs, 1963–64, Box 8, PBSL.

5. "Non-Military Nuclear Explosions," Apr. 12, 1961, 720/10/10 pt. 1, "Peaceful Nuclear Explosions in Australia—Operation Ploughshare," Series A1838, NAA-C.

6. AEC 811/71, "Plowshare Program," May 23, 1961, AEC Meetings—1961, Box 3, PDTO.

7. AEC Meeting No. 1616, May 3, 1960, vol. 24, RG 326, Minutes of the Meetings of the AEC, Box 13, NA-CP; AEC 811/71, "Plowshare Program." The deferral of Limestone and Ditchdigger became permanent. There apparently was no discussion of either experiment after 1961.

8. Alaska Conservation Society to Egan, Apr. 25, 1962, Radiation—Project Chariot, Papers of the Alaska Conservation Society, Box 18, UAF; Arthur Grahame, "A-Test Alaska Threat?," *Outdoor Life*, Jan. 1961, 10–11.

9. Wolfe to Kessel, Mar. 7 and 20, 1961, and Kessel to Wolfe, Mar. 14, 1961, Atomic Energy Commission, Correspondence, Div. Bio & Med., 1959–66, Project Chariot Collection, Box 1, and Campbell memo, "Project Chariot—Phase IV Environmental Program Proposals," Apr. 7, 1961, Atomic Energy Commission, Correspondence, 1960–63, Box 1, PCP.

10. O'Neill, *Firecracker Boys*, 189–90; Pruitt to Viereck, Swartz, and Kessel, Mar. 15, 1961, Other Documents from Archives, Box 10, PDTO.

11. O'Neill, *Firecracker Boys*, 186, 187; ACS *News Bulletin*, Mar. 1961, Project Chariot, RJCAE, General Correspondence, Box 506, NA.

12. Brina to Al, Apr. 2, 1961, Albert Johnson's Correspondence File, Box 9, and Pruitt to Foote, May 10, 1961, D. C. Foote Collection Documents, Box 10, PDTO; O'Neill, *Firecracker Boys*, 195.

13. Smith to Seaborg, June 17, 1961, Wayburn to Egan, June 13, 1961, and Twyne to the President, July 7, 1961, AEC Meetings—1961, Box 3, PDTO.

14. Eville Gorham, "Accumulation of Radioactive Fall-out by Plants in the English Lake District," *Nature*, May 31, 1958, 1523–24; Eville Gorham, "Comparison of Lower and Higher Plants as Accumulators of Radioactive Fall-Out," *Canadian Journal of Botany*, March 1959, 327–29T. Hvinden and A. Lillegraven, "Cesium-137 and Strontium-90 in Precipitation, Soil and Animals in Norway," *Nature*, Dec. 23, 1961, 1144–46.

15. O'Neill, *Firecracker Boys*, 209–10.

16. Kirsch, *Proving Grounds*, 104–6.

17. Committee on Nuclear Information, "Project Chariot" 3, nos. 4–7 (June 1961): 1–12, AT 3 Peace Promotion General, WHCF, Subject File, Box 10, JFKL.

18. Minutes of the Eighty-Seventh Meeting of the Advisory Committee for Biology and Medicine, June 9–10 1961, AEC Meetings—1961, Box 3, PDTO; Teller to McLaughlin, June 8, 1961, Reading File, Apr.–June 1961, Box 422, PET; "Project Chariot: Two Groups of Scientists Issue 'Objective' but Conflicting Reports," *Science*, June 23, 1961, 2000–2001; Robert C. Cowen, "A-Bombs and Eskimos," *Christian Science Monitor*, Aug. 21, 1961.

19. "Caribou May Bar Alaska A-Blasts," *New York Times*, June 4, 1961. For analyses of media coverage of Chariot, see Marrs, "Project Chariot"; and Rodgers, "From a Boon to a Threat."

20. Francis to Viereck, June 28, 1961, Alaska Conservation Society, 1961, Box 1, PWOP.

21. Wild, *Pioneer Conservationists of Western America*, 174, 178.

22. "Stewart Udall," *Daily Telegraph* (London), Mar. 23, 2010; Matt Schudel, "Interior Secretary Was Guardian of America's Wilderness" *Washington Post*, Mar. 21, 2010; Udall, *Quiet Crisis*, 12.

23. Viereck to Francis, July 1, 1961, and Pruitt to Francis, July 7, 1961, Alaska Conservation Society, 1961, Box 1, PWOP; Bartlett to Seaton, Apr. 9, 1959, Correspondence—Albert Johnson, 1958–60, Box 1, PCP; J. Foote, "Project Chariot," Mar. 1, 1961, A.E.C. Project Chariot: Foote, Joe—Outline of Events, Box 10, PDCF.

24. O'Neill, *Firecracker Boys*, 229–30; Village Council of Point Hope to Udall, July 25, 1961, and Betts to Seaborg et al., May 15, 1961, Documents from Various Sources, Box 10, PDTO.

25. Francis to Viereck, Aug. 14, 1961, Alaska Conservation Society, Box 1, PWOP.

26. "Executive Summary, Plowshare Program," https://www.osti.gov/opennet/reports/plowshar.pdf, accessed Mar. 1, 2010; Dokos, *Negotiations for a CTBT*, 41; Foster to Committee of Principals, Apr. 15, 1963; Tal, *American Nuclear Disarmament Dilemma*, 180–81; Evangelista, *Unarmed Forces*, 74.

27. Oliver, *Kennedy, Macmillan, and the Nuclear Test-Ban Debate*, 19; Seaborg to McCloy, May 5, 1961, Nuclear Weapons Testing, 5/61, NSF, Subjects, Box 299, and Seaborg to the President, Oct. 12, 1961, Nuclear Weapons Testing, Nov. 1–28, 1961, NSF, Subjects, Box 299A, and Circular telegram, No. 767, Oct. 24, 1961, Nuclear Weapons Testing, Cables, Aug. 1961–June 1862, NSF, Subjects, Box 301, JFKL.

28. Szasz, "New Mexico's Forgotten Nuclear Tests," 354–55.

29. Seife, *Sun in a Bottle*, 69; "Summary Notes of Meeting of the Commissioners with the Plowshare Advisory Committee," Feb. 15, 1961, AEC Meetings—1961, Box 3, PDTO; Gladwin Hill, "U.S. Is Host to 200 at Atom Test Site," *New York Times*, Nov. 26, 1961; "A Reporter at Large," *New Yorker*, Jan. 6, 1962, 35–36.

30. "Swords into Plowshares," *Time*, Dec. 22, 1961, 29; Wendell D. Weart, interviewed by Mary Palevsky, Apr. 18, 2006, transcript, Nevada Test Site Oral History Project, University of Nevada, Las Vegas; Findlay, *Nuclear Dynamite*, 23; Skartvedt, "The Plowshare Program," 205; "A Reporter at Large," 36, 38, 49; Szasz, "New Mexico's Forgotten Nuclear Tests," 358.

31. "Peace Bomb Leaks Some Radioactivity," *Los Angeles Times*, Dec. 11, 1961; "Estimated Fallout in 1963 from Nuclear Weapons Tests," undated, Department of Energy, https://www.osti.gov/servlets/purl/16377245-wRNOgV/16377245.pdf, accessed Jan. 30, 2009; Bill Becker, "U.S. A-Bomb Test for Peaceful Use Frees Radiation," *New York Times*, Dec. 11, 1961. On the debate, see Miller, *Under the Cloud*, 313.

32. Brooks, *Pursuit of Wilderness*, 70.

33. Gerald Bowkett, "A-Blasting Harbor in Alaska Argued," *Christian Science Monitor*, Mar. 30, 1962.

34. Egan, *Barry Commoner and the Science of Survival*, 66–72.

35. Piper to Wolfe, Jan. 10, 1962, Plowshare, Water, RG 57, Project Chariot Files, 1958–63, Box 4, NA-A. For his full report, see Piper, *Potential Effects of Project Chariot*; Minutes of the Eighty-Ninth Meeting of the Advisory Committee for Biology and Medicine, U.S. Atomic Energy Commission, Dec. 8–9, 1961, https://www.osti.gov/opennet/servlets/purl/16107707-Djqo0ht/16107707.pdf, accessed Feb. 2, 2009.

36. O'Neill, *Firecracker Boys*, 195–96, 199, 201; Brina to Bill, Feb. 15, 1962, Pruitt to Kessel, Feb. 18, 1962, Pruitt to Wood, Mar. 2, 1962, Kessel to Pruitt, Mar. 29, 1962, Pruitt to Kessel, Mar. 30, 1962, and Wood to Pruitt, Apr. 4, 1962, Other Documents from Archives, Rasmuson Library, Box 10, PDTO.

37. O'Neill, *Firecracker Boys*, 201, 202.

38. Revelle to Francis and Carithers, Jan. 27, 1962, Alaska—Project Chariot, RG 75, OFACJEO, Box 3, NA.

39. Udall to Seaborg, Jan. 30, 1962, Plowshare, vol. 2, Sept. 1960, RJCAE, General Correspondence, Box 504, NA; Seaborg to Udall, undated, Alaska—Project Chariot, RG 75, OFACJEO, Box 3, NA.

40. Francis to Viereck, Aug. 14, 1961, Alaska Conservation Society, 1961, Box 1, PWOP; Sharon to Don, May 28, 1962, Correspondence: U.S. Dept. of Interior, Office of the Secretary, Box 11, PDCF; Miller to Quinn, Feb. 9, 1962, Alaska—Project Chariot, RG 75, OFACJEO, Box 3, NA. Miller's emphasis.

41. Kirsch, *Proving Grounds*, 112; AEC 811/104, "Plowshare Program (Project Chariot)," July 10, 1962, AEC Meetings—1962, Box 3, PDTO.

42. Foote to Francis, Feb. 11, 1962, Correspondence: U.S. Dept. of Interior, Office of the Secretary, Box 11, PDCF; Campbell to Philip, Apr. 25, 1962, Lawrence Livermore National Laboratory Documents, Box 10, PDTO; Paul Brooks and Joseph Foote, "The Disturbing Story of Project Chariot," *Harper's*, Apr. 1962, 60–67.

43. Lawrence E. Davies, "A-Blast to Dig Alaska Harbor May Be Deferred," *New York Times*, May 13, 1962; Kirsch, "Experiments in Progress," 275, 277; O'Neill, *Firecracker Boys*, 250; AEC 811/104, "Plowshare Program (Project Chariot)."

44. Seife, *Sun in a Bottle*, 69; *Plowshare Program*, Jan. 1963, 3-2 Federal Agencies, Atomic Energy Commission, Plowshare, RG 57 Mission Control Files, Box 231, NA-CP; Marvin Miles, "Giant H-Bomb Shot Rips Crater in Nevada Desert," *Los Angeles Times*, July 7, 1962; "For the Record: A History of the Nuclear Test Personnel Review Program, 1978–1986," Aug. 1, 1986, https://www.osti.gov/opennet/servlets/purl/16389340-T673cu/16389340.pdf, accessed Feb. 1, 2009; "Hydrogen Explosion Set Off Underground in Nevada," *New York Times*, July 7, 1962.

45. Kirsch, "Experiments in Progress," 269; Skartvedt, "Plowshare Program," 56, 130; Wasserman et al., *Killing Our Own*, 114; Johnson to Pastore, Nov. 27, 1963, Canal Study—Plowshare, RJCAE, 1946–77, General Correspondence, Box 506, NA.

46. John W. Gofman, interviewed by Karoline Gourley and Loretta Hefner, Dec. 20, 1994, www.hss.doe.gov/healthsafety/ohre/roadmap/histories/0457/0457toc.html, accessed Sept. 1, 2009; Wasserman et al., *Killing Our Own*, 114.

47. Raymond J. Crowley, "Strong Eskimo Protests Shelve 'Atomic' Harbor," *Anchorage Daily Times*, Aug. 24, 1962; "Harbor-Blasting Project in Alaska Put Off by U.S.," *New York Times*, Aug. 25, 1962; Seaborg to President, Aug. 28, 1962, Atomic Energy Commission, Subject, Biweekly Reports to the President, 1962, NSF, Box 268, JFKL; "Dr. Teller Predicts A-Blasts Will Move Earth for Builders," *New York Times*, Nov. 29, 1962; Johnson, "Technological Development of Nuclear Explosives Engineering," 15; O'Neill, "Project Chariot," 36–37; Kelly to Conway, May 2, 1963, Project Chariot, RJCAE, General Correspondence, Box 506, NA.

48. Greene, *Eisenhower, Science Advice, and the Nuclear Test-Ban Debate*, 238; Oliver, *Kennedy, Macmillan, and the Nuclear Test-Ban Debate*, 129.

49. Seaborg, *Kennedy, Khrushchev, and the Test Ban*, 175–79, 191–92; Tal, *American Nuclear Disarmament Dilemma*, 217–20.

50. Seaborg, *Kennedy, Khrushchev, and the Test Ban*, 195–96.

51. Seaborg with Seaborg, *Adventures in the Atomic Age*, 180; Sylves, *Nuclear Oracles*, 69.

52. Seaborg with Seaborg, *Adventures in the Atomic Age*, 184–85, 229.

53. Seaborg, *Kennedy, Khrushchev, and the Test Ban*, 94–95; Tal, *American Nuclear Disarmament Dilemma*, 171.

54. Seaborg, *Kennedy, Khrushchev, and the Test Ban*, 196; Foster to Seaborg, Mar. 28, 1963, Limited Test Ban Treaty, Subject Files, Box 854, PGTS.

55. Memorandum of Conversation, Apr. 17, 1963, ACDA, Disarmament, Committee of Principals, Memos of Conversation, Mar. 1961–Nov. 1963, NSF, Departments and Agencies, Box 267, JFKL.

56. Ibid.

57. "Implications of Recent AEC Proposal for Nuclear Tests for Peaceful Purposes Conducted under a Comprehensive Nuclear Test Ban," undated, ACDA, Disarmament, General, Apr. 15–May 31, 1963, NSF, Departments and Agencies, Box 258, JFKL.

58. Seaborg, *Kennedy, Khrushchev, and the Test Ban*, 209–11.

59. *PPPUS, John F. Kennedy*, 1963, 463; *Plowshare Program during 1963*, undated, 3-2 Fed. Agencies, Atomic Energy Comm., Plowshare, RG 57, Mission Control Files, Box 230, NA-CP; "Memorandum of Decisions at the Meeting on Test Preparations, Etc., on June 18, 1963," June 19, 1963, Limited Test Ban Treaty, Subject Files, Box 854, PGTS.

60. Dokos, *Negotiations for a CTBT*, 43; Greene, *Eisenhower, Science Advice, and the Nuclear Test-Ban Debate*, 239–40; Seaborg, *Kennedy, Khrushchev, and the Test Ban*, 244–47.

61. McKesson to Bundy, Aug. 10, 1963, Panama, General, Aug.–Nov. 1963, NSF, Countries, Box 150, JFKL; Bisset to Timbs, Aug. 13, 1963, 1961/1568 Peaceful Uses of Nuclear Explosives—Operation Plowshare, Series A5628, NAA-C.

62. AEC 811/97, "Plowshare Program," Feb. 7, 1962, and Batzel to Kelly, Jan. 9, 1962, AEC Meetings—1962, Box 3, PDTO; Seaborg to Holifield, Feb. 27, 1962, Plowshare, vol. 2, Sept. 1960 (General), RJCAE, 1946–77, General Correspondence, Box 504, NA; Szasz, "New Mexico's Forgotten Nuclear Tests," 360; *Plowshare Program during 1963*.

63. "Executive Summary, Plowshare Program"; Dokos, *Negotiations for a CTBT*, 41; Borg, "Nuclear Explosions for Peaceful Purposes," 62, 64.

64. Wittine and Summ, "Prelude," 25; LaFeber, *Panama Canal*, 127–28, 133, 136.

65. U.S. Congress, Senate, Committee on Foreign Relations, *Nuclear Test Ban Treaty*, 206, 210; Memorandum for the President re Sea Level Canal, undated, Panama Restricted Data, Inter-Oceanic/Panama Canal Negotiations, NSF, Country File, Box 71, LBJL; SIPRI, *Ten Years of the Partial Test Ban Treaty*, 14–15.

66. Seaborg with Loeb, *Stemming the Tide*, 317.

67. Terchek, *Making of the Test Ban Treaty*, 100; U.S. Congress, *Nuclear Test Ban Treaty*, 418–24, 427.

68. Sale, *The Green Revolution*, 18; Terchek, *Making of the Test Ban Treaty*, 118, 147, 156–60.

69. "Excerpts from Documents on the Nuclear Test Ban Treaty Related to Nuclear Excavation Experiments," undated, Plowshare Nuclear Excavation Program, Box 495, PWAH; Kaufman, *Henry M. Jackson*, 151–52.

70. Findlay, *Nuclear Dynamite*, 61–62; Seaborg to the President, Oct. 22, 1963, Atomic Energy Commission, Biweekly Reports to the President, 1963, NSF, Subjects, Box 268, JFKL; National Security Action Memorandum 269, Oct. 31, 1963, Nuclear Testing—Plowshare Events (Cabriolet), NSF, Subject File, Box 29, LBJL.

71. Memorandum of Conversation, Nov. 22, 1963, Panama, General, Aug.–Nov. 1963, NSF, Countries, Box 150, JFKL.

72. Seaborg with Seaborg, *Adventures in the Atomic Age*, 198.

CHAPTER 5

1. Wittine and Summ, "Prelude," 26–27; LaFeber, *Panama Canal*, 138–40.

2. Johnson, *Vantage Point*, 181; Brands, *Wages of Globalism*, 31–33; "Panama Crisis—1964," Panama Crisis 1964 Chronology 1-30, NSF, National Security Council History, Panama Crisis 1964, Box 1, LBJL.

3. Telephone conversation between Johnson and Chiari, Jan. 10, 1964, *FRUS, 1964–1968*, 31:778–80.

4. Telephone conversation between Johnson, Mann, and Dungan, Jan. 15, 1964, and Memorandum of Conversation, Jan. 13, 1964, *FRUS, 1964–1968*, 31:792–93, 803, 804; Dallek, *Flawed Giant* 94; Woods, *LBJ*, 498.

5. Memorandum of Conference, Jan. 13, 1964, 31:797.

6. Author e-mail correspondence with Harold Brown, Dec. 12, 2009; Memorandum for the Record, Jan. 28, 1964, Panama Canal Policy and Relations with Panama, RG 185.8, Planning Documents for Construction of an Inter-Ocean Sea Level Canal and Lock Canal, Box 3, NA-CP.

7. Memorandum for the Record, Jan. 28, 1964 Administrative History, Atlantic-Pacific Interoceanic Canal Study Commission, no box number, LBJL.

8. Administrative History, Atomic Energy Commission, undated, vol. 1, Administrative History, pt. 1, chaps. 1–7, no box number, LBJL; Kramish, *Peaceful Atom in Foreign Policy*, 123; *Plowshare Program during 1963*, undated, 3-2 Fed. Agencies, Atomic Energy Commission, Plowshare, RG 57, Mission Control Files, Box 230, NA-CP; "Executive Summary, Plowshare Program," undated, https://www.osti.gov/opennet/reports/plowshar.pdf, accessed Sept. 29, 2009.

9. *Plowshare Program during 1964*, undated, 3-2 Fed. Agencies, Atomic Energy Commission, Plowshare, RG 57, Mission Control Files, Box 230, NA-CP; Skartvedt, "Plowshare Program," 109, 112, 123.

10. Koop, "Plowshare and the Nonproliferation Treaty," 797; "Executive Summary, Plowshare Program"; AEC press release, May 6, 1964, Atomic Energy Commission—Press Releases, Articles, Reports, etc., NSF, Files of Charles E. Johnson, Box 2, LBJL; John W. Finney, "Cost of Atom-Dug Sea-Level Canal Is Put at $500 Million," *New York Times*, Jan. 21, 1964

11. "Draft Testimony for S. 2497 Chairman's Statement," Panama Memos and Mis., 2/64, NSF, Country File, Boxes 65–66, LBJL; "Use of A-Bombs to Dig Canal Called Just Talk," *Los Angeles Times*, Feb. 27, 1964.

12. U.S. Congress, Senate, Committee on Commerce, *Second Transisthmian Canal*, 33–34.

13. U.S. Congress, Joint Committee on Atomic Energy, *AEC Authorizing Legislation Fiscal Year 1965*, 56–57, 78, 1202–3, 1213, 1216–18; "Plowshare: AEC Program for Peaceful Nuclear Explosives Slowed Down by Test Ban Treaty," *Science*, Mar. 13, 1964, 1154; Seaborg journal, Feb. 25, 1964, Peaceful Nuclear Explosions and Plowshare Programs, 1963–64, Box 8, PBSL.

14. U.S. Congress, *AEC Authorizing Legislation Fiscal Year 1965*, 1218, 1231.

15. "Panama Review Group Meeting," Apr. 7, 1964, Panama Memos and Misc., vol. 4, Apr.–May 1964, NSF, Country File, Boxes 65–66, LBJL; Fleming to Collins, May 24, 1964, Panama Canal Policy and Relations with Panama, RG 185.8, Planning Documents for Construction of an Inter-Oceanic Sea Level Canal and Lock Canal, Box 3, NA-CP.

16. Brands, *Wages of Globalism*, 38–41; "Editorial Note," *FRUS, 1964–1968*, 31:813–14; "Panama Crisis—1964"; Liss, *Canal*, 153.

17. Hedrick Smith, "U.S. and Colombia Join in Sea-Level-Canal Study," *New York Times*, Apr. 17, 1964; Richard Eder, "Panama Irked by U.S. Proposal to Survey for Canal in Colombia," *New York Times*, Apr. 18, 1964.

18. Special National Intelligence Estimate 84–64, Mar. 11, 1964, and Vaughn to Secretary of State, Oct. 8, 1964, *FRUS, 1964–1968*, 31:845, 880; Liss, *Canal*, 155–56.

19. Vaughn to Secretary of State, Oct. 8, 1964; Ministry of Foreign Relations to Chiari, July 28, 1964, *Memoria que el Ministro de Relaciones Exteriores*, Annex 2-1, FMA-P.

20. Ministry of Foreign Relations to Chiari, July 28, 1964; *Memoria que el Ministro de Relaciones Exteriores* (Panama: Republic of Panama, 1965), 31, FMA-P; Memorandum for the President re Sea Level Canal, undated, Panama Restricted Data, Inter-Oceanic/Panama Canal Negotiations, NSF, Country File, Box 71, LBJL.

21. Central Intelligence Agency, "A New Interoceanic Canal—Area Political Considerations," June 11, 1965, and *First Annual Report of the Atlantic-Pacific Interoceanic Canal Study Commission*, Panama, vol. 1, Inter-Oceanic/Panama Canal Negotiations, NSF, Country File, Box 70, and Untitled memo re choices regarding the canal, undated, Panama, vol. 1, Memos and Misc., Apr.–May 1964, NSF, Country File, Box 66, Administrative History of the Atlantic-Pacific Interoceanic Canal Study Commission, LBJL; "Chronology of Isthmian Canal Related Events: Jan 9, 1965–Feb 3, 1965," undated, Panama: A Documentary, NSF, Country File, Box 71, LBJL; Administrative History, Atlantic-Pacific Interoceanic Canal Study Commission; U.S. Congress, Senate, Committee on Appropriations, *Supplemental Appropriations Bill for 1965*, 392, 402.

22. "Panama Canal Studies, 1964, Appendix 1," Sept. 1964, Report Isthmian Canal Studies 1964, Box 271, PRBA.

23. "Isthmian Canal Studies, 1964, Appendix 1"; Neal Sanford, "Nuclear 'Plow' Readied," *Christian Science Monitor*, Jan. 16, 1965; Gerber et al., *Plowshare*, 35–36; *Plowshare Program during 1963*; Reynolds to Kelly, Aug. 1, 1962, AEC Meetings—1962, Box 3, PDTO.

24. "Isthmian Canal Studies, 1964, Appendix 1"; "Executive Summary, Plowshare Program."

25. "Isthmian Canal Studies, 1964, Appendix 1"; Lindsay-Poland, *Emperors in the Jungle*, 90.

26. Wilson, Pender, and Carter, *Peaceful Uses of Nuclear Explosives*, 55, 57–58.

27. "Isthmian Canal Studies, 1964, Appendix 1"; U.S. Congress, *Second Transisthmian Canal*, 18; Lawrence Galton, "A New Canal—Dug by Atom Bombs," *New York Times Magazine*, Sept. 29, 1964; Memorandum for the President re Sea Level Canal.

28. Galton, "New Canal," 74; "Isthmian Canal Studies, 1964, Appendix 1."

29. "Isthmian Canal Studies, 1964, Appendix 1."

30. Herring, *America's Longest War*, 138–39.

31. "Chronology of Isthmian Canal Related Events: Jan 9, 1965–Feb 3, 1965."

32. *PPPUS, Lyndon B. Johnson, 1963–1964*, 1663–65; "Texts of Johnson State and Address by Robles," *New York Times*, Dec. 19, 1964; Tad Szulc, "U.S. Plans to Open Parleys on Canal Early in January," *New York Times*, Dec. 12, 1964.

33. "Executive Summary, Plowshare Program."

34. "Report on Sulky," Dec. 24, 1964, Nuclear Testing—Plowshare Events (Sulky and Palanquin), NSF, Subject File, LBJL; U.S. Congress, Joint Committee on Atomic Energy, *AEC Authorizing Legislation Fiscal Year 1966*, 541.

35. Seaborg to Bundy, Jan. 15, 1964, Peaceful Nuclear Explosions and Plowshare Programs, 1963–64, Box 8, PBSL; Chayes to Johnson, Feb. 7, 1964, *FRUS, 1964–1968*, 11:14.

36. Johnson to Bundy, Apr. 30, 1964, and Johnson to the Secretary, undated, Plowshare Nuclear Excavation Program, PWAH, Box 495PBSL; ACDA, "Memorandum re Interpretation of Test Ban Treaty Provision on Causing 'Radioactive Debris to Be Present outside the Territorial Limits' of a State," Apr. 17, 1964, Nuclear Testing—General, NSF, Subject File, Box 14, LBJL; Chayes to Johnson, Feb. 7, 1964; National Security Action Memorandum 282, Feb. 11, 1964, www.lbjlib.utexas.edu/johnson/archives.hom/NSAMs/nsam282.asp, accessed Mar. 3, 2010.

37. Seaborg to Bundy, June 5, 1964, Peaceful Nuclear Explosions and Plowshare Programs, 1963–64, Box 8, PBSL; Brown to Bundy, June 26, 1964, Nuclear Testing–Plowshare

(General), and "Analysis of Project Sulky," and Bundy to Chairman, U.S. Atomic Energy Commission, Oct. 13, 1964, Nuclear Testing–Plowshare Events (Sulky and Palanquin), NSF, Subject Files, Box 29, LBJL.

38. "Editorial Note," *FRUS, 1964–1968*, 11:153–54; Bundy to Chairman, U.S. Atomic Energy Commission, Oct. 13, 1964. Under NSAM 307 of June 1964, the president expanded the membership of the Review Committee, adding the director of the Bureau of the Budget to its membership. For a copy of NSAM 307, see www.lbjlib.utexas.edu/Johnson /archives.hom/NSAMs/nsam307.asp, accessed Mar. 30, 2010.

39. "A.E.C. Conducts Test of Nuclear Excavation," *New York Times*, Dec. 20, 1964; *Plowshare Program during 1964*; "Report on Sulky"; U.S. Congress, Joint Committee on Atomic Energy, *Peaceful Applications of Nuclear Explosives—Plowshare*, 40; Seaborg journal, Dec. 24, 1964.

40. Desert Research Institute, *Forty-Three Off-Site Plowshare and Vela Uniform Projects with Potential Environmental Restoration Liabilities*, Sept. 2004, 43 Off-Site Plowshare & Vela, no box number, LLNL; U.S. Congress, *AEC Authorizing Legislation Fiscal Year 1965*, 1615, 1618; "Summary of Background Paper on the Plowshare Program," Nuclear Testing—Plowshare (General), NSF, Subject File, Box 29, LBJL; Neal Stanford, "Project Carryall," *Christian Science Monitor*, Jan. 4, 1964.

41. Smith, "Advertising the Atom," 251; "Summary of Background Paper on the Plowshare Program."

42. Stanford, "Project Carryall"; Ronald J. Ostrow, "Atom Now Ready for Earth-Moving," *Los Angeles Times*, Aug. 25, 1965.

43. U.S. Congress, *AEC Authorizing Legislation Fiscal Year 1965*, 1243.

44. "Summary of Background Paper on the Plowshare Program."

45. Johnson to Conway, June 8, 1965, Folder 48, Atomic Energy Commission, Box 6, PGJ.

46. On this score, see Johnson to Harriman, undated, and Denney to the Secretary, Feb. 25, 1964, Plowshare Nuclear Excavation Program, Box 495, PWAH.

47. Seaborg to Ball, Feb. 12, 1965, Peaceful Nuclear Explosions and Plowshare Programs, 1965–66, Box 8, PBSL; Memorandum of Conversation, Dec. 21, 1964, Disarmament, vol. 3, Committee of Principals, NSF, Subject File, Box 14, LBJL.

48. U.S. Congress, *Peaceful Applications of Nuclear Explosives—Plowshare*, 19–20.

49. Ibid., 22–26.

50. NSAM 323, Jan. 8, 1965, *FRUS, 1964–1968*, 31:896–99.

51. Vaughn to Secretary of State, Jan. 15, 1965, Panama, vol. 6, Cables, Aug. 1964–Jan. 1965, NSF, Country File, Box 67, LBJL.

52. Secretary of State to AmEmbassy Panama, Jan. 18, 1965, Panama, vol. 6, Cables, Aug. 1964–Jan. 1965, NSF, Country File, Box 67, LBJL

53. "Chronology of Isthmian Canal Related Events: Jan 9, 1965–Feb 3, 1965"; Memoranda of Conversation, Jan. 28 and 29, 1965, Panama Jan.–Mar. 1965, Box 262, PRBA.

54. Memoranda of Conversation, Jan. 30, 1965, Panama Jan.–Mar. 1965, Box 262, PRBA.

55. Memoranda of Conversation, Feb. 1, 1965, Panama Jan.–Mar. 1965, Box 262, PRBA.

56. George Natanson, "Latin Shrugs Greet Our Talk of New Canal," *Washington Post*, Feb. 7, 1965.

57. De la Rosa to Eleta, Mar. 6, 1965, and Resumen No. 5, Apr. 23, 1965, *Memoria que el Ministro de Relaciones Exteriores*, Annex 2-1, FMA-P; Jorden, *Panama Odyssey*, 97–98.

58. Kirsch, *Proving Grounds*, 163; *Plowshare Program during 1964*.

59. Stine, *Mixing the Waters*, 55–56.

60. Ibid., 56; *Plowshare Program during 1964*.

61. Kirsch, *Proving Grounds*, 166–67.

62. Desert Research Institute, *Forty-Three Off-Site Plowshare and Vela Uniform Projects*. Though Phaeton reappeared around 1968, once again the AEC was unable to find a site. See ibid.

63. Desert Research Institute, *Forty-Three Off-Site Plowshare and Vela Uniform Projects*; "Executive Summary, Plowshare Program."

64. "Analysis of Project Palanquin," undated, Seaborg to Bundy, Feb. 3, 1965, and "Supplement to the Palanquin Analysis of February 3, 1965," Nuclear Testing—Plowshare Events (Sulky and Palanquin), NSF, Subject File, Box 29, LBJL.

65. Hornig to Members of Review Committee on Underground Nuclear Tests, Mar. 2, 1965, and Johnson to Bundy, Mar. 2, 1965, Nuclear Testing—Plowshare (Sulky & Palanquin), NSF, Subject File, Box 29, LBJL.

66. Findlay, *Nuclear Dynamite*, 83; M. D. Nordyke, "The Soviet Program for Peaceful Uses of Nuclear Explosives," Sept. 1, 2009, www.bibliotecapleyades.net/ciencia/ciencia_uranium27.htm, accessed Nov. 19, 2011.

67. Fisher to Acting Secretary of State, Oct. 25, 1966, Nuclear Testing—Plowshare (General), NSF, Subject File, Box 29, LBJL; Keeny to Bundy and Hornig, May 4, 1965, Seaborg to Bundy, Feb. 19, 1965, and Keeny to Bundy, Mar. 3, 1965, Nuclear Testing—Plowshare Events (Sulky & Palanquin), NSF, Subject File, Box 29, LBJL; Seife, *Sun in a Bottle*, 58; "Chronology of Isthmian Canal Related Events: Jan 9, 1965—Feb 3, 1965."

68. Seaborg to Bundy, Mar. 24, 1965, and Bundy to Chairman, U.S. Atomic Energy Commission, Mar. 31, 1965, Nuclear Testing—Plowshare Events (Sulky and Palanquin), NSF, Subject File, Box 29, LBJL.

69. Kirsch, *Proving Grounds*, 153; McEwan, "Environmental Effects of Underground Nuclear Explosions," 76; Seaborg to the President, Apr. 16, 1965, and Seaborg journal, Apr. 15, 1965; "U.S. Test Releases Some Radioactivity," *New York Times*, Apr. 18, 1965; Northrup to Chief of Staff, May 3, 1965, Nuclear Testing—Plowshare Events (Sulky and Palanquin), NSF, Subject File, Box 29, LBJL.

70. Memorandum of Conversation, Apr. 29, 1965, and Aide-mémoire, undated, Nuclear Testing—Plowshare Events (Sulky and Palanquin), and Fisher to Acting Secretary of State, Oct. 25, 1966, Nuclear Testing—Plowshare (General), NSF, Subject File, Box 29, LBJL; Memorandum for the Files by Bruner, Jan. 29, 1969, https://www.osti.gov/opennet/servlets/purl/16108304-5ahki1/16108304.pdf, accessed Jan. 30, 2009.

71. "Panama Crisis—1964"; Bundy to Johnson, May 10, 1965, *FRUS, 1964–1968*, 31:902; Rusk to the President, June 22, 1965, Panama Inter-Oceanic Panama Canal Negotiations, vol. 1, NSF, Country File, Boxes 69–70, LBJL.

72. Administrative History, Atlantic-Pacific Interoceanic Canal Study Commission; Second Annual Report of the Atlantic-Pacific Interoceanic Canal Study Commission, July 31, 1966, Panama—Annual Report of the Atlantic-Pacific Interoceanic Canal Study Commission, NSF, Country File, Box 71, LBJL; Anderson to Rusk, Sept. 30, 1965, Interoceanic Studies IUCS Sept. 1962–Dec. 1968, RG 185.8, Box 3, NA-CP; "Panama Crisis—1964."

73. Herring, *America's Longest War*, 155, 157–58; Olson and Roberts, *Where the Domino Fell*, 122.

74. Rubinoff, "Mixing Oceans and Species," 69–72.

75. Gerber et al., *Plowshare*, 4–5.

CHAPTER 6

1. Manathunga, "Evolution of Irish Disarmament Initiatives at the United Nations," 99–100; Evgeny M. Chossudovsky, "The Origins of the Treaty on the Non-Proliferation of

Nuclear Weapons," 116, 122, 124; "Atom Arms Curb Urged by Ireland," *New York Times*, Sept. 20, 1958.

2. Quoted in Schwartz, *Lyndon Johnson and Europe*, 18.

3. Greb, "Survey of Past Nuclear Test Ban Negotiations," 103; Oral message from Khrushchev to Johnson, Feb. 28, 1964, *FRUS, 1964–1968*, 11:31–32.

4. Memorandum of Conversation, June 16, 1964, *FRUS, 1964–1968*, 11:79.

5. Brands, *Wages of Globalism*, 86–87; Seaborg, *Stemming the Tide*, 84; Young, "Killing the MLF?," 295–96; Policy Planning Staff Paper, undated, *FRUS, 1964–1968*, 30:57; Memorandum of Conversation, Feb. 27, 1964, *FRUS, 1964–1968*, 11:26.

6. "Negotiation of the Non-Proliferation Treaty," undated, Atomic Energy Commission, vol. 1, pt. 2, Administrative History, Box 1, LBJL; Memoranda of Conversation, Dec. 5, 1964, and Jan. 7, 1965, and "A Report to the President by the Committee on Nuclear Proliferation," Jan. 21, 1965, *FRUS, 1964–1968*, 11:26, 130, 155, 174.

7. Middeke, "Anglo-American Nuclear Cooperation after the Nassau Conference," 72–73, 77; Young, "Killing the MLF?," 296, 305, 311; Memorandum of Conversation, Mar. 22, 1965, *FRUS, 1964–1968*, 11:195.

8. Report by Foster, "Summary of Session of United Nations Disarmament Commission," June 18, 1965, *FRUS, 1964–1968*, 11:214; *PPPUS, Lyndon B. Johnson*, 1965, 790; Findlay, "Peaceful Nuclear Explosions and the NPT," 222; Conference of the Eighteen-Nation Committee on Disarmament, "Final Verbatim Record of the Two-Hundred and Thirty-Fourth Meeting," Sept. 16, 1965, http://quod.lib.umich.edu/cgi/t/text/text-idx?c=endc;cc=endc;view=toc;idno=4918260.0234.001, accessed Aug. 22, 2010.

9. Young, "Killing the MLF?," 313, 318–19; Epstein, *The Last Chance*, 69–70.

10. "A Report to the President by the Committee on Nuclear Proliferation," Jan. 21, 1965, 176, Memoranda of Conversation, Mar. 22 and 30 and May 19, 1965, and Minutes of Meeting of the Committee of Principals, Aug. 25, 1965, *FRUS, 1964–1968*, 11:176, 196, 198, 205, 238; Sam Pope Brewer, "U.S. Supports Call by Key U.N. Group for a Full Test Ban," *New York Times*, Nov. 27, 1965.

11. "Negotiation of the Non-Proliferation Treaty"; Palfrey oral history, undated, untitled folder, Box 15, PJGP; Seaborg journal, Jan. 12, 1965, Peaceful Nuclear Explosions and Plowshare Programs, Box 8, PBSL.

12. Keeny to Bundy, Nov. 6, 1964, Nuclear Testing—Plowshare (General), NSF, Subject File, Box 29, LBJL; NSAM 320, Nov. 25, 1964; "A Report to the President by the Committee on Nuclear Proliferation," *FRUS, 1964–1968* 11:126, 181.

13. Memorandum for the Record, Apr. 12, 1966, Nuclear Testing—Plowshare Events (Cabriolet), NSF, Subject File, Box 29, LBJL.

14. Central Intelligence Agency, "A New Interoceanic Canal—Area Political Considerations," June 11, 1965, Panama, vol. 1, Inter-Oceanic/Panama Canal Negotiations, NSF, Country File, Box 70, LBJL; Sheffey to Rostow et al., and Anderson to the President, Mar. 27, 1967, Panama, vol. 8, Memos and Misc., Sept. 1966–May 1967, NSF, Country File, Box 68, LBJL; Atlantic-Pacific Interoceanic Canal Study Commission, "Summary Report: Construction of an Isthmian Sea-Level Canal by Nuclear Methods, Route 8, Nicaragua–Costa Rica," no folder, RG 77, Nuclear Cratering Group, Technical Reports, 1963–71, Box 1, NA-SB.

15. "Atlantic-Pacific Interoceanic Canal Study Commission," undated, Administrative History of the Atlantic-Pacific Interoceanic Canal Study Commission, no box number, LBJL; Ted Bell, "Delay Likely in Study for Sea Level Canal," *Los Angeles Times*, May 19, 1966.

16. "Trends . . . ," *Christian Science Monitor*, Aug. 29, 1966; "Scientists Fearful of Effect of Level Canal on Oceans," *New York Times*, Sept. 4, 1966.

17. Resumen No. 37, Aug. 2–3, 1966, *Memoria que el Ministro de Relaciones Exteriores*, Annex No. 2-2, FMA-P; Memorandum of Conversation, May 11, 1967, Panama, Jan.–June 1967, Box 263, PRBA.

18. U.S. Congress, Joint Committee on Atomic Energy, *AEC Authorizing Legislation Fiscal Year 1967*, 1365.

19. Physics Report, Headquarters Field Command, Defense Atomic Support Agency, Sandia Base, Albuquerque, New Mexico, Nov. 18, 1965, https://www.osti.gov/opennet /servlets/purl/16004685_UTBOhe/16004685.pdf, accessed Feb. 1, 2009; "U.S. May Try Atomic Shot in Excavation Test," *Los Angeles Times*, Jan. 25, 1966; Glenn to Mac, Nov. 22, 1965, and "Concept for Project Cabriolet," undated, Nuclear Testing—Plowshare Events (Cabriolet), NSF, Subject File, Box 29, LBJL.

20. Physics Report, Headquarters Field Command, Nov. 18, 1965; Glenn to Mac, Nov. 22, 1965; Glenn to Mac, Feb. 15, 1966, Nuclear Testing—Plowshare Events (Cabriolet), NSF, Subject File, Box 29, LBJL; "Concept for Project Cabriolet."

21. "Editorial Note," *FRUS, 1964–1968*, 11:211; U.S. Congress, Joint Committee on Atomic Energy, *Peaceful Applications of Nuclear Explosives—Plowshare*, 42–43; "Notes on K Civ. Meeting," undated, Plowshare Meeting, no box number, LLNL; Foster to Bundy, Feb. 21, 1966, Hornig to the President, Apr. 4, 1966, and Cy to Don, Mar. 7, 1966, Nuclear Testing—Plowshare Events (Cabriolet), NSF, Subject File, Box 29, LBJL; Seaborg journal, Mar. 7, 1966..

22. "Cabriolet," undated, Peaceful Nuclear Explosions and Plowshare Programs, 1965–66, Box 8, PBSL; Memorandum for the Record, Apr. 12, 1966; Holifield to Seaborg, Mar. 28, 1966, and Seaborg to Holifield, Apr. 1, 1966, Peaceful Nuclear Explosions and Plowshare Programs, 1965–66, Box 8, PBSL; "U.S. May Try Atomic Shot in Excavation Test," *Los Angeles Times*, Jan. 25, 1966; U.S. Congress, *AEC Authorizing Legislation Fiscal Year 1967*, 1693.

23. Seaborg journal, Apr. 12, 1966; Seaborg to Dean, Apr. 12, 1966, and Memo, "Cabriolet," undated, Peaceful Nuclear Explosions and Plowshare Programs, 1965–66, Box 8, PBSL; Memorandum for the Record, Apr. 12, 1966; Rostow to the President, Apr. 20, 1966, Nuclear Testing—Plowshare Events (Cabriolet), NSF, Subject File, Box 29, LBJL.

24. Hornig to Rusk, Apr. 12, 1966, and Keeny to Rostow, Apr. 20, 1966, Nuclear Testing—Plowshare (General), and Hornig to the President, Apr. 4, 1966, Nuclear Testing—Plowshare Events (Cabriolet), NSF, Subject File, Box 29, LBJL.

25. Hornig to the President, Apr. 4, 1966; Memorandum for the President, Apr. 20, 1966, Nuclear Testing—Plowshare Events (Cabriolet), NSF, Subject File, Box 29, LBJL; Rostow to the President, Apr. 20, 1966.

26. "Memorandum on Cabriolet," undated, Rusk to Seaborg, May 28, 1966, and Seaborg to Rusk, June 2, 1966, Peaceful Nuclear Explosions and Plowshare Programs, 1965–66, Box 8, PBSL; Minutes of the Eleventh Meeting of the Atlantic-Pacific Interoceanic Canal Study Commission, June 23, 1966, Minutes of Interoceanic Canal Studies, June 1965–Dec. 1967, RG 185.8, Box 3, NA-CP.

27. Seaborg journal, Aug. 24 and Sept. 1, 1966.

28. U.S. Congress, Joint Committee on Atomic Energy, *AEC Authorizing Legislation Fiscal Year 1968*, 1796.

29. Desert Research Institute, *Forty-Three Off-Site Plowshare and Vela Uniform Projects with Potential Environmental Restoration Liabilities*, Sept. 2004, 43 Off-Site Plowshare & Vela, no box number, LLNL; Neal Stanford, "Underground Nuclear Blasts to Aid Industry," *Christian Science Monitor*, Nov. 29, 1967; U.S. Congress, Joint Committee on Atomic Energy, *Frontiers in Atomic Energy Research*, 41, 44.

30. Desert Research Institute, *Forty-Three Off-Site Plowshare and Vela Uniform Projects*; Stanford, "Underground Nuclear Blasts to Aid Industry"; *Plowshare Program during*

1965, *Plowshare Program during 1966*, and *Plowshare Program during 1967*, 3-2 Fed. Agencies, Atomic Energy Commission, Plowshare, RG 57, Mission Control Files, Box 230, NA-CP.

31. "El Paso Natural Says '65 Operation Revenue Climbed to a New High," *Wall Street Journal*, Feb. 9, 1966; U.S. Congress, *AEC Authorizing Legislation Fiscal Year 1967*, 1352, 1353; Bupp, *Priorities in Nuclear Technology*, 207.

32. *Plowshare Program during 1965*; U.S. Congress, *AEC Authorizing Legislation Fiscal Year 1967*, 1352; Szasz, "New Mexico's Forgotten Nuclear Tests," 361; Neal Stanford, "Peaceful Use of Nuclear Explosives Explored," *Christian Science Monitor*, Dec. 8, 1966.

33. Alfred Balk, "Mountains of Oil," *Rotarian* 107 (Dec. 1965): 41; Woods, *LBJ*, 769; U.S. Congress, *AEC Authorizing Legislation Fiscal Year 1967*, 1352.

34. *Plowshare Program during 1965*; "Atomic Blast Termed Able to Boost Output of Gas Well Sevenfold," *Wall Street Journal*, June 17, 1965; Dallek, *Flawed Giant*, 308–9; U.S. Congress, *AEC Authorizing Legislation Fiscal Year 1967*, 1349–51, 1353.

35. U.S. Congress, *AEC Authorizing Legislation Fiscal Year 1967*, 1356–57, 1379, 1381–82.

36. Ibid., 1394; "A Brave New World," *New York Times*, Mar. 11, 1965.

37. U.S. Congress, House of Representatives, *Authorizing Appropriations for the Atomic Energy Commission for Fiscal Year 1967*, 35–36; Virginia to Strauss, May 24, 1966, Gas Buggy, 1966–68, Atomic Energy Commission Series, Box 30, PLLS.

38. "Summary Notes of Commissioners' Meeting with El Paso Natural Gas Co.," Nov. 18, 1966, Summary Notes of Meetings, Nov.–Dec. 1966, Box 638, PGTS.

39. "Summary Notes of Meeting with Representatives of Continental Oil Company, Austral Oil Company and GER Geonuclear Corporation," Dec. 6, 1966, Summary Notes of Meetings, Nov.–Dec. 1966, Box 638, PGTS.

40. Seaborg to the President, Feb. 14, 1967, Peaceful Nuclear Explosions and Plowshare Programs, 1967, Box 8, PBSL; *Proceedings for the Symposium on Public Health Aspects of Peaceful Uses of Nuclear Explosives*, Apr. 7–11, 1969, 3-2, Fed. Agencies, Atomic Energy Commission, RG 59, Records of the Geological Survey Conservation Division, Mission Control Files, Box 67, NA-CP.

41. *Proceedings for the Symposium*; "Project Gasbuggy: A Government-Industry Natural Gas Production Stimulation Experiment Using Nuclear Explosives," Sept. 15, 1967, Joint Committee on Atomic Energy—Operation Gasbuggy, Box 850, PCPA.

42. *Proceedings for the Symposium*.

43. Woods, *LBJ*, 702; Telegram, Rusk to Amembassy Moscow, Aug. 22, 1967, and Memo, Johnson to Smith, Oct. 30, 1967, Nuclear Testing—Plowshare (General), NSF, Subject File, Box 29, LBJL; Gene Smith, "Project Gasbuggy Seeks a Wider Source of Fuel," *New York Times*, Sept. 22, 1967.

44. Mark Forrest, "Town Wants to Dig Cave with A-Bomb," *Washington Post*, Mar. 12, 1967.

45. Desert Research Institute, *Forty-Three Off-Site Plowshare and Vela Uniform Projects*; Teller et al., *Constructive Uses of Nuclear Explosives*, 264; *Project Ketch*, July 1967, no folder or box number, and Tarr to Goddard, Apr. 21, 1966, and "Report on Project Ketch—Nuclear Excavation for Underground Gas Storage," Sept. 12, 1966, Ketch, 1966, no box number, PJBK; *Plowshare Program during 1966*; Stanford, "Underground Nuclear Blasts."

46. Krygier, "Project Ketch," 313–14.

47. *Proceedings for the Symposium*.

48. Underwood to Forrest, Feb. 16, 1967, Ketch, 1967, no box number, PJBK; *Proceedings for the Symposium*.

49. Desert Research Institute, *Forty-Three Off-Site Plowshare and Vela Uniform Projects.*

50. "Canal Unit Seeking Extension," *New York Times,* Aug. 16, 1966; "Executive Summary, Plowshare Program," https://www.osti.gov/opennet/reports/plowshar.pdf, accessed Mar. 1, 2010.

51. Rusk to the President, Sept. 16, 1966, Rostow to the President, Sept. 23, 1966, and Hornig to the President, Sept. 22, 1966, Nuclear Testing—Plowshare Events (Cabriolet), vol. 2, NSF, Subject File, Box 29, LBJL; Administrative History, Atlantic-Pacific Interoceanic Canal Study Commission, undated, LBJL.

52. Hornig to the President, Sept. 20 and 22, 1966, Hornig et al. to the President, Sept. 20, 1966, and Rostow to the President, Sept. 23, 1966, Nuclear Testing—Plowshare Events (Cabriolet), vol. 2, NSF, Subject File, Box 29, LBJL.

53. Rostow to Katzenbach, Oct. 3, 1966, and Katzenbach to Rostow, Oct. 8, 1966, Nuclear Testing—Plowshare Events (Cabriolet), NSF, Subject File, Box 29, LBJL; Seaborg, *Stemming the Tide,* 332; Kathleen Teltsch, "U.S. and Russians to Seek U.N. Plea on Atomic Spread," *New York Times,* Oct. 15, 1966.

54. Seaborg journal, Nov. 14, 1966.

55. Untitled memorandum on questions regarding Plowshare, undated, Thompson to the Secretary, Nov. 22, 1966, and Rusk to the President, undated, Nuclear Testing—Plowshare (General), NSF, Subject File, Box 29, LBJL; Seaborg journal, Nov. 29, 1966.

56. Seaborg journal, Nov. 29, 1966; Rostow to the President, Dec. 10, 1966, Panama, vol. 8, Memos and Misc. (con't. Sept. 1966–May 1967), NSF, Countries File, Box 68, LBJL; Acting Secretary to Rostow, Dec. 10, 1966, and Rostow to the President, Dec. 12, 1966, Nuclear Testing—Plowshare Events (Cabriolet), NSF, Subject File, Box 29, LBJL.

57. Seaborg journal, Dec. 20, 1966.

58. Bible, Cannon, and Baring to Seaborg, Jan. 26, 1967, Seaborg to Bible, Feb. 3, 1967, Peaceful Nuclear Explosions and Plowshare Programs, 1965–66, Box 8, PBSL; Seaborg journal, Feb. 1, 1967; Memorandum by Tape re Cabriolet, Jan. 18, 1967, "Draft Announcement," undated, and Telegram to U.S. Ambassadors of Colombia and Panama, Jan. 23, 1967, Interoceanic Canal Studies, Jan. 1967–Mar. 1969, RG 185.8, Box 3, NA-CP.

59. Seaborg journal, Feb. 9, 1967.

60. Ibid.; Herring, *America's Longest War,* 182, 201–9.

61. Teltsch, "U.S. and Russians to Seek U.N. Plea"; "U.N. Assembly Votes Plea for Atomic Curb Treaty," *New York Times,* Nov. 5, 1966; "The Atom," *New York Times,* Jan. 21, 1967; John W. Finney, "Atom Test Delayed to Aid Treaty Hopes at Geneva Parley," *New York Times,* Feb. 11, 1967; Foster to Rusk, Jan. 11, 1967, *FRUS, 1964–1968,* 11:418–21; Philip Shabecoff, "Atom Pact Hope Is Voiced in Bonn," *New York Times,* Jan. 4, 1967; Seaborg journal, Feb. 9, 1967.

62. Dallek, *Flawed Giant,* 446–47; Seaborg journal, Feb. 28, 1967.

63. Seaborg journal, Feb. 28, 1967; J. B. Knox, "Long Range Plan—Plowshare Excavation Program (Book #1—1966/1967 Excavation Program Binder)," Sept. 7, 1967, https://www.osti.gov/opennet/servlets/purl/459335_CUF35A/webviewable/459335.pdf, accessed Jan. 30, 2009; Katzenbach to President, Apr. 11, 1967, Rostow to President, Apr. 15, 1967, and Rostow to Secretary of State and Chairman, Atomic Energy Commission, Mar. 17, 1967, Nuclear Testing—Plowshare Events (Cabriolet), NSF, Subject File, Box 29, LBJL.

64. Seaborg to Rostow and Seaborg to the President, Apr. 10, 1967, and Katzenbach to the President, Apr. 11, 1967, Nuclear Testing—Plowshare Events (Cabriolet), and Schultze to Seaborg, Apr. 20, 1967, Nuclear Testing—Plowshare (General), NSF, Subject File, Box 29, LBJL.

65. "Report on Project Ketch Meeting, Nuclear Excavation for Underground Gas Storage," Jan. 24, 1967, Ketch, 1967, no box number, PJBK. As late as 1990 the federal government owned or administered over 50 percent of the land in those eleven states, including 86 percent of the acreage in Nevada. See Milner, O'Connor, and Sandweiss, *Oxford History of the American West*, 6, 496.

66. *Proceedings for the Symposium*; Krygier, "Project Ketch," 311, 315–16, 317–18; Darrow to Nordyke, Apr. 11, 1966, Ketch, 1966, no box number, PJBK; Forrest, "Town Wants to Dig Cave with A-Bomb."

67. Kruger, "A Survey of University Courses in Nuclear Civil Engineering," 239–56.

68. Findlay, *Nuclear Dynamite*, 114–16; Adrian S. Fisher, "Nuclear Peaceful Uses 'Service' Offered to Nonnuclear States," *Department of State Bulletin*, Sept. 5, 1966, 351–53.

CHAPTER 7

1. U.S. Congress, Senate, Committee on Commerce, *Atlantic-Pacific Interoceanic Canal Study Commission*, 2–3; "House Unit Rejects Canal Study Funds," *New York Times*, Oct. 21, 1967.

2. LaFeber, *Panama Canal*, 147–48; John W. Finney, "U.S. and Panama Agree on New Canal Treaties," *New York Times*, June 27, 1967; Jorden, *Panama Odyssey*, 116–17.

3. John W. Finney, "2 Leaders Stress Need for A-Pact," *New York Times*, June 24, 1967; Seaborg, *Stemming the Tide*, 274.

4. "China Announces It Has Exploded a Hydrogen Bomb," *New York Times*, June 18, 1967; Raymond H. Anderson, "Announcement of Chinese Blast Startles and Worries Russians," *New York Times*, June 18, 1967; Finney, "2 Leaders Stress Need for A-Pact"; Epstein, *Last Chance*, 71, 72–74; "Nuclear Milestone at Geneva," *New York Times*, Aug. 25, 1967.

5. Anderson to the President, July 25, 1967, Panama, vol. 9, Memos and Misc., June 1967–Apr. 1968, NSF, Country File, Box 68, LBJL; Benjamin Welles, "150 in House Oppose 3 Panama Canal Treaties," *New York Times*, Aug. 9, 1967.

6. "Executive Summary, Plowshare Program," https://www.osti.gov/opennet/reports /plowshar.pdf, accessed Mar. 1, 2010; U.S. Congress, House of Representatives, Committee on Merchant Marine and Fisheries, *Canal Commission Authorization—1969*, 57.

7. Seaborg to Walt, July 11, 1967, Jager to Rostow, Oct. 17, 1967, Seaborg to Rostow, Oct. 10, 1967, Rostow to the Secretary of State et al., Oct. 12, 1967, and Johnson and Keeny to Rostow, Oct. 12, 1967, Nuclear Testing—Plowshare Events (Cabriolet), NSF, Subject File, Box 29, LBJL.

8. "Notes for Discussion of Nuclear Excavation Experiments," undated, Nuclear Testing—Plowshare Events (Cabriolet), NSF, Subject File, Box 29, LBJL; Ealy, *Yanqui Politics and the Isthmian Canal*, 132–33; Henry Giniger, "Canal Pacts Face Snags in Panama," *New York Times*, July 14, 1967; Welles, "150 in House Oppose 3 Panama Canal Treaties"; Clyde H. Farnsworth, "5 in Euratom Lift Barrier to A-Pact," *New York Times*, Oct. 28, 1967; "5 in Euratom Give Terms for A-Pact," *New York Times*, Nov. 1, 1967; Farnsworth and McKenney, *U.S.-Panama Relations*, 51.

9. "Editorial Note," *FRUS, 1964–1968*, 11:519; Telegram, Goldberg to Secretary of State, Oct. 18, 1967, and Katzenbach to Rostow, and Hornig to Rostow, and Schultze to Rostow, Oct. 20, 1967, Nuclear Testing—Plowshare Events (Cabriolet), vol. 2, NSF, Subject File, Box 29, LBJL.

10. "Editorial Note," *FRUS, 1964–1968*, 11:519; Rostow to the President, Oct. 24, 1967, and Helms to Rostow and Anderson to Rostow, Oct. 20, 1967, NSF—Plowshare Events (Cabriolet), NSF, Subject File, Box 29, LBJL.

11. Rostow to the President, Oct. 25, 1967, and Memorandum for the Record, Oct. 26, 1967, Nuclear Testing—Plowshare Events (Cabriolet), NSF, Subject File, Box 29,

LBJL; "The Atlantic-Pacific Interoceanic Canal Study Commission during the Administration of Lyndon B. Johnson," Administrative History of the Atlantic-Pacific Interoceanic Canal Study Commission, LBJL.

12. "Notes of the President's Meeting on Cabriolet," Nov. 28, 1967, *FRUS, 1964–1968*, 11:529–32.

13. Seaborg journal, Dec. 6, 1967, Peaceful Nuclear Explosions and Plowshare Programs, Box 8, PBSL; Rostow to the President, Dec. 6 and 8, 1967, Nuclear Testing—Plowshare Events (Cabriolet), NSF, Subject File, Box 29, LBJL.

14. Seaborg journal, Dec. 16 and 19, 1967, and Jan. 18, 1968.

15. Seaborg journal, Jan. 18, 1968; Farley to the Secretary, Jan. 5, 1968, and Keeny to Rostow, Jan. 6, 1968, Nuclear Testing—Plowshare Events (Cabriolet), NSF, Subject File, Box 29, LBJL; Findlay, *Nuclear Dynamite*, 75.

16. "Cabriolet Review," undated (ca. Jan. 1968) and Augustine to Hamburger, Feb. 13, 1968, Nuclear Testing—Plowshare Events (Buggy 1) (Schooner), NSF, Subject File, Box 30, LBJL; Rostow to the President, Jan. 26, 1968, and "Preliminary Report on Cabriolet," Jan. 30, 1968, Nuclear Testing—Plowshare Events (Cabriolet), NSF, Subject File, Box 29, LBJL; "Nevada Atom Blast Digs Crater in Test," *Los Angeles Times*, Jan. 27, 1968; Seaborg journal, Jan. 26, 1968.

17. Howard Simons, "AEC, Pleased by Test, Plans for Two More," *Washington Post*, July 7, 1962; "Preliminary Report on Buggy," JCAE #9543, Mar. 27, 1953, Peaceful Uses of Atomic Energy, Project Plowshare, RJCAE , Declassified Material from Classified Boxes, Box 43, NA; J. B. Know, "Long Range Plan—Plowshare Excavation Program (Book #1—1966/1967 Excavation Program Binder)," Sept. 7, 1967, https://www.osti.gov/opennet/servlets/purl/459335-CUF35A/webviewable/459335.pdf, accessed Jan. 30, 2009; U.S. Congress, Joint Committee on Atomic Energy, *AEC Authorizing Legislation Fiscal Year 1968*, 1795; Howard Simons, "AEC Outlines 4-Year Peaceful Nuclear Plan," *Los Angeles Times*, Jan. 31, 1963; Wheeler to Secretary of Defense, Aug. 22, 1966, Nuclear Testing—Plowshare (General), NSF, Subject File, Box 29, LBJL.

18. Seaborg journal, Oct. 11 and Nov. 14 and 21, 1966; Keeny to Rostow, Dec. 21, 1966, Nuclear Testing—Plowshare Events (Cabriolet), vol. 2, NSF, Subject File, Box 29, LBJL.

19. "Executive Summary, Plowshare Program"; U.S. Congress, *AEC Authorizing Legislation Fiscal Year 1968*, 1795; Foster to Acting Secretary of State, Apr. 7, 1967, and Draft Memorandum for the President, undated, Nuclear Testing—Plowshare Events (Cabriolet), NSF, Subject File, Box 29, LBJL.

20. Seaborg to Rostow, Feb. 2, 1968, Johnson to Rostow, Feb. 15, 1968, and Memo, "Analysis of Project Buggy," undated, Nuclear Testing—Plowshare Events (Buggy 1) (Schooner), NSF, Subject File, Box 30, LBJL.

21. Weaver to Director, Division of Peaceful Nuclear Explosives, AEC, Feb. 12, 1968, Keeny to Rostow, Feb. 16, 1968, and Rostow to Secretary of State et al., Feb. 16, 1968, Nuclear Testing—Plowshare Events (Buggy 1) (Schooner), NSF, Subject File, Box 30, LBJL.

22. Epstein, *Last Chance*, 77, 93; "Arms Parley Gets U.S.-Soviet Draft for Atom Treaty," *New York Times*, Jan. 19, 1968.

23. Epstein, *Last Chance*, 77–78.

24. Foster to Rostow, Feb. 21, 1968, Nuclear Testing—Plowshare Events (Buggy 1) (Schooner), NSF, Subject File, Box 30, LBJL.

25. Nitze to the President, Feb. 22, 1968, Katzenbach to Rostow, Feb. 24, 1968, Anderson to Rostow, undated, and Rostow to the President, Feb. 28, 1968, Nuclear Testing—Plowshare Events (Buggy 1) (Schooner), NSF, Subject File, Box 30, LBJL; *Fourth Annual Report of the Atlantic-Pacific Interoceanic Canal Study Commission*, July 31, 1968, Panama—Annual Report of the Atlantic-Pacific Interoceanic Canal Study Commission,

NSF, Country File, Box 71, LBJL; U.S. Congress, *Canal Commission Authorization—1969*, 1–2, 11–13; U.S. Congress, House of Representatives, Subcommittee on Panama Canal of the Committee on Merchant Marine and Fisheries, *Canal Tolls and Route Studies*, 2–3; Epstein, *Last Chance*, 79.

26. "A.E.C. Postpones Blast," *New York Times*, Mar. 10, 1968; Memo, "Preliminary Report on Buggy," undated, "Buggy Review," undated, and Rostow to the President, Mar. 14, 1968, Nuclear Testing—Plowshare Events (Buggy 1) (Schooner), NSF, Subject File, Box 30, LBJL; "Five Nuclear Devices Dig 800-Foot Nevada Trench," *New York Times*, Mar. 13, 1968; U.S. Congress, Joint Committee on Atomic Energy, *AEC Authorizing Legislation Fiscal Year 1970*, 327–28; Seaborg journal, Mar. 22, 1968.

27. Norman Carlisle and Jon Carlisle, "Project Gasbuggy," *Popular Mechanics* 128 (Sept. 1967): 104, 105, 222; Gene Smith, "Project Gasbuggy Seeks a Wider Source of Fuel," *New York Times*, Sept. 22, 1967.

28. Werth to Kelly, Feb. 3, 1967, https://www.osti.gov/opennet/servlets/purl/451788_ 2Gbjb0/webviewable/451788.pdf, accessed Aug. 3, 2008.

29. "Mining by Atomic Explosion: A $4.5-Million Experiment," *U.S. News and World Report*, Nov. 20, 1967, 107.

30. Szasz, "New Mexico's Forgotten Nuclear Tests," 363; Johnson to Smith, Oct. 30, 1967, Nuclear Testing—Plowshare (General), NSF, Subject File, and Seaborg to the President, Nov. 28, 1967, Atomic Energy Commission—General, vol. 2, NSF, Agency File, Box 29, LBJL; Gene Smith, "A-Blast Set Off in Earth to Spur Recovery in Gas," *New York Times*, Dec. 11, 1967; "Gasbuggy Bomb Detonation Is Rescheduled by A.E.C.," *New York Times*, Dec. 7, 1967; "Project Gasbuggy Participants Obtain Preliminary Technical Data," undated, FG 202 Jan. 1–May 31, 1968, WHCF, Box 202, LBJL.

31. Szasz, "New Mexico's Forgotten Nuclear Tests," 362–63, 365; Schulte, *Wayne Aspinall and the Shaping of the American West*, 247; Foote, Hays, and Klepinger, *Gasbuggy*, 4–7; *Plowshare Program during 1967*, 3-2 Fed. Agencies, Atomic Energy Commission, Plowshare, RG 57, Records of the Geological Survey Conservation Division, Mission Control Files, Box 230, NA-CP.

32. "Project Gasbuggy Participants"; Hubert G. Lawson, "Early Success of Project Gasbuggy Point to Success; Gas Flow Tests Are Planned," *Wall Street Journal*, Apr. 22, 1968; U.S. Congress, Joint Committee on Atomic Energy, *AEC Authorizing Legislation Fiscal Year 1969*, 1134; Kelly to Seaborg et al., Apr. 26, 1968, Cooperation 3-2, Federal Agencies, Atomic Energy Commission, Plowshare, RG 57, Records of the Geological Survey Conservation Division, Mission Control Files, Box 229, NA-CP; Johnson to Libby, Jan. 10, 1968, Libby, Willard F., Box 6, PGJ.

33. Peter Metzger, "Project Gasbuggy and Catch-85," *New York Times Magazine*, Feb. 22, 1970; Kreith and Wrenn, *Nuclear Impact*, 62; Skartvedt, "The Plowshare Program," 240; Victor Cohn, "Atom Blast Contaminated Gas," *Washington Post*, Nov. 13, 1968. How much radioactivity to which an average person would have been exposed remains a matter of debate, for it depended on the amount of tritium and the extent to which it was possible to dilute the radioactive gas. Evaluating several studies, Kreith and Wrenn have stated that it might have been as high as 170 mrem, the maximum allowed under federal guidelines (*Nuclear Impact*, 66–67).

34. Kreith and Wrenn, *Nuclear Impact*, 62; Metzger, "Project Gasbuggy."

35. U.S. Congress, *AEC Authorizing Legislation Fiscal Year 1970*, 301; U.S. Congress, Joint Committee on Atomic Energy, *Nuclear Explosion Services for Industrial Applications*, 180.

36. Szasz, "New Mexico's Forgotten Nuclear Tests," 363, 364; Metzger, "Project Gasbuggy"; Skartvedt, "Plowshare Program," 236–37; Kreith and Wrenn, *Nuclear Impact*,

54–55; Herbert G. Lawson, "Early Results of Project Gasbuggy Point to Success; Gas Flow Tests Are Planned," *Wall Street Journal*, Apr. 22, 1968.

37. Desert Research Institute, *Forty-Three Off-Site Plowshare and Vela Uniform Projects with Potential Environmental Restoration Liabilities*, Sept. 2004, 43 Off-Site Plowshare & Vela, no box number, LLNL; *Plowshare Program during 1967*; Neal Stanford, "Underground Nuclear Blasts to Aid Industry," *Christian Science Monitor*, Nov. 29, 1967.

38. Seaborg to the President, July 23, 1968, Peaceful Nuclear Explosions and Plowshare Program 1968–69, Box 9, PBSL; "Plowshare Program Meeting, 6 January 1969," Plowshare Meeting, no box number, LLNL; Dougan to Coffer, Dec. 2, 1968, Pinnell to Hank, Dec. 9, 1968, Glass to Grier, Dec. 9, 1968, Barlow to Young, Dec. 20, 1968, Kuhn to Coffer, Jan. 29, 1969, Elkins to Grier, Mar. 10, 1969, Pforzheimer to Grier, Mar. 17, 1969, and Steele to Grier, Mar. 19, 1969, 3-2-1 Federal Agencies, Atomic Energy Commission, Plowshare, Bronco, Colo. Correspondence, RG 57, Records of the Geological Survey Conservation Division, Mission Control Files, Box 232, NA-CP.

39. Desert Research Institute, *Forty-Three Off-Site Plowshare and Vela Uniform Projects; Plowshare Program during 1967*; U.S. Congress, Joint Committee on Atomic Energy, *AEC Authorizing Legislation Fiscal Year 1968*, 1799.

40. "Report on Project Ketch Meeting, Nuclear Excavation for Underground Gas Storage," Jan. 24, 1967, Ketch, 1967, no box number, PJBK.

41. *Project Ketch*, July 1967, no folder or box number, PJBK.

42. Ibid.; Johnstud, "A Political Geography of the Nuclear Power Controversy," 277.

43. "Report on Project Ketch Meting, Nuclear Excavation for Underground Gas Storage"; Krygier, "Project Ketch," 315, 316.

44. Freeman, *Nuclear Witnesses*, 63–64.

45. Krygier, "Project Ketch," 315; Tarr to Goddard, July 13, 1967, Bowers to Jones, July 28, 1967, Subcommittee on Project Ketch to Jones, July 31, 1967, Bielo to Jones, Aug. 2, 1967, Georges to Jones, Aug. 4, 1967, and Shafer to Seaborg, Aug. 11, 1967, Ketch, 1967, no box number, PJBK; Wilt to Tarr, July 31, 1967, Ketch: Lease and Misc., no box number, PJBK; Desert Research Institute, *Forty-Three Off-Site Plowshare and Vela Uniform Projects*.

46. Johnstud, "A Political Geography of the Nuclear Power Controversy," 279–81; Deily to Goddard, June 28, 1968, Ketch, 1968, no box number, PJBK; Desert Research Institute, *Forty-Three Off-Site Plowshare and Vela Uniform Projects*.

47. Kelly to Seaborg et al., June 7, 1968, "Remarks of S. Orlofsky at the Project Ketch Forum at Lock Haven State College on February 16, 1968," and "Dress Mom with the Money You Save with Gas," undated, Ketch, 1968, no box number, PJBK.

48. Orlofsky to Shafer, July 5, 1968, Ketch, 1968, no box number, PJBK,

49. Desert Research Institute, *Forty-Three Off-Site Plowshare and Vela Uniform Projects*; "Plowshare Program Meeting"; *Proceedings for the Symposium on Public Health Aspects of Peaceful Uses of Nuclear Explosives*, Apr. 7–11 1969, 3-2, Fed. Agencies, Atomic Energy Commission, RG 59, Records of the Geological Survey Conservation Division, Mission Control Files, Box 67, NA-CP.

50. Desert Research Institute, *Forty-Three Off-Site Plowshare and Vela Uniform Projects*; "Plowshare Program Meeting"; Kelly to Seaborg et al., Apr. 26, 1968, Cooperation, 3-2, Federal Agencies, Atomic Energy Commission, Plowshare, RG 57, Records of the Geological Survey Conservation Division, Mission Control Files, Box 229, NA-CP.

51. Desert Research Institute, *Forty-Three Off-Site Plowshare and Vela Uniform Projects*.

52. Ibid.

53. Epstein, *Last Chance*, 80–84.

54. Lindsay-Poland, *Emperors in the Jungle*, 91–92.

55. "House Passes Bill on Canal," *New York Times*, Nov. 21, 1967; "Johnson Signs Bill Setting Later Date on Canal Report," *New York Times*, Jan. 4, 1968; *Fourth Annual Report of the Atlantic-Pacific Interoceanic Canal Study Commission*, July 31, 1968, Panama—NSF, Country File, Box 71, LBJL.

56. "Analysis of Project Schooner," undated, Nuclear Testing—Plowshare Events (Buggy I) (Schooner), NSF, Subject File, Box 30, LBJL; Skartvedt, "Plowshare Program," 40.

57. "Editorial Note," *FRUS, 1964–1968*, 11:620; "Executive Summary, Plowshare Program"; "Analysis of Project Schooner," undated, Nuclear Testing—Plowshare Events (Buggy I) (Schooner), NSF, Subject File, Box 30, Nuclear Testing—Plowshare Events (Cabriolet), NSF, Subject File, Box 29, LBJL.

58. "Editorial Note," *FRUS, 1964–1968*, 11:620.

59. Ibid.; "Executive Summary, Plowshare Program"; "Analysis of Project Schooner"; Foster to Rostow, Oct. 30, 1968, Nuclear Testing—Plowshare Events (Cabriolet), NSF, Subject File, Box 29, LBJL.

60. Seaborg to Rostow, Oct. 16, 1968, Nuclear Testing—Plowshare Events (Cabriolet), NSF, Subject File, Box 29, LBJL.

61. Katzenbach to Rostow, Nov. 5, 1968, and Hornig to the President, Nov. 15, 1968, Nuclear Testing—Plowshare Events (Cabriolet), NSF, Subject File, Box 29, LBJL; Rostow to the President, Nov. 16, 1968, Nuclear Testing—Plowshare Events (Buggy I) (Schooner), NSF, Subject File, Box 30, LBJL; "Editorial Note," *FRUS, 1964–1968*, 11:621.

62. "Nuclear Test Postponed," *New York Times*, Dec. 6, 1968; "Nuclear Canal-Digging Test Blasts Huge Crater in Desert," *Los Angeles Times*, Dec. 9, 1968; "U.S. Blasts Crater in Peaceful A-Test," *New York Times*, Dec. 9, 1968; Skartvedt, "Plowshare Program," 159; U.S. Congress, *AEC Authorizing Legislation Fiscal Year 1970*, 328; Seaborg to Pastore, Jan. 16, 1969, Project Schooner, RJCAE, General Correspondence, Box 570, NA; Seaborg journal, Dec. 10, 1968, Box 9, PBSL.

63. Telegram, No. 9903, Department of State to Moscow, Jan. 22, 1969, *FRUS, 1969–1972*, E-2; Memorandum of Conversation, Jan. 22, 1969, Peaceful Nuclear Explosions and Plowshare Programs, 1968–69, Box 9, PBSL.

64. "Ninety-Day Paper: Panama Canal Negotiations," undated, Panama July–Dec. 1968, Box 263, PRBA.

CHAPTER 8

1. Untitled memorandum on questions regarding Plowshare, undated, Nuclear Testing—Plowshare (General), NSF, Subject File, Box 29, LBJL.

2. U.S. Congress, Joint Committee on Atomic Energy, *Peaceful Applications of Nuclear Explosives—Plowshare*, 49; "The Cape Keraudren Feasibility Study," 720/10/10/1, Mar. 21, 1969, pt. 3, Operation Ploughshare, Cape Keraudren, Series A1838, NAA-C; "Summary Notes of Meeting with Pote Sarasin, Thai Minister for National Development," Oct. 10, 1966, Summary Notes of Meetings, June–Oct. 1966, Box 638, PGTS; Plowshare Program Meeting, Mar. 15, 1967, Plowshare Meeting, no box number, LLNL.

3. Borg, "Nuclear Explosions for Peaceful Purposes," 66; Keeny to Bundy, Feb. 11, 1966, Nuclear Testing—Plowshare (General), NSF, Subject File, Box 29, LBJL.

4. Elliott to Reid, Nov. 12, 1959, 12H Peaceful Uses Subject File: 17b, Project Plowshare, 1959, RG 59, SASEOS, Records Relating to Atomic Energy Matters, 1944–63, Box 218, NA-CP; Keeny to Bundy, Feb. 11, 1966, Nuclear Testing—Plowshare (General), NSF, Subject File, Box 29, LBJL.

5. Keeny to Bundy, Feb. 11, 1966; Palfrey oral history, undated, untitled folder, Box 15, PJGP; U.S. Congress, Joint Committee on Atomic Energy, *Request for Supplemental Fiscal Year 1975 Funds for AEC Nuclear Weapons Testing*, 27.

6. Siracusa and Coleman, *Australia Looks to America*, 85; Oliphant to Timbs, Aug. 29, 1960, E1355 Operation "Plowshare" Use of Nuclear Explosion for Civilian Purposes, Series A987, NAA-C.

7. Biography of Harold George Raggatt, www.asap.unimelb.edu.au/bsparcs /aasmemoirs/raggatt.htm, accessed Sept. 6, 2010; "Harold Raggatt," *Encyclopedia of Australian Science*, www.eoas.info/biogs/P000728b.htm, accessed Sept. 6, 2010; "Operation Plowshare—Informal Meeting," Mar. 20, 1961, and Minute by Raggatt, Nov. 11, 1960, Folder E1355, Operation "Plowshare" Use of Nuclear Explosion for Civilian Purposes, Series A987, NAA-C.

8. Raggatt to Martin et al., Mar. 14, 1961, Raggatt to Hudson, Feb. 27, 1961, "Operation Plowshare—Informal Meeting," Mar. 20, 1961, and "Use of Nuclear Explosives for Civil Works," Mar. 22, 1961, E1355 Operation "Plowshare" Use of Nuclear Explosives for Civilian Purposes, Series A987, NAA-C; Bisset to Timbs, Mar. 21, 1961, Meeting at Dept. of National Development, Canberra re "Plowshare" Proposals—Use of Nuclear Explosives in Engineering Work, Series MP 1084/4, NAA-M.

9. Minute by Cook, Apr. 6, 1961, Minute by Harry, Apr. 7, 1961, and Tange to Buntin, Apr. 17, 1961, 720/10/10 pt. 1, Peaceful Nuclear Explosions in Australia—Operation Ploughshare, Series A1838, NAA-C; Timbs to Tange, Apr. 26, 1961, E1335A, Operation "Plowshare" Use of Nuclear Explosion for Civilian Purposes, Series A987, NAA-C.

10. "Record of Discussion on Project Plowshare," June 19, 1961, E1335, Operation "Plowshare" Use of Nuclear Explosion for Civilian Purposes, Series A987, NAA-C.

11. "Notes for Cabinet Submission: Application of Plowshare to Construction of Western Australian Harbor," undated, 1962/1911, pt. 5, Operation Plowshare—Use of Nuclear Explosives for Civilian Purposes, Series A1690, and Raggatt to Hudson, July 25, 1962, 1961/1568, Peaceful Uses of Nuclear Explosions—Operation Plowshare, Series A5628, NAA-C; Raggatt to Lewis, Apr. 6, 1962, 1961/401, Meeting at Department of National Development, Canberra re "Plowshare" Proposals—Use of Nuclear Explosives in Engineering Work, Series MP 1084/4, NAA-M.

12. See O'Meara to the Deputy Director-General, July 31, 1962, Lewis to Raggatt, Aug. 7, 1962, and Raggatt to Lewis, Aug. 16, 1962, Meeting at Department of National Development, Canberra re "Plowshare" Proposals—Use of Nuclear Explosives in Engineering Work, Series MP 1084/4, NAA-M.

13. Seaborg to Beale, Oct. 25, 1962, 1961/1568, Peaceful Uses of Nuclear Explosions—Operation Plowshare, Series A5628, and Spooner to Cabinet, undated, and Beale to Seaborg, undated, 720/10/10 pt. 2, IAEA—Peaceful Nuclear Explosions in Australia—Operation "Plowshare," Series A1838, and Cabinet Minute, Decision No. 772, May 7, 1963, vol. 16, Agendum 625, Peaceful Use of Nuclear Explosives, Decision 772, Series A5819, NAA-C; Wilson et al., *Peaceful Uses of Nuclear Explosives*, 1.

14. Bisset to Timbs, Aug. 13, 1963, 1961/1568, Peaceful Uses in Nuclear Explosives—Operation Plowshare, Series A5628, and Memorandum of Conversation, Aug. 21, 1963, 720/10/10 pt. 2, IAEA—Peaceful Nuclear Explosion in Australia—Operation "Plowshare," Series A1838, NAA-C.

15. Leech to Baxter, Apr. 26, 1968, Plowshare: General Correspondence, G67/2827, Australian Atomic Energy Commission, General Records File, NAA-S; Wilson to Timbs, Oct. 14 and 15, 1963, 186/1/128, United States Plan for Exploiting Nuclear Explosives for Peaceful Purposes—"Operation Plowshare," Series A1945, NAA-C.

16. Leech to Baxter, Apr. 26, 1968. For a copy of the report, see Wilson et al., *Peaceful Uses of Nuclear Explosives*.

17. Pender to Chief Engineer, Civil Design and Scientific Services, Snowy Mountains Hydro-Electric Authority, July 14, 1964, 1961/1568, Peaceful Uses of Nuclear Explosions—Operation Plowshare, Series A5628, NAA-C.

18. "Brand, Sir David," *Australian Dictionary of Biography,* http://adbonline.anu.edu .au/biogs/A130280b.htm, accessed Sept. 6, 2010; Cablegram No. 1033, Department of External Affairs to Australian Embassy, Washington, Apr. 16, 1964, Booker to the Minister, undated, and Cablegram No. 1111, Australian Embassy, Washington, to Department of External Affairs, Apr. 17, 1964, 720/10/10 pt. 2, IAEA—Peaceful Nuclear Explosion in Australia—Operation "Plowshare," Series A1838, NAA-C; "Notes for Cabinet Submission: Application of Plowshare to Construction of Western Australian Harbor," undated, 1962/1911 pt. 5, Operation Plowshare—Use of Nuclear Explosives for Civilian Purposes, Series A1690, NAA-C.

19. Memo by Warner, "Report on Visit to Western Australia in Connection with Possible Nuclear Excavated Harbour for Shipping Iron Ore," Apr. 13, 1966, 186/1/28, United States Plan for Exploiting Nuclear Explosives for Peaceful Purposes—"Operation Plowshare," Series A1945, NAA-C; McLennan to Raggatt, Aug. 27, 1964, and Raggatt to McLennan, Sept. 2, 1964, 1962/1911 pt. 5, Operation Plowshare—Use of Nuclear Explosives for Civilian Purposes, Series A1690, NAA-C.

20. Minute by Wilson, " 'Plowshare'—Discussion with U.S.A.E.C. Officials 29th/30th March, 1965," 1962/1911, pt. 5, Operation Plowshare—Use of Nuclear Explosives for Civil Purposes, Series A1690, NAA-C; "Notes K Div. Meeting," undated, Plowshare Meeting, no box number, LLNL.

21. Booker to the Minister, undated, 720/10/10 pt. 2, IAEA—Peaceful Nuclear Explosion in Australia—Operation "Plowshare," Series A1838, NAA-C; Bett to Timbs, Apr. 14, 1965, and "Plowshare Project—Western Australia," July 2, 1965, 1962/1911 pt. 5, Operation Plowshare—Use of Nuclear Explosives for Civilian Purposes, Series A1690, NAA-C; "Report on Visit to Western Australia in Connection with Possible Nuclear Excavated Harbour for Shipping Iron Ore," Apr. 13, 1966, 186/1/28, United States Plan for Exploiting Nuclear Explosives for Peaceful Purposes—"Operation Plowshare," Series A1945, NAA-C.

22. "Report on Visit to Western Australia in Connection with Possible Nuclear Excavated Harbour for Shipping Iron Ore"; Court to the Premier, May 21, 1965, and "Notes of Meeting in Savoy Plaza Hotel, New York," Apr. 28, 1965, 1962/1911 pt. 5, Operation Plowshare—Use of Nuclear Explosives for Civilian Purposes, Series A1690, NAA-C.

23. Bett to Timbs, July 7, 1965, and Fairbairn to Menzies, May 24, 1965, 1962/1911 pt. 5, Operation Plowshare—Use of Nuclear Explosives for Civilian Purposes, Series A1690, NAA-C; "Statement by Dr. Glenn T. Seaborg, Chairman, U.S. Atomic Energy Commission, on Plowshare Program before the Joint Committee on Atomic Energy, January 5, 1965," Cooperation, 3-2, Federal Agencies, Atomic Energy Commission, Plowshare, RG 57, Records of the Geological Survey Conservation Division, Mission Control Files, Box 229, NA-CP.

24. "Report on Visit to Western Australia in Connection with Possible Nuclear Excavated Harbour for Shipping Iron Ore"; "Record of Meeting Held at U.S.A.E.C., 3rd November 1965, to Discuss the Subject of Accommodations under the Limited Nuclear Test Ban Treaty," "Record of Meeting Held at Department of State, 4th November to Discuss Effect of Limited Test Ban Treaty on Harbour Construction Using Nuclear Explosives," and Furlonger to Secretary, Department of External Affairs, Nov. 9, 1965, 186/1/128, United States Plan for Exploiting Nuclear Explosives for Peaceful Purposes—"Operation Plowshare," Series A1945, NAA-C.

25. "Notes on Visit to Western Australia in Connection with Possible Nuclear Excavated Harbour," Feb. 9, 1966, 1974/7951, Australian Atomic Energy Commission—Plowshare Policy, Series A3211, NAA-C.

26. "Trip Report: Australia, Thailand, India, and Pakistan, January 3 through January 14, 1967," Atomic Energy Commission—General, vol. 2, NSF, Agency File, Box 29, LBJL; Leech to Baxter, Apr. 26, 1968.

27. "Canberra Backs N-Blast Plan for Harbour," *West Australian* (Perth), Jan. 24, 1969; "Nuclear Blasting of New Harbour in W.A. Possible," *Kalgoorlie Miner*, Jan. 31, 1969; Telegram, No. AP 40, Apr. 18, 1969, 1966/1847, Operation Plowshare—Use of Nuclear Explosives for Civilian Purposes, Series A1690, NAA-C; Timbs to Hewitt, Dec. 20, 1968, 1974/7951, Australian Atomic Energy Commission—Plowshare Policy, Series A3211, NAA-C; Alvy to Hope, May 8, 1967, 260/69, Sentinel Mining Company, General Correspondence, Department of Industrial Development, SROWA.

28. Timbs to Hewitt, Dec. 20, 1968, 1974/7951, Australian Atomic Energy Commission—Plowshare Policy, Series A3211, NAA-C.

29. Minister for Industrial Development and the North-West to the Premier, Dec. 2, 1968, 494/68, Cabinet Minutes and Decisions, Oct. 21, 1968–Jan. 28, 1969, Premier's Department, State Cabinet Papers, SROWA; Brand to Gorton, Dec. 5, 1968, and Gorton to Brand, Jan. 6, 1969, and "Text of Australian Embassy's Note of 22 January, 1969," 720/10/10/1 pt. 3, Operation Plowshare—Cape Keraudren, Series A1838, NAA-C.

30. Desert Research Institute, *Forty-Three Off-Site Plowshare and Vela Uniform Projects with Potential Environmental Restoration Liabilities*, Sept. 2004, 43 Off-Site Plowshare & Vela, no box number, LLNL; "Canberra Backs N-Blast Plan for Harbour"; Seaborg to Nixon, Feb. 5, 1969, *FRUS, 1969–1972*, E-2; Kirsch, *Proving Grounds*, 194.

31. U.S. Congress, Joint Committee on Atomic Energy, *AEC Authorizing Legislation Fiscal Year 1969*, 1140–41; *Seventeenth Annual Report of the Australian Atomic Energy Commission, for Year 1968–69*, 76; Seaborg to the President, Feb. 5 and 10, 1969, and Seaborg journal, Dec. 16, 1968, Box 9, PBSL; Anthony Ripley, "A.E.C. Aide Scoffs at Radiation Fears," *New York Times*, Jan. 13, 1970; Seaborg to Holifield, Feb. 17, 1969, Plowshare, vol. 4, RJCAE, General Correspondence, Box 504, NA.

32. See, for instance, Minutes of Cabinet Meeting, Apr. 29 1960, AWF, Cabinet Series, Box 16; Memorandum of Conversation, July 7, 1960, 1960 Meetings with the President vol. 2, WHO, Office of the Special Assistant for National Security Affairs, Special Assistant Series, Presidential Subseries, Box 2, DDEL; Kistiakowsky, *Scientist in the White House*, 365.

33. Memorandum of Conversation, July 7, 1960; Memoranda of Conversation, Jan. 22 and 28, 1969, Peaceful Nuclear Explosions and Plowshare Programs, 1968–69, Box 9, PBSL.

34. Hosmer to the President, Dec. 27, 1968, Australia—Cape Keraudren Harbor Pres Rel./Article/Clips, no box number, LLNL; "A-Blast Weighed to Dig Australia Port," *New York Times*, Jan. 24, 1969.

35. Unger and Unger, *LBJ*, 465; Dallek, *Flawed Giant*, 554; Ambrose, *Nixon*, 2:225.

36. "Summary of Meeting on 28 Jan. 1969," 1969/3025 pt. 1, Project Plowshare—Proposal to USE Nuclear Weapons to Excavate Harbour at Cape Keraudren, West Australia, Series A432, NAA-C; "Text of United States Note of 3 February, 1969," 720/10/10/1 pt. 3, Operation Ploughshare—Cape Keraudren, Series A1838, NAA-C; Seaborg with Loeb, *Atomic Energy Commission under Nixon*, 17; Seaborg journal, Jan. 31, 1969, Box 1, PBSL; Cawte, *Atomic Australia*, 122, 123.

37. Hubbard, "From Ambivalence to Influence," 532; Martin, *Nuclear Knights*, 50.

38. Walsh, "Surprise Down Under," 12.

39. Joel Bateman, "Australian Prime Ministers and Deposition: John Gorton and Bob Hawke Compared," paper presented at the Australasian Political Studies Association Conference, Adelaide, 2004, www.adelaide.edu.au/apsa/docs_papers/Others/Bateman .pdf, accessed Oct. 1, 2010; Hubbard, "From Ambivalence to Influence," 533–34.

40. Hubbard, "From Ambivalence to Influence," 532, 534.

41. Nuclear Nonproliferation Treaty, 1968, Articles I, III–V; Telegram, No. AP 40, Apr. 18, 1969; "Keraudren Blast May Be First of Series," *West Australian* (Perth), Jan. 25, 1969.

42. "Text of United States Note of 3 February, 1969"; "Record of Discussion at Luncheon, 21 February 1969," 720/10/10/1 pt. 2, AAEC—Operation Ploughshare—Cape Keraudren, and "Message Delivered by Mr. Pollack. 11.30 Washington Time This Evening," Feb. 6, 1969, 720/10/10/1 pt. 1, AAEC—Operation Ploughshare—Cape Keraudren, and Minute by McIntyre, Feb. 6, 1969, 720/10/10/1 pt. 4, AAEC—Operation Ploughshare—Cape Keraudren, Series A1838, NAA-C; "A Meaty Question," *Wall Street Journal*, Jan. 13, 1969.

43. Boswell to the Minister, Feb. 10, 1969, 1969/3025 pt. 1, Project Plowshare—Proposal to Use Nuclear Weapons to Excavate Harbour at Cape Keraudren, Western Australia, Series A432, and "The Cape Keraudren Feasibility Study," Feb. 18, 1969, 720/10/10/1 pt. 3, Operation Ploughshare—Cape Keraudren, Series A1838, NAA-C.

44. Boswell to the Minister, Feb. 10, 1969.

45. Cablegram, No. 1004, Australian Embassy to Atomcom, Feb. 20, 1969, 1974/7951, Australian Atomic Energy Commission—Plowshare Policy, Series No. A3211, NAA-C; "Cape Keraudren Project," undated, 720/10/10/1 pt. 2, AAEA—Operation Ploughshare—Cape Keraudren, Series A1838, NAA-C; Handwritten, undated note, Australia—Cape Keraudren Plowshare Project, 1969, undated, Box 1, PBSL; Seaborg with Loeb, *Atomic Energy Commission under Nixon*, 25.

46. Savingram AP 40, "The Cape Keraudren Feasibility Study," Apr. 18, 1969, 1966/1847, Operation Plowshare—Use of Nuclear Explosives for Civilian Purposes, Series A1690, NAA-C; Memorandum of Conversation, AUSTL, Mar. 18, 1969, OS-AUSTL 69 (inc. Cape Keraudren Project), RG 59, Subject Files of the Office of Australia, New Zealand, and Pacific Island Affairs, 1959–74, Box 30, NA-CP.

47. "Blasting Out a Port," *West Australian* (Perth), Jan. 27, 1969; "Harbour from Nuclear Blast," *Kalgoorlie Miner*, Jan. 15, 1969; Findlay, *Nuclear Dynamite*, 148–49.

48. Siracusa and Coleman, *Australia Looks to America*, 85–86.

49. "Broadcast A.B.C. Saturday 15th February 1969 8.15 A.M. Interview Dr W. D. L. Ride by Dr Peter Pockley A.B.C.," 244/69, Fisheries—Cape Keraudren Plowshare Operation, Department of Fisheries and Fauna, SROWA; Cawte, *Atomic Australia*, 123.

50. Brodine, "Unsung Harbor," 34–35.

51. *Parliamentary Debates*, Representatives, 26th Parliamentary, 2nd session, 1969, vol. H of R. 62, pp. 10–11, 317, 823.

52. Seaborg journal, Mar. 26, 1969, Box 1, PBSL; "Nuclear Doubts," *Sydney Morning Herald*, Apr. 2, 1969.

53. Atomcom to Prime Ministers Dept., Mar. 11, 1969, 1969/3025 pt. 1 Project Plowshare—Proposal to Use Nuclear Weapons to Excavate Harbour at Cape Keraudren, West Australia, Series A432, NAA-C; Gorton to Fairbairn, Mar. 25, 1969, 720/10/10/1 pt. 3, Operation Ploughshare—Cape Keraudren, Series A1838, NAA-C.

54. Cablegrams, No. 1802, Australian Embassy Washington to Department of External Affairs, Mar. 27, 1969, No. 1149, Department of External Affairs to Australian Embassy Washington, Mar. 27, 1969, and No. 1837, Australian Embassy Washington to Department of External Affairs, Mar. 28, 1969, 1969/3025 pt. 2, Project Plowshare—Proposal to Use Nuclear Weapons to Excavate Harbour at Cape Keraudren, West Australia, Series A432, NAA-C.

55. "Cape Keraudren Co-ordinating Committee 5th Meeting, Canberra, 21st April, 1969," 720/10/10/1 pt. 3, Operation Ploughshare—Cape Keraudren, Series No. A1838,

NAA-C; U.S. Congress, Joint Committee on Atomic Energy, *AEC Authorizing Legislation Fiscal Year 1970*, 337–38.

56. McCay to the Minister, July 29, 1969, 1966/1847 Operation Plowshare—Use of Nuclear Explosives for Civilian Purposes, Series A1690, NAA-C; Report by Wilson et al., "Proposed Nuclear Excavation of Harbour at Cape Preston, Western Australia," July 1969, 1969/3025 pt. 3, Project Plowshare—Proposal to Use Nuclear Weapons to Excavate Harbour at Cape Keraudren, West Australia, Series A432, NAA-C.

57. McCay to Lawrence, Sept. 26, 1969, 1966/1847 Operation Plowshare—Use of Nuclear Explosives for Civilian Purposes, Series A1690, NAA-C; "National Bulk Pulls Out of Joint Australia Project," *Wall Street Journal*, July 15, 1969.

58. Ira Rubinoff, "Central American Sea-Level Canal: Possible Biological Effects," *Science*, Aug. 30, 1968, 857–61; Robert W. Topp, "Interoceanic Sea-Level Canal: Effects on the Fish Faunas," *Science*, Sept. 26, 1969, 1324–27; "Panama's Sea-Level Canal," *Science*, Nov. 1, 1968, 511–13; "Fish-Eye View of a New Panama Canal," *New York Times*, Sept. 15, 1968; "New Canal: What about Bioenvironmental Research," *Science*, Jan. 10, 1969, 165–67.

59. U.S. Congress, *AEC Authorizing Legislation Fiscal Year 1970*, 16, 308; U.S. Congress, Joint Committee on Atomic Energy, *Nuclear Explosion Services for Industrial Applications*, 161; "Panama Review Group Meting, June 11, 1969: Summary of Discussion," Panama Jan.–June 1969, Box 264, PRBA.

60. Anderson to Seaborg, Aug. 23, 1968, Nuclear Testing—Plowshare Events (Buggy I) (Schooner), NSF, Subject File, Box 30, LBJL; Memorandum of Conversation, July 22, 1969, Summary Notes of Meetings, June–Oct. 1969, Box 640, PGTS; Skartvedt, "Plowshare Program," 161; Seaborg to Richardson, Sept. 11, 1969, Peaceful Nuclear Explosions and Plowshare Programs, 1968–69, Box 9, PBSL.

61. Seaborg with Loeb, *Atomic Energy Commission under Nixon*, 23–25; Victor Cohn, "A-Canal Dealt Blow," *Washington Post*, Apr. 13, 1970.

62. "Executive Summary, Plowshare Program," undated, https://www.osti.gov/opennet /reports/plowshar.pdf, accessed June 9, 2009; U.S. Congress, Joint Committee on Atomic Energy, *AEC Authorizing Legislation Fiscal Year 1972*, 2345.

63. Seaborg with Loeb, *Atomic Energy Commission under Nixon*, 24; Skartvedt, "Plowshare Program," 164; *Annual Report to Congress of the Atomic Energy Commission for 1970*, Jan. 1971, [oversize attachments] [Annual Report to the Congress for 1970], WHCF, Subject Files, FG 78, Box 4, NPMP.

64. Anderson et al. to the President, Dec. 1, 1970, Interoceanic Canal Studies, Jan. 1966–Nov. 1970, RG 185.8, Box 3, NA-CP.

65. Richard Halloran, "Route Is Chosen for New Panama Canal," *New York Times*, Nov. 13, 1970.

CHAPTER 9

1. Gene Smith, "Natural Gas Reserves Down 2%; Paper Output at a Record Level," *New York Times*, Apr. 7, 1969; Small, *Presidency of Richard Nixon*, 201; Reeves, *President Richard Nixon*, 43; Crane, et al., *Imported Oil and U.S. National Security*, 26–27.

2. U.S. Congress, Joint Committee on Atomic Energy, *AEC Authorizing Legislation Fiscal Year 1972*, 2307.

3. U.S. Congress, Joint Committee on Atomic Energy, *AEC Authorizing Legislation Fiscal Year 1975*, 45.

4. Sale, *Green Revolution*, 20–21.

5. Smith, "Advertising the Atom," 253.

6. Wellock, *Preserving the Nation*, 172–73; Rothman, *Saving the Planet*, 127–28; "The Cities: The Price of Optimism," *Time*, Aug. 1, 1969, 41.

7. Seaborg with Loeb, *Atomic Energy Commission under Nixon*, 26–27.

8. "Austral Oil Stock Sold, Quickly Doubles in Price," *Wall Street Journal*, Oct. 15, 1968; Kreith and Wrenn, *Nuclear Impact*, 73, 75; Dennis Webb, "40 Years Later, Dust Still Hasn't Settled from Project Rulison Nuclear Blast," *Grand Junction (Colo.) Daily Sentinel*, Sept. 6, 2009.

9. Neal Stanford, "Peaceful Use of Nuclear Explosives Explored," *Christian Science Monitor*, Dec. 8, 1966; Borg, "Nuclear Explosions for Peaceful Purposes," 63; U.S Congress, Joint Committee on Atomic Energy, *AEC Authorizing Legislation Fiscal Year 1969*, 1135; Kreith and Wrenn, *Nuclear Impact*, 110; Skartvedt, "Plowshare Program," 240.

10. Seaborg to the President, Mar. 26, 1969, Australia—Cape Keraudren Plowshare Project, 1969, undated, Box 1, PBSL; U.S. Congress, Joint Committee on Atomic Energy, *AEC Authorizing Legislation Fiscal Year 1970*, 302–3; "Bombs Away," *Newsweek*, Sept. 15, 1969, 106; Kreith and Wrenn, *Nuclear Impact*, 75, 78–79.

11. Kreith and Wrenn, *Nuclear Impact*, 87–88; James, *Our Own Generation*, 99–100.

12. Kreith and Wrenn, *Nuclear Impact*, 88–89; Peter Metzger, "Project Gasbuggy and Catch-85," *New York Times Magazine*, Feb. 22, 1970.

13. Metzger, "Project Gasbuggy and Catch-85."

14. "Colorado Is Divided on Proposal for A-Blast to Free Natural Gas," *New York Times*, Aug. 24, 1969; Anthony Ripley, "Aspen Awaiting Nearby A-Blast," *New York Times*, Sept. 3, 1969; Buys, "Isaiah's Prophecy," 33–33, 34; Seaborg with Loeb, *Atomic Energy Commission under Nixon*, 19–20.

15. Buys, "Isaiah's Prophecy," 34; Schulte, *Wayne Aspinall and the Shaping of the American West*, 244–45; U.S. Congress, Joint Committee on Atomic Energy, *Nuclear Explosion Services for Industrial Applications*, 82–83, 109; "Underground Nuclear Blast for Natural Gas Delayed to September," *Wall Street Journal*, May 8, 1969; Seaborg with Loeb, *Atomic Energy Commission under Nixon*, 19.

16. U.S. Congress, *Nuclear Explosion Services for Industrial Applications*, 83–84.

17. Anthony Ripley, "4 Seek to Block Atomic Test Shot," *New York Times*, Aug. 26, 1969; Seaborg with Loeb, *Atomic Energy Commission under Nixon*, 20; U.S. Congress, *Nuclear Explosion Services for Industrial Applications*, 734–42.

18. Anthony Ripley, "Winds Again Bar Atom Explosion," *New York Times*, Sept. 6, 1969; "Underground Nuclear Test Delayed Again in Colorado," *New York Times*, Sept. 8, 1969; "Nuclear Test Delayed Again," *New York Times*, Sept. 9, 1969; Shwiller to Bauser, Sept. 8, 1969, Project Rulison, vol. 2, RJCAE, General Correspondence, Box 509, NA.

19. Kreith and Wrenn, *Nuclear Impact*, 103; Jennie Lay, "Drilling Could Wake a Sleeping Giant," *High Country News* (Paonia, Colo.), Mar. 2005; Schulte, *Wayne Aspinall*, 248; Anthony Ripley, "Protestors Camped Near A-Blast Site," *New York Times*, Sept. 7, 1969; Webb, "40 Years Later"; Anthony Ripley, "A Nuclear Device Fired in Colorado," *New York Times*, Sept. 11, 1969, 1.

20. Jollingsworth to Holifield, Sept. 30, 1969, Project Rulison, vol. 2, RJCAE, General Correspondence, Box 509, NA; Seaborg with Loeb, *Atomic Energy Commission under Nixon*, 20; Kreith and Wrenn, *Nuclear Impact*, 117; U.S. Congress, Joint Committee on Atomic Energy, *AEC Authorizing Legislation Fiscal Year 1973*, 992; U.S. Congress, Joint Committee on Atomic Energy, *AEC Authorizing Legislation Fiscal Year 1971*, 620.

21. Jollingsworth to Holifield, Sept. 30, 1969; Seaborg with Loeb, *Atomic Energy Commission under Nixon*, 20; *Congressional Record*, 91st Cong., 2nd sess., 1970, 116, pt. 7.

22. "Summary Notes of Briefing on Gas Stimulation," Dec. 21, 1970, Summary Notes of Meetings, Nov. 1970–Feb. 1971, Box 640, PGTS; *Annual Report to Congress of the Atomic Energy Commission for 1970*, (oversize attachments) (Annual Report to the Congress for 1970), NPMP, WHCF, Subject Files, FG 78, Box 4, NA-CP; Metzger, "Project

Gasbuggy," 2; Kreith and Wrenn, *Nuclear Impact*, 127, 128; Seaborg with Loeb, *Atomic Energy Commission under Nixon*, 21–22.

23. U.S. Congress, *AEC Authorizing Legislation Fiscal Year 1972*, 2375, 2376–77.

24. Metzger, "Project Gasbuggy," 80.

25. *Congressional Record*, 92nd Cong., 2nd sess., 1972, 118, pt. 16; "Roncalio Loses Fight to Stop Wagon Wheel," *Casper (Wyo.) Star-Tribune*, June 10, 1972.

26. Borg, "Nuclear Explosions for Peaceful Purposes," 64; Desert Research Institute, *Forty-Three Off-Site Plowshare and Vela Uniform Projects with Potential Environmental Restoration Liabilities*, Sept. 2004, 43 Off-Site Plowshare & Vela, no box number, LLNL.

27. Small, *Presidency of Richard Nixon*, 206–9; Herbert G. Lawson, " 'Plowshare' Payoff?," *Wall Street Journal*, June 8, 1972; U.S. Congress, *AEC Authorizing Legislation Fiscal Year 1971*, 3; Desert Research Institute, *Forty-Three Off-Site Plowshare and Vela Uniform Projects*.

28. Seaborg with Seaborg, *Adventures in the Atomic Age*, 214–15, 217, 222, 252; James M. Naughton, "Seaborg Resigns as Head of A.E.C.," *New York Times*, July 22, 1971; Seaborg, *Chemist in the White House*, 80.

29. U.S. Congress, *AEC Authorizing Legislation Fiscal Year 1973*, 1002; Guzzo, *Is It True What They Say about Dixy?*, 87.

30. Guzzo, *Is It True What They Say about Dixy?*, 1–5, 94.

31. Ibid., 7.

32. "Report of Ad Hoc Plowshare Review Committee," undated, 120th General Advisory Committee Meeting, RG 326, General Advisory Committee, Minutes and Reports of Meetings, Box 12, NA-CP; Desert Research Institute, *Forty-Three Off-Site Plowshare and Vela Uniform Projects;* Findlay, *Nuclear Dynamite*, 186–87.

33. *Annual Report to Congress of the Atomic Energy Commission for 1970*; Lawson, " 'Plowshare' Payoff?"; "Nuclear Blast to Seek Gas Slated in Colorado May 17," *New York Times*, May 1, 1973; U.S. Congress, Senate, Subcommittee on Public Lands of the Committee on Interior and Insular Affairs, *Nuclear Stimulation of Natural Gas*, 55.

34. Perlstein, *Nixonland*, 460–61; Hoff, *Nixon Reconsidered*, 21; *PPPUS, Richard Nixon*, 1970, 2.

35. Sale, *Green Revolution*, 24.

36. Grier to Lincoln, Russell, and Seaborg, Dec. 24, 1970, JCAE—Plowshare, Box 854, PRBA; Lawson, " 'Plowshare' Payoff?"; U.S. Congress, *AEC Authorizing Legislation Fiscal Year 1973*, 989–90.

37. U.S. Congress, *AEC Authorizing Legislation Fiscal Year 1973*, 95, 99; Lawson, " 'Plowshare Payoff?"; Skartvedt, "Plowshare Program," 246.

38. "Nuclear Gas Stimulation Development Program Planning Document," Feb. 17, 1972, 120th GAC Meeting, RG 326, General Advisory Committee, Minutes and Reports of Meetings, Box 12, NA-CP; "Meeting Minutes—Ad Hoc Committee on Project Rio Blanco," Mar. 16, 1971, Plowshare-NGS-Project Rio Blanco Opposition Campaign, Box 53, PMW.

39. AEC, "Draft Environmental Statement, Rio Blanco Gas Stimulation Project, Rio Blanco County, Colorado," Jan. 1972, RG 326, Secretariat, Folder 6, and "Transcript, Informal Public Hearings on Project Rio Blanco, Mar. 24 and 27–28, 1972, RG 326, Secretariat, Folder 7, Box 7826, DOE; James P. Sterba, "Nuclear Blast Rocks a Colorado Town before It Occurs," *New York Times*, May 16, 1973; U.S. Congress, *Nuclear Stimulation of Natural Gas*, 57, 140; "Testimony Prepared for the United States Atomic Energy Commission for the Purpose of Providing Information Regarding the Proposed Project Rio Blanco," Mar. 27, 1972, Plowshare-NGS-Project Rio Blanco Opposition Campaign, Box 53, PMW.

40. U.S. Congress, *Nuclear Stimulation of Natural Gas*, 4, 55–56; AEC, "Environmental Statement, Rio Blanco Gas Stimulation Project, Rio Blanco County, Colorado," Mar. 1973, RG 326, Secretariat, Folder 4, Box 7933, DOE; "BLM Set to Withdraw 360 Acres for Test Site," *Rocky Mountain News* (Denver, Colo.), Mar. 21, 1973.

41. U.S. Congress, *Nuclear Stimulation of Natural Gas*, 141–43.

42. Ibid., 169, 181, 235–37, 240–41; *Congressional Record*, 93rd Cong., 1st sess., 1973, 119, pt. 11; James P. Sterba, "Atom Test Blast Set in Colorado," *New York Times*, May 13, 1973; Steve Wynkoop, "Will Gas Well Blasts Destroy Oil Shale Future?," *Denver Post*, Mar. 21, 1973.

43. U.S. Congress, *Nuclear Stimulation of Natural Gas*, 7–8, 13–16, 47–50; *Congressional Record*, 93rd Cong., 1st sess., 1973, 119, pt. 11.

44. U.S. Congress, *Nuclear Stimulation of Natural Gas*, 45–46.

45. Lawson, "'Plowshare' Payoff?"; Sterba, "Nuclear Blast Rocks a Colorado Town before It Occurs."

46. U.S. Congress, *Nuclear Stimulation of Natural Gas*, 6, 17, 46, 73–75, 143, 156.

47. Ibid., 6–7, 57–58, 61–62, 245.

48. Ibid., 56, 63–64, 232–33.

49. Ibid., 125; U.S. Congress, *AEC Authorizing Legislation Fiscal Year 1973*, 992.

50. U.S. Congress, *AEC Authorizing Legislation Fiscal Year 1973*, 987–88; U.S. Congress, *Nuclear Stimulation of Natural Gas*, 216; AEC, "Environmental Statement, Rio Blanco Gas Stimulation Project," Mar. 1973, Plowshare-NGS-Project Rio Blanco Assessment, Environmental Impact Statement," Box 7, PMW.

51. Milo D. Nordyke, "Technical Summary of the Third Stage of the Soviet-American Technical Talks on the Peaceful Uses of Nuclear Explosives," Aug. 23, 1971, Miscellaneous: Nuclear Stimulation, General, Box 49, PTR; U.S. Congress, *Nuclear Stimulation of Natural Gas*, 52.

52. U.S. Congress, *Nuclear Stimulation of Natural Gas*, 200–202; Sterba, "Nuclear Blast Rocks a Colorado Town."

53. U.S. Congress, *Nuclear Stimulation of Natural Gas*, 124, 125; Sterba, "Atom Test Blast Set in Colorado"; "A.E.C. Gets Permission for Underground A-Blast," *New York Times*, May 15, 1973.

54. Kreith and Wrenn, *Nuclear Impact*, 197; U.S. Congress, *Nuclear Stimulation of Natural Gas*, 232–33.

55. James P. Sterba, "A-Blast in Colorado Does Less Damage Than Was Expected," *New York Times*, May 18, 1973; Buys, "Isaiah's Prophecy," 36; Broad, *Teller's War*, 72.

56. Desert Research Institute, *Forty-Three Off-Site Plowshare and Vela Uniform Projects*; U.S. Congress, *Nuclear Explosion Services for Industrial Applications*, 190, 191, 209, 211.

57. McDonald to Anderson, Aug. 22, 1968, Joint Committee on Atomic Energy—Operation Gasbuggy, Box 850, PCPA; Seaborg to Hansen, Jan. 5, 1971, AT Atomic Energy, 1/1/71, WHCF, Subject Files, Atomic Energy, Box 1, NPMP.

58. Lederer, "Project Wagon Wheel," 27; Desert Research Institute, *Forty-Three Off-Site Plowshare and Vela Uniform Projects*.

59. Desert Research Institute, *Forty-Three Off-Site Plowshare and Vela Uniform Projects*; *AEC Authorizing Legislation Fiscal Year 1973*, 127; AEC, "Draft Environmental Statement, Wagon Wheel Gas Stimulation Project, Sublette County, Wyoming," Jan. 1972, RG 326, Secretariat, Folder 6, Box 7826, DOE; Lederer, "Project Wagon Wheel," 27; U.S. Congress, *AEC Authorizing Legislation Fiscal Year 1972*, 2373.

60. Roncalio to Schlesinger, Mar. 14, 1972, Project Wagon Wheel Correspondence—Atomic Energy Commission, Box 52, PTR.

61. Lederer, "Using Public Policy Models to Evaluate Nuclear Stimulation Projects," 9–10; interviews of Sally Hill Mackey, Mary Ann Steele and Floyd Bousman, Jan. 5, Feb.

17 and Mar. 15, 1994, respectively, interviewed by C. L. Rawlins, Subject Files: Wagon Wheel Information Committee, Wagon Wheel Information Committee, Box 13, WWICP; Steele to Hansen, Mar. 30, 1972, Correspondence: Federal Congress, Box 6, WWICP; and "Wagon Wheel, Pinedale, March 20, 1972," Loose Wagon Wheel Material, Box 54, PTR; Smith to Morey and Judy, Aug. 22, 1971, and Smith to Mary, Rick, and all, May 4, 1972, Nuclear Controversy GE Nuclear Engineers, Box 7, PMW.

62. Hathaway to Birr, Mar. 21, 1972, Correspondence: State Governors, Box 6, WWICP; "Welcome Wagon Wheel," *Casper (Wyo.) Star-Tribune*, Mar. 25, 1972.

63. Steele to Schlesinger and Steele to Ruckelshaus, Apr. 3, 1972, and Dubois to Steel, Apr. 21, 1972, Correspondence: Federal Agencies, Box 5, WWICP; Desert Research Institute, *Forty-Three Off-Site Plowshare and Vela Uniform Projects*; U.S. Congress, *AEC Authorizing Legislation Fiscal Year 1973*; Lederer, "Using Public Policy Models," 29; AEC, "Environmental Statement: Wagon Wheel Gas Stimulation Project, Sublette County, Wyoming," Apr. 1972, RG 326, Secretariat, Folder 6, Box 7826, DOE; Lederer, "Project Wagon Wheel," 27, 30.

64. Lederer, "Project Wagon Wheel," 30; Hathaway to Mackey, Apr. 5, 1972, Correspondence: State Governors, Box 6, WWICP; "Wait for the Wagon," *Casper (Wyo.) Star-Tribune*, May 11, 1972, loose Wagon Wheel material, Box 54, PTR.

65. U.S. Congress, *AEC Authorizing Legislation Fiscal Year 1973*, 127–29.

66. Judy Skalla, "Dr. Edward Teller Defends Wagon Wheel," *Casper (Wyo.) Star-Tribune*, Sept. 17, 1972.

67. Lederer, "Project Wagon Wheel," 30–31; "Press Conference, Nov. 30, 1972 with Dr. Philip Randolph, EPNG, during Wyoming Association of Soil Conservation Districts State Meeting at the Hitching Post in Cheyenne, Wyoming," Project Wagon Wheel Correspondence, Box 55, PTR.

68. "Democrats Are Irked by Physicist's Talk," *Casper (Wyo.) Star-Tribune*, Sept. 26, 1972; "This Week's Offering!," *High Country News* (Paonia, Colo.), Sept. 29, 1972.

69. Lederer, "Project Wagon Wheel," 32; "Press Conference, Nov. 30, 1972."

70. "Tape Transcription of a Meeting with Senator Hansen and the Wagon Wheel Information Committee—on Saturday, December 2, 1972, at 7:00 p.m. in the Sublette County Library, Pinedale, Wyoming," and "Monday—February 5, 1973," Chronological File, Wagon Wheel, Box 3, WWICP; Statement by H. F. Steen, Feb. 7, 1973, Correspondence: Corporations, Box 5, WWICP; "KK Notes from Wagon Wheel Meeting Feb. 7, 1973," and "Transcript of Wagon Wheel Information Committee/AEC Meeting," Feb. 7, 1973, Wagon Wheel Meetings—Pinedale, Box 54, PTR; interview with Bousman; U.S. Congress, *Nuclear Stimulation of Natural Gas*, 40–41; interview with Steele; Lederer, "Project Wagon Wheel," 32.

71. U.S. Congress, *Nuclear Stimulation of Natural Gas*, 9, 32, 34–36; U.S. Congress, *AEC Authorizing Legislation Fiscal Year 1975*, 45, 49.

72. "CER Geonuclear to Test New Gas-Output Method," *Wall Street Journal*, Mar. 29, 1974.

73. "Notes on Washington Press Club: April 28, 1973," Project Wagon Wheel, Notes on Washington Press Club, Dixy Lee Ray, Box 55, PTR; Leonard Larsen, "AEC's Wagon Wheel Test Plan Dormant," *Denver Post*, Feb. 20, 1974.

74. Layton O'Neill, interview by Suzanne Becker, July 23, 2004, transcript, NTSOHP; Richard Schneider, "New Rio Blanco Radioactive Leak Found," *Rocky Mountain News* (Denver, Colo.), Nov. 20, 1974; Donald C. Kirkman, "Demise of AEC's Nuclear Gas Stimulation on Horizon," *Rocky Mountain News* (Denver, Colo.), July 18, 1974; Kreith and Wrenn, *The Nuclear Impact*, 209; Bill Strabala, "Cement to Seal Well of Project Rio Blanco Forever," *Denver Post*, June 13, 1976; Comptroller General of the United States, "Progress and Problems in Developing Nuclear and Other Experimental Techniques for

Recovering Natural Gas in the Rocky Mountain Area," Apr. 2, 1974, Folder 5, RG 326, Secretariat, Box 7933, DOE.

CONCLUSION

1. "Prof. E. Teller," undated, no folder, Box 385, PET.

2. "Trip Report: Australia, Thailand, India, and Pakistan, January 3 through January 14, 1967, by Glenn T. Seaborg," Atomic Energy Commission—General, vol. 2, NSF, Agency File, Box 29, LBJL; "Prof. E. Teller."

3. Borg, "Nuclear Explosions for Peaceful Purposes," 65; Milo D. Nordyke, "Plowshare and Edward Teller," no folder, Box 386, PET.

4. Seaborg with Loeb, *Stemming the Tide*, 347; Skartvedt, "Plowshare Program," 70–71; Lindsay-Poland, *Emperors in the Jungle*, 100, 101.

5. Findlay, *Nuclear Dynamite*, 68; U.S. Congress, Joint Committee on Atomic Energy, *Peaceful Applications of Nuclear Explosives—Plowshare*, 25; "Executive Summary, Plowshare Program," undated, https://www.osti.gov/opennet/reports/plowshar.pdf, accessed June 9, 2009.

6. U.S. Congress, Senate, Subcommittee on Public Lands of the Committee on Interior and Insular Affairs, *Nuclear Stimulation of Natural Gas*, 44.

7. Keeny to the Director, Jan. 21, 1971, *FRUS, 1969–72*, vol. E-2.

8. Seaborg with Loeb, *Stemming the Tide*, 226; Comptroller General of the United States, "Progress and Problems in Developing Nuclear and Other Experimental Techniques for Recovering Natural Gas in the Rocky Mountain Area," Apr. 2, 1974, Folder 5, RG 326, Secretariat, Box 7933, DOE; Gulf Universities Research Consortium, *PNE (Peaceful Nuclear Explosion) Activity Projections for Arms Control Planning*, 1:12.

9. El Paso Natural Gas Company, "Interim Report: Gasbuggy 1973 Production Test," Aug. 30, 1973, Folder No. 3: Miscellaneous, Project Gasbuggy, Box 47, PTR.

10. Kirsch, "Project Plowshare," 212.

11. Ibid., 213.

12. Johnson, "Technological Development of Nuclear Explosives Engineering," 15.

13. "Nuclear Dynamite," undated, www.facetofacemedia.ca/files/6quotes.pdf, accessed Oct. 10, 2010.

14. Comptroller General of the United States, "Progress and Problems in Developing Nuclear and Other Experimental Techniques for Recovering Natural Gas in the Rocky Mountain Area."

15. Seaborg with Loeb, *Atomic Energy Commission under Nixon*, 27.

16. Sylves, *The Nuclear Oracles*, 209; Kirsch, "Project Plowshare," 215.

17. Seife, *Sun in a Bottle*, 72; Findlay, *Nuclear Dynamite*, 83–87; Nastassia Astrasheuskaya, Ben Judah, and Alina Selyukh, "Special Report: Should BP Nuke Its Leaking Well?," Reuters online, July 2, 2010, www.reuters.com/assets/print?aid=USTRE6611RF20100702, accessed Dec. 4, 2011.

18. William J. Broad, "A Soviet Company Offers Nuclear Blasts for Sale to Anyone with the Cash," *New York Times*, Nov. 7, 1991; Zuberi, "Nuclear Non-Proliferation Regime in Crisis," 130–31.

19. Skartvedt, "Plowshare Program," 159; Kirsch, *Proving Grounds*, 210.

20. O'Neill, *Firecracker Boys*, 177–84; Timothy Egan, "Eskimos Learn They've Been Living amid Secret Pits of Radioactive Soil," *New York Times*, Dec. 6, 1992.

21. Szasz, "New Mexico's Forgotten Nuclear Tests," 366.

22. Ibid., 360–61; Miller, *Under the Cloud*, 313.

23. Department of Energy, "Environmental Management: Rio Blanco and Rulison Sites," www.em.doe.gov/bemr/BEMRSites/prbs.aspx, accessed Aug. 10, 2010; Dennis

Webb, "40 Years Later, Dust Still Hasn't Settled from Project Rulison Nuclear Blast," *Grand Junction (Colo.) Daily Sentinel*, Sept. 6, 2009; Catherine Tsai, "Legacy of Nuke Drilling Site in Colorado Lingers," Associated Press online, July 22, 2010; David O. Williams, "Rio Blanco and Garfield Counties: A Tale of Two Gas Blasts," *Colorado Independent*, July 1, 2009, http://coloradoindependent.com/32409/rio-blanco-and-garfield-counties-a-tale-of-two-nuclear-gas-blasts, accessed Aug. 10, 2010; Mark Jaffe, "Plans Moving Ahead for Drilling Near Underground Atomic Blast," *Denver Post*, Dec. 24, 2009.

24. James Quinn, "Barack Obama Sends Nuclear Experts to Tackle BP's Gulf of Mexico Oil Leak," *Telegraph* (London), May 14, 2010; Astrasheuskaya et al., "Special Report."

25. Bryan Walsh, "The Gas Dilemma," *Time*, Apr. 11, 2011, 40–48; Andre Gsponer and Jean-Pierre Hurni, *Fourth Generation Nuclear Weapons*, 5th ed., http://nuclearweapon archive.org/News/INESAPTR1.html, accessed Nov. 14, 2011. Although the United States has signed the Comprehensive Test Ban Treaty, it has yet to ratify it.

PRIMARY SOURCES

Manuscript Collections and Government Archives

American Heritage Center, University of Wyoming, Laramie

Papers of Teno Roncalio
Wagon Wheel Information Committee Papers

Department of Energy Archive, Germantown, Maryland

Records of the Atomic Energy Commission

Dwight D. Eisenhower Library, Abilene, Kansas

Ann Whitman File
Papers of Fred A. Seaton
Papers of Robert B. Anderson
Papers of the White House Office, Office of the Staff Secretary
White House Central File

Foreign Ministry Archive, Panama City, Panama

Memoria que el Ministro de Relaciones Exteriores
Memoria que el Ministro de Relaciones Exteriores, Annex 2-1

Herbert Hoover Library, West Plains, Iowa

Papers of Lewis L. Strauss

Hoover Institution, Stanford University, Stanford, California

Papers of Edward Teller

John F. Kennedy Library, Boston

National Security File
Papers of John G. Palfrey
White House Central File

Lawrence Livermore National Laboratory, Livermore, California

Library of Congress, Washington, D.C.

Papers of Benjamin S. Loeb
Papers of Clinton P. Anderson
Papers of Glenn T. Seaborg
Papers of W. Averell Harriman

Lyndon B. Johnson Library, Austin, Texas

Administrative Histories
National Security File
White House Central File

National Archives and Records Service, Anchorage, Alaska

Records of the U.S. Geological Survey

National Archives and Records Service, College Park, Maryland

General Records of the Department of State
Nixon Presidential Materials Project
Records of the Atomic Energy Commission
Records of the Canal Zone Government and the Panama Canal Company
Records of the U.S. Geological Survey

National Archives and Records Service, San Bruno, California

Records of the Office of the Chief of Engineers

National Archives and Records Service, Washington, D.C.

Records of the Bureau of Indian Affairs
Records of the Joint Committee on Atomic Energy

National Archives of Australia, Canberra

Series A432
Series A987
Series A1690
Series A1838
Series A1945
Series A3211
Series A5628
Series A5819

National Archives of Australia, Melbourne

Series 1084/4

National Archives of Australia, Sydney

Papers of the Australian Atomic Energy Commission

Norlin Library, University of Colorado, Boulder

Papers of Morey Wolfson

Papers of John B. Krygier, Columbus, Ohio

Rasmuson Library, University of Alaska, Fairbanks

Papers of Daniel T. O'Neill
Papers of Don C. Foote
Papers of Leslie Viereck
Papers of William O. Pruitt
Project Chariot Papers

San Diego State University, San Diego, California

Papers of Gerald Johnson

State Record Office of Western Australia, Perth

Papers of the Department of Fisheries and Fauna
Papers of the Department of Industrial Development
Papers of the Premier's Department

Published Archival and Governmental Documents

Congressional Record
Department of State Bulletin

Foote, R. G., W. W. Hays, and R. W. Klepinger. *Gasbuggy: Analysis of Ground Motions and Close-in Physical Effects*. Alexandria, Va.: Environmental Research Corporation, 1970.

Foreign Relations of the United States. Washington, D.C.: Government Printing Office, 1948–72.

Gerber, Carl R., Richard Hamburger, and E. W. Seabrook Hull. *Plowshare*. Oak Ridge, Tenn.: Atomic Energy Commission, 1966.

Glasstone, Samuel, ed. *The Effects of Nuclear Weapons*. Washington, D.C.: Atomic Energy Commission, 1957.

Gulf Universities Research Consortium. *PNE (Peaceful Nuclear Explosion) Activity Projections for Arms Control Planning*. Vol. 1. Galveston, Tex.: Consortium, 1975.

Hedman, William, and Charles Diters. *The Legacy of Project Chariot*. Anchorage: Bureau of Indian Affairs, Alaska Region, 2007.

Piper, Arthur M. *Potential Effects of Project Chariot on Local Water Supplies, Northwestern Alaska*. Washington, D.C.: Government Printing Office, 1966.

Seventeenth Annual Report of the Australian Atomic Energy Commission, for Year 1968–69. Canberra: Commonwealth Government Printing Office, 1969.

U.S. Congress. House of Representatives. *Authorizing Appropriations for the Atomic Energy Commission for Fiscal Year 1967*. 89th Cong., 2nd sess., 1966.

————. Committee on Merchant Marine and Fisheries. *Canal Commission Authorization—1969*. 90th Cong., 2nd sess., 1968.

————. Subcommittee on Panama Canal of the Committee on Merchant Marine and Fisheries. *Canal Tolls and Route Studies*. 90th Cong., 1st sess., 1967.

U.S. Congress. Joint Committee on Atomic Energy. *AEC Authorizing Legislation Fiscal Year 1965*. 88th Cong., 2nd sess., 1964.

————. *AEC Authorizing Legislation Fiscal Year 1966*. 89th Cong., 1st sess., 1965.

————. *AEC Authorizing Legislation Fiscal Year 1967*. 89th Cong., 2nd sess., 1966.

————. *AEC Authorizing Legislation Fiscal Year 1968*. 90th Cong., 1st sess., 1967.

————. *AEC Authorizing Legislation Fiscal Year 1969*. 90th Cong., 2nd sess., 1968.

————. *AEC Authorizing Legislation Fiscal Year 1970*. 91st Cong., 1st sess., 1969.

————. *AEC Authorizing Legislation Fiscal Year 1971*. 91st Cong., 2nd sess., 1970.

————. *AEC Authorizing Legislation Fiscal Year 1972*. 92nd Cong., 1st sess., 1971.

————. *AEC Authorizing Legislation Fiscal Year 1973*. 92nd Cong., 2nd sess., 1972.

————. *AEC Authorizing Legislation Fiscal Year 1975*. 93rd Cong., 2nd sess., 1974.

————. *Frontiers in Atomic Energy Research*. 86th Cong., 2nd sess., 1960.

————. *Nuclear Explosion Services for Industrial Applications*. 91st Cong., 1st sess., 1969.

————. *Peaceful Applications of Nuclear Explosives—Plowshare*. 89th Cong., 1st sess., 1965.

————. *Request for Supplemental Fiscal Year 1975 Funds for AEC Nuclear Weapons Testing*. 93rd Cong., 2nd sess., 1974.

U.S. Congress. Senate. Committee on Appropriations. *Supplemental Appropriations Bill for 1965*. 88th Cong., 2nd sess., 1964.

————. Committee on Commerce. *Atlantic-Pacific Interoceanic Canal Study Commission*. 90th Cong., 1st sess., 1967.

————. Committee on Commerce. *Second Transisthmian Canal*. 88th Cong., 2nd sess., 1964.

————. Committee on Foreign Relations. *Nuclear Test Ban Treaty*. 88th Cong., 1st sess., 1963.

————. Subcommittee of the Committee on Foreign Relations. *Control and Reduction of Armaments*. 85th Cong., 2nd sess., 1958.

————. Subcommittee on Public Lands of the Committee on Interior and Insular Affairs, *Nuclear Stimulation of Natural Gas*, 93rd Cong., 1st sess., May 11, 1973.

U.S. Congress. Subcommittee on Research and Development of the Joint Committee on Atomic Energy. *Frontiers in Atomic Energy Research*. 86th Cong., 2nd sess., 1960.

Wilson, A. B. W., E. B. Pender, and E. K. Carter. *Peaceful Uses of Nuclear Explosives—An Evaluation, for Australian Purposes, of Proposed Civil Engineering and Mining Applications*. Sydney: Australian Atomic Energy Commission, 1964.

Memoirs and Polling Data

Anderson, Clinton P., with Milton Viorst. *Outsider in the Senate: Senator Clinton Anderson's Memoirs*. New York: World, 1970.

Gallup, George H. *The Gallup Poll: Public Opinion, 1935–1971*. Vol. 2. New York: Random House, 1972.

Johnson, Lyndon B. *Vantage Point: Perspectives of the Presidency*. New York: Holt, Rinehart and Winston, 1971.

Jorden, William J. *Panama Odyssey*. Austin: University of Texas Press, 1984.

Kistiakowsky, George B. *A Scientist in the White House: The Private Diary of President Eisenhower's Special Assistant for Science and Technology*. Cambridge, Mass.: Harvard University Press, 1976.

O'Neill, Dan. *Project Chariot: A Collection of Oral Histories*. Alaska and Polar Regions Department, Rasmuson Library, UAF, 1989.

Seaborg, Glenn T. *A Chemist in the White House: From the Manhattan Project to the End of the Cold War*. Washington, D.C.: American Chemical Society, 1998.

Teller, Edward, with Judith Shoolery. *Memoirs: A Twentieth Century Journey in Science and Politics*. Cambridge, Mass.: Perseus, 2001.

Weizman, Ezer. *The Battle for Peace*. New York: Bantam, 1981.

SECONDARY SOURCES

Books and Articles

Ambrose, Stephen E. *Eisenhower*, vol. 2: *The President*. New York: Simon and Schuster, 1984.

————. *Nixon*, vol. 2: *The Triumph of a Politician, 1962–1972*. New York: Simon and Schuster, 1989.

Blumberg, Stanley A., and Louis G. Panos. *Edward Teller: Giant in the Golden Age of Physics*. New York: Scribner's, 1990.

Borg, Iris Y. P. "Nuclear Explosions for Peaceful Purposes." In *Nuclear Weapons Tests: Prohibition or Limitation?*, edited by Jozef Goldblat and David Cox, 59–74. New York: Oxford University Press, 1988.

Brands, H. W., Jr. "Testing Massive Retaliation: Credibility and Crisis Management in the Taiwan Strait." *International Security* 12 (1988): 124–51.

————. *The Wages of Globalism: Lyndon Johnson and the Limits of American Power*. New York: Oxford University Press, 1995.

Broad, William J. *Teller's War: The Top-Secret Story behind the Star Wars Deception*. New York: Simon and Schuster, 1992.

Brodine, Virginia. "Unsung Harbor." *Environment* 11 (1969): 34–36.

Bromley, Michael L. *William Howard Taft and the First Motoring Presidency, 1909–1913*. Jefferson, N.C.: McFarland, 2003.

Brooks, Paul. *The Pursuit of Wilderness*. Boston: Houghton Mifflin, 1971.

Bupp, Irvin C. *Priorities in Nuclear Technology: Program Prosperity and Decay in the United States Atomic Energy Commission, 1956–1971*. New York: Garland, 1988.

Buys, Christian J. "Isaiah's Prophecy: Project Plowshare in Colorado." *Colorado Heritage,* no. 1 (1989): 28–39.

Carson, Rachel. *Silent Spring*. 40th anniversary ed. Boston: Houghton Mifflin, 2002.

Cawte, Alice. *Atomic Australia, 1944–1990*. Kensington, NSW, Australia: NSW Press, 1992.

Chernus, Ira. *Eisenhower's Atoms for Peace*. College Station: Texas A&M Press, 2002.

Chossudovsky, Evgeny M. "The Origins of the Treaty on the Non-Proliferation of Nuclear Weapons: Ireland's Initiative in the United Nations (1958–61)." *Irish Studies in International Affairs* 3 (1990): 111–35.

Crane, Keith, et al. *Imported Oil and U.S. National Security*. Santa Monica, Calif.: RAND, 2009.

Dallek, Robert. *Flawed Giant: Lyndon Johnson and His Times, 1961–1973*. New York: Oxford University Press, 1998.

Divine, Robert A. *Blowing on the Wind: The Nuclear Test Ban Debate, 1954–1960*. New York: Oxford University Press, 1978.

————. *Eisenhower and the Cold War*. New York: Oxford University Press, 1981.

Dokos, Thanos P. *Negotiations for a CTBT, 1958–1994: Analysis and Evaluation of American Policy.* Lanham, Md.: University Press of America, 1995.

Dunlap, Thomas R. *DDT: Scientists, Citizens, and Public Policy.* Princeton, N.J.: Princeton University Press, 1981.

Ealy, Lawrence O. *Yanqui Politics and the Isthmian Canal.* University Park: Pennsylvania State University Press, 1971.

Egan, Michael. *Barry Commoner and the Science of Survival: The Remaking of American Environmentalism.* Cambridge, Mass.: MIT Press, 2007.

Eisenbud, Merril, and Thomas Gesell. *Environmental Radioactivity: From Natural, Industrial, and Military Sources.* 4th ed. San Diego, Calif.: Academic Press, 1997.

Epstein, William. *The Last Chance: Nuclear Proliferation and Arms Control.* New York: Free Press, 1976.

Evangelista, Matthew. *Unarmed Forces: The Transnational Movement to End the Cold War.* Ithaca, N.Y.: Cornell University Press, 1999.

Farnsworth, David N., and James W. McKenney. *U.S.-Panama Relations, 1903–1978: A Study in Linkage Politics.* Boulder, Colo.: Westview, 1983.

Fetter, Steve. *Toward a Comprehensive Test Ban.* Cambridge, Mass.: Ballinger, 1988.

Findlay, Trevor. *Nuclear Dynamite: The Peaceful Nuclear Explosions Fiasco.* New York: Pergamon, 1990.

———. "Peaceful Nuclear Explosions and the NPT: Letting a Dead Letter Lie." *Arms Control* 10 (1989): 219–34.

Freeman, Leslie J. *Nuclear Witnesses: Insiders Speak Out.* New York: Norton, 1981.

Frenkel, Stephen. "A Hot Idea? Planning a Nuclear Canal in Panama." *Ecumene* 5 (1998): 303–9.

Froehle, Bryan T. "Backdrop: The Historical Context." In *The Good Neighbors: America, Panama, and the 1977 Canal Treaties*, edited by G. Harvey Summ and Tom Kelly, 1–21. Athens: Ohio University Center for International Studies, Latin American Studies Program, 1988.

Gaddis, John Lewis. *Strategies of Containment: A Critical Appraisal of American National Security Policy during the Cold War.* 2nd ed. New York: Oxford University Press, 2005.

Goertzel, Ted, and Ben Goertzel. *Linus Pauling: A Life in Science and Politics.* New York: Basic Books, 1995.

Gorham, Eville. "A Comparison of Lower and Higher Plants as Accumulators of Radioactive Fall-Out." *Canadian Journal of Botany* 37 (1959): 327–29.

Gosnell, Harold F. *Truman's Crises: A Political Biography of Harry S. Truman.* Westport, Conn.: Greenwood Press, 1980.

Greb, G. Allen. "Survey of Past Nuclear Test Ban Negotiations." In *Nuclear Weapons Tests: Prohibition or Limitation?*, edited by Jozef Goldblat and David Cox, 95–117. New York: Oxford University Press, 1988.

Greene, Benjamin P. *Eisenhower, Science Advice, and the Nuclear Test-Ban Debate, 1945–1963.* Stanford, Calif.: Stanford University Press, 2007.

Guzzo, Louis R. *Is It True What They Say about Dixy? A Biography of Dixy Lee Ray.* Mercer Island, Wash.: Writing Works, 1980.

Hager, Thomas. *Force of Nature: The Life of Linus Pauling.* New York: Simon and Schuster, 1995.

Herring, George C. *America's Longest War: The United States and Vietnam, 1950–1975.* 4th ed. Boston: McGraw-Hill, 2002.

Hewlett, Richard G., and Jack M. Holl. *Atoms for Peace and War, 1953–1961: Eisenhower and the Atomic Energy Commission.* Berkeley: University of California Press, 1989.

Hietala, Thomas R. *Manifest Design: Anxious Aggrandizement in Late Jacksonian America*. Ithaca, N.Y.: Cornell University Press, 1985.

Hoff, Joan. *Nixon Reconsidered*. New York: Basic Books, 1994.

Hubbard, Christopher. "From Ambivalence to Influence: Australia and the Negotiation of the 1968 Nuclear Nonproliferation Treaty." *Australian Journal of Politics and History* 50 (2004): 526–43.

James, Ronald A. *Our Own Generation: The Tumultuous Years, University of Colorado, 1963–1976*. Boulder: University of Colorado Press, 1979.

Johnson, Gerald W. "Nuclear Explosions in Science and Technology." *Bulletin of the Atomic Scientists* 16 (1960): 155–61.

———. "Technological Development of Nuclear Explosives Engineering." In *Education for Peaceful Uses of Nuclear Explosives*, edited by Lynn E. Weaver, 11–21. Tucson: University of Arizona Press, 1970.

Johnson, Rebecca. *Unfinished Business: The Negotiation of the CTBT and the End of Nuclear Testing*. New York: UNIDIR, 2009.

Jolly, J. Christopher. "Linus Pauling and the Scientific Debate over Fallout Hazards." *Endeavour* 28 (2002): 149–53.

Kaufman, Robert G. *Henry M. Jackson: A Life in Politics*. Seattle: University of Washington Press, 2000.

Kirsch, David A. "Project Plowshare: The Cold War Search for a Peaceful Nuclear Explosive." In *Science, Values, and the American West*, edited by Stephen Tchudi, 191–222. Reno: Nevada Humanities Committee, 1997.

Kirsch, Scott. "Experiments in Progress: Edward Teller's Controversial Geographies." *Ecumene* 5 (1998): 267–85.

———. *Proving Grounds: Project Plowshare and the Unrealized Dream of Nuclear Earthmoving*. New Brunswick, N.J.: Rutgers University Press, 2005.

Kline, Benjamin. *First along the River: A Brief History of the U.S. Environmental Movement*. 2nd ed. Lanham, Md.: Acada, 2000.

Koop, Jacob. "Plowshare and the Nonproliferation Treaty." *Orbis* 12 (1968): 792–815.

Kramish, Arnold. *The Peaceful Atom in Foreign Policy*. New York: Harper and Row, 1963.

Kreith, Frank, and Catherine B. Wrenn. *The Nuclear Impact: Case Study of the Plowshare Program to Produce Gas by Underground Nuclear Stimulation in the Rocky Mountains*. Boulder, Colo.: Westview, 1976.

Kruger, Paul. "A Survey of University Courses in Nuclear Civil Engineering." In *Education for Peaceful Uses of Nuclear Explosives*, edited by Lynn E. Weaver, 239–56. Tucson: University of Arizona Press, 1970.

Krygier, J. B. "Project Ketch: Project Plowshare in Pennsylvania." *Ecumene* 5 (1998): 311–22.

LaFeber, Walter. *The Panama Canal: The Crisis in Historical Perspective*. New York: Oxford University Press, 1978.

Lederer, Adam. "Project Wagon Wheel: A Nuclear Plowshare for Wyoming." *Annals of Wyoming: The Wyoming History Journal* 70 (1998): 24–33.

Lindsay-Poland, John. *Emperors in the Jungle: The Hidden History of the U.S. in Panama*. Durham, N.C.: Duke University Press, 2003.

Liss, Sheldon B. *The Canal: Aspects of United States Panamanian Relations*. Notre Dame, Ind.: Notre Dame University Press, 1967.

Lutts, Ralph H. "Chemical Fallout: Rachel Carson's 'Silent Spring,' Radioactive Fallout, and the Environmental Movement." *Environmental Review* 9 (1985): 211–25.

Manathunga, Catherine. "The Evolution of Irish Disarmament Initiatives at the United Nations, 1957–1961." *Irish Studies in International Affairs* 7 (1996): 97–113.

Marrs, John Merton. "Project Chariot, Nuclear Zeal, Easy Journalism and the Fate of
    Eskimos." *American Journalism* 16 (1999): 71–98.
Martin, Brian. *Nuclear Knights*. Dickson, Australia: ACT, 1980.
McEwan, A. C. "Environmental Effects of Underground Nuclear Explosions." In *Nuclear
    Weapons Tests: Prohibition or Limitation?*, edited by Jozef Goldblat and David
    Cox, 75–91. New York: Oxford University Press, 1988.
Middeke, Michael. "Anglo-American Nuclear Cooperation after the Nassau Conference:
    The British Policy of Interdependence." *Journal of Cold War Studies* 2 (2000): 69–96.
Miller, Richard L. *Under the Cloud: The Decades of Nuclear Testing*. New York: Free
    Press, 1986.
Milner, Clyde A., II, Carol A. O'Connor, and Martha A. Sandweiss. *The Oxford History
    of the American West*. New York: Oxford University Press, 1994.
Morgan, Lael. *Art and Eskimo Power: The Life and Times of Alaskan Howard Rock*.
    Fairbanks, Alaska: Epicenter Press, 1988.
Oliver, Kendrick. *Kennedy, Macmillan, and the Nuclear Test-Ban Debate, 1961–1963*.
    New York: St. Martin's, 1998.
Olson, James S., and Randy Roberts. *Where the Domino Fell: America and Vietnam,
    1945–2006*. 5th ed. Maplecrest, N.Y.: Brandywine, 2006.
O'Neill, Dan. *The Firecracker Boys: H-bombs, Inupiat Eskimos and the Roots of the
    Environmental Movement*. New York: St. Martin's, 1994.
———. "Project Chariot: How Alaska Escaped Nuclear Excavation." *Bulletin of the
    Atomic Scientists* 45 (1989): 28–37.
Perlstein, Rick. *Nixonland: The Rise of a President and the Fracturing of America*.
    New York: Scribner, 2008.
Pfau, Richard. *No Sacrifice Too Great: The Life of Lewis L. Strauss*. Charlottesville:
    University of Virginia Press, 1985.
"Project Plowshare: Peaceful Uses of Nuclear Explosives." *Bulletin of the Atomic Scientists*
    16 (1960): 416.
Reeves, Richard. *President Richard Nixon: Alone in the White House*. New York: Simon
    and Schuster, 2001.
Reines, Frederick. "Are There Peaceful Engineering Uses of Atomic Explosives?" *Bulletin
    of the Atomic Scientists* 6 (1950): 171–72.
Rodgers, Ron. "From a Boon to a Threat: Print Media Coverage of Project Chariot,
    1958–1962." *Journalism History* 30 (2004): 11–19.
Rothman, Hal K. *Saving the Planet: The American Response to the Environment in the
    Twentieth Century*. Chicago: Ivan R. Dee, 2000.
Rubinoff, Ira. "Mixing Oceans and Species." *Natural History* 74 (1965): 69–72.
Sale, Kirkpatrick. *The Green Revolution: The American Environmental Movement,
    1962–1992*. New York: Hill and Wang, 1995.
Schulte, Steven C. *Wayne Aspinall and the Shaping of the American West*. Boulder:
    University Press of Colorado, 2002.
Schwartz, Thomas. *Lyndon Johnson and Europe: In the Shadow of Vietnam*. Cambridge,
    Mass.: Harvard University Press, 2003.
Scolfield, C. I., ed. *Holy Bible: Authorized King James Version*. New York: Oxford
    University Press, 1967.
Seaborg, Glenn T., with Benjamin S. Loeb. *The Atomic Energy Commission under Nixon:
    Adjusting to Troubled Times*. New York: St. Martin's, 1993.
———. *Kennedy, Khrushchev, and the Test Ban*. Berkeley: University of California Press,
    1981.
———. *Stemming the Tide: Arms Control in the Johnson Years*. Lexington, Mass.:
    Lexington Books, 1971.

Seaborg, Glenn T., with Eric Seaborg. *Adventures in the Atomic Age: From Watts to Washington.* New York: Farrar, Straus and Giroux, 2001.

Seife, Charles. *Sun in a Bottle: The Strange History of Fusion and the Science of Wishful Thinking.* New York: Viking, 2008.

Serafini, Anthony. *Linus Pauling: A Man and His Science.* New York: Paragon House, 1989.

SIPRI. *Ten Years of the Partial Test Ban Treaty.* Stockholm: SIPRI, 1973.

Siracusa, Joseph M., and David G. Coleman. *Australia Looks to America: Australian-American Relations since Pearl Harbor.* Claremont, Calif.: Regina, 2006.

Small, Melvin. *The Presidency of Richard Nixon.* Lawrence: University Press of Kansas, 1999.

Smith, Denis. *Rogue Tory: The Life and Legend of John G. Diefenbaker.* Toronto: MacFarlane Walter and Ross, 1995.

Smith, Gaddis. *Morality, Reason, and Power: American Diplomacy in the Carter Years.* New York: Hill and Wang, 1986.

Smith, Michael. "Advertising the Atom." In *American Technology,* edited by Carroll Pursell, 209–37. Maiden, Mass.: Blackwell, 2001.

Sorensen, Theodore. *Kennedy.* New York: Harper and Row, 1965.

Stine, Jeffrey K. *Mixing the Waters: Environment, Politics, and the Building of the Tennessee-Tombigbee Waterway.* Akron, Ohio: University of Akron Press, 1993.

Strong, Douglas H. *Dreamers and Defenders: American Conservationists.* Lincoln: University of Nebraska Press, 1988.

Strong, Robert A. "Eisenhower and Arms Control." In *Reevaluating Eisenhower: American Foreign Policy in the 1950s,* edited by Richard A. Melanson and David Mayers, 241–66. Urbana: University of Illinois Press, 1987.

Sylves, Richard T. *The Nuclear Oracles: A Political History of the General Advisory Committee of the Atomic Energy Commission, 1947–1977.* Ames: Iowa State University Press, 1987.

Szasz, Ferenc M. "New Mexico's Forgotten Nuclear Tests: Projects Gnome (1961) and Gasbuggy (1967)." *New Mexico Historical Review* 73 (1998): 347–70.

Tal, David. *The American Nuclear Disarmament Dilemma, 1945–1963.* Syracuse, N.Y.: Syracuse University Press, 2008.

Teller, Edward, with Allen Brown. *The Legacy of Hiroshima.* Westport, Conn.: Greenwood, 1962.

Teller, Edward, Wilson K. Talley, Gary H. Higgins, and Gerald W. Johnson. *The Constructive Uses of Nuclear Explosives.* New York: McGraw-Mill, 1968.

Terchek, Ronald J. *The Making of the Test Ban Treaty.* The Hague: Martinus Nijhoff, 1970.

Tsutsui, William. *Godzilla on My Mind: Fifty Years of the King of Monsters.* New York: Palgrave Macmillan, 2004.

Udall, Stewart L. *The Quiet Crisis.* New York: Holt, Rinehart and Winston, 1963.

Unger, Irwin, and Debi Unger. *LBJ: A Life.* New York: Wiley, 1999.

Walsh, Jim. "Surprise Down Under: The Secret History of Australia's Nuclear Ambitions." *Nonproliferation Review* 5 (1997): 1–20.

Wasserman, Harvey, and Norman Solomon, with Robert Alvarez and Eleanor Walters. *Killing Our Own: The Disaster of America's Experience with Atomic Radiation.* New York: Delacorte, 1982.

Wellock, Thomas R. *Preserving the Nation: The Conservation and Environmental Movements, 1870–2000.* Wheeling, Ill.: Harlan Davidson, 2007.

Wild, Peter. *Pioneer Conservationists of Western America.* Missoula, Mont.: Mountain Press, 1979.

Wittine, Eric C., and G. Harvey Summ. "Prelude: Early Negotiations, 1958–1974." In *The Good Neighbors: America, Panama, and the 1977 Canal Treaties*, edited by G. Harvey Summ and Tom Kelly, 23–38. Athens: Ohio University Center for International Studies, Latin American Studies Program, 1988.

Woods, Randall B. *LBJ: Architect of American Ambition*. Cambridge, Mass.: Harvard University Press, 2006.

Worster, Donald. *Nature's Economy: The Roots of Ecology*. San Francisco: Sierra Club Books, 1977.

Young, John W. "Killing the MLF? The Wilson Government and Nuclear Sharing in Europe, 1964–66." *Diplomacy and Statecraft* 14 (2003): 295–324.

Zoellner, Tom. *Uranium: War, Energy, and the Rock That Shaped the World*. New York: Viking, 2009.

Zuberi, Martin, "The Nuclear Non-proliferation Regime in Crisis." In *Weapons of Mass Destruction: Options for India*, edited by Raja Menon, 129–97. Thousand Oaks, Calif.: Sage, 2004.

Unpublished Materials

Bateman, Joel. "Australian Prime Ministers and Deposition: John Gorton and Bob Hawke Compared." Paper presented at the Australasian Political Studies Association Conference, Adelaide, Australia, 2004.

Johnstud, Judith Ann Hays. "A Political Geography of the Nuclear Power Controversy: The Peaceful Atom in Pennsylvania." MA thesis, Pennsylvania State University, 1977.

Lederer, Adam. "Using Public Policy Models to Evaluate Nuclear Stimulation Projects: Wagon Wheel in Wyoming." MA thesis, University of Wyoming, 1998.

Skartvedt, Stephen. "The Plowshare Program: Environmental Perceptions and Impacts." MA thesis, San Francisco State University, 1992.

Nevada Test Site Oral History Project (online)

Herbert York
Layton O'Neill

Index